Pyongyang

Wonsan

Kosong

38°   38°
            Kaesong   Uijongbu   1 Oct 50
                               Chunchon
                        Seoul
15 Sept 50   Inchon   Samchok
X CORPS   Suwon   Wonju

                            Chungju
                    Chonan   26 Sept
                                   Andong   50
                            Sangju Yongdok
YELLOW   Taejon   23 Sept
SEA   50
            Kunsan   Pohang – Dong   16 Sept
               Chonju   Taegu   50

                    Kwangju   Chinju Masan   EIGHTH   SEA
                      Sunchon   Pusan ARMY OF
            Mokpo   JAPAN

U. S. MARINE OPERATIONS IN KOREA

1950–1953

VOLUME II

The Inchon-Seoul Operation

by

LYNN MONTROSS

and

CAPTAIN NICHOLAS A. CANZONA, USMC

Historical Branch, G–3

Headquarters U. S. Marine Corps

Washington, D. C., 1955

Foreword

THE INCHON LANDING was a major amphibious operation, planned in record time and executed with skill and precision. Even more, it was an exemplification of the fruits of a bold strategy executed by a competent force. The decision to attack at Inchon involved weakening the line against enemy strength in the Pusan Perimeter in order to strike him in the rear. It involved the conduct of an amphibious attack under most difficult conditions of weather and geography.

The stakes were high and the risk was fully justified. Had it not been for the intervention of the Chinese Communist Army, the offensive generated by the Inchon attack would have resulted in a complete victory for our arms in Korea. A study of the record of this operation will disclose, with arresting clarity, the decisive power that is to be found in highly trained amphibious forces when their strength is applied at the critical place and time.

LEMUEL C. SHEPHERD, JR.,
General, U. S. Marine Corps,
Commandant of the Marine Corps.

Preface

THIS IS THE second volume of a series dealing with United States Marine Operations in Korea during the period 2 August 1950 to 27 July 1953. Volume II presents in detail the operations of the 1st Marine Division and the 1st Marine Aircraft Wing as a part of X Corps, USA, during and immediately following the Inchon Landing on 15 September 1950.

In order to tell a complete story of this historic amphibious opera-tion, the authors have described the mobilization of the Marine Corps reserves to form the components of the Division and Aircraft Wing; the movement to the staging area and the hurried planning for an amphibious landing; the withdrawal of the 1st Provisional Brigade and Marine Air Group 33 from the embattled Pusan Perimeter to amalgamate with the larger force for D-day at Inchon; the seizure of Seoul and its environs, and finally the withdrawal on 7 October to prepare for the Wonsan operation.

Again, this is primarily a Marine Corps story. Activities of other services are presented in sufficient detail only to set this operation in its proper perspective.

Grateful acknowledgment is made for the valuable information furnished by the scores of officers and men consulted by interview or letter and for the assistance provided by the Current History Branch of the Office of the Chief of Military History, Department of the Army.

Maps included herein were prepared by the Reproduction Section, Marine Corps Schools, Quantico, Virginia.

T. A. WORNHAM,
Major General, U. S. Marine Corps,
Assistant Chief of Staff, G-3.

Contents

Appendixes

Illustrations

Photographs

Sixteen-page sections of photographs follow pages 68 and 180.

Maps and Sketches

Contents

CHAPTER I

The Communist Challenge

Authorization of Marine Brigade—First Conference on Inchon Landing—General Shepherd in Tokyo—Request for a Marine Division—America's Force-in-Readiness—Planning for the Pohang Landing

No spot on earth could have seemed farther removed from war's alarms than Yellowstone Park on the tranquil Sunday afternoon of 25 June 1950. Yet it was here that Lieutenant General Lemuel C. Shepherd, Jr., Commanding General of Fleet Marine Force, Pacific (FMFPac), had his first news of Communist armed aggression in Korea and the resulting threat to world peace.

Appointed to his new command only nine days before, he was motoring from the Marine Corps Schools at Quantico to the West Coast. From Yellowstone Park he advised Admiral Arthur W. Radford, Commander in Chief, U. S. Pacific Fleet, of his readiness to proceed to Hawaii and the Far East. His offer was accepted, and a Marine plane from El Toro transported him from Salt Lake City to San Francisco. There he boarded the first available plane to Pearl Harbor, arriving in the early morning hours of 2 July.[1]

On this date, with the Korean conflict only a week old, the armed forces of the United States were already committed. From the outset the United Nations had viewed the Red Korean invasion of the Republic of Korea as a challenge issued to free nations by World Communism. The so-called North Korean People's Republic had been set up after World War II as a Communist puppet state, and the army of invasion was both trained and armed by Soviet Russia.

More than half of the troops in the original North Korean People's Army (NKPA) were veterans of the victorious Chinese Communist

[1] FMFPac *Historical Diary, 1–31 Aug 50.*

1

forces in the Chinese Civil War. Weapons and equipment, all the way from T–34 tanks to Tokarev pistols, had been made available by the Soviet Union; and Soviet instructors prepared the invading army for its surprise attack of 25 June on the Republic of Korea.[2]

There could have been little doubt as to the outcome. Although the ROK army included eight divisions and a regiment, estimated at some 98,000 men in all, it could not compare with the NKPA establishment of about equal numbers. The difference lay in the purposes for which the two forces had been organized during the joint Soviet-American occupation of Korea after World War II. While Red Army officers created the NKPA as an instrument of aggression, American instructors trained the ROK troops for frontier defense and internal security. They had neither tanks nor combat aircraft, and their heaviest artillery consisted of a few battalions of 105mm howitzers. It was scarcely more than a lightly armed constabulary which crumpled at the first shock of NKPA columns led by Soviet-made tanks and supported by Soviet-made bombing planes. The four ROK divisions deployed along the frontier were routed, and Seoul fell to the invaders on the third day.

The reaction of the United Nations was prompt and decisive. On 27 June the UN Security Council denounced the NKPA attack as a breach of world peace and called upon member nations to aid the Republic of Korea. The United States and 52 other nations approved this resolution, which was opposed only by the Soviet Union and two of its satellites.[3]

As the NKPA tanks entered Seoul, just evacuated by American nationals, President Truman ordered American air and sea forces in the Far East to support the shattered ROK army. With the U. S. Seventh Fleet protecting Formosa, Task Force 77 bombed and bombarded points on the Korean coast. Far East Air Forces (FEAF), consisting of eight and a half combat groups commanded by Lieutenant General George E. Stratemeyer, USAF, flew interdictory strikes meanwhile from bases in Japan against NKPA supply lines.

Within a few days the NKPA air force, consisting of about 100 Yak-type planes, was driven from the skies except for occasional night raids. It would appear that a mountainous peninsula of few good

---

[2] For a more detailed account of the organization of the NKPA and ROK forces, see v. I of this series, *The Pusan Perimeter*, ch. II.

[3] US Dept of State, *Guide to the U. N. in Korea* (Washington, 1951).

roads would be a favorable area for strategic bombing, since our naval forces were denying the sea lanes to the enemy. Yet the FEAF bombers could not prevent the aggressors from bringing up supplies at night by means of truck, animal, and human transport. The columns of invasion were doubtless hampered, but they continued to roll on southward in spite of interdictory strikes.

General of the Army Douglas MacArthur, Commander in Chief, Far East (CinCFE), concluded on 29 June, during his first flying visit to the front, "that air and naval action alone could not be decisive, and that nothing short of the intervention of U. S. ground forces could give any assurance of stopping the Communists and of later regaining the lost ground."[1] Unfortunately, he had only the four understrength divisions of the Eighth U. S. Army at his disposal in the Far East. During the two World Wars the United States had been able to raise and train armies while allies held the line. But no such respite was forthcoming in Korea, and the first U. S. ground forces at the front consisted of a small task force flown from Japan— an incomplete battalion reinforced by a battery of artillery.

The date was 2 July 1950. And on this same Sunday, CinCFE sent a request to Washington for the immediate dispatch of a Marine regimental combat team (RCT) with appropriate air to the Far East.

Authorization of Marine Brigade

It is not quite a coincidence that 2 July happened also to be the date of General Shepherd's arrival at Pearl Harbor. Previous decisions in Washington had made it virtually certain that General MacArthur's request would be granted, and CG FMFPac was on his way to the Far East to prepare for the reception of the Marine reinforcements.

The first step had been taken on 28 June. General Clifton B. Cates, Commandant of the Marine Corps, conferred at the Pentagon with Admiral Forrest P. Sherman, Chief of Naval Operations. He urged that troops of the Fleet Marine Force be employed, and CNO promptly informed Vice Admiral C. Turner Joy, Commander of

---

[1] Quoted from report of Chief of Staff, FECOM: LtGen Edward M. Almond (USA), *United Nations Military Operations in Korea, 29 June 1950–31 December 1951* (Carlisle Barracks, 1952), 10–11. (Hereafter, Almond, *UN Mil Ops.*)

Naval Forces, Far East (ComNavFE), that a Marine RCT could be made available if General MacArthur desired it.[5]

CinCFE had hoped that an entire Marine division could be sent to the Far East. But after being briefed by Admiral Joy as to the limitations of Marine Corps numbers, he had to content himself with the request for an RCT.

Admiral Sherman acted at once. With the approval of JCS and the President, he ordered Admiral Radford to transport the Marine units across the Pacific. This was the inception of the 1st Provisional Marine Brigade (Reinf.), which was activated on 7 July with three squadrons of Marine Aircraft Group 33 as its air component.[6]

First Conference on Inchon Landing

While General Shepherd stopped for a few days at Pearl Harbor, the possibility of an Inchon amphibious operation was mentioned officially for the first time at a conference in Tokyo attended by two Marine officers.

On 4 July a party given by the American colony was interrupted by a message for Brigadier General William S. Fellers, commanding general of Troop Training Unit, Amphibious Training Command, Pacific Fleet, and Colonel Edward S. Forney, commanding Mobile Training Team Able of that organization. As specialists in amphibious techniques, they were summoned along with Army and Air Force officers to a meeting at Headquarters, FECOM, presided over by General MacArthur's chief of staff, Major General Edward M. Almond, USA.[7]

The Marine officers were in Japan as a result of General MacArthur's belief in the efficacy of amphibious tactics. Early in 1950, several months before the outbreak of the Korean conflict, he had foreseen the necessity of recovering lost ground by means of a ship-to-shore assault if an enemy ever won a foothold in the Japanese Islands. His request for amphibious instructors to train U. S. Army troops in Japan

---

[5] Gen C. B. Cates ltr to authors, 7 Apr 54.
[6] For the full story of the 1st ProvMarBrig, see *The Pusan Perimeter, op. cit.*
[7] Col Edward S. Forney *Transcript of Special Report*, n. d., Part II.

had found the Navy and Marine Corps ready with units set up for just such a purpose.[8]

The oldest was the TTU organization of the Phib Tra Pac established originally on 15 August 1943 to prepare Army as well as Navy and Marine forces for amphibious operations. After making a distinguished record in World War II, TTU created a permanent place for itself during the following five years.[9]

A group of TTU officers and enlisted men under the command of Colonel Forney made up Mobile Training Team Able in the spring of 1950. Sailing from San Diego in April, these Marines were accompanied by a second group of amphibious specialists, the ANGLICO (Air and Naval Gunfire Liaison Company) instruction team commanded by Lieutenant Edward B. Williams, USN.[10]

The ANGLICOs, composed of both Navy and Marine Corps personnel, evolved in 1949 to assist Army units lacking the forward air control and naval gunfire control units which are integral in Marine divisions. Growing out of the responsibility of the Marine Corps for the development of those phases of landing force operations pertaining to tactics, techniques, and equipment employed by landing forces, the first company was formed in answer to the request of Lieutenant General Mark W. Clark, USA, for a unit capable of giving an Army division this sort of amphibious fire support. After taking part in the MIKI exercises with the Sixth Army in Hawaii during the autumn of 1949, this ANGLICO split up into instruction teams assigned to various Army units.[11]

Training Team Able and Lieutenant Williams' ANGLICO team reached Japan just in time to cooperate with a third organization of amphibious specialists, Rear Admiral James H. Doyle's Amphibious Group (PhibGru) One of the Pacific Fleet. The three teams were given a mission of training one regiment from each of the four Eighth Army divisions in Japan. But the instruction program had only been launched when it was interrupted by the Korean conflict.

---

[8] In the autumn of 1946 a TTU team of 35 Marine officers and 40 enlisted men had been sent to Yokosuka, Japan, at MacArthur's request, to train Army troops in amphibious techniques.

[9] Joint Landing Force Board, Project No. 13-52, Annex Able, 28-30; see also FMFPac, *Historical Outline of the Development of FMFPac 1941-1950* (Preliminary), 15-16 (hereafter, FMFPac *History*); and Maj Gen W. S. Fellers memo to authors, 16 Feb. 55.

[10] Capt E. P. Stamford interv with HistDiv HQMC, 16 Mar 51.

[11] *Ibid.* The amphibious functions of the Marine Corps, as outlined by National Security Act of 1947 and the Key West Conference of 1948, are discussed in the following chapter.

PhibGru One and the ANGLICO team were immediately assigned to new duties in connection with the sea lift of Eighth Army troops to Korea. They had just begun this task when orders came for Admiral Doyle and his staff, in the USS *Mount McKinley* at Sasebo, to proceed by air on 4 July to the conference at Tokyo.[12] There at FECOM Headquarters, they met General Fellers, Colonel Forney, and the Army officers who had been summoned from the Independence Day celebration of the American colony.

At the conference it was made plain that the concept of an Inchon landing had originated with General MacArthur. Even at this early date, he envisioned not only a ship-to-shore assault on some east or west coast seaport, preferably Inchon, but also a drive inland to cut enemy communications and envelop Seoul. The Joint Strategic Plans and Operations Group (JSPOG) headed by Brigadier General Edwin K. Wright, U. S. A. (FECOM G-3) was then drawing up the outline of such an amphibious attack plan. Code-named Operation BLUE-HEARTS, it called for a landing in the Inchon area by a Marine RCT and an Army assault force in coordination with a frontal attack from the south by the 24th and 25th Divisions. Inchon had been designated the objective area for the amphibious assault, and the date would depend upon the availability of troops· for the combined operation.[13]

It would be an understatement to say that the naval and Marine officers were impressed by the boldness of MacArthur's thinking. At a time when he could send only a battalion-size force to the aid of the shattered ROK army, his mind had soared over obstacles and deficiencies to the concept of an amphibious operation designed to end the war at a stroke.

It was an idea that fired the imagination. But the amphibious specialists of TTU and PhibGru One had been trained to view the risks with a realistic appraisal. Their admiration was tempered by caution, therefore, when they took into account the difficulties.[14]

---

[12] ComPhibGru-1 (CTF 90), "Rpt of Ops for 25 Jun 50 to 1 Jan 51," in CinCPacFlt, *Interim Evaluation Report No. 1*, v. XV, Annex Able Able. (Hereafter, PacFlt *Interim Rpt No. 1*, XV:Able Able. For detailed description and location of major reports, see the bibliography.)

[13] LtGen Edward M. Almond (USA, Ret.) ltr to authors, 10 Feb 55; Col Edward S. Forney interv, 7 Dec 54. (Unless otherwise noted, all interviews were conducted by the authors of this work.)

[14] Forney interv, 7 Dec 54.

The end of World War II had found the United States at a peak of military strength never before attained in the Nation's history. Then, within a year, the popular clamor for the immediate discharge of citizen-soldiers had left the Army with scarcely enough troops for the occupation of strategic areas in the Far East. It took vigorous recruiting to fill the ranks in time of peace, and on 25 June 1950 the U. S. Eighth Army in Japan included the 7th, 24th, and 25th Infantry Divisions and the 1st Cavalry (dismounted) Division. Infantry regiments were limited to two battalions.

In the lack of trained amphibious assault troops, a definite decision could not be reached at the conference of 4 July. But it was proposed by FECOM officers that Major General Hobart H. Gay's 1st Cavalry Division be employed as the Army assault force of the proposed Inchon operation. PhibGru One and Training Team Able were to give the troops all possible amphibious training, and Colonel Forney was assigned on 5 July as the G–5 (Plans) of the division.[15]

General Shepherd in Tokyo

The activation of the 1st Provisional Marine Brigade on 7 July freed General Shepherd to continue his trip to the Far East. That evening, accompanied by his G–3, Colonel Victor H. Krulak, he took off from the Pearl Harbor area on the flight to Tokyo.

Upon his arrival, CG FMFPac was acquainted by General Almond with the deteriorating military situation. As a first step toward sending U. S. ground forces to Korea, CinCFE had set up the GHQ Advanced Command Group under the command of Brigadier General John H. Church, USA. After beginning the reorganization of the ROK forces, it was absorbed on 3 July by Headquarters, U. S. Armed Forces in Korea. And with the establishment next day of the Pusan Logistical Command (Brigadier General Crump Garvin, USA), a start was made toward handling the mountains of supplies which would be required.[16]

On 4 July the initial contact of U. S. ground forces with the enemy took place near Osan. The little task force from Major General William F. Dean's 24th Infantry Division could not attempt anything

---

[15] *Ibid.*
[16] USMA, Dept of Mil Art and Engr, *Operations in Korea* (West Point, 1953).

more ambitious than delaying actions. But preparations were afoot to send the rest of the division to Korea as soon as possible, to be followed by Major General William B. Kean's 25th Infantry Division.

The first fire fights occurred on 5 and 6 July in the vicinity of Osan. It was evident at once that the enemy held a great superiority in arms and equipment. Lieutenant General Walton H. Walker, USA, who had been one of Patton's favorite subordinates, commented after his first visit to the Korean front that the NKPA units appeared equal to the Germans who were his adversaries in World War II.[17]

Accounts of the early actions in Korea were depressing to FECOM officers.[18] Many plausible excuses may be found for men snatched from occupation duties and rushed piecemeal into action against great material odds. The nation as a whole must share the blame when willing troops are sent to the firing line without adequate preparation, as were the first U. S. units. Eighth Army officers had done their best under the circumstances, but a scarcity of maneuver areas in Japan had restricted training exercises to the battalion and company levels. Divisions with barely 70 percent of their full complement of troops were armed with worn World War II weapons, some of which proved unserviceable for lack of spare parts and maintenance personnel. Division tank units, equipped with light M–24 tanks because of poor roads and bridges in Japan, operated at a handicap against the enemy's new Soviet T–34 tanks; and American 2.36-inch rocket launchers knocked out NKPA armor only at fairly close ranges.[19]

At this stage the ground forces were particularly dependent upon air support because of shortages of artillery. But since the mission of the Air Force in Japan had been primarily of a defensive nature, neither the organization nor equipment was available for effective air-ground cooperation on the tactical level. As a consequence, FEAF units had to confine their tactical efforts largely to targets of opportunity, and 24th Infantry units had to do without such support when it was most needed.[20]

Altogether, the so-called "police action" in Korea proved to be one of the toughest assignments ever given to American soldiers.

---

[17] CG FMFPac *Report of Liaison Visit to the Far East*, 10–11 Jul 50.
[18] Several of these encounters are realistically described from firsthand interviews in a study sponsored by the Chief of Military History, USA: Capt R. A. Gugeler, *Combat Actions in Korea* (Washington, 1954), 3–19.
[19] USMA, *op. cit.*, 7–8.
[20] *Ibid.*

Request for a Marine Division

General Shepherd's few days in Tokyo were filled with conferences, and history was made on 10 July during the course of a conversation with General MacArthur at FECOM Headquarters.

The commander in chief was not optimistic about the situation at the front. Not only had the NKPA invasion developed into a formidable threat at the end of the first two weeks, but the possibility of Red Chinese or Soviet armed intervention could not be dismissed.

President Truman had named General MacArthur as supreme commander of UN forces after the Security Council passed a resolution on 7 July calling for a unified effort in Korea. General Walker was soon to be appointed to the command of the Eighth Army in Korea (EUSAK), assuming control of all ROK ground forces.

The personnel situation had grown critical. After being completely routed, the ROK troops were now in process of reorganization into five divisions. Meanwhile, the U. S. 25th Infantry Division was being sent to Korea as rapidly as possible; and it had been decided to withdraw the 1st Cavalry Division from consideration as the landing force of the proposed Inchon operation. Not only were these troops lacking in amphibious training, but they were needed as infantry reinforcements. Thus it was planned for the combat-loaded 1st Cavalry Division to make a landing at the East Coast port of Pohang-dong, under the direction of ComPhibGru One and Mobile Training Team Able, before proceeding to the front. This would leave only the 7th Infantry Division in Japan, and it was being stripped of troops to fill out units of the other three.

The outweighed UN forces were still limited to delaying actions. But General MacArthur hoped that space could be traded for time until the arrival of stateside units enabled him to take the offensive. At his urgent request, the 2d Infantry Division and 2d Engineer Special Brigade had been alerted in the United States for immediate movement to the Far East. Port dates commencing on 20 July had been assigned, and General Wright expressed his opinion that these units might be employed along with the recently activated 1st Provisional Marine Brigade to initiate the first UN counterstroke.[21]

The only hope of an early UN decision, General MacArthur told CG FMFPac at their conference of 10 July, lay in the launching of an

---

[21] CG FMFPac memo to CMC, 11 Jul 50.

amphibious assault to cut supply lines in the enemy's rear. This situation, he added, reminded him of the critical days of World War II in the Pacific, when troops trained in amphibious techniques were urgently needed to make ship-to-shore landings on Japanese-held islands.

In a reminiscent mood, MacArthur recalled the competence shown by the 1st Marine Division while under his control during the New Britain operation of 1943–1944. If only he had this unit in Japan, he said, he would employ it at his first opportunity as his landing force for the Inchon assault.

Shepherd, who had been assistant division commander of the 1st Marine Division during the New Britain landings, immediately suggested that the UN supreme commander make a request that the 1st Marine Division with appropriate Marine air be assigned to him. This possibility had apparently been put aside by MacArthur after being limited to an RCT in his request of 2 July. He asked eagerly if the Marine general believed that the division could be made available for an Inchon landing as early as 15 September. And Shepherd replied that since the unit was under his command, he would take the responsibility for stating that it could be sent to Korea by that date, minus the infantry regiment and other troops of the Brigade.[22]

Thus was history made without pomp or ceremony during the conference at FECOM Headquarters.

The date was 10 July, but it was already D-minus 67 for thousands of American young men. On farms and in offices, in cities and villages from coast to coast, these civilians had no inkling that just 67 days later they would be fighting their way ashore in a major amphibious operation. For they were Marine reservists, and the 1st Marine Division could not be brought up to full strength without calling them back into uniform.

Shepherd realized, even while assuring MacArthur that the division could be made combat-ready by 15 September, that the activation of the Brigade had left the division with less than the strength of a single RCT. Nearly as many men would be required to bring it up to full strength as were contained at present in the entire Fleet Marine

---

[22] USMC, MarCorps Board, *An Evaluation of the Influence of Marine Corps Forces on the Course of the Korean War* (4 Aug 50–15 Dec 50), v. 1, 1–B–1. (Hereafter, MarCorps Board *Study*.)

Force.[23] But so great was his confidence in the Marine Corps Reserve that he did not hesitate to take the responsibility.

Nor did MacArthur lose any time at making up his mind. That very day, 10 July, he sent his first request to the Joint Chiefs of Staff for a Marine division.

As the conference ended, Shepherd found the UN supreme commander "enthusiastic" about the prospect of employing again the Marine outfit that had been his reliance seven years before in the New Britain operation. He planned to stabilize the front in Korea as soon as possible, he said, as a prelude to the landing in the NKPA rear which he believed would be decisive.[24]

America's Force-in-Readiness

Long before the New Britain landing, Cates and Shepherd had learned from first-hand experience as junior officers how decisive a force-in-readiness can be. The lieutenant from Tennessee and the lieutenant from Virginia took part in June 1918 with the Marines who stopped the Germans by counterattacking at Belleau Wood. In terms of human tonnage, two Marine regiments did not cut much of a figure in the American Expeditionary Force. What counted was the *readiness* of the Marines and a few outfits of U. S. Army regulars at a time when most of the American divisions had not yet finished training.

More than three decades later, as CMC and CG FMFPac, both Marine generals were firm advocates of the force-in-readiness concept as a basic mission of the Marine Corps. It was a mission that had evolved from practice rather than theory. During the half century since the Spanish-American War, there had been only two years when U. S. Marines were not on combat duty somewhere. It had long been a tradition that the Marines, as transitory naval forces, might land on foreign soil without the implication of hostilities usually associated with invasion. This principle was invoked, along with a liberal interpretation of the Monroe Doctrine, by the State Department from 1906 to 1932 in the Caribbean and Central America. As a means of

---

[23] For statistics on Reserve mobilization, see Ernest H. Giusti, *The Mobilization of the Marine Corps Reserve in the Korean Conflict.*) (HistBr. G–3 HQMC, 1952). (Hereafter, Giusti.)

[24] CG FMFPac memo to CMC, 11 Jul 50.

supervising unstable governments in sensitive strategic areas, Marines were sent to Cuba, Mexico, Haiti, the Dominican Republic, Nicaragua, and China for long periods of occupation.[25]

U. S. Marines were not only web-footed infantry during these over-seas operations; they also distinguished themselves as scouts, can-noneers, constabulary, engineers, and horse marines. As modern war-fare grew more complex, however, the time came when the Leather-necks could no longer sail on a few hours' notice as a "gangplank expeditionary force" made up of men detailed from the nearest posts and stations. No longer could such light weapons as machine guns, mortars, and mountain howitzers serve as the only armament neces-sary for seizing a beachhead.

The Fleet Marine Force evolved in 1933, therefore, to fill the need for a corps of highly-trained amphibious specialists capable of carry-ing out a major ship-to-shore assault against modern defensive weapons. New landing craft as well as new landing tactics and tech-niques were developed during the next ten years, and the reputation of the Marine Corps as a force-in-readiness was upheld in the amphib-ious operations of World War II.

During these three eventful decades of Marine development, Gen-eral Cates and General Shepherd had participated in all the stages while ascending the ladder of command. Thus in the summer of 1950, they were eminently qualified for leadership in the task of build-ing the 1st Marine Division up to war strength for the amphibious operation which General MacArthur hoped to launch on 15 September.

As a prerequisite, the sanction of Congress and authorization of the President had to be obtained before the Marine Corps Reserve could be mobilized. General MacArthur's request of 10 July for a Marine division went to the Joint Chiefs of Staff, who referred it to General Cates. The Commandant could only reply that it would be necessary to call out the Reserve, and no action was taken on this first request. It was enough that a beginning had been made, and CMC put his staff to work on the necessary studies and plans.

General Shepherd was meanwhile winding up his visit to Tokyo by conferring with Admirals Joy and Doyle and Generals Almond and Stratemeyer. The Air Force general tentatively confirmed (sub-

---

[25] For a detailed discussion of this subject, see US Dept of State, Office of the Solicitor, *Right to Protect Citizens in Foreign Countries by Landing Forces*, 3d rev. ed. with sup. app. to 1933 (Washington, 1934). (State Dept Pub. No. 538.)

ject to discussion with his staff) the assignment of Itami Airfield in Japan to Marine air units. He also informed CG FMFPac that he accepted as valid the principle of employing Marine air in support of Marine ground forces.[26]

The air situation in Korea had struck General Shepherd as abounding in paradoxes. He noted that "B-29's are employed against tactical targets to the dissatisfaction of all concerned—the Air Force because of misemployment of its planes, and the ground forces because of the results achieved. Carrier aircraft, despite the wealth of close support targets available, were committed against deep and semi-strategic targets. Jet fighters, with little enemy air to engage, have been assigned to close support work despite a fuel restriction which holds them to no more than 15 minutes in the combat zone. Only a very limited number of aircraft adaptable to tactical support missions are available (F-51 and B-26) and there appears to be urgent need for suitable close support aircraft along with competent air-ground liaison units." [27]

These conclusions had much to do with a Marine policy, dating back to World War II, of insisting whenever possible on Marine close air support for Marine ground forces. Without disparaging other techniques, Marines believed that their own fliers, trained in Marine infantry methods, could provide the most effective tactical air for Marine infantry.

Planning for the Pohang Landing

While General Shepherd was flying back to Pearl Harbor, a succession of sleepless nights awaited the officers of PhibGru One, the ANGLICO group, and Training Team Able. Upon the shoulders of these amphibious specialists fell the task of drawing up the orders, planning the loading, and mounting out the troops of the 1st Cavalry Division for its landing of 18 July at Pohang-dong.

It was not even certain, when the division commenced loading at Yokohama on 14 July, that Pohang-dong could be held by the ROKs long enough for a landing to be effected. Three reinforced NKPA divisions were making the enemy's main thrust down the Seoul-

[26] CG FMFPac memo to CMC, 11 Jul 50.
[27] *Ibid.*

Taejon axis. They were opposed only by weary 24th Infantry Division units fighting delaying actions while falling back on Taejon and the line of the river Kum. Along the east coast and the mountains of the central sector, five regrouped and reorganized ROK divisions held as best they could. Two of these units in the center were being relieved by the U. S. 25th Infantry Division, which completed its movement to Korea on the 14th.

As a preliminary step in the Pohang landing, a reconnaissance party of Army, Navy, and Marine officers flew from Tokyo on 11 July into the objective area. They returned two days later with valuable information about the beaches, depths of water, and unloading facilities.

"Because of the extraordinary speed with which the landing at Pohang-dong was conceived, planned, and executed," said the report of ComPhibGru One, "there was no opportunity for conventional and orderly planning. . . . Since all echelons of the planning force were installed in offices at GHQ in Tokyo, it was possible to employ the quickest and most informal ways of doing business. Telephone conversations and oral directives were used in place of dispatches, letters, and formal orders." [28]

Lack of amphibious shipping in the area made it a Herculean labor to provide boat servicing gear, general securing gear, debarkation nets, towing bridles, and boat and vehicle slings in less than a week. By 14 July, however, enough shipping to move the four embarkation groups of the division had been assembled at Yokohama—two MSTS transports, two AKAs, six LSUs, and 16 LSTs in addition to LCVPs and LCMs.

The transport group and screen got under way on the 15th for a rendezvous near the objective area on D-day with the tractor group. Naval aircraft of Rear Admiral John M. Hoskins' carrier group of the Seventh Fleet were on call to provide support; but at 0558 on the 18th, the armada was unopposed as it steamed into Yongil Bay. CTF 90 signaled orders for the carrying out of Plan Baker, calling for a landing against little or no enemy resistance. By midnight the *Mount McKinley, Union, Oglethorpe,* and *Titania* had been completely unloaded, and the LSTs had accounted for 60 per cent of their cargoes. Altogether, 10,027 troops, 2,022 vehicles, and 2,729 tons of bulk cargo were put ashore on D-day.

---

[28] PacFlt *Interim Rpt No. 1,* XV:Able Able.

The Second Echelon consisted of six LSTs, three APs, and four Japanese freighters, while six LSTs made up the Third Echelon. These ships discharged their cargo from 23 to 29 July, having been delayed by Typhoon GRACE. And on the 30th, ComPhibGru One, as CTF 90, reported that the operation had been completed and no naval units were now at the objective.[29]

Viewed superficially, the uncontested Pohang landing may have seemed a tame affair to stateside newspaper readers. Nevertheless, it was a timely demonstration of Navy and Marine Corps amphibious know-how and Army energy, and it came at a critical moment. The important communications center of Taejon had to be abandoned by 24th Infantry Division units on 20 July, and it was growing apparent that the Eighth Army would be hard-pressed to retain a foothold in Korea until reinforcements from the States could give the United Nations a material equality. It was a time when every platoon counted, and the fresh regiments of General Gay's division were rushed to the Yongdong area two days after their landing to relieve weary and battered elements of the 24th Infantry Division.

---

[29] *Ibid.*

CHAPTER II

The Minute Men of 1950

Expansion to Full Peace Strength—Mobilization of Marine Corps Reserve—The Influx at Camp Pendleton—Embarkation of 1st Marine Division—Build-up of 7th Marine Regiment— Staff Groups Flown to Japan

ON 18 JULY 1950, it was D-minus 59 for the Marine reservists who would hit the beaches at Inchon. These young civilians were doubtless more interested in major league baseball standings at the moment than in hydrographic conditions at the Korean seaport they would assault within two months. Yet the proposed amphibious operation moved a long step closer to reality on the 18th when Major General Oliver P. Smith left Washington under orders to assume command of the 1st Marine Division at Camp Pendleton, California.

A graduate of the University of California in 1916, General Smith had been commissioned a Marine second lieutenant at the age of 24 in the first World War. After serving in Guam during that conflict, he saw duty at sea and in Haiti during the early 1920's, followed by studies at the Army Infantry School, Fort Benning, Georgia, and duty as an instructor in the Marine Corps Schools at Quantico.

In Paris, while attached administratively to the office of the U. S. Naval Attaché, he took the full two-year course at the École Superieure de Guerre, and afterwards he was an instructor for three more years at the Marine Corps Schools. He had an extensive experience of hard-fought amphibious operations during World War II as a regimental commander in the Talasea, New Britain, landing, as ADC of the 1st Marine Division at Peleliu, and as deputy chief of staff of the U. S. Tenth Army on Okinawa. Returning with the rank of brigadier, he became Commandant of the Marine Corps Schools; and after putting up a second star, the tall, slender, white-haired general served as Assistant Commandant at Marine Corps Headquarters in Washington.

At the outbreak of the Korean conflict, Major General Graves B. Erskine had commanded the 1st Marine Division. Following his assignment to a secret State Department mission in southeast Asia, General Smith was named as his relief.

The division had meanwhile been reduced to 3,386 officers and men as compared to a strength of 7,789 on 30 June 1950. It had been stripped of its principal operating elements to build up the 1st Provisional Marine Brigade, which numbered about 5,000 officers and men when it sailed from San Diego to the Far East on 14 July under the command of Brigadier General Edward A. Craig.[1]

At El Toro, the near-by Marine Corps Air Station, it was the same story. The 1st Marine Aircraft Wing, with a total strength of 4,004 officers and men on 30 June, provided most of the 1,548 officers and men of Marine Aircraft Group 33, the air component of the Brigade, commanded by Brigadier General Thomas J. Cushman, who was also deputy Brigade commander.[2]

Expansion to Full Peace Strength

General Smith had known before his arrival at Pendleton that his first task would be the building up of the 1st Marine Division to full peace strength. As early as 12 July, a dispatch from CNO had warned CinCPacFlt that this expansion would take place, including the elements of the Brigade.[3] And on 15 July General Shepherd directed Brigadier General Harry B. Liversedge, temporary CG 1st Marine Division, to extend the work day and work week while intensifying training and making preparations to expand.[4]

The 15th was also the date of General MacArthur's second request for a war-strength Marine division with its own air for employment in his proposed Inchon amphibious assault. General Shepherd advised CMC that same day as to the composition of cadres to facilitate the rapid expansion of the 1st Marine Division.[5]

---

[1] PacFlt *Interim Rpt No. 1*, XV:Zebra. Estimates of Brigade numbers will be found to vary according to different stages of the build-up.

[2] *Ibid.*; see also XV:Charlie Charlie.

[3] CNO disp to CinCPacFlt, 12 Jul 50.

[4] CG FMFPac disp to CG 1st MarDiv, 14 July 50.

[5] CG FMFPac disp to CMC, 15 Jul 50; CG FMFPac ltr to CMC, 16 Jul 50.

Already it was becoming apparent that this build-up would allow little time for training. Fortunate it was, therefore, that the Division and the 1st Marine Aircraft Wing had participated in an intensive training program during recent months. Following are the principal exercises:

Oct	1949	Air lift field exercise involving movement of a reinforced battalion and air command to San Nicholas Island, Calif. One Marine aircraft group carrier-embarked for participation in Operation MIKI with Sixth Army in Hawaii.
Nov	1949	Field exercise involving a reinforced regiment and supporting aircraft.
Dec	1949	Combined field exercise—a simulated amphibious assault extending over a period of seven days—involving all principal elements of the Division and Wing.
Jan	1950	Participation by elements of Division in Operation MICOWEX 50, stressing the use of the transport submarine and helicopter in amphibious operations.
Feb	1950	Field exercise involving a reinforced regiment with supporting air.
Mar	1950	Land plane and seaplane air-lift exercise involving seizure of San Nicholas Island by a reinforced battalion and a Marine air command.
May	1950	Participation by a majority of Division and Wing elements in DEMON III, an amphibious demonstration for students of Command and General Staff College, Fort Leavenworth. Participation by Wing in two-week major advanced base field exercise, with intensive training in close support.
Jun	1950	Continuation of training in lesser air-ground problems, field exercises and command post exercises.[8]

Counterparts of nearly all of these exercises might have been found in the training program for the 2d Marine Division and 2d Marine Aircraft Wing on the North Carolina coast. Operation CAMID at Little Creek, Va., was similar to DEMON III. All principal FMFLant elements participated in Operation CROSSOVER at Camp Lejeune, North Carolina, in the spring of 1950, and a Marine aircraft group was embarked aboard a carrier in the Mediterranean. Other elements of the Wing took part in PORTREX, an Army-Navy amphibious exercise in the Caribbean, and in SWARMER, an Army-Air Force airborne exercise in North Carolina. Units of both the Division and the Wing were represented in the annual Amphibious Command Post Exercise at Lejeune; and throughout the winter and

[8] PacFlt *Interim Rpt No. 1*, XV:Zebra, 3–5.

spring a succession of smaller ground, air, and air-ground exercises
emphasized close support and amphibious landings.

Posts and stations were meanwhile conducting annual weapons
qualification firing tests and individual training as required by USMC
General Order No. 10. This program was designed to maintain the
basic military proficiency of men not serving with the Fleet Marine
Force. It is significant, however, that a large proportion of them had
reported to such duty directly from FMF units, in accordance with the
rotation policy.

The program for the Organized Reserve included both armory and
active duty summer training. Air and ground units of reservists were
"adopted" during their summer training by similar units of the Fleet
Marine Force, which supervised the exercises and provided instructors. By the summer of 1950, a large proportion of the reservists had
progressed beyond basic training into advanced individual and unit
training, so that they could be classed as "nearly combat ready" at the
time of the 1st Marine Division expansion.[7]

Mobilization of Marine Corps Reserve

Shortcomings in quantity rather than quality of Marine personnel
made expansion a problem on 19 July 1950, when General MacArthur
sent his third request to the Pentagon for a Marine division with
appropriate air. Again the Joint Chiefs referred the matter to General Cates, who was prepared with two plans worked out in detail by
his staff—Plan ABLE, providing third rifle companies and replacements for the Brigade; and Plan BAKER, designed to bring the 1st
Marine Division up to full war strength by calling reservists to active
duty.

These plans were based on the personnel statistics of 30 June 1950.
The grand total of 74,279 Marines on active duty at that time (97
per cent of authorized strength) was distributed as follows:

Operating Forces—engaged directly in carrying out assigned missions
   and tasks 40,36/
Supporting Establishment—comprising trained administrative and
   supply personnel 24,552

---
[7] *Ibid.*

Special Assignment—including all personnel serving with organizations outside the regular establishment 3,871

Non-Available—made up of personnel hospitalized, confined, or en route 5,492

Total 74,279

A breakdown of the Operating Forces reveals that the Fleet Marine Force numbered 27,703 men, the security detachments included 11,087, and 1,574 Marines were afloat. Of the 11,853 in FMFPac, 7,779 were in the 1st Marine Division, and 3,733 in the 1st Marine Aircraft Wing. The 15,803 Marines in FMFLant included 8,973 in the 2d Marine Division and 5,297 in the 2d Marine Aircraft Wing.[8]

These figures make it evident that the 1st Marine Division could not be brought up to war strength of about 25,000 troops without drawing upon the 33,527 (77 per cent of authorized strength) in the ground forces of the Organized Reserve, and the 6,341 (94 per cent of authorized strength) in the aviation forces. The ground personnel were distributed among these units:

Twenty-one infantry battalions; 16 rifle companies; seven 105mm howitzer battalions; five 155mm howitzer battalions; one 155mm gun battalion; two 40mm gun batteries; two tank battalions; three amphibian tractor battalions; one amphibian truck company; one signal company (supplementary); six signal companies; one engineer battalion; 15 women's reserve platoons.

Aviation units consisted of 30 Marine fighter squadrons (VMF) and 12 Marine ground control intercept squadrons (MGCI).

The Organized Reserve was exceeded as a reservoir of potential man power by the Volunteer Marine Corps Reserve, which had a total of 90,044 men and women on 30 June 1950. This total included 2,267 volunteer reservists on continuous active duty with the regular establishment, about 5,000 training in some 200 volunteer training units, and 1,316 in the Fleet Reserve.

Altogether, the strength of all Marine reserve components (less volunteer reservists on active duty) amounted to a total of 128,959, or nearly double the number of Marines in the regular establishment.[9]

Behind every Marine regular, figuratively speaking, stood two reservists who were ready to step forward and fill the gaps in the ranks.

[8] Giusti, 1–2.
[9] *Ibid.*, 1–5, 6.

Thus it was scarcely far-fetched when some inspired public information officer coined the phrase "Minute Men of 1950" for these recent
civilians who made it possible for the 1st Marine Division to hit the
beaches at Inchon.

Events moved swiftly on 19 July. Only a few hours after the
receipt of CinCFE's third request, the mobilization of the Marine
Corps Reserve was authorized by President Truman with the sanction of Congress. Headquarters Marine Corps, on the hill overlooking the Pentagon, was ablaze with lights that summer night; and
decisions were made which enabled four important steps to be taken
next day:

(1) a warning to Reserve District directors that the Organized Reserve
would soon be ordered to active duty;

(2) notification to commanding generals to expect some 21,000 Organized
Reservists shortly at Marine Barracks, Camp Pendleton, and about 5,800
at Marine Barracks, Camp Lejeune;

(3) orders issued by CMC, with the approval of CNO, to discontinue the
practice of discharging reservists at their own request;

(4) the first reservists—22 units with a total strength of 4,830 men—ordered
to active duty with a delay of ten days.[10]

The Joint Chiefs of Staff were still not convinced that a Marine force
could be embarked to meet General MacArthur's deadline of 10 September without stripping FMFLant units to a dangerous extent. On
the advice of Admiral Sherman, they informed CinCFE on 20 July
that a Marine division could not be sent before November or even
December.

General Shepherd had a great deal to do with shaping the ultimate decision. On the 20th, when CNO conferred with Admiral
Radford on the question of a Marine division, the Commander of the
Pacific Fleet in his turn asked the opinion of the Marine general.
General Shepherd replied that a Marine amphibious striking force
could be raised for the proposed Inchon landing without seriously
weakening the Fleet Marine Force as a whole. This striking force,
he predicted, would prove to be "the key of achievement of a timely
and economical decision for our arms." [11]

The Marine general's statement was one of the main factors in
causing the Joint Chiefs to advise MacArthur on the 22d that they

---

[10] *Ibid.*, II–2.
[11] CG FMFPac memo to CinCPacFlt, 20 Jul 50.

were reconsidering their stand. During the next 48 hours, as dispatches sped back and forth across the Pacific, a compromise was reached. CinCFE was promised his Marine division in time for his target date—but it was to be a division minus one RCT. In other words, the infantry regiment of the Brigade would be supplemented by another RCT and supporting troops with appropriate Marine air. But the Joint Chiefs were adamant in their decision that MacArthur must wait until autumn or even winter for his third RCT.

These preliminaries cleared the way so that General MacArthur's request was finally approved by JCS on 25 July, the day when General Smith took over command of the 1st Marine Division. The Marine Corps was directed to build the division (less one RCT) up to full war strength, and a date of departure of 10–15 August for the Far East was set.

A 50 percent reduction in Marine security forces within the continental limits of the United States was authorized by CNO on that same date. This meant that an additional 3,630 regulars would be enabled to report for service with the 1st Marine Division.

On the morning of the 26th a courier from Washington arrived at Camp Pendleton with a communication for General Smith indicating that the expanded 1st Marine Division would be composed of four types of personnel: (1) Brigade units, to be combined with the Division upon arrival in the Far East; (2) units of the 2d Marine Division, to be ordered to Camp Pendleton to augment elements of the 1st; (3) regular personnel to be called in from posts and stations; and (4) final deficiencies to be filled by men from the Marine Corps Reserve who met minimum combat experience requirements.[12]

Congress passed legislation on 27 July authorizing the President to extend for one year all enlistments in the armed forces, both regular and reserve, which were due to expire before 9 July 1951. This gave the assurance of a stable body of troops.

On the 31st, with the first reservists arriving at Camp Pendleton and

---

[12] MajGen Oliver P. Smith, *Notes on the Operations of the 1st Marine Division during the First Nine Months of the Korean War, 1950–1951* (MS), 3–4. (Hereafter, O. P. Smith, *Notes.*) Among the most valuable sources of the present book are the *Chronicle of the Operations of the 1st Marine Division During the First Nine Months of the Korean War, 1950–1951* (MS), (hereafter, O. P. Smith, *Chronicle*), and *Notes* prepared in typescript by the commanding general of the division. The *Chronicle* is a day-by-day account of planning, command decisions, and resulting events, while the *Notes* are an analytical review of the relative facts, statistics, and directives. Combining accuracy with a keen sense of historical values, the Marine general by his knowledge of shorthand was able to keep a fairly complete record in the field which he later checked with official reports.

the first contingents leaving Camp Lejeune for the West Coast, the Joint Chiefs of Staff directed CNO to expand the 2d Marine Division to war strength while increasing the number of Marine tactical air squadrons from 16 to 18.[13]   Obviously, the 1st and 2d Divisions could not be built up simultaneously without serious delays, and priority must be given to the 1st.   It was equally obvious, moreover, that this expansion must be largely accomplished during the first week of August if the troops were to be made ready for embarkation between the 10th and 15th.

The Influx at Camp Pendleton

The first build-up troops to reach Camp Pendleton were three Organized Reserve units which arrived on 31 July—the 13th Infantry Company, of Los Angeles; the 12th Amphibian Tractor Company, of San Francisco; and the 3d Engineer Company, of Phoenix, Arizona.   This was the beginning of an inundation which kept the camp keyed to a 24-hour day and a 7-day week.   A torrent of troops poured into the vast military reservation by bus, train, and plane at all hours of the day and night.   Confusion seemed to reign from the tawny California hills to the blue Pacific; and yet this seeming chaos was under the control of veteran officers and NCOs who had mounted out before. Accommodations for the newcomers were not de luxe, but men were being processed, assigned, fed, and equipped as rapidly as they arrived. The tramp of feet could be heard all night long as details of troops drew clothing and equipment or reported for medical examinations.

A total of 13,703 Marines reached Camp Pendleton during this busy week.   Counting the personnel already on hand, troops of four categories were represented:

Officers and men remaining in 1st Marine Division at Camp Pendleton after dispatch of the Brigade   3,459

Officers and men reporting from posts and stations up to 4 August . . .   3,630

Officers and men reporting from the 2d Marine Division from 3 to 6 August   7,182

Officers and men selected as combat-ready out of the total of about 10,000 reservists reporting by 7 August   2,891

Total   17,162

---

[13] Giusti, II–2.

The expansion took place in two phases. First, of course, came the bringing of the 1st Marine Division (less one RCT) up to war strength, including augmentation personnel and supplies for the units of the Brigade. Next, the organization of a third reinforced infantry regiment, the 7th Marines, was directed by a letter from CMC to CG 1st Marine Division on 4 August.[14]

Headquarters Marine Corps naturally foresaw the necessity for replacement and rotation troops. The importance of the Reserve in this long-range expansion program may be seen by glancing ahead at the statistics of the next few months. Units of these recent civilians continued to report at such a rate that by 11 September 1950 the Organized Reserve (Ground) had in effect ceased to exist! In other words, all acceptable personnel had already reported for active duty, and the total of 33,528 officers and men represented a 90.02 percentage of availability.

The record of the Volunteer Reserve proved to be equally good after it was ordered to active duty on 15 August 1950. During the next seven and a half months, down to 31 March 1951, the Volunteer Reserve furnished 51,942 of the 84,821 reservists on active duty. As to the quality of these troops, about 99 per cent of the officers and 77.5 per cent of the enlisted were veterans of World War II.[15]

Many of the first reservists to report at Camp Pendleton made unusual sacrifices. Although they had the privilege of being discharged at their own request as late as 18 July 1950, the unexpectedness of the Korean conflict worked hardships in some instances. Reservists with several dependents or just establishing themselves in a business or profession had to settle their affairs hurriedly. There was little applause when the Minute Men of 1950 departed from home communities which were on a basis of business and pleasure as usual. The Korean conflict was still regarded as a "police action" which would be ended shortly. Nobody dreamed that within its first year it would become the fourth largest military effort of our nation's history.

The Marine Corps was as lenient as could reasonably be expected when it came to granting delays and deferments. On 1 August a board of eight officers at Marine Corps Headquarters initiated daily meetings to consider such requests emanating from the various Reserve

---

[14] O. P. Smith, *Notes*, 5–6.
[15] Giusti, III–2, 7.

districts. Two weeks later the Commandant gave Reserve District directors the authority to grant delays for periods up to six months after judging each case on its individual merits. But even after every concession had been made that could be reconciled with the national interest, it was a wrench for hundreds of reservists to make the sudden plunge from civil into military life.

There were instances of men seeking deferment by using political influence or pleading physical disability. But such cases were rare as compared to the great majority who reported promptly and declared themselves combat-ready.

In the selection of reservists for the division, two categories were recognized—combat-ready and noncombat-ready. The first applied to men whose records proved that they had been members of the Organized Reserve for two years and had attended one summer camp and 72 drills or two summer camps and 32 drills. Veterans of more than 90 days' service in the Marine Corps also qualified. All other reservists were classified as noncombat-ready.

When lost or incomplete records complicated the equation, a reservist's own opinion could not be accepted as proof of his fitness for combat. This ruling had to be made because so many men were found to have more spunk than training. Officers of a reservist's unit were questioned before a decision was reached, and any man feeling the need of further training could be removed without prejudice from immediate consideration for combat.

Standards were so strictly observed that only about half of the reservists qualified as being combat-ready. This group broke down into the 15 per cent accepted for the 1st Marine Division and the 35 per cent assigned to posts and stations to relieve regulars who joined the division. The remaining 50 per cent consisted of men placed in the noncombat-ready or recruit class.[16]

The emergency found the Organized Aviation Reserve with 30 VMF and 12 GCI squadrons generally up to peacetime strength. Of the 1,588 officers, about 95 per cent were combat-experienced, and only about 10 per cent of the enlisted men stood in need of basic training. It was a comparatively simple task, therefore, to comply with the order of 23 July calling for six VMF and three GCI squadrons to report to El Toro. Their mission was to build up to war strength

---

[16] Andrew Geer, *The New Breed* (New York, 1952), 103–105.

the units of the 1st MAW which had been stripped to mount out MAG-33.

On 3 August the remaining nine GCI squadrons of the Organized Aviation Reserve were ordered to El Toro.[17] By this time the build-up was so well in hand that Major General Field Harris, commanding the 1st Marine Aircraft Wing, conferred with General Smith about aviation shipping for the embarkation.

This veteran Marine pilot, a native of Kentucky, had been commissioned a second lieutenant in 1917 after graduating from the U. S. Naval Academy. Three years of service with Marine ground forces in Cuba and the Philippines were followed by Headquarters duty at Washington and flight training at Pensacola. Designated a naval aviator in 1929, he held various Marine air commands before participating as colonel and brigadier general in the Guadalcanal, Northern Solomons, and Green Island air operations of World War II. On his return, he was appointed Assistant Commandant (Air) and Director of Aviation.

In the autumn of 1946, after Operation CROSSROADS had given a glimpse into the tactical future, Generals Shepherd, Harris, and Smith were named as a Special Board "to orient the effort of the Marine Corps away from the last war and toward the next." The result was recommendations leading to experiments with rotary wing aircraft as a means of tactical dispersion in amphibious operations against an enemy employing atomic weapons. Thus the Marine Corps worked out new helicopter combat techniques which were soon to create tactical history with the Brigade and Division in Korea.[18]

Embarkation of 1st Marine Division

It is a curious circumstance that not until 8 August did General Smith himself have his first information as to the Inchon landing. The basic directive of 25 July had merely specified that the main body of the Division would embark from San Diego, prepared for combat. The commanding general did not learn even unofficially about the time and the place of the proposed operation until he was told by General Fellers. While reporting at Camp Pendleton on his return from

[17] Giusti, III-2.
[18] Lynn Montross, *Cavalry of the Sky* (New York, 1954), 51–53.

Japan, the TTU commander gave General Smith an informal account of the conference which took place on 4 July at FECOM Headquarters in Tokyo.[19]

On the following day, 9 August, the Division issued Operation Order No. 1–50, which provided for the movement of the Division (less the Brigade and one RCT) to the Far East to report upon arrival to CinCFE for operational control. Embarkation was to be carried out in accordance with Embarkation Plan No. 1–50 of 6 August.

By this date, 17,162 Marines in Camp Pendleton were eligible for reassignment to the 1st Marine Division. There was no time, of course, for much training. On 2 August the Division issued Training Bulletin No. 36–50 as a general guide providing for some rudiments of individual and small-unit instruction. But about all that could be accomplished was conditioning training and test firing of weapons. As a result, many of the weapons issued directly to units were found to be defective, having been in storage since 1945.[20]

The war news from Korea at this time lent an atmosphere of grim realism to preparations at Camp Pendleton. On 2 August the 1st Provisional Marine Brigade had landed at Pusan, the day following the debarkation of two U. S. Army units, the skeletonized 2d Infantry Division and the 5th RCT. The original destination of the Marines had been Japan, but during the voyage the military situation deteriorated so rapidly that on 25 July a landing in Korea was ordered by CinCFE.

Following the capture of Taejon on 20 July, the Red Korean columns of invasion speeded up their "end run" around the Eighth Army's open left flank. Driving eastward as well as southward, the enemy made such progress during the next ten days that on 31 July the UN forces were pushed back into a chain of defensive positions in southeast Korea. This was the Pusan Perimeter, which must be held if the vital line of communications from the supply port to Taegu was to be maintained.

The Marines jumped off east of Masan on 7 August with the Army 5th RCT and elements of the 25th Infantry Division in the first sustained counterattack mounted by UN forces. General Craig had control of Army as well as Marine units during the most critical period of the initial two days, and carrier-based MAG–33 squadrons provided

[19] O. P. Smith, *Notes*, 18, 41.
[20] *Ibid.*, 16–17.

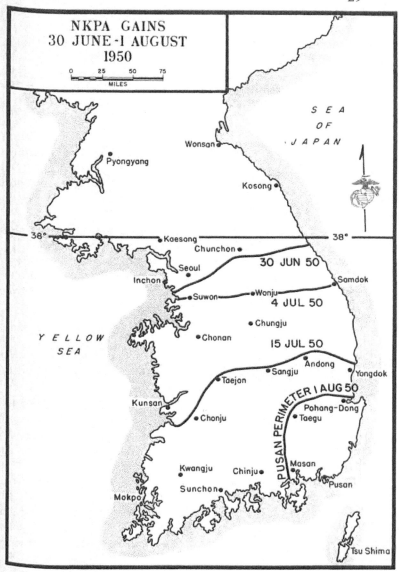

**NKPA GAINS
30 JUNE - 1 AUGUST
1950**

0   25   50   75
MILES

SEA OF JAPAN

Wonsan

Pyongyang

Kosong

38°   38°

Kaesong

Chunchon

Seoul   30 JUN 50

Inchon   Samdok

Suwon   Wonju   4 JUL 50

Chungju

YELLOW
SEA   Chonan   15 JUL 50

Andong

Sangju   Yongdok

Taejon

PUSAN PERIMETER 1 AUG 50

Kunsan

Pohang-Dong

Chonju   Taegu

Kwangju   Chinju   Masan

Sunchon   Pusan

Mokpo

Tsu Shima

tactical air support. Enemy resistance was so shattered by the 9th that the Red Korean machine of invasion went into reverse for the first time.

From the 9th to the 13th, when they were relieved, parallel columns of Army and Marine assault troops drove from Chindong-ni nearly to Chinju, a distance of about 40 miles by the seacoast route. It was only a local setback for the enemy, to be sure, but it had a heartening effect for tired UN forces which had known only delaying actions so far.

It also added to the problems of staff officers at Camp Pendleton and Pearl Harbor, since replacements must be sent to the Brigade. With this in mind, the Commandant had begun the organization of the 1st Replacement Draft of approximately 800 men on the date of Brigade activation. These troops, however, were absorbed into the 1st Marine Division when it expanded to war strength, as was a second draft (also designated the 1st Replacement Draft) of 3,000 men.[21]

On 3 August the 1st Marine Division was directed by FMFPac to send 10 officers and 290 enlisted men to the Brigade by airlift. This draft was to be ready to move from Camp Pendleton by MATS planes on 9 August, but not until five days later did it finally proceed to San Francisco by rail and fly to Japan.

On the 23d another draft of 10 officers and 300 enlisted men from Marine posts in Hawaii and Guam was sent by air to Japan, these troops being replaced by the same number of noncombat-ready Marines airlifted from Camp Pendleton. This process was twice repeated early in September, when two more drafts totaling 20 officers and 590 men flew to Japan to provide replacements and third companies for the 5th Marines of the Brigade.[22]

Logistics offered as many problems as personnel at Camp Pendleton, since both the Brigade and Division units had been on peace tables of organization and equipment. The 30-day replenishment stock, held in readiness for such an emergency, was also based on peace strength tables. Thus it was found that the specification of "requirements" was best determined in most instances by making out requisitions based on the difference between T/E for peace and war.

Narrow time limits did not permit the assembly of supplies and equipment delivered at Camp Pendleton under the relentless pressure

---

[21] PacFlt *Interim Rpt No. 1*, XV:Zebra, 8–9.
[22] *Ibid.*; Col A. L. Bowser ltr to CMC, 11 Feb 55.

of urgent deadlines. FMFLant air and ground units arriving from Camp Lejeune brought their own organization equipment, which was staged through the Recruit Depot at San Diego. Much of the heavy equipment from the Barstow, California, Annex, Depot of Supplies, was delivered dockside and loaded without further inspection. Not until arrival at Kobe, Japan, were such items as the LVTs finally given a mechanical checkup.[23]

Ammunition was delivered from the depots to the Naval Station, San Diego, for loading. The following units of fire were specified by Division Embarkation Plan 1–50:

  (1) 3 UF in hands of 1st Marines, LVT, tank, and artillery units;
      1 UF in hands of all other units;
  (2) 2 UF in hands of 1st Ordnance Bn for the 1st Marines, LVT, tank, and
      artillery units;
  (3) 4 UF in the hands of the 1st Ordnance Bn for other units.[24]

Even after all items of initial supply had been assembled, the problem was by no means solved. Since the Division and Wing would be operating under Army and Air Force control, it became necessary to establish a long-range policy for resupply. The best answer seemed to be the procedure adopted by the Brigade, providing that the Army and Air Force furnish all supplies not peculiar to the Marine Corps. The latter would be provided by Marine or Navy agencies automatically in 30-day increments, with 120 days of resupply allotted to ground units and 90 days to air units. Thereafter, supply was to be requisitioned as needed. And in the lack of a service command as such, the G–4 section of FMFPac was committed to the task of preparing and submitting resupply requisitions for items in this category.[25]

Five hundred civilians were employed to help with the reconditioning of motor transport and other heavy equipment which had been "in mothballs" at Barstow since the end of World War II. Such items had to be put through the shops in many instances and restored to operating condition before delivery. The enormous supply depot in the California desert erupted with activity as trains of flatcars and long columns of motor trucks were routed to San Diego.

---

[23] PacFlt *Interim Rpt No. 1*, XV:Zebra, 18–22.
[24] 1st MarDiv *Embarkation Plan 1–50*, 6 Aug 50, Annex Charlie.
[25] PacFlt *Interim Rpt No. 1*, XV:Zebra, 12.

The actual loading and embarkation were conducted almost according to schedule in spite of such handicaps as inadequate dock facilities, the reception of supplies and equipment from a variety of sources, a shortage of stevedores, and piecemeal assignments of shipping.   Only 54 stevedore crews were available out of the 90 requested, and commercial ships were necessary to supplement naval shipping.   Nevertheless, the loading began on 8 August and was completed by the 22d.   The following 19 ships were employed to mount out the main body of the 1st Marine Division:

LST 845; LSM 419; two APAs, the USS *Noble* and USS *President Jackson;* five APs, the USNS *General Buckner,* USNS *General Weigel,* USS *Marine Phoenix,* USNS *General Meigs* and USS *General Butner;* and ten AKs, the SS *Dolly Thurman,* SS *Green Bay Victory,* SS *Noonday,* SS *African Patriot,* SS *Twin Falls Victory,* SS *Southwind,* SS *American Press,* SS *American Victory,* SS *Alma Victory,* and SS *Belgian Victory.*[26]

Generals Shepherd and Cates arrived for the main embarkation on the 13th and 14th respectively, accompanied by Major General Franklin A. Hart and Brigadier General Edwin A. Pollock.   While these general officers were being acquainted with the progress made so far, the AKA *Titania* blew out two boilers after being about 20 percent loaded.   Since the repairs would require about ten days, a commercial freighter was provided as a last-minute replacement.

Build-up of 7th Marine Regiment

One of the purposes of General Shepherd's visit was to discuss with General Cates the problems of organizing and embarking the 7th Marines (Reinf.).   The activation of this unit had been directed on 10 August 1950, when an officer of the G–1 Section, Headquarters FMFPac, delivered orders to Camp Pendleton.[27]

This was the result of a change of mind on the part of the Joint Chiefs of Staff.   After reconsideration, they decided that it would be

[26] 1st Marine Division *Special Action Report for the Inchon-Seoul Operation,* 20 Apr 51, sec. 1.   (Hereafter, 1st MarDiv *SAR.*)
[27] FMFPac *Operation Order (Opn O) 3–50,* 11 Aug 50.

feasible to raise a third RCT much sooner than had at first seemed possible, though not in time for MacArthur's assault landing. Arrival in Japan about 20 September seemed to be the earliest date that could be managed.

Of the 17,162 eligible Marines at Camp Pendleton at that time, the regulars in excess of those required to mount out between the 10th and 15th were placed in the rear echelon of the division as a cadre for the third infantry regiment.[28] The following troops were made available to draw upon for the formation of the 7th Marines:

Officers and men from 2d Marine Division	1, 822
Officers and men of 3d Bn, 6th Marines in the Mediterranean	735
Officers and men of Marine Corps Reserve selected as combat-ready	1, 972
Officers and men of rear echelon of Division, and from posts and stations	1, 109
Total	[29] 5, 638

Colonel Homer L. Litzenberg was designated as commanding officer on the date of activation, 17 August 1950. The Chief of Naval Operations directed the regiment to embark for the Far East not later than 3 September. These components were included in the build-up:

3d Battalion, 11th Marines; Company D, 1st Tank Battalion; Company D, 1st Engineer Battalion; Company C, 1st Shore Party Battalion (including two Shore Party communication teams from Signal Company, Signal Battalion); Company D, 1st Motor Transport Battalion; Company E, 1st Medical Battalion.

Forming the nucleus of the regiment, the 6th Marines, at peace strength and less two battalions, arrived from Camp Lejeune on 16 August. The 3d Battalion of this FMFLant regiment, then stationed afloat in the Mediterranean, was ordered to proceed through the Suez Canal to become part of the 7th Marines upon arrival in Japan.

While the other elements were being absorbed at Camp Pendleton, a conference attended by General Smith, Major General Alfred H. Noble, and Colonel Litzenberg was held to discuss rear echelon personnel and the formation of RCT-7. The following troops were

---

[28] See Appendix B for the build-up of the 1st Marine Division and Appendix C for the Task Organization.
[29] This account of the build-up of the 7th Marines is based on the summary in PacFlt *Interim Rpt No. 1*, XV:Zebra, pt. V.

found to be available to take care of casuals and retain custody of such division supplies and equipment as had not yet been embarked:

MARINE CORPS		NAVY	
Off.	*Enl.*	*Off.*	*Enl.*
224	1,029	11	35

Not included in these figures were 197 noneffective enlisted personnel, a rocket battery, a motor transport company, and the organizational rear echelon of eight officers and 28 men. It was decided that General Noble, as FMFPac representative, would examine MOSs, to determine how many men would be transferred to the 7th Marines or retained for FMF units to be activated later. The need was also foreseen for rear echelon working parties to relieve personnel of units mounting out.[30]

Staff Groups Flown to Japan

Although the 1st Marine Division had enough problems at Camp Pendleton to keep a full war-strength staff busy, several of the key members were in Korea with the Brigade. The complete Division staff was never integrated until after the landing at Inchon. On 7 August, however, a dispatch from CinCFE requested that the "Commanding General, 1st Marine Division, and planning group capable of developing Division embarkation and landing plans be airlifted" to the Far East.[31]

General Smith decided that this flight could best be made in two echelons. The first, which took off for Japan at 1400 on 16 August 1950, included a group of 12 officers and six enlisted men selected to initiate planning:

	Officers	*Enlisted*
G–2	Col B. T. Holcomb, Jr	TSgt W. O'Grady
Ass't G–2	Maj J. G. Babashanian	Cpl J. N. Lareau
G–3	Col A. L. Bowser, Jr	Sgt G. O. Davis, Jr.
Ass't G–3	LtCol F. R. Moore	
Ass't G–4	LtCol C. T. Hodges	
Ass't Emb Off	Capt R. E. Moody	PFC H. J. McAvinue

[30] O. P. Smith, *Notes*, 36–37.
[31] CinCFE disp to CinCPacFlt, 7 Aug 50, info CNO, CMC, CG 1st MarDiv, CG FMFPac, and ComNavFE.

	Officers	Enlisted
Shore Pty Off............	Maj J. G. Dibble	
Signal Off	LtCol A. Creal...........	Cpl L Shefchik
Ass't G–1	LtCol B. D. Godbold	
Fire Sup Coord..........	LtCol D. E. Reeve........	SSgt P. Richardson
Naval Gunfire Off.......	LtCol L. S. Fraser	
Air Off................	Capt W. F. Jacobs	

General Smith stayed at Camp Pendleton for two more days until he was assured that the main body of the Division had sailed. Then he accompanied the second echelon of planners which departed by air at 1410 on 18 August:

	Officers	Enlisted
CG	MajGen O. P. Smith	
C/S..................	Col G. A. Williams........	Cpl C. V. Irwin
Aide to CG.............	Capt M. J. Sexton.........	PFC W. D. Grove
G–1.................	Col H. S. Walseth........	Cpl W. P. Minette
Ass't Signal Off..........	Capt A. J. Gunther.........	MSgt F. J. Stumpges
G–4	Col F. M. McAlister	
Engineer Off............	Maj E. P. Moses, Jr.	
Embark Off............	Maj J. M. Rouse	
Amtrac Off	Maj A. J. Barrett	
Motor Trans Off........	Maj H. W. Seeley, Jr.	
Ordnance Off............	Maj L. O. Williams [32]	

The departure of the commanding general coincided with the closing of the Division CP at Camp Pendleton. There were still several thousand Marines of the rear echelon left under the control of General Noble in the sprawling installation, but the brown California hills looked down upon a scene of strange and brooding quiet as compared to the activity of the past three weeks.

It was D-minus 28 for the men of the 1st Marine Division.

---

[32] O. P. Smith, *Notes*, 37–38.

CHAPTER III

Operation Plan CHROMITE

Interview with General MacArthur—Conferences in Tokyo—
Inception of X Corps—Final Conference on Inchon—Brigade
Victory in Korea—The Marine Amphibious Mission

THE SCARS OF WAR heal rapidly. From the air General Smith could see jungle covering the battlefields of Guam. Iwo Jima looked as untouched as if it had never been the scene of Marine casualties exceeding the losses of the Union army at Gettysburg. Even fire-blasted Tokyo had recovered to a surprising extent from the terrible bombings of 1945.

Now, five years later, the United States had entered upon a new military effort. As the Marine general landed at Haneda Airfield on the afternoon of 22 August 1950, he was met by Admiral Doyle and driven to the *Mount McKinley*, tied up at the dock in Tokyo harbor. And though assigned to the cabin reserved for the landing force commander, CG 1st MarDiv found it an ironical circumstance that he did not yet know the prospective D-day and H-hour of the landing.[1]

He had not long to wait for such data. The advance section of the Marine planning group being already aboard the *Mount McKinley*, he was quickly informed by Colonel Bowser, the G–3 of the incomplete Division staff. D-day at Inchon had been tentatively set for 15 September, and the landing must be made during the high tide of late afternoon. It meant assaulting a port of 250,000 prewar population over the mud flats and seawalls, with little opportunity to consolidate positions before nightfall. Nor would there be time for training and rehearsals, since the troops would reach Japan barely in time to unload and reload in amphibious shipping before proceeding to the objective area.

---

[1] O. P. Smith, *Chronicle*, 22 Aug 50.

General Smith learned further that a new command structure, to be known as X Corps, was being hastily erected by FECOM especially for the operation. No announcement had been made of a project still classified as Top Secret, but it was known to the planning group that General Almond would command a corps not yet activated. The 1st Marine Division would be under his control as the landing force.

Admiral Doyle, an old hand at amphibious warfare, was not happy about Inchon when he considered the naval aspects. Initiated at Guadalcanal and Tulagi in 1942, he had taken part in some rugged ship-to-shore assaults of World War II. Afterwards, as Commander of Amphibious Shipping for the Pacific Fleet, he had made a career of it. And Admiral Doyle considered Inchon a hard nut to crack. He refused to admit that any amphibious operation was impossible as long as the United States Navy remained afloat, but he did maintain that Inchon bristled with risks.

In twenty minutes that Tuesday afternoon General Smith heard enough to convince him that the forthcoming assault would take a great deal of doing. But there was no time for discussion. For at 1730, just two hours after stepping from his plane, he had an appointment with the commander in chief.

Interview with General MacArthur

Arriving on the minute at the Dai Ichi building, General Smith reported to FECOM Headquarters. He was met by an aide, who escorted him to General Almond's office. On the way down echoing corridors, he responded at frequent intervals to the salutes of sentries who presented arms with fixed bayonets.[2]

The offices of CinCFE and his chief of staff were connected by an imposing conference room with paneled walls and pillars along one side. General Smith had an opportunity to survey his surroundings at leisure before General Almond appeared. The new X Corps commander explained that his chief had a habit of taking a long afternoon break and would arrive later.

Of medium height and stocky build, Almond gave the impression at the age of 58 of a buoyant temperament and restless energy. A

---

[2] This section is based upon: O. P. Smith, *Notes*, 45–51, *Chronicle*, 22 Aug 50, and interv, 13 Jan 55.

native Virginian and graduate of the Virginia Military Institute, he had been an ETO division commander in World War II. After joining MacArthur's staff, he became one of the most loyal officers of a group noted for devotion to their famous chief.

Almond greeted the reserved, white-haired Marine general cordially. He launched at once into the topic of the Inchon operation, expressing the utmost confidence in the ability of the UN forces to prevail.

It was the initial contact of the two men. Mutual respect was not lacking, but differences in temperament made it inevitable that these generals would not always see eye to eye. History teaches that this is by no means a deplorable situation when kept within reasonable bounds. Character can be as decisive a factor as logistics, and some of the greatest victories of the ages have been won by colleagues who did not agree at times. Friction, in fact, is more likely to sharpen than to blunt military intellects; and Smith's precision had potentialities of being a good counterpoise for Almond's energy.

While they were discussing the tactical problems, the commander in chief returned to his office. He summoned his chief of staff for a brief conference, then requested that Smith be presented.

MacArthur shook hands warmly, grasping the Marine general's elbow with his left hand. Without the celebrated "scrambled eggs" cap, he looked his 70 years in moments of fatigue, but the old fire and dash were not lacking. The very simplicity of his attire—shirtsleeves and open collar—made a dramatic contrast to the military pomp and ceremony surrounding him in this former Japanese commercial building, one of the few earthquake-proof and air-conditioned structures in Tokyo.

In a cigarette-smoking age, both MacArthur and Smith preferred the calm comfort of a pipe. The commander in chief lit up and puffed reflectively a moment. Then he leaned back in his chair and gave his concept of the Inchon operation. But it was more than a concept in the usual military sense; it was a vision of a victory potent enough to end the Korean conflict at a stroke. And it was more than confidence which upheld him; it was a supreme and almost mystical faith that he could not fail.

He granted, of course, that there were difficulties and risks. Evidently Almond had mentioned Smith's reservations, for he proceeded to reassure the Marine general. His voice full of feeling, he expressed his deep conviction that the war could be won in a month at Inchon, and that the 1st Marine Division could win it. The enemy, he explained, had committed nearly all of his troops in the Pusan Perimeter. Thus the Marines would not be heavily opposed when they stormed ashore at Inchon and drove inland to cut the main NKPA line of communications at Seoul.

MacArthur said he knew that the Marines had high standards, having commanded them in the New Britain operations of the last war. He realized that the Marines strove for perfection, and the Inchon landing was bound to be somewhat helter-skelter by the very nature of things. But there was no doubt, he affirmed, that the victory soon to be gained by the 1st Marine Division would make 15 September 1950 a glorious date in American history.

His voice was charged with fervor as it rose and fell eloquently. Once General Smith made a move as if to depart, but the commander in chief motioned him back to his chair. At last he brought the conversation to a close by standing suddenly, grasping the Marine general's hand, and bidding him a cordial good-bye.

Conferences in Tokyo

It was sometimes an awkward situation for Navy and Marine officers in general, and Admiral Doyle and General Smith in particular. In many respects they appeared doubters and pessimists in contrast to FECOM staff officers who reflected General MacArthur's shining confidence. But as amphibious specialists, carrying a heavy load of responsibility for the landing, they had to give serious thought to the risks at Inchon.

This was brought home forcibly to the Marine general on the morning of the 23d, when he attended a meeting conducted by Major General Clark L. Ruffner, Chief of Staff of the future X Corps. Although the conference proceeded according to the usual form, General Smith felt that it departed at times from the realism which he considered an essential of sound amphibious planning. It was announced, for instance, that after taking Inchon, the 1st Marine Division was to cross the Han and attack Seoul, although X Corps had neither equipment nor materiel for bridging the sizeable river.[3]

---

[3] O. P. Smith, *Chronicle*, 23 Aug 50.

A review of the background disclosed that after CinCFE decided on 10 July not to use the 1st Cavalry Division as his landing force, he briefly considered two other Army outfits. The 2d Infantry Division, commanded by Major General Lawrence B. Keiser, was then under orders to embark from the West Coast. Some of the personnel had been given amphibious training by an ANGLICO instruction team and had taken part in Operation MIKI, but the division as a whole was much understrength. The same difficulty led to the elimination of Major General David G. Barr's 7th Infantry Division in Japan, which had supplied troops to units at the front until only a cadre remained.

The assurance on 25 July of a war-strength Marine division took care of the *who* question. Next came the problems of *when* and *where* an amphibious assault could be best mounted. JANIS (Joint Army and Navy Intelligence Studies) reports indicated that the east coast of Korea, though of lesser importance in military respects, offered such hydrographic advantages as unusually moderate tides and a general absence of shoals. In forbidding contrast, the shallow west coast waters could be navigated at most points only by means of narrow channels winding through the mud flats.[4]

Of all the west coast seaports, Inchon was probably the least desirable objective when considered strictly from the viewpoint of hydrographic conditions. From first to last, however, Inchon was Douglas MacArthur's choice. FECOM staff officers ventured to suggest two alternatives, Wonsan on the east coast and Kunsan on the west coast, but the commander in chief replied that neither was close enough to the enemy's main line of communications to suit his purposes. He would settle for nothing less than Inchon.

So much for the place. As to the time, the choice was even more limited. The tidal range varied from an average spring tide[5] height of 23 feet to an occasional maximum of 33 feet. Landing craft required a tide of 25 feet to navigate the mud flats of the harbor, and the LSTs must have 29 feet. Only during a few days in the middle of September and October were those depths provided by spring tides of the next 12 weeks. MacArthur rejected an October date as being

---

[4] JANIS No. 75, ch. IV, *Theater Study, Korean Coast and Beaches*.

[5] A spring tide is a higher than normal tide caused by the sun and moon being in conjunction or opposition, as at new moon and full moon. Conversely, when the moon is at first or third quarter the tide (neap tide) is smaller than usual.

too late in the season, so that 15 September became D-day by virtue of elimination.

A late afternoon H-hour was also a choice of necessity. Islands, reefs, and shoals restricted the approach to the outer harbor, and currents ranging from three to six knots multiplied the chances of confusion. This meant that daylight landings were necessary for all but small groups.

Much of the inner harbor was a vast swamp at low water, penetrated by a single dredged channel 12 to 13 feet deep.[6] The duration of spring tides above the prescribed minimum depth averaged about three hours, and during this interval the maximum in troops and supplies must be put ashore. Every minute counted, since initial landing forces could not be reinforced or supplied until the next high water period.

Time and tide seemed to have combined forces to protect Inchon from seaborne foes. As if such natural obstacles were not enough, the target area provided others. Two islands, Wolmi-do and Sowolmi-do, located in a commanding position between the inner and outer harbors, were linked to each other and to Inchon by a causeway. In advance of intelligence reports, it must be assumed that rocky, wooded Wolmi-do would be honeycombed with hidden emplacements for enough guns to create a serious menace for the landing craft.

This critical terrain feature must somehow be reduced as a preliminary to the main landing during the high tide of late afternoon. Inchon being situated on a hilly promontory, the "beaches" were mere narrow strips of urban waterfront, protected by seawalls too high for ramps to be dropped at any stage of the tide. Once past these barriers, the troops would have about two hours of daylight in which to secure an Oriental city with a population comparable to that of Omaha.

But the amphibious assault was only the first phase of the operation as conceived by CinCFE. After taking Inchon the landing force had the task of driving some 16 miles inland, without loss of momentum, to assault Korea's largest airfield before crossing a tidal river to assault Korea's largest city.

And even this ambitious undertaking was not the whole show. For a joint operation was to be carried out meanwhile by Eighth Army forces thrusting northward from the Pusan Perimeter to form a junction with the units of the Inchon-Seoul drive. This double-

---

[6] JANIS No. 75, ch. V.

barreled assault, it was believed, would shatter North Korean resistance
and put an end to the war.

Inception of X Corps

The time, the place, the landing force, the main objectives—these
essentials of the proposed Inchon-Seoul operation had been pretty
well settled, at least to General MacArthur's satisfaction, by the first
week of August. But even though he had his assault troops, there
was as yet no headquarters organization.

Admiral Sherman urged early in August that the commander in
chief call upon General Shepherd and the facilities of the FMFPac
organization at Pearl Harbor. Since there was so little time left before
D-day—only a fraction of the time usually allotted to the planning
phase of a major ship to shore assault—he felt that amphibious know-
how and experience were required. He proposed, therefore, that
steps be taken to obtain the approval of Admiral Radford, who had
jurisdiction over FMFPac.

The need for a headquarters organization was discussed on 7 August
by the Joint Strategic Plans and Operations Group (JSPOG) of
FECOM. Brigadier General Wright, G-3 of FECOM, received a
memorandum from the other members of the staff recommending
that the gap be filled in one of two ways—either by putting into effect
Admiral Sherman's plan, or by sponsoring the organization of a provisional corps headquarters. General Wright favored the first course
of action, as did Brigadier General Doyle G. Hickey, FECOM deputy
chief of staff. Ultimately, however, the FECOM chief of staff decided
in favor of the latter command arrangement.[7]

Final Conference on Inchon

The questions of *when* and *where* and *who* had been answered to some
extent. But as late as 23 August, a good many variations of opinion
existed as to *how* the amphibious assault was to be accomplished.

The natural obstacles of the Inchon harbor area were so disturbing
that Doyle suggested an alternative to MacArthur and Almond. Since

[7] OCMH, Dept of Army (Maj J. F. Schnabel), *The Korean Conflict* (MS), v. I, ch. I.

the purpose of the landing was to drive inland and cut the enemy's communications, urged ComPhibGru One, why not select a west coast objective with fewer hydrographic difficulties? He proposed the Posung-Myon area, about 30 miles south of Inchon on the west coast, where better approach channels and beaches were believed to be available in a more lightly populated locality. A landing at this point, Doyle contended, would not be attended by the risks and restrictions of Inchon, yet after securing a beachhead the troops would be in position to strike inland at the enemy's main line of rail and highway communications in the vicinity of Osan.[8]

Smith was favorably impressed. He brought up the subject on 23 August, when he and Barr had a meeting with Almond. The X Corps commander did not concur, though conceding that Posung-Myon had possibilities as an area for a subsidiary landing in connection with the Inchon assault. Nor was Doyle able to obtain MacArthur's consent to the alternate objective.

It was the Marine general's third conference of the day. From the X Corps meeting he had gone directly to the regular conference at GHQ, and thence to the talk with Almond and Barr. He came away from all three meetings with the conviction that CinCFE and his staff were not to be swerved by his objections. It was definitely to be Inchon on 15 September, and Smith instructed his planning group to proceed accordingly.

Doyle made a last attempt at 1730 that afternoon to present a comprehensive picture of the risks and difficulties inherent at Inchon. This final conference on the subject of a west coast landing was attended by some of the nation's highest ranking officers—General J. Lawton Collins, Army Chief of Staff; Admiral Forrest P. Sherman, Chief of Naval Operations; General Shepherd, CG FMFPac; Lieutenant General Idwal H. Edwards, U. S. Air Force; as well as other high-ranking staff officers who had flown out from Washington. It was no secret in Tokyo military circles that the Joint Chiefs of Staff were present for the purpose of studying General MacArthur's plans for the Inchon landing. It was also generally known that doubts and misgivings had been expressed at various times when the project was discussed at the Pentagon. General Collins stated candidly at a later date that the purpose of his Tokyo visit was ". . . to find out exactly

---

[8] O. P. Smith, *Chronicle*, 23 Aug 50, *Notes*, 51–52. A *myon* is comparable to our county, being a Korean political subdivision containing several towns or villages.

what the plans were. Frankly, we were somewhat in the dark, and as it was a matter of great concern, we went out to discuss it with General MacArthur. We suggested certain alternate possibilities and places. . . ." [9]

Admirals Joy and Doyle also attended the meeting, and FECOM was represented by Generals Almond, Ruffner, and Wright. The conference room on the sixth floor of the Dai Ichi building proved too small for the audience, and members of the PhibGru One team had to wait their turn in Almond's adjoining office. One by one, at eight-minute intervals, Doyle's officers took turns at being presented to MacArthur, who listened gravely while puffing at his pipe. The following amphibious specialists were heard:

Cdr Edmund S. L. Marshall, USN......... Navigation
Lt Charles R. Barron, USN............. Aerology
LtCol William E. Benedict, USMC......... Military Aspects
LCdr Jack L. Lowentrout, USN.......... Beach Study
LCdr M. Ted Jacobs, Jr., USN............ Seabees Pontoon Causeway Plans
LCdr Clyde E. Allmon, USN............. Ship to Shore Plans
LCdr Arlie G. Capps, USN.............. Gunfire Support
Cdr Theophilus H. Moore, USN.......... Air Support [10]

The officers spoke of the natural obstacles. They asserted that it would be the peak of optimism to hope for a strategic surprise at Inchon, for the enemy also knew that only a few days each autumn month offered a tidal range sufficient to float the landing craft and supply ships over the mud flats of the harbor.

They contended that even a tactical surprise was out of the question, since Wolmi-do must be neutralized before landings could be made on the mainland. Otherwise, the vulnerable column of landing craft would be exposed to a slaughter from the flanking fire of the island's guns.

The Navy group pointed out further that it must also be assumed that the enemy would not neglect a good opportunity to sow both moored and magnetic mines in the channels the shipping must take. And to cap all the other natural and man-made risks, there

---

[9] MacArthur Hearings, 1295, quoted by Major Schnabel in *The Korean Conflict* (MS), v. I, ch. I.

[10] The description of the conference has been derived from: LCdr Frank A. Manson (USN) interv, 22 Apr 52; Capt Walter Karig (USNR), *et al., Battle Report: The War in Korea* (New York, 1952), 165–168 (hereafter, Karig, *Korea*); VAdm Arthur D. Struble ltr to authors, 25 Apr 55.

was danger at the height of the typhoon season that Nature would intervene and scatter the amphibious armada during its approach to the objective area.

The presentation lasted for nearly an hour and a half. At the conclusion, Admiral Doyle summed up by giving his opinion. "The best I can say," he told the commander in chief, "is that Inchon is not impossible."

General MacArthur heard the amphibious specialists to a finish without his imperturbability being shaken. Even the onlookers who could not partake of his perfect faith were impressed. There was something magnificent about this old warrior in shirtsleeves and open collar, calmly smoking his pipe while hearing his plan dissected. Daring and optimism are supposed to be the exclusive prerogatives of youth, yet this smiling septuagenarian was not only the oldest officer at the conference, he was also the most confident and assured! After the PhibGru One presentation ended, he took 45 minutes for his comments. Speaking with eloquence, he declared that the natural obstacles and practical difficulties of the proposed Inchon operation were more than balanced in the strategic scale by the psychological advantages of a bold stroke. About 90 percent of the NKPA forces were fighting in the Pusan Perimeter. A combined offensive by X Corps and the Eighth Army would have the effect of placing the enemy between the hammer and anvil.

Referring to the Kunsan landing favored by General Collins and Admiral Sherman, CinCFE asserted that this objective was too far south for a fatal blow to be dealt the invaders. He cited a historical precept in Wolfe's victory at Quebec, made possible by audacity in overcoming natural obstacles that the enemy regarded as insurmountable. He recalled the amphibious victories he himself had won in the Southwest Pacific, with the Navy and sometimes the Marine Corps sharing in the glory. And he ended on a dramatic note with a single, prophetic sentence spoken in a tense voice:

"We shall land at Inchon and I shall crush them!" [11]

As the officers filed out into the noisy, teeming Tokyo street, most of them felt certain that the last word had been said. It was still possible, of course, for the Joint Chiefs to overrule CinCFE; and it was

---

[11] Karig, *Korea*, 165–168.

not likely that all of their doubts had been laid to rest. Nevertheless, the Navy and Marine planners proceeded on the basis that a final decision had been reached that August afternoon.

Brigade Victory in Korea

Before his arrival at Tokyo, General Shepherd had paid a flying visit to the headquarters of the Brigade in Korea immediately after the Marines stormed and seized Obong-ni Ridge. Just as General Craig's men had taken part from 7 to 13 August in the first sustained UN counterattack, so this Army and Marine effort a week later became the first rout of a major NKPA unit. After putting up a fierce struggle to hold their bridgehead on the east bank of the river Naktong, the veteran troops of the NKPA 4th Division were shattered by repeated Marine attacks. Carrier-borne Corsairs of MAG–33 had a turkey shoot at the expense of panic stricken enemy soldiers who abandoned their arms in a wild flight. Some of the fugitives were shot down while trying to swim the river.

Despite this encouraging little victory, it was still nip and tuck on the central front of the Pusan Perimeter. With the U. S. 2d Infantry Division and 5th RCT now in line, the Eighth Army strategy of trading space for time had resulted in whittling down the enemy's material superiority. But the invaders still held the material advantage, and there were signs that they would soon launch an all-out effort to smash through to Pusan.

The Marine Amphibious Mission

General Shepherd, after being informed as to the Tokyo conferences, accompanied General Smith on the morning of 24 August to a meeting with Admirals Sherman, Radford, Joy, and Doyle. It was generally agreed that not enough weight had been given to amphibious considerations in the final decision to attack at Inchon. Navy opinion held that one more attempt should be made to propose another landing point with fewer hydrographic objections. The area south of Inchon had been investigated by Navy UDT and Marine amphibious scouts of the Reconnaissance Company, 1st Marine Division, who had sailed to the Far East with the Brigade. As a preliminary, this group had embarked on the USS *Horace A. Bass* (APD–124) and gone ashore undetected to stage several raids during the period 12–16 August on the enemy's main line of communications along the west coast. Three tunnels and two railway bridges were destroyed without the loss of a man.[12]

Next the raiders successfully carried out a survey and reconnaissance of available landing beaches during the period 22–25 August in the Posung-Myon area. Their findings impressed General Shepherd so much that before his departure from Tokyo he called on CinCFE to make a last plea for reconsideration of the landing area. General MacArthur, however, remained firm in his preference for Inchon.[13]

The meeting of the admirals and Marine generals on the 24th broke up with a general agreement that the decision as to Inchon on 15 September must be accepted as the basis for final planning. That same afternoon General Smith instructed his planning group to begin work on a scheme of maneuver.

Modern amphibious tactics were in their infancy during World War I when an appalling object lesson seemed to have been left by the Allied disaster at Gallipoli in 1915–16. Brilliant in strategic conception, this major amphibious operation might have knocked Turkey out of the war and opened the unlocked back door of Austria and Germany. Unfortunately, the execution fell short; and the failure was too often charged to amphibious warfare itself rather than a wholesale violation of its basic principles.

In 1920 the new Marine Corps Schools at Quantico became the center of Marine amphibious study and research. Marine units participated in fleet problems at Panama and Culebra during the postwar years; and in 1927 the Joint Board of the Army and Navy (forerunner of JCS) stated in a directive that the Marine Corps had the mission of "special preparation in the conduct of landing operations."[14]

During the early 1920s the writings of a brilliant Marine officer, Major Earl H. Ellis, had a tremendous influence on current amphibious thought. Predicting that Japan would strike first in the Pacific and win initial successes, he drew up a strategic plan for assaults on Japanese-mandated islands which was approved by Major General John A.

---

[12] CTF 90 *Opn O 13–50*, in PacFlt *Interim Rpt No. 1*, XV:Able, 6.

[13] O. P. Smith, *Chronicle*, 24 Aug 50.

[14] BrigGen Eli K. Cole, "Joint Overseas Operation," *US Naval Institute Proceedings*, 55, No. 11 (Nov 29):927.

Lejeune, Commandant of the Marine Corps. Later known as Operation Plan No. 712, this Top Secret document helped to shape the ORANGE plans adopted by the Joint Board of the Army and Navy for offensive operations against Japan if it came to war.

After making good progress in the early 1920s, with landing exercises being held annually, the Marine amphibious program bogged down from 1927 to 1932 because of the necessity of sending expeditionary forces to China and Nicaragua. The turning point came in 1933, a memorable date in the evolution of modern amphibious warfare. It was then that Major General John H. Russell, Assistant Commandant of the Marine Corps, urged that a staff be set up at Quantico to plan for the organization of a mobile Marine striking force. This force, under the Commandant, and fully prepared for service with the fleet, was to be in readiness for tactical employment subject to the orders of the Commander in Chief, U. S. Navy. General Russell further proposed that the old name "Expeditionary Force" be discontinued and "Fleet Marine Force" adopted as a name better expressing this mission.[15]

After the acceptance of these recommendations, the Commandant ordered classes discontinued at the Marine Corps Schools and a concerted effort applied to the preparation of a new amphibious manual. Both the Army and Navy had treated some of the procedures in existing manuals, but it remained for the Marine Corps in 1934 to put out the first complete work of the sort. Known as the *Tentative Manual on Landing Operations,* it became either directly or indirectly the guide for exercises and maneuvers of the Navy and Marine Corps down to World War II.

Most of its suggested procedures were endorsed with revisions in the Navy's *Fleet Training Publication 167,* published in 1938. This work in its turn became the model three years later for the Army's first basic field manual for landing operations.[16]

Training exercises were held every year, usually at Culebra or Vieques in the Caribbean and San Clemente Island off San Diego. At the suggestion of the Fleet Marine Force, the Navy purchased Bloodsworth Island in Chesapeake Bay as the first amphibious gunfire range used for that purpose alone.

---

[15] J. A. Isely and P. A. Crowl, *The U. S. Marines and Amphibious War* (Princeton, 1951), 21–24, 33–34.

[16] FMFPac, *History,* 6–9.

Schools were set up to train Army and Navy as well as Marine officers as specialists in fire control parties. Air support was closely integrated with naval gunfire, shore artillery, and troop movements. Technology came to the aid of tactics when the Fleet Marine Force encouraged and supervised the designing of strange new amphibious craft and vehicles. Concepts were actually based in several instances on landing craft not yet developed and the confidence of the Marine Corps in American inventiveness proved to be justified.

Thus the Nation entered World War II with a system of offensive tactics which opened Europe, Africa, and the islands of the Pacific to American invasion without incurring a single major defeat. Not only was the United States ahead of the enemy in the development of amphibious operations but the Axis Powers never found the key to an adequate defense. In an often quoted summary, the British military critic and historian, Major General J. F. C. Fuller, has asserted that these techniques were "in all probability . . . the most far-reaching tactical innovation of the war."[17]

During the next few years the Marine Corps was twice officially given the major responsibility for American amphibious tactics. The National Security Act of 1947 made it the function of the Corps "to provide fleet marine forces of combined arms, together with supporting air components, for service with the fleet in the seizure and defense of advanced naval bases and for the conduct of such land operations as may be essential to the prosecution of a naval campaign."[18]

At the so-called Key West Conference the following spring (March 11–14, 1948), the Secretary of Defense and Joint Chiefs of Staff restated the Marine Corps' mission to include that of developing "in coordination with the Army, the Navy, and the Air Force, the tactics, technique, and equipment employed by landing forces in amphibious operations. The Marine Corps shall have primary interest in the development of those landing force tactics, techniques, and equipment which are of common interest to the Army and the Marine Corps."[19]

During these post-war years, the Marine Corps was grappling with the new amphibious problems posed by atomic weapons. It was fitting, therefore, that the three men who formed the Special Board

---

[17] MajGen J. F. C. Fuller, *The Second World War* (London, 1948), 207.

[18] 61 *U. S. Stat. at L.* (1947), 495.

[19] OAFIE, OSD, *The United States Marine Corps* (Washington, 1950). (Armed Forces Talk No. 317.)

for this research—Generals Shepherd, Harris, and Smith—should have been at the forefront in 1950 when the Marine Corps faced its next amphibious test. As veterans of World War II operations, they could recall the scramble for the beaches of Bougainville, the fight for Bloody Nose on Peleliu, the off-the-cuff landing on Oroku Peninsula in Okinawa. There had been some tense moments in those battles, but never had Marine generals contemplated an objective which held more potentialities for trouble than the harbor area at Inchon.

CHAPTER IV

The Planning Phase

Working Around the Clock—X Corps Scheme of Maneuver—
Intelligence Planning for Inchon—The Landing Force Plan—
Naval Gunfire and Rockets—Plans for Air Support

T HE CHAMPION GLOBE-TROTTERS of the 1st Marine Division were the
men of the 3d Battalion, 7th Marines. Before returning to their
homes from Korea, these military tourists would have traveled entirely
around the world by various forms of land, water, and air transportation.

The unit was originally an element of the 6th Marines, FMFLant,
serving afloat with the Sixth Fleet in the Mediterranean. On 12
August 1950 the CP aboard the USS *Yellowstone* at Suda Bay, Crete,
received a message from CNO ordering the battalion to the Far East.
Lieutenant Colonel Frederick R. Dowsett, deputy commander, noted
that the dispatch had bypassed such channels as CMC and the Sixth
Fleet.[1] This irregularity, he learned later, was explained by the
urgency of an order which had been framed by Admiral Sherman
while General Cates was present. It directed that the APA *Bexar*
arrive on 14 August at Suda Bay and depart two days later with the
troops.

The rub was that these Marines were dispersed on various ships
all over the Mediterranean.

Given the rush job of picking up the scattered elements of the
battalion was the USS *Leyte*, which was due to return to Norfolk
for refitting afterwards and thence to the Far East via the Panama
Canal. Not only did the carrier complete its assignment before the
deadline, but the *Bexar* also arrived at Suda Bay on the evening of

---

[1] The battalion commander, Colonel Reynolds H. Hayden, had a deputy because of the
administrative set-up within the Sixth Fleet and did not accompany the unit to the Far East.

the 14th. Both ships had hardly dropped anchor when the LCVPs and LCMs were shuttling troops and cargo to the transport and the AKA *Montague,* which was to accompany it to the Far East.[2]

On the 16th the two vessels departed according to schedule by way of Port Said and the Suez Canal. Security regulations were rigidly enforced, with only one stop being made when the vessels anchored at Ceylon for six hours to take on fuel. Marine officers were figuratively as well as literally at sea, since they had no idea of the specific mission awaiting the battalion in the Far East. Unaware of plans for the Inchon landing, they envisioned the troops being employed as the ship-based raiding party of some American task force.

Meanwhile their future teammates of the 7th Marines were preparing to embark from San Diego. Colonel Litzenberg and his officers had made a good start at Camp Pendleton even before the activation date of 17 August 1950. In order to build up from cadres of former 6th Marines' troops, this regiment received the largest proportion of combat-ready reservists of any major unit in the 1st Marine Division—about 50 per cent, counting the augmentation personnel to bring 3/6 up to war strength when it would be taken into the outfit in Japan.[3]

CNO had set 3 September as the date of embarkation. But Headquarters, FMFPac, prepared the embarkation plans while the regimental staff solved problems of organization and equipment so effectively that the 7th Marines sailed on the 1st, thus beating the deadline by two days.[4]

Orders came to El Toro on 16 August for the overseas movement of the remaining elements of the 1st MAW. Units affected were Wing Headquarters Squadron 1 and MAG–12, comprising Headquarters Squadron 12, Service Squadron 12, VMF–312, VMF–212, VMF(N)–542, and the rear echelon of VMF(N)–513.

VMF–312 and the rear echelon of VMF(N)–513 were loaded on the USS *Sitkoh Bay* with their aircraft and sailed on 24 August. Three days later VMF–212 and VMF(N)–542 embarked on the USS *Cape Esperance,* and the USNS *General Morton* weighed anchor with the remaining components on 1 September.[5] This completed the overseas

---

[2] This description is based upon: Col F. R. Dowsett interv, 2 Nov 54.
[3] Giusti, II–5.
[4] PacFlt *Interim Rpt No. 1,* XV:Zebra, 15.
[5] *Ibid.,* XV:Charlie Charlie, 4.

movement of the 1st MAW, since General Harris and his staff had departed from El Toro by air for Japan the day before.

Working Around the Clock

The first echelon of the 1st Marine Division planning group had its preliminary briefing on 19 August, and the tractor elements of the Attack Force were scheduled to sail for the objective area on 9 September. This left an interval of 20 days for most of the Inchon planning—probably the shortest period ever allotted to a major amphibious assault.

Less than one-fourth of the officers and men of the 1st Marine Division staff were on the *Mount McKinley* when planning commenced. At that time the distribution of the staff was as follows:

	With the 1st Prov Mar Brig in Korea	Aboard USS *Mount McKinley* in Tokyo	En route by sea to Japan	Total
Div Cdr Section		2		2
Asst Div Cdr Section	2			2
Chief of Staff Section	2	1	1	4
General Staff Section:				
G–1	2	2	1	5
G–2	2	2	7	11
G–3	2	2	1	5
G–4	2	2	2	6
Special Staff Section:				
Adjutant	4		7	11
Air & Air Observers	2	1	2	5
Amph Trac	*a* 1	*a* 1		2
Anti-Tank	*b* 1		1	1
Armored Amtracs			*a* 1	1
Artillery	*a* 1	*a* 1	*a* 1	3
Chaplains	*b* 1		1	1
Chem War & Radiol Def			1	1
Dental	*b* 1		1	1
Embarkation	*b* 1	2	1	3
Engineer		*a* 1		1
Food Director			1	1
Hq Comdt	*a* 1		*a* 2	3
Inspector			2	2
Legal	*b* 1		1	1
Liaison	3			3
Medical	2		1	3
Mtr Trans	1	1		2

See footnotes at end of table.

	With the 1st Prov Mar Brig in Korea	Aboard USS *Mount McKinley* in Tokyo	En route by sea to Japan	Total
Special Staff Section—Continued				
Nav Gunfire		1		1
Ordnance	[b] 1	1		1
Post Ex			[a] 1	1
Pub Info	[b] 1		1	1
Prov Marshal			[a] 1	1
Shore Party		[a] 1		1
Signal	6	2		8
Spec Serv	[b] 1		3	3
Sup & Disb	[b] 2		9	9
Tank	[b] 1		[a] 1	1
Total	33	23	51	107

[a] Carried in other Brigade, Division, or Force units.

[b] Additional duty basis; not counted in total.[6]

[a] O. P. Smith, *Notes*, 54–55.

The Marine planners aboard the *Mount McKinley* were short on elbow room as well as personnel, time, and equipment. Although it was an advantage to have the planning groups of the Attack Force and Landing Force together, the ship did not provide enough space for both without crowding. Moreover, the already undermanned Marine contingent had to be further reduced late in August by sending several officers to Kobe to meet incoming units. Thus the G–2 section, to cite one example, consisted of only two officers, one of whom was detached on this duty for a week.

"The issuance of and adherence to a planning schedule was utterly impossible," commented the 1st Marine Division report. "Only by a virtual 'around the clock' working day, concurrent . . . planning by Attack Force (ComPhibGru One) and Landing Force (1st MarDiv), willing teamwork by both, and especially the amphibious 'know-how' of key staff members gained by long experience, was it possible to complete and issue . . . plans and orders for a most difficult . . . landing operation. The time-space factor denied any co-ordinated orientation, prohibited even the most elementary re-hearsal, made it difficult to distribute orders, and gave subordinate units very little time for formulation and distribution of their plans." [7]

[7] 1st MarDiv *SAR*, basic rpt.

Command relationships during the embarkation and assault phases were as follows:

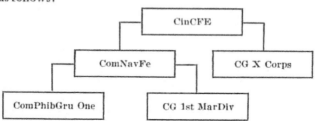

All the top commanders were concentrated in Tokyo with the arrival of Admiral Struble on 25 August. This facilitated the planning and allowed important decisions to be worked out in conferences between the principal commanders.[8]

Planning was based mainly on studies made by ComPhibGru One as prospective Attack Force Commander. It was conducted entirely on a concurrent basis by the Attack Force and Landing Force groups aboard the *Mount McKinley*. No step was taken by either without the full knowledge and consent of the other.

X Corps Scheme of Maneuver

Army planning had been initiated by the Joint Strategic Plans and Operations Group until 16 August, when the "Special Planning Staff" was set up at GHQ to issue directives for Operation Plan CHROMITE. Published on 12 August as CinCFE Operation Plan No. 100–B, it was based on these assumptions:

(a) that the North Korean ground advance would be stopped in time to permit the build-up of our forces in South Korea;

(b) that our forces in South Korea would be built up to the capability of mounting effective offensive operations against NKPA forces opposing them;

(c) that we retain air and naval supremacy in the area of operation;

(d) that the NKPA ground forces would not receive major reinforcements from the USSR or Red China;

(e) that there would be no major change in the basic disposition of the NKPA forces.[9]

---

[8] Struble ltr. 25 Apr 55.
[9] MarCorps Board *Study*, v. II–B, 13–17.

It was understood from the beginning that the Special Plans Staff, headed by General Ruffner, would be the nucleus of the future X Corps staff. In order to have the benefit of specialized amphibious knowledge, ten Marine and two Navy officers of TTU Mobile Training Team Able were assigned on 19 August:

Col H. A. Forney	Deputy Chief of Staff
LtCol J. Tabor	Asst Coordinator, FSCC
LtCol C. E. Warren	Asst G–4
Maj J. N. McLaughlin	Asst G–3
Maj J. F. Warner	Asst G–3
Maj C. P. Weiland	Air Officer, FSCC
Maj V. H. Vogel	Asst G–4
Capt H. S. Coppedge	Asst G–2
Capt T. A. Manion	Asst Signal Officer, FSCC
Capt V. J. Robinson	Target Info Officer
Lt L. N. Lay, USN	Asst Surgeon
Lt W. A. Sheltren, USN	Asst NGF Officer, FSCC [10]

These officers did not begin their new assignment in time to contribute to the preliminary X Corps over-all scheme of maneuver. The main provisions, as communicated to General Smith at General Ruffner's briefing conference of 23 August, were as follows:

(1) The 1st Marine Division, as the landing force, was to seize the urban area of Inchon (line A–A); to capture a beachhead (line B–B); to advance as rapidly as possible and seize Kimpo Airfield (line C–C); to clear out the south bank of the Han River (line D–D); to cross the river, seize Seoul and secure the commanding ground to the north (E–E); and, finally, to fortify and occupy this line with reduced forces until relieved (apparently by the 3d Infantry Division, still in the United States), whereupon the Division was to recross the Han and seize a line (F–F) about 25 miles southeast of Seoul.

(2) The 7th Infantry Division was to land behind the Marines and advance on their right flank to seize the commanding ground south of Seoul and the south bank of the river (line D–D); to continue the advance to phase line (E–E); and to conduct a reconnaissance in force to the south (line F–F). There, on the line from Suwon to Kyongan-ni, the 7th Infantry Division and 1st Marine Division would form the strategic anvil as Eighth Army forces advanced from the Pusan Perimeter in the role of hammer.

(3) The 1st Marine Aircraft Wing was to furnish air support, air direction, and air warning for the Corps with units operating from Kimpo Airfield. It was also to be prepared to operate a control center ashore on order.[11]

---

[10] MarCorps Board *Study*, v. II, app. 67.
[11] *Ibid.*, v. I, III–B–8, and v. II, app. 16; O. P. Smith, *Notes*, 48–49.

The Special Plans Staff gave General Smith a study explaining the purposes of these maneuvers. "The B–B line in this study appeared to be a suitable beachhead line," he commented, "and we decided to concentrate our efforts on plans for its seizure. Subsequent operations would be reserved for later consideration." [12]

Intelligence Planning for Inchon

Good planning, of course, depended on accurate intelligence. All possible information about the objective area had been gathered by the staff of PhibGru One before the arrival of the 1st Marine Division planners. Air Force planes had taken hundreds of photographs at every stage of the tide. Hydrographic reports and navigation charts had been studied. Army and Navy men familiar with Inchon during the American occupation after World War II were interrogated as well as NKPA prisoners captured by the Eighth Army.

Although a great deal of useful data was compiled, some disturbing questions remained. How high were the sea walls of Inchon? Were the mud flats suitable for landing either troops or vehicles at low tide? Approximately how many NKPA guns were hidden on Wolmi-do? . . . These were some of the intelligence gaps which must be filled before an effective plan could be drawn up for an assault landing.

PhibGru One made its material available to the G–2 Section of the 1st Marine Division, and the two staffs worked together on the *Mount McKinley* in close cooperation. Attached were the 163d Military Intelligence Service Detachment (MISD) and the 441st Counter Intelligence Corps (CIC) Team. Both of these units had been furnished by FECOM and consisted of Army commissioned and enlisted personnel as well as native Koreans serving in liaison, interpretation, and translation capacities.

Even when a question could not be answered conclusively, it was up to the G–2 sections of the Attack Force and Landing Force to arrive at a conclusion for planning purposes. For instance, it was never satisfactorily determined from available sources—JANIS publications, strategic engineering studies, Naval Attaché reports, and photographic interpretation reports—whether LVTs would be able to

---

[12] O. P. Smith, *Notes*, 50.

traverse the mud flats of the Inchon harbor area. And since there remained some doubt, planning proceeded on the assumption that the answer was negative. This proved to be the correct as well as the prudent decision, later developments revealed.

Another G–2 planning problem concerned the effect that the height of the sea walls would have upon the landing. Photographs at hourly stages of the tide made it appear that the masonry was too high for the dropping of ramps at any time. As a solution, G–2 officers hit upon a device reminiscent of the storming of castles during the Middle Ages. Scaling ladders were recommended with the suggestion that they be built of aluminum with hooks at one end to be attached to the masonry. Construction was started at Kobe, but the order could be only partially filled before D-day, and wooden ladders were built as substitutes.

It is hardly necessary to point out the importance of estimates as to the numbers and defensive capabilities of the enemy. Yet the G–2 sections on the *Mount McKinley* were up against a peculiar situation cited in the 1st Marine Division report:

"Our accumulated knowledge of the enemy's military tactics, prior to our landing at Inchon on 15 September 1950, consisted almost in its entirety of knowledge about the enemy's offense. . . . With but few exceptions, UN forces were forced to take a defensive stand and denied the opportunity to study large scale enemy defensive tactics from actual combat. Thus it was that our assault landing was made with relatively little prior knowledge regarding the enemy's probable reaction to a large-scale offensive of this nature, particularly when it involved the penetration into the very heart of his newly acquired domain." [13]

Photographic coverage showed the Inchon harbor area to be honey-combed with gun positions and other defensive installations. On the other hand, daily aerial observation indicated that most of them were not occupied.

G–2 conclusions during the planning phase often had to be based on such conflicting evidence, even though the penalties of faulty inter-pretation might be drastic. But after being viewed with due suspicion, signs of negative enemy activity were finally accepted as valid in esti-mates of light to moderate NKPA resistance.

---

[13] This account of G–2 planning for Inchon is based upon 1st MarDiv *SAR*, Annex Baker.

"Sadly lacking as was information on the objective area," commented the Division G–2 report, "more so was that on the enemy in the area." Early in September, however, the Attack Force and Landing Force concurred in the initial X Corps estimate of 1,500 to 2,500 NKPA troops in the immediate area, consisting largely of newly raised personnel.[14]

Radio reports of first-hand observations in the objective area, though coming too late for initial planning purposes, confirmed some of the G–2 estimates. This dangerous mission was undertaken by Lieutenant Eugene F. Clark, a naval officer on General MacArthur's JSPOG staff. U. S. and British Marines provided an escort on 1 September when the British destroyer *Charity* brought him from Sasebo to a point along the coast where the South Korean patrol vessel PC 703 waited to land him at Yonghung-do, an island about 15 miles southwest of Inchon.[15]

Clark went ashore with a small arsenal of firearms, grenades and ammunition, as well as 30 cases of C rations and 200 pounds of rice. He quickly made allies of the 400 friendly Korean inhabitants of the island and organized his own private little "army" of about 150 youths from 14 to 18 years old. These "troops" were posted about Yonghung-do for security, since the near-by island, Taebu-do, was occupied by 400 NKPA soldiers within wading distance at low tide.

The naval officer had no illusions as to what his fate might be in the event of capture. Day and night, he kept a grenade within reach, since he did not intend to be taken alive. When the long expected enemy attack from Taebu-do materialized, he commandeered a "onelung" South Korean motor sampan and fought it out with the NKPA motor sampan escorting boats filled with soldiers. The enemy began the strange "naval" battle with a few badly aimed rounds from a 37mm tank gun. Clark and his crew of three friendly Koreans finished it with a long burst from a .50 caliber machine gun. After sinking the NKPA motor sampan, he destroyed another boat with 18 soldiers aboard and captured three prisoners for questioning.

One night the intrepid lieutenant rowed a dinghy to the Inchon sea wall. When the tide went out, he tested the mire by wading in it up to his waist. This experience led to the sending of a radio report,

---

[14] See Appendix I for the Order of Battle of the units which opposed the 1st Marine Division throughout the Inchon-Seoul operation, listing them in chronological order as to area of employment, strength, and effectiveness.

[15] This account is based upon: Capt James B. Soper interv, 16 Aug 54; and Karig, *Korea*, 176–191.

"Inchon not suitable for landing either troops or vehicles across the mud."

Korean youths, posing as fishermen, brought intelligence which Clark included in his daily radio messages. One of these spies made an effort to count the guns on Wolmi-do and describe the locations. Others took measurements of the Inchon sea wall and penetrated as far inland as Seoul to report numbers and positions of NKPA troops.

Clark declined all offers to evacuate him. As the climax of his exploit, he managed to restore the usefulness of the lighthouse on Palmi Island which the enemy had put out of commission. This structure, the former entrance beacon for Inchon by way of Flying Fish channel, served him as a refuge when he had to leave Yonghung-do hurriedly just ahead of NKPA troops who landed in force and butchered 50 civilians of both sexes. Clark, who received a Silver Star, stuck it out on Palmi until midnight of 14 September, when he turned on the beacon light to guide the amphibious task force.

The Landing Force Plan

The decisions behind the Landing Force Plan—1st Marine Division OpnO 2-50—obviously had to be made without benefit of Lieutenant Clark's reports, since the publication date was 4 September 1950.[16] It is to the credit of these conclusions, therefore, that so few of them had to be corrected in the light of first-hand evidence from the objective area.

Although CG X Corps was the assigned Expeditionary Troops Commander, planning on the Corps level was concerned almost entirely with the exploitation phase following the seizure of the beachhead. All Landing Force planning was done on the *Mount McKinley* by the Division in close coordination with PhibGru One.

The first consideration, as viewed by the Navy planners, was that the tides, currents, and tortuous channels of Inchon made necessary a four-hour daylight approach to the transport area. This meant that 1130, at low tide, was the earliest hour of arrival; and not until about 1700 would the next high tide provide enough water for an assault landing.

---

[16] See Appendix G for a chronological list of all 1st Marine Division operation orders during the Inchon-Seoul operation.

On 15 September a maximum high tide of 31 feet could be expected
at 1919. Evening twilight came at 1909. It was estimated initially
that 23 feet of water would take the LCVPs and LVTs over the mud
flats, but that 29 feet were necessary for the beaching of the LSTs.

In view of these conditions, PhibGru One planners concluded that
1700 was the best time for landing the LCVPs and LVTs, and it was
decided to beach the LSTs at about 1900. Simultaneous landings of
troops on Wolmi-do and the mainland were contemplated.

This was the point of departure for Division planners. They maintained that Wolmi-do was the key terrain feature, and that it should
be secured first in a separate landing. The logical course, according
to the Marines, would be to utilize the morning high tide for the
seizure of this island commanding the waterfront. The enemy would
be given the whole day in which to prepare for the attack on the mainland; but the Landing Force could also utilize this period for cleaning
up Wolmi-do and moving in supporting artillery.

It was typical of the harmony prevailing between the two planning
groups on the *Mount McKinley* that PhibGru One immediately
accepted the concept of a double-barreled attack. The rub was that
a night approach would be necessary to assault Wolmi-do at 0600 on
the morning high tide, and the Navy doubted the feasibility of a
movement of the slow-moving and unmaneuverable APAs, AKAs,
and LSTs through winding, mud-lined channels in the darkness.

At length a compromise was reached with the decision to employ
DD, APD, and LSD types primarily, which were more maneuverable
in addition to being equipped with radar navigational instruments.[17]

The morning landing on Wolmi-do was to be made with a single
battalion of the 5th Marines, to be designated by the Brigade. On
the mainland the remaining two battalions would land with the
evening high tide on RED Beach, just north of the causeway connecting the island with the city, while two battalions of the 11th
Marines landed in support on Wolmi-do. Meanwhile the 1st Marines
was to hit BLUE Beach, southeast of the urban area. And after
driving rapidly inland to consolidate their positions before nightfall,
the two Marine regiments were to make a junction in the morning and

---

[17] This summary of Landing Force planning is based upon: 1st MarDiv *SAR*, basic rpt;
MarCorps Board *Study*, v. I, II–B, 13–16; O. P. Smith, *Notes*, 58–62; PacFlt *Interim Rpt No. 1*,
XV:Able Able, 6–7.

seize the beachhead while the 17th ROK Regiment (later replaced by 1st KMC Regiment) mopped up the city streets.

Marine G–4 planners suggested one of the most daring of all the calculated risks. This was the decision to use LCVPs for the RED Beach landings because their comparative speed would clear the landing area for the beaching of eight LSTs—all that could be crammed into the narrow confines of this strip of urban waterfront. Each was to be loaded with ammunition, rations, water, and fuel. Obviously these Navy workhorses, nicknamed "large slow targets", would be easy marks for NKPA shore guns, but this was a chance that had to be taken if the assault troops were to be adequately supplied.

There was not time, of course, to unload and retract the ships during the period of evening high tide. They must be unloaded during the night and taken out on the morning tide.

Since it was not considered feasible to land LSTs on BLUE Beach, that area would not be developed beyond the needs of the immediate assault. For this purpose, 16 preloaded LVTs were to be used as floating dumps until the 1st Marines could link up with the other regiment.

These were the essentials of the Landing Force plan. H-hour was ultimately determined from a study of late photographs which brought about a slight change in estimates. Since a tide of 25 feet (two feet higher than the initial estimate) appeared to be necessary for the LCVPs and LVTs to reach the sea wall, H-hour was set at 1730 instead of 1700. The completed Landing Force plan provided for these steps:

(1) BLT–3 of RCT–5 to land on Beach GREEN at L-hour on D-day and seize Wolmi-do.

(2) RCT–5 (– BLT–3) to land on Beach RED at H-hour, seize Objective O–A, effect a juncture with RCT–1, and prepare for further operations to the east in coordination with RCT–1 to seize the FBHL.

(3) RCT–1, to land on Beach BLUE, with two battalions in assault, seize Objective O–1, and prepare for further operations to the east in coordination with RCT–5 to seize the FBHL.

(4) 11th Marines (– 3d Bn) (96th F. A. Bn, USA, attached) to land 1st and 2d Bns on Beach GREEN at H-hour, occupy positions on Wolmi-do and support seizure of the beachhead with priority of fires to RCT–1. Remainder of artillery to land on call.

(5) ROK Marines, initially in Division reserve, to land over Beach RED on call and conduct operations to occupy the city of Inchon in coordination with RCT–5.

(6) 1st Tank Bn (–) (Reinf.) to be prepared to land on order one company in LSU on Beach GREEN, remainder of battalion on order on beaches to be designated.

(7) 1st Engr Bn (–) to land on Beach RED or in harbor on order, assume control of detached companies on order, and support seizure of beachhead as directed. Priority to opening and maintaining MSR along southern edge of the city to RCT–1 zone of action.

(8) 1st Shore Party Bn (–) to land on order on Beach RED or in harbor and assume control of shore party activities on Beaches RED and GREEN.

(9) 1st Amph Trac Bn to transport and land elements of RCT–1 on Beach BLUE and continue support of RCT–1 until released.

(10) 2d Engr Spl Brig, USA (Reinf.) to furnish ships platoons and augment Division shore party as requested. After landing and when directed, to assume operational control of Division shore party and responsibility for control of all port operations. To provide logistical support of 1st MarDiv.

Availability of Brigade Troops

The old recipe for rabbit stew began, "First, catch your rabbit." And while the Landing Force plan was being formulated, General Smith had no assurance for a few days that he could count on having the whole of his landing force available.

General Almond informed the Marine general on 23 August that the release of the 1st Provisional Marine Brigade for participation in the Inchon landing would depend on the military situation. He seemed doubtful and added that the withdrawal of the Marines would be bad for Eighth Army morale.

The Attack Force and Landing Force began their planning, however, on the basis of Brigade availability. It had been the intention of CinCFE to employ a full Marine division, but an embarkation date of 1 September would not permit the 7th Marines to arrive in time. This left the 1st Marines as the only RCT of the Landing Force unless the 5th Marines and other Brigade units could be released.

On 30 August, Smith brought up the issue again in a dispatch to X Corps, whereupon CinCFE issued an order making the Brigade troops available to the Division on 4 September.

This might have settled the issue if the enemy had not launched an all-out offensive on 1 September to smash through the Pusan Perimeter. Although the Brigade had already sent heavy equipment to Pusan for embarkation, the Marines were rushed up to the front on 2 September as a mobile reserve. That same day the order for their release was revoked.

There could be no doubt about the gravity of the military situation. Thirteen NKPA divisions were making a final effort, and the Marines were needed in the Naktong Bulge sector, where the Korean Reds were attempting to cut the Pusan-Taegu lifeline.

On the other hand, time was also running out for the Inchon planners. Colonel Forney, the new deputy chief of staff for X Corps, informed Smith on 2 September that Almond planned to use the 32d Infantry of the 7th Infantry Division if the 7th Marines could not arrive in time for the Inchon landing. Recently, the cadres of this Army division had been brought up to strength with 8,000 South Koreans. The remaining 12,000 U. S. troops had received no adequate amphibious training, though instructors from Training Team Able had made a start with some of the units.

This turn of affairs resulted in a meeting in General Almond's office. The Navy was represented by Admirals Joy, Struble, and Doyle; the Army by Generals Almond, Ruffner, and Wright; and the Marines by General Smith.

Wright opened the discussion by stating that Walker needed the Brigade troops urgently as a mobile reserve to hold the line in the current NKPA offensive. Almond conceded that the question of Brigade availability must be decided on a basis of Eighth Army requirements and tactical considerations. But if the 5th Marines could not be released, he reiterated his decision to substitute the 32d Infantry for the Inchon operation.

Admiral Joy declared that the success of the Inchon assault depended on the employment of Marines trained in amphibious techniques; and he called upon Smith for his opinion. The Marine general said that a hastily instructed unit could not be expected to take the place of a combat-experienced regiment in the Landing Force, and that last-minute substitutions of this sort could not be made in complicated ship-to-shore landings without courting trouble. He added that it would be necessary in such an event to land in column on one beach instead of two, with the 1st Marines in advance of the 32d Infantry. These comments had the support of Doyle, who agreed that the availability of the 5th Marines might mean the difference between success and failure at Inchon.

At this point Admiral Struble commented that the issue boiled down to the need for a mobile Eighth Army reserve. He suggested as a compromise that a regiment of the 7th Infantry Division be embarked and moved to Pusan as a floating reserve to be landed in an emergency as a substitute for the 5th Marines. This solution was accepted. Almond called up Eighth Army Headquarters immediately, and within an hour Wright telephoned to inform Smith that the Brigade would be relieved at midnight on 5 September.[18]

As it turned out, the 17th Infantry of the 7th Infantry Division was embarked and transferred to Pusan to substitute for the 5th Marines, with Marine officers of Training Team Able assisting in the outloading. After the amphibious assault, the regiment landed administratively at Inchon to rejoin its parent unit.

Naval Gunfire and Rockets

At a conference on 1 September called by Admiral Struble and attended by Admirals Richard W. Ruble, John M. Higgins, and Sir William G. Andrewes (RN)[19] in addition to Generals Ruffner and Smith, it was tentatively agreed that the cruisers would begin the bombardment on the morning of D-minus 1, and the destroyers that afternoon after a napalm air strike had been conducted against Wolmi-do on D-minus 4.

At another naval gunfire conference two days later, the napalm strike was delayed until D-minus 3. On 8 September, when Admiral Struble held his final meeting, PhibGru One and the 1st Marine Division agreed on the scope and timing of naval gunfire support. It was decided, therefore, that the bombardment would commence on D-minus 2 and be repeated if necessary on D-minus 1.[20]

During the following week, plans were worked out in detail. The beachhead was divided into 52 target areas, including two on Wolmi-do and one on Sowolmi-do. In the channel to the west and southwest of the port, imaginary lines marked off three fire support areas for the ships, numbered in order from south to north.

---

[18] O. P. Smith, *Notes*, 74–80, *Chronicle*, 31 Aug–3 Sep 50; Forney *Special Rpt*, II, 4.
[19] See Appendix E for Naval Task Organization giving components, ships, and commanders of JTF-7.
[20] O. P. Smith, *Notes*, 72–74.

68

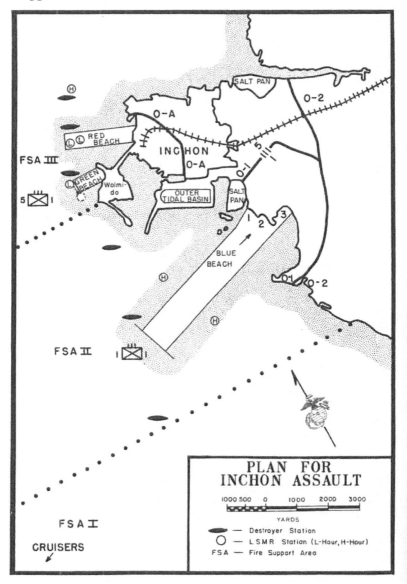

PLAN FOR
INCHON ASSAULT

1000 500   0   1000   2000   3000

YARDS

⬭ — Destroyer Station
◯ — L S M R Station (L-Hour, H-Hour)
FSA — Fire Support Area

Call to Arms—Marine reservists fall in near railway station in Seattle for departure to Camp Pendleton (U. S. Navy Photo).

A1

The Invasion Fleet—Above, Marines board troopship in Japan for voyage to objective; and, below, Marines eating breakfast on transport at 3:30 on the morning of D-Day (Marine Corps Photos).   A2

The Invasion Fleet—Above, Marines board troopship in Japan for voyage to objective; and, below, Marines eating breakfast on transport at 3:30 on the morning of D-Day (Marine Corps Photos).

Smiles of Victory—General MacArthur shows his approval of the Wolmi-do landing; behind him (left to right) are Vice Admiral Struble, Brigadier General Wright, and Major General Almond (U. S. Navy Photo).   A3

Action on Wolmi-do—Above, Marine using flame thrower on enemy cave; and, below, assault troops mopping up on the island (Marine Corps Photos).

H-Hour—Above, the first wave of LCVPs heads for the beaches at Inchon; and, below, grounded LSTs bring supplies to captured Wolmi-do (U. S. Navy Photos).

Hitting the Beaches—Above, Marines in landing craft on way to BLUE Beach with scaling ladders; and, below, assault troops using ladders to climb seawall at RED Beach (Marine Corps Photos).

A6

Ashore at Inchon—Above, an LST brings supplies to RED Beach on heels of assault troops (Marine Corps Photo): and, below, Marines hoisting tank over seawall, with LST 802 in background (U. S. Navy Photo).

A7

Bombardment of Inchon—Above, railway station in flames (U. S. Army Photo); and, below, burning factory buildings (U. S. Navy Photo).

Inchon Secured—Above, enemy gun emplacement (U. S. Navy Photo); and, below, troops of 5th Marines advancing in streets of Inchon (U. S. Army Photo).

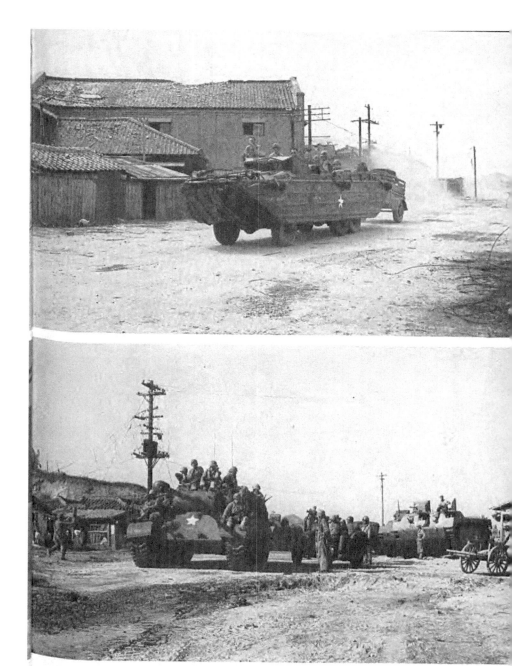

Advance to Force Beachhead Line—Above, assault troops of 1st Marines move up in DUKWs; and, below, Marine tanks and amtracs northeast of Inchon (U. S. Army Photos).

Upper Command Level—Above, Generals Almond (left) and Shepherd go ashore in launch of USS Mount McKinley; *and, below, General Smith and Admiral Doyle confer on the USS* Rochester *(U. S. Navy Photos).*

Inchon Harbor Scenes—Above, a VMO-6 helicopter gives a lift to a Marine officer on LCP; and, below, LST 1123 stranded at low tide (U. S. Navy Photos).

A12

Interludes—Above, Hospitalman Philip A. Barome, USN, shares his "C" rations with a Korean youngster (U. S. Navy Photo); and, below, Private G. W. Febrey and Corporal Charles E. Burris of 1st Marine Division, fill can at captured Yongdungpo brewery (U. S. Army Photo).   A13

D-Plus 2—Above, Marine tank-infantry team searches houses in Korean village (Marine Corps Photo); and, below, stripped NKPA prisoners are marched past killed enemy tank (U. S. Army Photo).

A14

RED Beach—LSTs unloading and Marine trucks taking supplies to advancing troops on D-plus 2 (U. S. Army Photo).

On D-day the four cruisers would stand in from 13,000 to 15,000 yards offshore in Fire Support Area I, while the destroyers in FSAs II and III manned stations 800 to 6,000 yards from the beach. The three LSMRs would first support the Wolmi-do landing from close-in positions to the north and west of the island. Later, for H-hour, one of the rocket ships was to remain northward to soften up RED Beach, and the other two would displace to the vicinity of BLUE Beach.[21]

From L-minus 45 to L-minus 2, the cruisers and destroyers would dump a total of 2,845 shells on Inchon and its outlying island, each ship concentrating on specifically assigned target areas. From L-minus 15 to L-minus 2, each of the three LSMRs would saturate Wolmi-do with 1,000 5-inch rockets. Most of the ships were to cease fire two minutes before the landing on GREEN Beach, when Marine planes strafed possible enemy positions for final shock effect. Four of the destroyers would continue to pound Inchon targets with 55 shells during the short air attack.

Another intricate piece in the mosaic of destruction was the mission assigned to one LSMR for the period immediately preceding and following the landing of 3/5. The lone rocket ship would lumber parallel to Wolmi-do's shoreline, across the front of the advancing first wave, and pour 40mm shells into the beach area. Clearing the route of approach to GREEN Beach just in time for the landing craft to speed by, the LSMR was to continue southward along the coast and direct its heavy automatic fire at the slopes in advance of the attacking troops.

Once Wolmi-do was secured, the full fury of the support ships would rain down on targets in the Inchon area. From H-minus 180 to H-minus 5, the cruisers and destroyers were scheduled to blast their assigned targets with a total of 2,875 shells. Chiming in at H-minus 25 with 2,000 rockets apiece, the LSMRs would pulverize RED and BLUE Beaches until five minutes before the landings by the two Marine regiments. At that time, all ships must cease fire to clear the way for strafing Corsairs and Navy Skyraiders.

The meticulous planning left nothing to chance, even with the assumption that a foothold would be successfully established by darkness. During the night of D-day, the cruisers would expend an additional 250 shells on interdictory missions, and the destroyers were

---

[21] This summary of naval gunfire planning is derived from: ComPhibGru One *OpnO 14-50*, Annex George. app. II, III.

authorized to fire a total of 300 5-inch rounds on call from the infantry. To help thwart any possible enemy ambitions at dawn of D-plus 1, the cruisers would be prepared to unload 300 shells for interdiction and call fires, while the destroyers stood poised with the same number of high-explosive missiles plus 300 illuminating shells.

Other details of the elaborate plan dealt with the coordination of naval gunfire, air, artillery, mortars, and rockets. At certain times, for example, Marine and Navy gunners could fire only below a maximum trajectory of 1100 feet, so that planes, whose minimum altitude was set at 1500 feet, could pass safely over Inchon during strikes on adjacent areas. During those periods when close support Corsairs were scheduled to descend on beachhead targets, all other heavy weapons would fire completely clear of broad circles defining strike areas for the air missions.

More tables and instructions in the formidable appendixes of Admiral Doyle's operation order assigned shore fire control parties their ships and radio frequencies, ships their battery missions and ammunition allowances, and a host of other tasks and responsibilities.

Air Support for Inchon

Air support, of course, was closely related to naval gunfire planning. After the arrival of CG 1st MAW and his staff at Tokyo on 3 September, part of the group proceeded at once to Itami Air Force Base while General Harris and selected staff members remained at Tokyo for planning conferences.

Air support planning for Inchon was based on the decision that the sky over the objective area was to be divided between the organic air units of JTF-7 and X Corps.

JTF-7 counted on its fast carrier task force, TF-77, to gain air supremacy and furnish deep support and interdiction strikes. Close support for the landing was to be provided by the two squadrons of TG-90.5, on board the CVEs *Sicily* and *Badoeng Strait,* which had been the main air components of MAG-33 in support of the 1st Marine Provisional Brigade. In addition, the Attack Force commander could also call upon the aircraft of TF-77 for close support.

Organic air support for X Corps was to be the mission of the Tactical Air Control set up under the operational control of the corps commander and the direct command of General Cushman. The inspiration for this organization came from Marine officers on the staff of X Corps. Their suggestions were accepted by General Almond, who used his authority as FECOM chief of staff to put the idea into effect.

MAG–33 was designated by General Harris from the Forward Echelon, 1st MAW, to serve as TAC X Corps, with VMFs 212 and 312 in addition to VMF(N)–542 and the rear echelon of VMF(N)–513. These units were not to be assigned, however, until X Corps assumed control of operations in the objective area, whereupon they would be based at Kimpo Airfield. Meanwhile, they remained under the administrative control of ComNavFE and MAG–12, with headquarters at the Itami AFB in Japan. The two Marine carrier-based squadrons and the forward echelon of VMF(N)–513, having come out to Korea in August as units of MAG–33, continued to be assigned temporarily to that group for administrative purposes.[22]

TAC X Corps was activated on 8 September, just six days before its components landed in Japan. 1st MAW planners designated the Air Support Section of MTACS–2, which had controlled air support for the Brigade, to continue in that capacity for the Landing Force and later for the entire X Corps. Arrangements were made with the Combat Cargo Command, FEAF, to airlift aviation fuel and ammunition from Japan to Kimpo Airfield, after its capture, until such supplies could be transported by sea.

Marine air units were also affected, of course, by the planning which the 1st Marine Division air and naval gunfire representatives of the Fire Support Coordination Center had already accomplished. Working aboard the *Mount McKinley* in conjunction with their opposite numbers of PhibGru One, the FSCC group had been busy since its arrival in Japan on 18 August. Planning was conducted with the CO 11th Marines after the artillery regiment landed in Japan, and the resulting decisions coordinated with air and naval gunfire plans.

The 1st MAW completed its planning on 9 September. General Cushman was designated Tactical Air Commander, X Corps, on that date and departed for the objective area the next day with the air elements scheduled to proceed by ship.

---

[22] 1st MAW *SAR*, basic rpt and Annex Able; PacFlt *Interim Rpt No. 1*, XV:Charlie Charlie, 4–5.

CHAPTER V

Embarkation and Assault

Landing of 1st Marine Division—Plan to Seize Kimpo Air-field—Shipping Assigned to Marines—Movement to the Objective Area—Strikes and Bombardments—Marine Land-ings on GREEN Beach—The Two Harbor Islands Secured

O N 30 AUGUST, ComNavFE issued his Operation Plan 108–50, assigning to JTF–7, of which X Corps was a part, the mission of seizing by amphibious assault a beachhead at Inchon.

X Corps OpnO No. 1 was dated on the 28th, though not received by Division until the 30th. By that time, Division planning had made so much progress that Embarkation Order 1–50 was issued on the last day of the month, followed on 4 September by the final draft of Division OpnO 2-50. Operations orders of JTF–7 and TF–90 were issued concurrently.

This meant that the assault RCTs, contrary to amphibious doctrine, were to receive rigid landing plans drawn up completely by the Division. Lack of time caused this variation from usual procedure, but General Smith had confidence in the ability of his troops to over-come the handicap. "Under the circumstances," he asserted, "adop-tion of such methods was justified by the common background and training of all elements and individuals in amphibious doctrine, pro-cedures, tactics, and techniques." [1]

The most that could be done was to summon Brigade staff officers from Korea for a conference. Colonel Edward D. Snedeker (Chief of Staff), Captain Eugene R. Hering, Jr., USN (Brigade Surgeon), Lieutenant Colonel Arthur A. Chidester (G–4), and Major Donald

---

[1] 1st MarDiv *SAR*, Annex Charlie.

W. Sherman (G–1) arrived on board the *Mount McKinley* for a conference on 28 August and the following day. The Brigade G–3, Lieutenant Colonel Joseph L. Stewart, reported as liaison officer on the 31st. When he returned to the front, the 5th Marines was attacking, and he discussed landing schedules with Lieutenant Colonel Raymond L. Murray while the regimental commander directed the action.

"This," remarked General Smith, "was hardly in accordance with accepted procedure for planning amphibious operations." [2]

The recommendation of Brigade staff officers that the 3d Battalion, 5th Marines, be designated for the assault on Wolmi-do was accepted by Division planners. Colonel Snedeker also proposed that the 1st Korean Marine Corps (KMC) Regiment of nearly 3,000 men be substituted for the 17th ROK Regiment, which he said was committed in the Pusan Perimeter and might not be available. The change was approved by GHQ on 3 September, with the Eighth Army being directed to provide weapons for the newcomers.

This was the beginning of a relationship that would find the KMCs serving with distinction alongside the men of the 1st Marine Division and eventually becoming a fourth infantry regiment of the Division. Activated in 1949 by the Republic of Korea, the unit took part in anti-guerrilla operations until the NKPA invasion. After the outbreak of hostilities, the KMCs fought creditably in UN delaying actions in southwest Korea. The turning point came when they were attached to the 1st Marine Division and sent to Pusan for test-firing of their new weapons before embarking for Inchon. Immediately the Koreans commenced to model themselves after U. S. Marines so assiduously as to win respect for their spirit and rugged fighting qualities. [3] They were quick to learn, despite the language handicap, and showed aptitude in mechanical respects.

Landing of 1st Marine Division

The main body of the 1st Marine Division troops landed at Kobe from 29 August to 3 September. Marine officers sent in advance to that seaport had found the authorities there "very cooperative" and

---

[2] O. P. Smith, *Notes*, 82. See v. I of this series for a detailed account of the Brigade in the second battle of the Naktong and the embarkation from Pusan.

[3] 1st MarDiv, "1st KMC Regiment and its relationship to the 1st Marine Division," (Type "C" Rpt) 1–2.

brought back to Tokyo a billeting plan which General Smith approved. Since the facilities in and about Kobe were limited, two large APs were designated as barracks ships, thus making available a Marine labor pool at the docks.

At best, every hour was needed for the tremendous task of transferring cargo from merchant type shipping into assault shipping.[*] There was cause for anxiety, therefore, when a telephone message informed the command of the 1st Marine Division on 3 September that Typhoon JANE had struck Kobe with winds of 74 miles per hour. First reports had it that the *Marine Phoenix* was on the bottom with all of the Division's signal gear. Several ships were said to have broken their moorings and gone adrift; the docks were reported under 4 feet of water, and loose cargo on the piers had been inundated by breakers.

Later accounts proved to be less alarming. The *Marine Phoenix,* having merely developed a bad list as a result of shifting cargo, was soon righted. Nor was the other damage as serious as had at first been supposed. But 24 hours were lost from the tight reloading schedule while Typhoon JANE kicked up her heels, and time was one commodity that could not be replaced. All operations at Kobe had to be speeded up to pay for this delay.

On 4 September the *Mount McKinley* set sail for Kobe, arriving at 1445 the next day to be welcomed by an Army band at the pier. The soothing powers of music were needed by Marine officers who learned that fire had broken out in the hold of the *Noonday* as she belatedly approached Kobe. This "Jonah" had taken so long to load at San Diego that she lagged behind the others, and now large quantities of much-needed Marine clothing were apparently ruined by water when the fire was extinguished. Once again the Army came to the rescue with wholehearted cooperation by taking the water-soaked boxes to a reclamation depot where the garments were dried, repackaged and sent back to the docks in time for loading out on the originally scheduled ships.

Only the most basic troop training could be conducted at Kobe to supplement the individual and amphibious instruction the men had received on shipboard. At this time, moreover, an order from the

---

[*] As a time-saving measure, it was decided to combat-load only the assault elements, allowing the other elements to go as organization loads. This was considered an acceptable risk in view of the enemy's lack of effective air and submarine forces.

Secretary of the Navy made it necessary to reduce the size of the landing force by withdrawing about 500 Marines who had not yet reached their 18th birthday. They were transferred to the 1st Armored Amphibian Tractor Battalion, which was to be left behind at Kobe when the Division embarked for Inchon.

This unit had been organized at Camp Pendleton in accordance with a directive from the Commandant. It was found necessary, however, to transfer most of its combat-ready men to the 1st Tank Battalion in order to bring that outfit up to full strength. The tank battalion was given priority because its vehicles would be used throughout the operation while the armored amphibians might be employed only occasionally. As a consequence, the 1st Armored Amphibian Tractor Battalion left San Diego with new personnel lacking in the skills to make it fully combat ready.

Lieutenant Colonel Francis H. Cooper, the commanding officer, recommended at Kobe that the unit be withheld from action until drivers, gunners, and maintenance crews could be properly trained. General Smith and his staff concurred, having learned that a trained Army unit, Company A of the 56th Amphibian Tractor Battalion, could be made available. Orders were given for Cooper's battalion to remain at Kobe, therefore, with the 17-year-old Marines attached.

Several other U. S. Army units were to take part along with the Marines—the 96th Field Artillery Battalion, the 2d Engineer Special Brigade, the 73d Engineer (c) Battalion, the 73d Tank Battalion, the 50th Engineer Port Construction Company, and the 65th Ordnance and Ammunition Company. These units comprised a total of about 2,750 troops.

Plans called for the commanding officer of the 2d Engineer Special Brigade to head a logistical task organization which also included several Marine units—the 1st Shore Party Battalion, the 1st Combat Service Group, and the 7th Motor Transport Battalion. The Shore Party troops were to initiate unloading at the objective, whereupon the over-all control would pass to the 2d Engineer Special Brigade, on order, to insure continuity of development of unloading facilities.[5]

Division service units, in accordance with current directives, were to carry the 30-day replenishment of spare parts appropriate to the unit concerned. Although the Combat Service Group had neither

---

[5] 1st MarDiv *SAR*, sec. 1, and Annexes Dog and Jig; O. P. Smith, *Notes*, 101, 104, 107, 110–112.

spare parts nor supplies, it was to have custody of both after the land-ing. Thus the units would be freed immediately to move away from the beach in support of the Division as it drove toward Kimpo and Seoul.[6]

At Kobe the men of the 1st Marine Division were required to leave the full clothing bags they had brought from San Diego and embark for Inchon with field transport packs containing only the most essen-tial items. This meant that some 25,000 sea bags must be stored at the Japanese port in such a way that future casualties and rotation drafts could reclaim their personal effects without delay. As a re-minder of the grim task ahead, provisions must be also made to return to proper custody the effects of deceased personnel.

Plan to Seize Kimpo Airfield

Intelligence reports on the eve of embarkation did not depart from earlier estimates of a maximum of 2,500 NKPA troops in the objective area. From 400 to 500 were believed to be garrisoning Wolmi-do, 500 defending Kimpo, and the balance stationed in and about Inchon.[7] Despite the estimates of low to moderate enemy resistance, however, General Smith differed with the command of X Corps when a commando-type raid on Kimpo was proposed.

The question came up on 8 September at a conference held at Kobe on the *Mount McKinley* and attended by Generals Hickey and Smith, Admiral Doyle and Colonel Louis B. Ely, USA. Ely commanded the newly formed X Corps Special Operations Company composed of 124 U. S. Army troops briefly trained by TTU instructors in demo-litions, individual combat and ship-to-shore movements in rubber boats.[8] General Almond's plan called for this company, reinforced by Marines, to embark at Kobe on 10 September in a British frigate and transfer to a South Korean picket boat. Upon arrival at the objective area on D–day, the raiders were to paddle three miles in rubber boats to the north of the Attack Force, land under cover of darkness, and move inland for a surprise attack on Kimpo at dawn.

[6] See Appendix D for a list of supplies and equipment to be embarked in assigned shipping, as prescribed by 1st MarDiv Embarkation Order 1–50 of 31 Aug 50.
[7] 1st MarDiv *SAR*, Annex Baker.
[8] Col E. H. Forney, *Special Report*, 5–7.

General Almond felt it necessary to seize the airfield at the earliest possible moment. Surprise, he felt, would reduce the risks. General Smith pointed out, however, that Colonel Ely's men would have to row their rubber boats against a strong tide and cross a wide expanse of mud flats on foot. His radios could only reach four miles, and his presence in the 1st Marine Division's zone of action would restrict the use of naval gunfire and air support. Finally, said the Marine general, it was not certain that the raiders could hold the airfield even if they took it.[9]

This conference did not settle the issue. Colonel Williams, the Division chief of staff, was requested in a telephone call followed by a dispatch from the G–1 Section of GHQ to turn over 100 specially qualified Marines to Ely's company. Smith sent a dispatch requesting reconsideration. He cited the battle casualties of the Brigade, which had not been replaced, and the 500 under-age Marines to be left behind at Kobe. As a final objection, many of his best qualified men had already embarked on the LSTs.

General Shepherd sent a dispatch supporting the 1st Marine Division commander, and the order from GHQ was recalled.[10]

Another proposal by General Almond to speed up the drive inland from the beachhead was relayed to General Smith aboard the *Mount McKinley* on 9 September by Brigadier General Henry I. Hodes, ADC of the 7th Infantry Division. This was a plan to land a battalion of the 32d Infantry on GREEN Beach, Wolmi-do, with a mission of racing across the causeway on the late afternoon of D–day and moving rapidly down the road to seize the high ground south of Seoul, more than 20 miles inland. The 1st Marine Division was requested to furnish five tanks in support of the enterprise tentatively scheduled to take place while two battalions of Marine artillery were landing on Wolmi-do and two Marine rifle regiments were landing on the Inchon beaches.

This idea struck Smith as being extremely optimistic. Without going into the tactical objections, he decided that the scheme was logistically impracticable.[11]

---

[9] O. P. Smith, *Notes*, 92–95.

[10] *Ibid.* Colonel Ely actually did embark with his Special Operations Company and make the approach, but the landing was called off because of his last-minute decision that too great a distance had to be covered in rubber boats.

[11] *Ibid.* It later developed that the 32d Infantry, first regiment of the 7th Infantry Division ashore, did not land until D-plus 3.

Shipping Assigned to Marines

The embarkation at Kobe was not completed without some confusion. Much of the equipment was in its original containers and had never been checked or identified. Large quantities of Class I, III, and V supplies, distributed throughout the incoming shipping, had to be reassembled and reassigned for the outloading. In the lack of suitable storage areas near the piers, Classes III and V were off-loaded into Japanese barges and held in floating storage until they could be reloaded into assault shipping.[12]

Inter-pier transfer of cargo was avoided whenever possible by berthing incoming shipping so that units could load directly into assault shipping. Unfortunately, this could not be done in some instances, since the LST landing was outside but adjacent to the pier area.

Facilities for the embarkation of the Brigade at Pusan were satisfactory, with pier space for three APAs and one AKA at one pier and an LSD at another. All of the assigned LSTs could beach simultaneously along the sea wall.

Only Marine amphibious experience enabled the Division to complete its tremendous task at Kobe in spite of the time lost as a result of Typhoon JANE. The shipping tentatively assigned by X Corps consisted of one AGC, six APAs, eight AKAs, three LSDs, one LSM, three APDs, 12 LSUs, and 47 LSTs. This last figure included 17 Navy-manned and 30 SCAJAP (Japanese-manned) LSTs. The troop list of approximately 29,000 men was broken down by the Division into the following six embarkation groups with their assigned shipping:

Embarkation group	Principal units	Shipping
ABLE	Division Troops	1 AGC
	1st CSG	2 APAs
		5 AKAs
		9 LSTs
		1 LSM
		3 LSUs (towed to objective area by tugs)
BAKER	1st Marine (Reinf)	1 APA
	1st Amtrac Bn	12 LSTs
CHARLIE	5th Marines (Reinf)	3 APAs
	73d Tank Bn, USA	12 LSTs
		3 APDs
		1 LSD w/3 LSUs

[12] See Appendix D.

Embarkation group	Principal units	Shipping
DOG	11th Marines	1 AKA 6 LSTs
EASY	1st Tank Bn	2 LSDs w/3 LSUs each 4 LSTs (later increased to 6)
FOX	2d Engr Spec Brig, USA 96th FA Bn, USA	1 AKA 4 LSTs

Four of these groups were to embark from Kobe while CHARLIE mounted out from Pusan and FOX from Yokohama, Yokosuka, and Camp McGill in Japan.[13] The main body of the Division's third rifle regiment, the 7th Marines, was scheduled to land in Japan on 17 September. Colonel Litzenberg, the commanding officer, arrived at Itami Airfield on the 6th, having flown from Camp Pendleton ahead of his troops to make arrangements.

Movement to the Objective Area

Command relationships during the assault and embarkation phase were as follows:

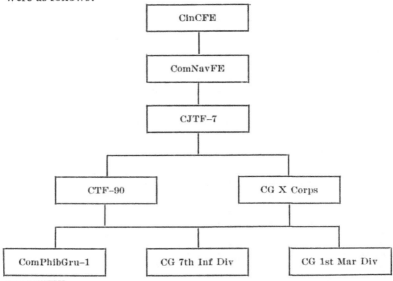

---
[13] 1st MarDiv *SAR*, sec. 1, and Annex Jig; O. P. Smith, *Notes*, 102, 117-119.

The movement of JTF-7 to the objective area was planned in the most exacting detail, owing to the dispersion of the ships to begin with, the need for secrecy, and the limited time. Another complication entered the picture at the last minute, when a second typhoon loomed on the Pacific horizon with considerably more menace than its exotic name would imply.

Navy meteorologists had been plotting the movement of Typhoon KEZIA since the first signs of turbulence near the Marianas Islands on 6 September. Generating winds of 100 miles per hour three days later, the typhoon was churning a steady course toward the East China Sea and Tsushima Strait, where it was expected to hit on 12 or 13 September. The timing could not have been worse as far as Admiral Doyle and General Smith were concerned. KEZIA threatened to strike the ships of the task force during the last stages of embarkation and the first phase of the approach to Inchon. And any serious disruption of the Navy's delicate timetable would place the 15 September deadline hopelessly beyond reach.

With the carriers, cruisers, and destroyers scheduled to be in the Yellow Sea, beyond the path of the storm, Admiral Doyle's amphibious vessels were the most imperiled elements. The Attack Force Commander planned to move his ships to the objective area in six increments, three of them loading in Japan, one in Pusan, and two at both places simultaneously. Because of the last two, certain rendezvous areas were designated so that fragments of a group could converge at sea to form the whole. Obviously, then, the mathematics of navigation was a dominant factor. Success hinged on coordination in terms of hours, not weeks or days.

Each of the six increments had its own time schedule for an independent voyage. The route to Inchon was marked off on maps by a chain of check points, the most significant of which bore the code names ARKANSAS, IOWA, and CALIFORNIA. The first two, lying in the East China Sea off the southwestern tip of Korea, formed the junction of the sea lanes from Japan and Pusan. Consequently, there was no alternative to their remaining fixed in the direct path of the oncoming typhoon. Point CALIFORNIA was important in that it marked the end of the open sea phase and the beginning of the treacherous offshore approach to Inchon via Flying Fish and East channels.[14]

---

[14] ComPhibGru-1; *OpOrder 14-50*, Annex Dog.

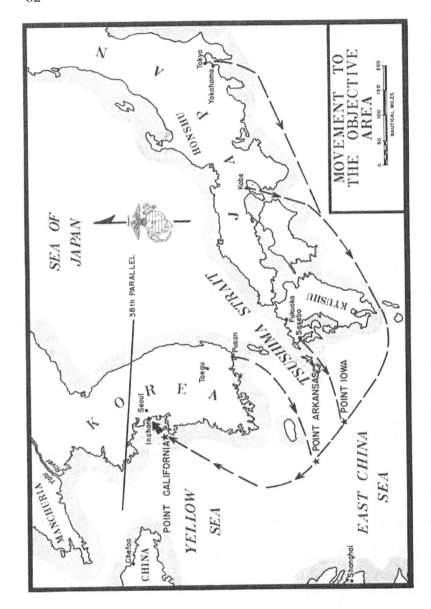

MOVEMENT TO
THE OBJECTIVE
AREA

The departure schedule for the Attack Force was set out in Doyle's Operation Order 14–50 as follows:

Unit	Port	Date
Pontoon Movement Group (2 ATFs, 3 LSUs, 1 YTB, 1 YW)	Yokohama	5 Sep
LSMR Movement Element (3 LSMRs)	....do	9 Sep
Tractor Movement Element A (LSM, 1 AMS, 1 AM, 1 ARS, 2 LSDs, 36 LSTs).	Kobe	10 Sep
Tractor Movement Element B (1 ARL, 1 PF, 1 PCEC, 12 LSTs)	....do	10 Sep
Transport Movement Group (5 APAs, 8 AKAs, 1 AP, 2 PFs)	....do	12 Sep
Advance Attack Group (Wolmi-do) (1 LSD, 3 APDs)	Pusan	13 Sep

The chart shows the basic pattern, which would evolve only after considerable shuffling and secondary routing. For instance, two vessels of the cumbersome Pontoon Movement Group, carrying vital equipment for the expansion of Inchon's port facilities, would not leave Sasebo until 11 September. They were to join the slow Yokohama convoy near Point IOWA the same day. Tractor Elements A and B, the latter trailing at a distance of six miles, would pick up the Pusan LSTs at IOWA on 13 September. The Kobe contingent of the Transport Movement Group was to pass through Point ARKANSAS on the 14th, joining the *Cavalier, Pickaway, Henrico,* and *Seminole* from Pusan.

All ship movements took place on schedule until the morning of 11 September, when angry ocean swells off the coast of Japan marked the approach of KEZIA. Winds at the center of the typhoon were estimated at 125 miles per hour, but Admiral Doyle based his decisions on the assumption that the storm would curve off to the north instead of colliding with the invasion armada in full force. He was taking a calculated risk, therefore, when he ordered the Transport Movement Group at Kobe to weigh anchor on the 11th, a day ahead of schedule, and proceed to the objective area. The LSTs, already on their way, were now out of danger; and Doyle believed that advancing the sailing date would enable the AKAs and APAs to escape the worst of the typhoon.

The *Mount McKinley,* with Doyle, Smith, and their staffs aboard, departed Kobe at 1030 on the 11th. As the ship rolled and pitched in heavy seas, the Attack Force Commander remarked that KEZIA was one of the worst storms he had ever encountered.[15]

---

[15] O. P. Smith, *Notes,* 127–129.

This was also the opinion of Captain Cameron Briggs, USN, then fighting it out with KEZIA in an effort to reach Sasebo with the carrier *Boxer* and its 96 planes plus 14 extra aircraft taken aboard at Pearl Harbor. It was necessary to launch these spares and land them on Okinawa before he could finally make port on the 12th and prepare to mount out two days later for Inchon.[16]

On 12 September the *Mount McKinley* overtook the AKAs and APAs. They had reversed course, apparently on the assumption that they could not get around the typhoon. If Doyle had not ordered the heaving vessels to circle about and follow the flagship through the storm, their chances for meeting the 15 September deadline at Inchon would have vanished like the wind-whipped spray.[17]

There was no joy in the troop compartments as the transports plowed through mountains of water. But Doyle was winning his gamble that the typhoon would slowly veer off to the north, and starting the Transport Group a day early proved to be a sound decision. Thanks to the admiral's judgment and resolution, every ship weathered the storm and approached Point ARKANSAS on schedule.

After rounding Kyushu on 12 September, the *Mount McKinley* docked at Sasebo that evening to pick up General MacArthur with his party of GHQ and X Corps officers. The proper ship for this purpose was Admiral Struble's flagship, the USS *Rochester*. But CinCFE preferred the *Mount McKinley* despite the fact that an AGC was designed for the staffs of an Attack Force and Landing Force and had no accommodations suited to a party including seven general officers. The ship was warped in by two tugs and CinCFE came aboard. General Shepherd had previously been assigned by General MacArthur to his staff for temporary duty as amphibious adviser and personal liaison officer to the 1st Marine Division. The Marine general was accompanied by Colonel V. H. Krulak, G–3 of FMFPac, and his personal aide, Major J. B. Ord.

In less than an hour the *Mount McKinley* was back on the high seas, straining through the darkness toward Korea.[18]

All elements of the Attack Force completed the last leg of the voyage without incident on 14 September. Headquarters of the 2d Battalion, 1st Marines, rode the only cripple, an LST partially incapaci-

---

[16] Karig, *Korea*, 197.
[17] O. P. Smith, *Notes*, 127–129.
[18] *Ibid*.

tated by an engine breakdown. Fortunately, an ocean-going tug was on hand to tow the ailing vessel at eight knots—sufficient speed to get her to the objective area on time.

The Yellow Sea was quiet as the columns of ships closed on Point CALIFORNIA and Korea's coastline. Nothing was taken for granted, and the approach was carefully screened to the very end by Admiral Andrewes' fast Blockade and Covering Force.

Air and Naval Bombardments

The softening up of Wolmi-do had begun on 10 September, when the Marine fliers of TG–95.5 made napalm attacks designed to burn off the trees screening NKPA artillery. Six planes of VMF–323 and eight planes of VMF–214 took off from the CVEs at 0600 and scorched the eastern side of the island. The next flight of 14 planes found it necessary to orbit for a few minutes until the smoke cleared sufficiently for them to continue the work of destruction.

Lieutenant Clark's reports had led G–2 officers to believe that enemy defensive installations on Wolmi-do were more formidable than had at first been supposed. As if in support of this conclusion, the Marine fliers of the second strike were greeted with small-caliber anti-aircraft fire both from the island and mainland. A third attack, launched from the decks of the *Sicily* and *Badoeng Strait* shortly before noon, left the hump-backed island in flames from one shore to another.

After the CVEs returned to Sasebo for replenishment the next day, the carrier-based Navy planes of TF–77 worked over both Wolmi-do and Inchon on 12 and 13 September. It was now the turn of the destroyers, and Admiral Higgins had planned a bold venture. Instead of risking collision or grounding in a night approach, he decided to forego the advantages of surprise and attack in broad daylight. And instead of avoiding NKPA fire, he intended to goad the enemy into retaliations which would reveal the positions of NKPA guns on Wolmi-do.

The hazards of the operation were increased by the fact that a ROK PC boat had discovered an NKPA craft laying mines on the morning of the 10th. This confirmed Admiral Struble's opinion that the Inchon area offered the enemy excellent opportunities for this form of warfare. Not only would the muddy waters make detection difficult, but crippled ships would block the narrow channel.

It was not a pleasant prospect. And the outlook became darker on the morning of 13 September when four mines were spotted in Flying Fish Channel. The U. S. cruisers *Toledo* and *Rochester* and the British cruisers *Kenya* and *Jamaica* had dropped off in support as the six destroyers carried out their mission. Pausing only to detonate the mines with 40mm rounds, the cans moved up within 800 yards of Wolmi-do to fire down the enemy's throat while the four cruisers poured in 6- and 8-inch salvoes and the planes of TF–77 made bombing runs.[19]

It had been long since the Navy issued the historic order "Prepare to repel boarders!" But Admiral Higgins did not overlook the possibility of NKPA infantry swarming out over the mud flats to attack a disabled and grounded destroyer. And though he did not issue pikes and cutlasses, the crews of the *Gurke, Henderson, Swanson, Collett, De Haven,* and *Mansfield* were armed with grenades and Tommy guns for action at close quarters.

The enemy endured half an hour of punishment before obliging Higgins by opening up with the shore guns of Wolmi-do. The *Gurke* and *DeHaven* took hits, and five NKPA shells found the *Collett.* The total damage was insignificant, however, and the casualties amounted to one man killed and eight wounded. These results cost the enemy dearly when the cruisers and destroyers silenced the NKPA guns shortly after they revealed their positions.

On the return trip the destroyers found eight more mines and exploded them. This proved to be all, for the enemy had neglected an opportunity to make the waters around Inchon dangerous for the attack force. The next morning, when the destroyers paid another visit to Wolmi-do, the shore guns appeared to have been effectually silenced. The DDs fired more than 1,700 5-inch shells and drew only a few scattered shots in reply. Meanwhile, the Marine planes of VMFs -214 and -323, having returned from Sasebo, cooperated by spotting for the cruisers and launching napalm strikes before and after the bombardment.

---

[19] Lynn Montross, "Fleet Marine Force Korea," *United States Naval Institute Proceedings,* 37, no. 9 (Aug 53):836–838.

On the evening of 14 September, after five days of continual pounding, Wolmi-do was a blasted piece of real estate as the Marines of 3/5 prepared to hit GREEN Beach in the morning.

Marine Landings on GREEN Beach

The pre-dawn stillness of the Yellow Sea was shattered as the Corsairs of VMFs–214 and –323 flashed up from the decks of the *Sicily* and *Badoeng Strait*. To the west the planes of Task Force 77 were assembling in attack formations above the *Valley Forge, Philippine Sea,* and *Boxer*. Squadron after squadron droned eastward through the blackness, and the first aircraft began orbiting over the objective area at 0454.[20]

Two hours earlier, Advance Attack Group 90.1, under Captain Norman W. Sears, USN, had glided into the entrance of Flying Fish channel. Led by the *Mansfield*, the column of 19 ships snaked through the treacherous passage while captains and navigators sweated over radar scopes. Lieutenant Clark's handiwork provided a welcome relief midway along the route, when the glimmering beacon on Palmi-do guided the vessels past one of the more dangerous points in the channel. Minutes after air cover began to form over Inchon, the ships eased into the narrows west of Wolmi-do and sought assigned battle stations. Training their big guns on the port city were the cruisers *Toledo, Rochester, Kenya,* and *Jamaica,* comprising one of the three Fire Support Units under Admiral Higgins. Other support vessels scattered throughout the waters of the objective area were the destroyers *Collet, Gurke, Henderson, Mansfield, De Haven, Swenson,* and *Southerland;* and this array of fire power was further supplemented by the three bristling rocket ships, LSMR's 401, 403, and 404.[21]

The control ship, *Mount McKinley,* its flag bridge crowded with star-studded commanders, steamed into the narrows just before dawn. No sooner had the gray shoreline become outlined in the morning haze than the 6- and 8-inch guns of the cruisers belched sheets of orange flame in the direction of Inchon; and at 0545, the initial explosions rocked the city and reverberated throughout the channel. There was

[20] ComAirSupGrp and ComCarDiv 15 *Report of Operations 6–21 Sep 50;* 1st MAW SAR, Annex Item:Baker, 4.
[21] 1st MarDiv *OpOrder 2–50;* Karig, *Korea,* 213.

a deafening crescendo as the destroyers hammered Wolmi-do with their 5-inch guns. Radio Hill, its seaward side already burnt and blackened from previous bombardments, was almost hidden by smoke when Marine planes streaked down at 0600 to smother the island with tons of rockets and bombs.[22]

Captain Sears, reporting to the *Mount McKinley,* confirmed L-hour at 0630. To this end, Lieutenant Colonel Robert D. Taplett's landing force was boated by 0600, and the LCVPs and LSUs rendezvoused while Marine air continued to soften up the target.[23]

Air attacks ceased at 0615, but Wolmi-do enjoyed only a momentary respite before the most unnerving blow of all. In strange contrast to the sleek men-o'-war and nimble aircraft, three squat LSMRs closed on the island from the north, a few hundred yards offshore. Phalanxes of rockets arose from the decks of the clumsy ships, arched steeply, and crashed down. One of the rocket ships, taking a southerly course, passed GREEN Beach and dumped salvo after salvo along the slopes and crest of Radio Hill.

When the LSMR cleared North Point of Wolmi-do, seven LCVPs darted across the line of departure and sped shoreward with 3/5's first wave.[24] Rockets and 40mm shells were still ripping the southern half of the island when one platoon of Company G and three platoons of Company H stormed GREEN Beach at 0633. Two minutes later, the second wave of landing craft ground to a halt on the sand, bringing the remainder of both assault companies.

The Marines were confronted by a scene of devastation almost devoid of enemy resistance. Only a few scattered shots greeted the assault force as it punched inland. The failure of UDT men to clear away all of the wrecked small craft cluttering the beach had left 3/5 a landing strip less than fifty yards wide. Consequently, each wave had to contract like an accordion, and there was considerable crowding during the first crucial minutes of the landing. But even at this stage, the potent Marine air arm offered a final measure of protection to the infantrymen splashing ashore. Pilots swung their F4Us fifty yards ahead of the assault troops and hosed the routes of advance with machine-gun bullets.

---

[22] 1st MarDiv *SAR*, sec. I; 1st MarDiv *C/S Journal, 15–20 Sep 50;* O. P. Smith, *Notes.*

[23] 1st MarDiv *SAR*, Annex Queen; and O. P. Smith, *Notes.*

[24] The following narrative is derived from 1st MarDiv *SAR*, Annexes Queen Queen and Oboe Oboe; 1st MAW *SAR;* 1st MarDiv *C/S Journal, 15–20 Sep 50;* Taplett interv, 25 Aug 54; Maj R. A. McMullen interv, 27 Jul 54; Capt J. D. Counselman memo to authors, 10 Mar 55; and MSgt E. L. Knox memo to authors, 10 Jan 55.

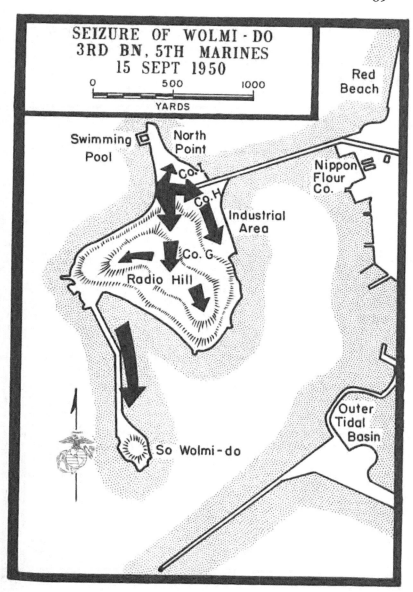

SEIZURE OF WOLMI - DO
3RD BN, 5TH MARINES
15 SEPT 1950

0   500   1000
YARDS

Red Beach

Swimming Pool

North Point

Co. I

Co. H

Nippon Flour Co.

Industrial Area

Co. G

Radio Hill

So Wolmi - do

Outer Tidal Basin

After a brief pause for reorganization at the beach, First Lieutenant Robert D. Bohn's Company G wheeled to the right and drove up the northern slopes of Radio Hill, Objective 1–A. Only half-hearted resistance was met along the way, most of the scattered and numb North Koreans preferring to surrender rather than face the inevitable. At 0655, Sergeant Alvin E. Smith, guide of the 3d Platoon, secured the American flag to a shell-torn tree on the crest.

At this point General MacArthur rose from the swivel chair in which he had been viewing the operation on the flag bridge of the *Mount McKinley*. "That's it," he said. "Let's get a cup of coffee."

Meanwhile, the Wolmi-do assault continued as Captain Patrick E. Wildman, after detaching a small force from Company H to clear rubble-strewn North Point, attacked across Wolmi-do toward the Inchon causeway with the rest of his unit. How Company's mission was to seize Objective 2–B, which included the eastern nose of Radio Hill and the shoreline industrial area facing Inchon.

At 0646, the three LSUs comprising the third wave squeezed into the narrow beach and disgorged the armored detachment of Company A, 1st Tank Battalion, under Second Lieutenant Granville G. Sweet. Ten tanks were landed in all—six M–26s, one flame-thrower, two dozers, and one retriever. The big vehicles crunched inland a short distance to await calls from the infantry.

Lieutenant Colonel Taplett ordered his free boat to the beach at 0650. Fifteen minutes later, he radioed the *Mount McKinley* and *Fort Marion* that his assault companies were advancing on schedule.

It was ironic that 3/5's reserve company should encounter the angriest hornets' nest on Wolmi-do. Landing in the fourth wave at 0659, Captain Robert A. McMullen's Company I moved through North Point in trace of the How Company detachment which supposedly had cleared the area. Suddenly a flurry of hand grenades clattered on the rubble, and the surprised Marines scattered for cover. Regaining their composure after the explosions, the infantrymen determined the source of trouble to be a by-passed string of enemy emplacements dug into a low cliff at the shoreline facing Inchon. There appeared to be about a platoon of North Koreans, who would rise from their holes intermittently, fling grenades inland, then disappear from sight.

Item Company's interpreter crawled toward the cliff during a lull, bellowing to the Reds that their predicament was hopeless and exhorting them to surrender. When the Communists responded to this advice by throwing more grenades, McMullen signalled Sweet's tanks into action. The M–26s and Marine riflemen took covering positions, while the dozer tank, directed by McMullen himself, rumbled into the troublesome pocket and systematically sealed the die-hard Reds in their holes.

Another bit of drama unfolded before the reserve troops when they closed on the causeway terminus in the wake of How Company's advance. From one of many caves drifted noises indicating the presence of several occupants, hitherto unnoticed. While riflemen covered the entrance, a Marine tank drove forward and fired two rounds into the interior.

Muffled explosions shook the area, and billows of black smoke streaked with flame rolled out of the cave. Wide-eyed, as though watching ghosts emerge, the Marines of Company I saw thirty enemy soldiers stagger out of the blazing recess and throw up their hands.

Less than an hour after landing, 3/5 controlled half of Wolmi-do. Company H, having cleared the causeway terminus, was pivoting southward to clean out the ruins of the industrial area. Engineers, close on the heels of the infantry, advanced 25 yards out on the pavement leading to Inchon and laid an antitank mine field. George Company had advanced about 400 yards and was clearing the northern crest of Radio Hill. Action up to this point is best summed up in Taplett's message to the *Mount McKinley* at 0745:

"Captured 45 prisoners. Meeting light resistance."

Nor did the situation change as Company G occupied the dominating peak of Radio Hill, some 105 meters high. The enemy lacked the will to fight, despite the fact that he had sufficient weapons and a formidable defensive complex from which to fire them. Frightened, dejected Red soldiers continued to surrender singly or in small groups, and Taplett exulted over the amazingly light casualties sustained by his battalion.

Since Company H found the going slow in the shambles of the industrial area, the battalion commander ordered Lieutenant Bohn to seize the whole of Radio Hill. Accordingly, George Company troops rushed across the ridgeline to the eastern spur. This done, Bohn dispatched a force to clear the western reaches of the high ground. By 0800, Radio Hill became the property of the 1st Marine Division, and with the prize went control of the island and Inchon Harbor.

When the news of 3/5's success blared from the loudspeaker on the flag bridge of the *Mount McKinley,* the commander in chief, wearing his famous leather jacket and braided campaign cap, withdrew to his cabin and penned a spirited message to Vice Admiral Struble aboard the *Rochester:*

"The Navy and Marines have never shone more brightly than this morning.

MacArthur"

Consolidation of Wolmi-do required the reduction of an enemy outpost on Sowolmi-do, the small lighthouse station connected to the southwestern tip of the island by a causeway 750 yards long and 12 yards wide. An islet of about 500 square yards, Sowolmi-do was topped by a low hill with the navigational beacon on the summit. Before bothering with this tiny, isolated target, Taplett put his larger house in order.

By previous plan, the three rifle companies of 3/5 took up defensive positions generally facing Inchon. Item Company occupied North Point, Wildman's unit the slopes above the industrial area, and Company G the crest of Radio Hill. While the battalion dug in, mopping-up operations throughout the island continued to net more prisoners and reveal the extent of North Korean fortifications. Radio Hill was ringed by mutually supporting trenches and emplacements, all of which had brought only a negligible return on the Reds' investment in time and labor. Parked on the western nose of the ridge were two intact 76mm antitank guns that could have wrought havoc on landing waves approaching GREEN Beach. Fortunately, these weapons had been exposed to the 40mm fire of the LSMR covering the beach assault, and their crews had lacked the stomach to man them.

More antitank guns were scattered around the terminus of the causeway leading to Inchon, leaving some question as to whether they had been rushed to the defense of the island or were marked for displacement to the city.

North Point, once a luxurious resort, was honeycombed with caves used both for storage and for bomb shelters. The swimming pool, one of the few structures still recognizable after the bombardment, was converted by the Marines into a prisoner-of-war stockade.

More than 300 cast-iron antipersonnel mines were found attached to the barbed wire entanglement stretched along the west coast at the base of Radio Hill. The explosives were removed and disarmed by

Technical Sergeant Edwin L. Knox and his detachment from Company A, 1st Engineer Battalion. Though the North Koreans had been helpful in placing these mines in so obvious a location, they had, oddly enough, failed to employ similar obstacles on the beaches, roads, and paths around the island.

Prior to the midmorning advance on Sowolmi-do, total casualties for the 3d Battalion were 14 wounded—an incredibly small price for a critical terrain feature commanding the approaches to Korea's major west coast port. Evacuation plans so carefully laid out by the 1st Medical Battalion worked smoothly. In the early phase of the operation, LCVPs returning from GREEN Beach delivered Marine casualties to the *Fort Marion,* whose normal medical complement had been augmented by a special surgical team. Men with particularly bad wounds were transferred to the *Mount McKinley* after being administered first aid. As the battle developed, navy medical corpsmen of 3/5 established a collecting point on a small pier which could be reached by ambulance boats even during low water.

Shortly before 1000, Taplett ordered Company G to seize Sowolmi-do. Bohn in turn assigned the mission to one infantry squad reinforced with machine guns and a section of tanks, all under the control of Second Lieutenant John D. Counselman, leader of George Company's 3d Platoon. Although the islet was by no means an objective of formidable proportions, the attackers eyed their route of approach over the long strip with misgivings. Their skepticism was not unfounded, for they neared the entrance to the causeway only to be stopped cold by heavy rifle and machine-gun fire from the other end. A platoon of North Koreans, almost literally at the end of a rope, preferred to fight it out.

Taplett ordered the tank-infantry team to hold up while he radioed a mission to Marine air. A few minutes later, Corsairs of VMF–214 nosed down and scorched the objective with napalm.

Sweet's tanks, preceded by an engineer mine-clearance team and followed by the column of infantrymen, rumbled onto the rock bed tracing the seaward edge of the causeway. As the task force filed across the exposed route, 81mm shells from 3/5's mortar platoon rattled overhead and tore into the Communist emplacements. Enemy fire was reduced to a light patter, and the observers on Radio Hill breathed a sigh of relief when the attackers gained the far end of the causeway at 1048.

Covered by tank fire, the Marine infantry quickly fanned out and closed with the defenders. There was a sharp outburst of small-arms racket, interspersed with the clatter of machine guns; then a few scattered volleys and the main fight was over at 1115. Mopping up with grenades and a flame thrower continued for almost another hour, owing to the number of caves and the determination of a few Red soldiers.

Nineteen North Koreans surrendered and 17 were killed, including some hapless warriors who tried to swim to the mainland. Despite the size of the islet, eight Reds succeeded in hiding out from the attackers; and General Craig, after landing on Wolmi-do with the ADC group in the evening, observed the fugitives escape to the mainland.[25]

The Two Harbor Islands Secured

Three Marines were wounded on Sowolmi-do, bringing 3/5's total casualties for the day to 17 WIA. In return, Taplett's battalion could count 136 prisoners and 108 enemy dead. Since interrogation of captives established the original number of Red defenders at 400, it could be concluded that some 150 more Communist fatalities lay entombed in sealed emplacements and caves throughout the island.

The Wolmi-do garrison was part of a 2,000-man force committed to the defense of Inchon by NKPA headquarters in Seoul. Represented were elements of the 226th Marine Regiment, to which two companies of the 2d Battalion, 918th Coast Artillery Regiment were attached with their Soviet-manufactured 76mm guns. The spiritless resistance encountered by 3/5 was the natural reaction of green troops to the awesome power of modern combined arms; for the North Korean marines and their artillerymen were largely recent conscripts with sketchy training and no experience. It remained to be seen how the other 1,600 Red troops would respond to the later assaults on RED and BLUE Beaches.

Mopping-up operations on the island were completed by noon, and with the support ships standing silent in the narrows, an oppressive quiet settled on the objective area. Gradually the phenomenal tide

---

[25] LtGen E. A. Craig memo to authors, 12 Jan 55.

rolled back from its morning high of more than 30 feet. By 1300 the waters had receded, leaving 3/5 perched on an island in a sea of mud. For the next several hours Taplett and his men were on their own, speculating whether an enemy force might suddenly rush out of Inchon's dead streets in an attempt to cross the mud flats, or whether a Red tank column would abruptly streak from the city and make for the causeway.

Nothing happened. The air of unreality caused by the stillness of the Oriental seaport weighed down on the nerves of the entire attack force. As the afternoon wore on, the Marines detected movement here and there, but the distant figures were identified as civilians more often than not. Captain McMullen, studying the RED Beach area from his OP on North Point, reported possible enemy "field pieces" on Cemetery Hill. What he actually sighted were the tubes of the mortar company of the 226th NK Marine Regiment, as will be shown later.

At Taplett's OP on Radio Hill, the Shore Fire Control Party Officer, Second Lieutenant Joseph R. Wayerski, searched Inchon intently through his binoculars. On one occasion he called down naval gunfire on small groups of people stirring in the inner tidal basin area to his right front, but when further observation revealed the figures to be civilians raiding a pile of rice, the Marine officer promptly cancelled the mission. Wayerski's lone tactical target of importance was a section of trench on Observatory Hill in which he once spotted about 20 enemy soldiers on the move. He smothered the earthworks with 30 5-inch shells from the *Mansfield*, and what North Koreans remained chose other avenues from that point on.

Taplett and others of his headquarters picked out enemy gun emplacements right at the waterfront near the Inchon dry dock. After the report went out to the *Mount McKinley*, red pencils throughout the task force circled the locale on maps for special attention during the pre-H-Hour bombardment.

Thus, the 3d Battalion enjoyed an almost uneventful interlude during its isolation. An occasional mortar round or long-range machine gun burst was the feeble reminder that Inchon still remained in enemy hands.

While the infantry lolled in relative ease and safety, service and support elements, attached to 3/5 for the landing, set the stage at GREEN Beach for the logistical follow-up so vital to amphibious operations. First Lieutenant Melvin K. Green's team from Shore Party Group A, having unloaded its LSUs in record time, established dumps for ammunition, rations, and other field necessities. Personnel of the Ordnance Battalion, Combat Service Group, and Service Battalion engaged in backbreaking toil to alleviate the headaches of a harried beachmaster. Signalmen scurried about, setting up their equipment and creating the familiar maze of wire. The reconnaissance detachment of the 11th Marines probed around the island's desolation in search of battery positions for the howitzers scheduled to roll ashore on the evening tide.

The narrow strip of sand on North Point would have appeared crowded and hopelessly confused to the inexperienced eye, but old hands knew that order would gradually emerge, as if by magic, from the "early rush hour"—that necessary evil inherent in all assault landings.

CHAPTER VI

Hitting the Beaches

*The Assault Plan—Beginning the Ship-to-Shore Movement—
Seizure of Cemetery Hill—RED Beach Secured—LSTs under
Enemy Fire—Fighting on Observatory Hill—1st Marines on
BLUE Beach—Ending the Ship-to-Shore Movement—Seizure
of the O-1 Line*

THE CONCEPT OF the amphibious envelopment of the North Korean Peoples Army, together with the actual assault on Inchon by United States Marines, constituted heresy to that school of wishful thinkers which sprang to life as World War II faded in the first brilliant flashes of the Atomic Age. Widely accepted and noisily proclaimed was the belief, perhaps sincere, perhaps convenient, that the nuclear and aeronautical sciences had relegated armies, navies, and man himself to insignificant positions in the waging of war. The massing of ships and field forces, it was argued, was a thing of the past; for the next war, if humanity dared risk another, would be decided in weeks or even days with the power unleashed by electronic and mechanical devices—many of which in 1950 were still in rudimentary stages on drawing boards.

This was the controversial "push-button" theory of war which left the peace-loving nations of the world unprepared in 1950 for violent aggression by the tough little peasant army of North Korea, supported by some 100 tanks and a few hundred artillery pieces. And to the premature acceptance of this theory by a large section of the American public may be attributed many of the major shortcomings of the Inchon assault, as it unfolded in the evening of 15 September. That the operation succeeded despite these shortcomings and the myriad natural handicaps amounts almost to a tactical miracle.

97

In the words of General Smith, ". . . half of the problem was in getting to Inchon at all."[1] The tremendous obstacles overcome in solving that "half of the problem" have already been treated at length; and it remains now, in the short space of a chapter, to show how the other half became history.

The Assault Plan

Aboard the *Henrico* and *Cavalier* in the Inchon narrows on 15 September were the 1st and 2d Battalions, 5th Marines, yanked out of the Pusan Perimeter ten days earlier. Having had no time for a rehearsal and only a few days for planning on the basis of admittedly sketchy intelligence, these two units would scale the sea wall of RED Beach and plunge into the dense waterfront area of the sprawling seaport.

The mission of the 5th Marines (less 3/5 on Wolmi-do) was to seize the O–A Line, a 3,000-yard arc encompassing Cemetery Hill on the left (north), Observatory Hill in the center, and thence extending the last 1,000 yards through a maze of buildings and streets to terminate at the inner tidal basin. Each battalion would land in a column of companies, Lieutenant Colonel George R. Newton's 1st, on the left, seizing Cemetery Hill and the northern half of Observatory Hill; while Lieutenant Colonel Harold S. Roise's 2d secured the remainder of the latter, the hill of the British Consulate, and the inner tidal basin.[2]

Landing nearly three miles southeast of the 5th Marines, the 1st Regiment would seize BLUE Beach, a north-south strip fronting a suburban industrial area. BLUE Beach One, on the left, was 500 yards wide, flanked on the north by the rock revetment of a salt evaporator that jutted into the water at a sharp angle to the shoreline. A wide drainage ditch, about which little was known besides the fact that it existed, formed the south boundary. Just inland a dirt road—the sole exit from the beach—skirted the north end of a steep knoll that ran the whole width of the landing site. There being no revetment at the waterline, Marine planners hoped that amphibian tractors could crawl ashore with the assault troops.[3]

---

[1] LtGen O. P. Smith memo to authors, 28 Feb 55.
[2] 1st MarDiv *SAR*, Annex Queen Queen.
[3] *Ibid.*, Annex Peter Peter.

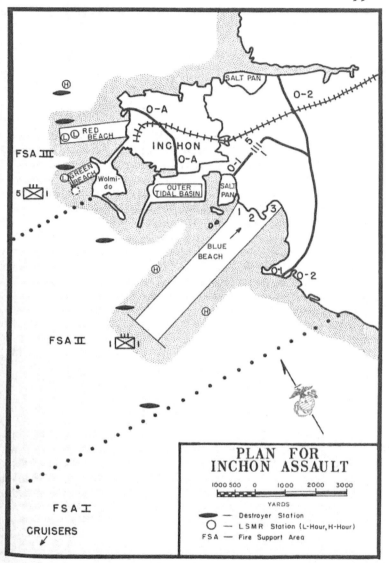

PLAN FOR
INCHON ASSAULT

1000 500   0   1000   2000   3000
YARDS

● — Destroyer Station
○ — LSMR Station (L-Hour, H-Hour)
FSA — Fire Support Area

BLUE Beach Two, connected to One by the drainage ditch, also extended 500 yards. Like RED Beach it was fronted by a rock sea wall. On the right half, the wall retained one side of a narrow ramp that jutted southward like a long index finger. Behind the ramp lay a cove, its shoreline at a right angle to the sea wall. During the assault, Marines would scale the waterfront of BLUE Two from LVTs, while the cove around the corner on the right, unofficially dubbed "BLUE Beach Three," was investigated as a possible supplementary landing site.[4]

Preceded by a wave of LVT(A)s of Company A (Reinf), 56th Amphibian Tractor Battalion, USA, the 2d and 3d Battalions, 1st Marines, would land abreast on BLUE One and Two respectively. With two companies initially in the assault, each of the infantry battalions was to drive forward and secure its portion of the O–1 Line. This four-mile arc bent inland as far as 3,000 yards to include four main objectives, assigned as follows:

2d Battalion (BLUE One)

ABLE	A critical road junction about 1,000 yards northeast of the beach.
DOG	Hill 117, 3,000 yards northeast of the beach, commanding Inchon's back door and the highway leading to Seoul, 22 miles away.

3d Battalion (BLUE Two)

CHARLIE	The seaward tip of Hill 233, a long east-west ridge beginning 1,500 yards southeast of the beach and blocking off the stubby Munhang Peninsula, which projected southward.
BAKER	A small cape, topped by Hill 94, to the right of Objective Charlie and flanking BLUE Beach.[5]

While a question may arise as to the choice of landing the 5th Marines in the very heart of Inchon, it must be remembered that immediate seizure of the port facilities was vital to the success of the operation. Hitting the beaches at only two-thirds infantry strength, the 1st Marine Division could not swell to the overwhelming proportions of an invasion force. A modern harbor for rapid build-up and exploitation by X Corps figured inherently in MacArthur's strategy.

---

[4] *Ibid.;* and Col T. L. Ridge ltr to authors, 11 May 55.
[5] 1st MarDiv *OpnO 2–50;* and 1st MarDiv *SAR,* Annex Peter Peter.

If RED Beach thus constituted the critical objective, then the selection of BLUE Beach for a supporting landing followed in logical sequence. Once on the O–1 Line, the 1st Marines would flank the single overland approach to the peninsular seaport, thereby presenting the NKPA garrison with the grim alternatives of early flight, capitulation, or strangulation. Without this leverage on Inchon's flank and rear, the 5th Regiment could easily be swallowed up by two square miles of dense urban area.

Four assault battalions would have two hours of daylight in which to bridge the gap between planning and reality. From overhead and behind they could expect a preponderance of heavy fire support, but ahead lay enemy and hydrographic situations still clouded by question marks.

Beginning the Ship-to-Shore Movement

As the early afternoon of 15 September wore on, the continued silence of Inchon beckoned temptingly to Lieutenant Colonel Taplett on Wolmi-do. Having studied the city over a prolonged period without detecting any significant evidence of Communist defensive capability, he radioed Division headquarters for permission to move a strong tank-infantry force across the causeway. The battalion commander believed that 3/5 could launch either an effective reconnaissance in force or an actual assault on RED Beach. Although his estimate of the enemy potential was shortly borne out, the degree of risk in Taplett's bold plan drew a firm "negative" from the *Mount McKinley*.[6]

Busy with last-minute details aboard the command ship, General Smith at noon had radioed General Craig instructions to land on Wolmi-do on the evening tide and set up an advance echelon of the division command post with the ADC group. Smith did not desire to land the remainder of his headquarters until D–plus 1, when there would be more room for dispersion within the expanding beachhead.[7]

The Landing Force Commander could look down from the flag bridge at 1400 and note the first signs of activity on the water. A few special landing craft were beating the forthcoming traffic rush as they sped toward the various ships to which they were assigned as command boats.

[6] Taplett interv, 25 Aug 54.
[7] O. P. Smith, *Notes*, 152.

At the same time, the central control vessel, *Diachenko* (APD 123), edged forward to its key station 3,000 yards southwest of the BLUE Beach line of departure. Lieutenant Commander Allmon checked the set and drift of the current and radioed his observations to Admiral Doyle. Estimated at three and a half knots, the run of current was heavier than expected. After receiving the Senior Control Officer's report, the Attack Force Commander confirmed 1730 as H-Hour.[8]

The confirmation went out to the entire Joint Task Force at 1430, and Admiral Higgins' fire support ships immediately commenced the final bombardment of Inchon. His four cruisers and six destroyers poured shells into the seaport for the next three hours, smashing every landmark of tactical importance and starting fires that blazed across the whole waterfront.

Under the calculating eyes of tactical air observers and coordinators in F4Us droning high above the objective area, VMFs–323 and –214 and three squadrons of Navy Skyraiders alternately blasted Inchon, integrating their strikes with naval gunfire from H-minus 180 minutes onward. Simultaneously, Fast Carrier Task Force 77 kept another 12 planes in the air continuously for deep support missions designed to freeze all enemy activity within a radius of 25 miles.

As if enough obstacles did not confront the landing force already, rain squalls began drifting past Inchon during the bombardment. Gradually the storm clouds merged with the thick smoke boiling up from the city, and heavy overcasts settled over large areas, particularly in the vicinity of BLUE Beach.[9]

Assault troops of the 5th Marines scrambled down cargo nets on the *Henrico* and *Cavalier* to fill landing craft splashing into the water from booms and davits. Nearly 200 LCVPs and 70 LCMs soon were joined by 12 LSUs and 18 LVT(A)s, 164 LVTs, and 85 DUKWs disgorged from the yawning wells of the LSTs, wherein the Marines of the 1st Regiment had made ready for battle.[10]

Guided by Lieutenant Commander Ralph H. Schneeloch, USNR, the *Horace A. Bass,* RED Beach control vessel, slowly steamed toward the line of departure, a long file of assault craft trailing behind like a brood of ducklings. Lieutenant Theodore B. Clark, USN, ordered the *Wantuck* to the head of the boat lane to BLUE Beach, and *PCEC*

---

[8] *Ibid.;* ComPhibGru–1 *OpnO 14–50;* and LCdr R. W. Berry ltr to authors, 17 Mar 55.
[9] 1st MarDiv *SAR,* Annex Peter Peter.
[10] ComPhibGru–1 *OpnO 14–50,* Annex Item; I.

896, under Lieutenant Reuben W. Berry, USN, took station off Wolmi-do to regulate the waves scheduled for the administrative landing on GREEN Beach.[11]

At 1645, the 18 Army LVT(A)s comprising the first wave of the 1st Marines crossed the line of departure and headed for BLUE Beach. Crawling at four knots, the armored vehicles had three quarters of an hour to cover the 5,500 yards to the target. The LCVPs, capable of twice the speed of the amphibian tractors, left the inner transport area near the *Diachenko's* station for the five-mile trip northward to the RED and GREEN boat lanes.[12]

The roar of the fire support ships increased in volume during the approach of the landing craft until, at 1705 (H-minus 25), Admiral Higgins signaled the LSMRs into action. At once the cruisers and destroyers fell silent. Again missiles soared from the squat rocket ships in high arcs that sent them plunging into the RED and BLUE landing areas. Upwards of 6,000 rockets detonated in the seaport during the next twenty minutes, further numbing the defenders but at the same time increasing the density and volume of the overcast.[13]

Seizure of Cemetery Hill

The critical moment of every amphibious assault was now at hand— the moment when intelligence and planning would be put to the test of actuality. On the bridge of the *Mount McKinley* high-ranking Army, Navy, and Marine Corps officers gathered again about General MacArthur, seated in a swivel chair. They listened for the second time that day as the loud speaker gave a blow-by-blow account of developments reported by aerial observers.

Everything that air attacks and naval gunfire could do to soften up the target had been done, yet no one could be sure just what sort of opposition the troops would encounter on RED and BLUE Beaches. It might be as fainthearted as that brushed aside by 3/5 on Wolmi-do; or it might be that another Tarawa awaited on those cramped strips of urban waterfront lying between the mud flats of the harbor and the dark, crooked streets of the Asiatic town and environs. The enemy

[11] *Ibid.*, VII; Cdr C. E. Allmon, USN, ltr to authors, 9 Mar 55; LCdr T. B. Clark, USN, ltr to authors, 11 Mar 55; and LCdr R. H. Schneeloch, USN, ltr to authors, 20 Mar 55.
[12] ComPhibGru-1 *OpnO 14–50*, Annex Item:VI.
[13] *Ibid.*, Annex George: II; and Schneeloch ltr, 20 Mar 55.

had been given ample time in which to prepare for a defense of the mainland.

Even the possibility of undetected mines or surprise NKPA air attacks at the last minute had not been overlooked. Although the Attack Force continued to exercise control from the TADC on the *Mount McKinley* of all aircraft operating in its assigned area, an alternate control agency had been installed on the USS *George Clymer*, utilizing an emergency hookup and a control unit attached to TAC, X Corps. All nets were manned and communications set up to permit a rapid shift of control to General Cushman in case of disaster.[14]

With H-hour only minutes away, the sky above the objective was murky and the wind whipped rain as well as stinging spray into the faces of the Marines in the assault waves. Only the Marine and Navy flyers upstairs could see the panorama of the waterborne attack—the cruisers and destroyers standing silent in the background, LSMR rocket flashes stabbing the false twilight ashore, the landing craft trailing pale wakes behind them like the tails of comets . The pilots observed the LCVPs to the left of Wolmi-do fan out at the line of departure and touch the sea wall of RED Beach minutes later. To the right of the little island, however, they saw the leading waves of the 1st Marines disappear in a blanket of gloom. For while the smoke and moisture-laden air had obscured parts of the 5th Marines' zone of action ashore, it had completely blotted out BLUE Beach and half the length of the 1st Regiment's boat lanes. Because of this development and other factors which posed special problems for the 1st Marines, the narrative will treat each landing separately, beginning with that of the 5th Regiment on the left.

Eight LCVPs had crossed the line of departure at H-minus 8 and sped toward RED Beach with the first wave of the 5th Marines. Starting from the left, boats numbered one through four carried parts of two assault platoons of Company A, 1st Battalion, whose mission was to seize Cemetery Hill and anchor the regimental left. In boats five through eight were troops of Company E, 2d Battalion, whose task included clearing the right flank of the beach and taking the hill of the British Consulate.[15]

---

[14] 1st MAW *SAR*, basic rpt; and LtGen (Ret) T. J. Cushman interv, 26 Jul 54.

[15] The RED Beach narrative, unless otherwise noted, is derived from: 1st Mar Div *SAR*, Annex Queen Queen; LtCol M. R. Olson interv, 29 Dec 54; Lt Col H. S. Roise intrev, 21 Dec 54; Maj J. R. Stevens interv, 1 Aug 54; Capt E. A. Deptula interv, 18 Jan 55; Capt G. C. McNaughton interv, 7 Jan 55; and 1stLt F. W. Muetzel interv, 6 Jan 54.

From Wolmi-do 3/5's machine guns, mortars, and supporting M-26s cut loose with a hail of bullets and high explosive to cover the landing. Technical Sergeant Knox lead an engineer team forward to clear the causeway, in order that the detachment of Able Company Tanks could advance to the mainland after the initial assault waves hit the beach.

As the landing craft passed the midway point of the 2,200-yard boat lane, the heaving LSMRs ceased firing, so that Lieutenant Colonel Walter E. Lischeid and Major Arnold A. Lund could lead in VMFs–214 and –323 for final strikes on both RED and BLUE Beaches. Navy Skyraiders joined in at the request of Captain John R. Stevens, commander of Company A; and the FAC of 1/5, First Lieutenant James W. Smith, controlled their strafing passes as the first wave came within 30 yards of the sea wall.[16]

Although the tide was racing in fast, the wall still projected about four feet above the ramps of the landing craft. The Marines readied their scaling ladders. On the right the boats of Company E touched the revetment at 1731. Up went the ladders as the assault troops hurled grenades over the wall. Following the explosions, the Marines from the four boats scrambled to the top of the barrier one by one. The ladders slipped and swayed as the LCVPs bobbed next to the wall. But they served their purpose, and in short order every man of Second Lieutenant Edwin A. Deptula's 1st Platoon was on the beach.

There were no casualties from the few stray bullets cracking through the air. Filtering through smoke and wreckage, the platoon moved inland to cover the landing of the second and third waves, carrying the remainder of Easy Company.

On the north of RED Beach, three of the four LCVPs with the leading elements of Company A bumped the sea wall at 1733. Boat number one, carrying Technical Sergeant Orval F. McMullen and half of his 1st Platoon, was delayed offshore by an engine failure. The remainder of the 1st, under the platoon guide, Sergeant Charles D. Allen, scaled the wall from boat number two in the face of heavy fire from the north flank and from submachine guns in a bunker directly ahead. Several Marines were cut down immediately, the others being unable to advance more than a few yards inland.

Boat number three, with Second Lieutenant Francis W. Muetzel and a squad of his 2d Platoon, touched a breach in the sea wall under

---

[16] 1st MAW *SAR*, Annex Item:Baker; and 1stLt (Ret) F. W. Muetzel ltr to CMC, 11 Apr 54.

the muzzle of an enemy machine gun protruding from a pillbox. The weapon did not fire as the Marines scrambled through the gap and onto the beach. A second squad and a 3.5-inch rocket section joined from boat number four. Gunfire crackled far off on the left, barely audible amid the road of fighter planes strafing fifty yards ahead. Muetzel and his men jumped into a long trench which paralleled the sea wall a few feet away. It was empty. Two Marines threw grenades into the silent pillbox, and the six bloody North Koreans who emerged in the wake of the hollow explosions were left under guard of a Marine rifleman.

Just beyond the beach loomed Cemetery Hill, its seaward side an almost vertical bluff. To avoid getting trapped if the enemy opened up from the high ground, Muetzel attacked toward his objective, the Asahi Brewery, without waiting for the remainder of his men in the tardy second wave. The skirmish line raced across the narrow beach, ignoring padlocked buildings and flaming wreckage. Passing to the south of Cemetery Hill, the 2d Platoon entered the built-up area of the city and marched unopposed up a street to the brewery.

On the left of Company A's zone, the beached half of the 1st Platoon made no progress against the flanking fire and the Communist bunker to the front. The 3d Platoon, under First Lieutenant Baldomero Lopez, landed in the second wave, and McMullen finally got ashore with the other half of the 1st. Both units crowded into the restricted foothold and casualties mounted rapidly. Enemy guns had felled Lopez as he climbed ashore and moved against the bunker with a grenade. Unable to throw the armed missile because of his wound, the young officer was killed when he smothered the explosion with his body to protect his men. Two Marines attacked the emplacement with flame throwers. They were shot down and their valuable assault weapons put out of action.

The situation on the left was at its worst when Captain Stevens landed in Muetzel's zone at H-plus 5. Learning of Lopez' death and unable to contact McMullen, he ordered his executive officer, First Lieutenant Fred F. Eubanks, Jr., to "take over on the left and get them organized and moving." [17] Time was of the essence, since Cemetery Hill, objective of the 1st Platoon, yet remained in enemy hands. Succeeding waves would be landing hundreds of Marines in the shadow

[17] Capt F. F. Eubanks, Jr., ltr to CMC, 2 Jun 55.

of the cliff within the next half hour. Stevens also radioed Muetzel, whose small force had just reached the brewery without suffering a casualty, and ordered the 2d Platoon back to the beach to help out.

Muetzel immediately formed his unit in column and struck out on the return trip to the waterfront. Nearing Cemetery Hill again, he noted that the southern slope of the vital objective was an excellent route of approach to the top. In planning Company A's part of the operation, Stevens had once told him that the 2d Platoon could expect to help seize the high ground if the job proved too rough for the 1st alone.[18] With a creditable display of judgment and initiative, Muetzel launched an assault on the key to RED Beach.

The Marines moved rapidly up the incline, flushing out about a dozen Red soldiers who surrendered meekly. Gaining the summit, they drove forward and saw the entire crest suddenly come alive with infantry-crewmen of the 226th NKPA Regiment's mortar company. Spiritless and dazed from the pounding by air and naval gunfire, the North Koreans to a man threw down their weapons, filed quietly from trenches and bunkers, and marched to the base of the hill where a small detachment kept them under guard. Hardly a shot had been fired by the 2d Platoon, still without a single casualty, and the capture of Cemetery Hill had required about ten minutes.

During the attack on the high ground, Eubanks had taken the situation in hand on the left of the beach. He first bested the bunker's occupants in a grenade duel, then ordered the emplacement fired by a flame thrower. Just as Muetzel prepared to dispatch assistance from the top of Cemetery Hill, the 1st and 3d Platoons broke out of the pocket, drove inland to the edge of the city, and made physical contact with the 2d.

At 1755, Stevens fired an amber star cluster signifying that Cemetery Hill was secured for the 5th Marines. The half-hour fight in the north corner of RED Beach had cost Company A eight killed and 28 wounded.

RED Beach Secured

After landing in 2/5's first wave, the 1st Platoon of Company E pushed inland 100 yards to the railroad tracks against no resistance whatso-

---

[18] Maj J. R. Stevens ltr to authors, 29 Mar 55.

ever. Captain Samuel Jaskilka was ashore with the rest of the Company by H-plus 10, and reorganization took place quickly near the Nippon Flour Company buildings, just south of the beach. Deptula's platoon then moved unopposed down the railroad tracks and seized the British Consulate, Regimental Objective C, at 1845. Simultaneously, another platoon cleared the built-up area across the tracks on the lower slopes of Observatory Hill. These rapid accomplishments secured the 5th Marines' right flank, giving an added measure of protection to 22 more waves of landing craft and LSTs scheduled for RED Beach.

Still in enemy hands, however, was Observatory Hill, reaching well over 200 feet above the center of the regimental zone to buttress the arc of the O–A Line. Company C of the 1st Battalion, landing in the fourth and fifth waves shortly before 1800, was to take Objective A, northern half of the critical terrain feature. To Dog Company of 2/5 was charged the southern half, designated Objective B.

That the attack did not go off as planned stemmed from a series of mishaps which began as far out as the line of departure. Despite the fact that Lieutenant Commander Schneeloch was using standard control procedures from the *Bass,* including radio contact with the beach, there was a mixing of waves starting with number four.[19] This development reflected the lack of a rehearsal in the hurried preparations for the operation, and the end result was that parts of Companies C and D, both in the second assault echelon, landed over the wrong beaches.[20] After landing, Charlie Company had the added disadvantage of being without its company commander for a crucial 12 minutes. Captain Poul F. Pedersen was delayed when the fifth-wave commander, who shared his boat, decided to tow a stalled LCVP left behind by the preceding formation.[21] When he finally reached his company, the job of reorganization was much more difficult than it would have been had he arrived at the beach on schedule. With troops pouring over the sea wall from succeeding waves, what had begun as intermingling at the point of overlap in the center of the landing area had grown to temporary congestion and confusion.

---

[19] Schneeloch ltr, 20 Mar 55.
[20] Col G. R. Newton ltr to CMC. 8 Apr 55.
[21] Capt P. F. Pedersen memo to CMC, 1 May 55.

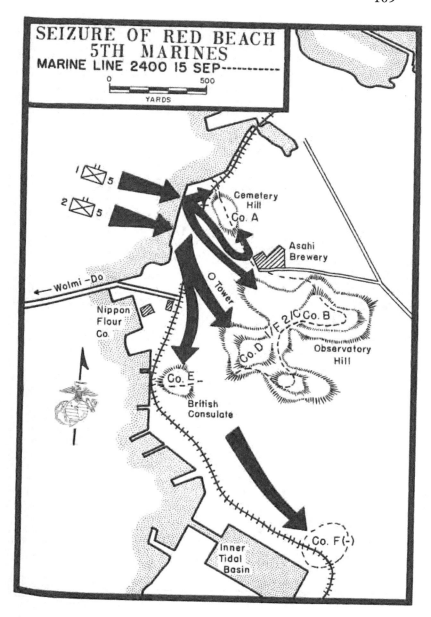

SEIZURE OF RED BEACH
5TH MARINES
MARINE LINE 2400 15 SEP----------

0   500
YARDS

Cemetery
Hill
Co. A

Asahi
Brewery

O Tower

Wolmi -Do

Nippon
Flour
Co.

1/C Co. B
F 2/C
Co. D

Observatory
Hill

Co. E

British
Consulate

Inner
Tidal
Basin

Co. F (-)

LSTs Under Enemy Fire

Out in the channel, the first of eight LSTs [22] heralded the climax of the ship-to-shore movement at 1830 by crossing the line of departure and heading for the sea wall. Prior to the approach, ships' officers had spotted the close fighting on the north flank of RED Beach as they peered through binoculars from their respective bridges. Later, noting the growing knot of Marines in the center of the waterfront area, they concluded that the assault troops could not advance inland. This impression was strengthened by an abrupt procession of gun flashes on Observatory Hill where, owing to the delay in the attack by Companies C and D, a handful of enemy soldiers had recovered from shock sufficiently to set up machine guns. A few North Korean mortar crews in the city also came to life and manned their weapons.

LST 859, leading the pack, came under mortar and machine-gun fire as it waddled toward its berth about 1835. Gun crews on the ship reacted by opening up with 40mm and 20mm cannon, spraying Cemetery and Observatory Hills and the right flank of the beach. Next in the column of ships, LSTs 975 and 857 likewise commenced firing after taking hits from mortars and machine guns. Enemy automatic weapons touched off a fire near ammunition trucks on LST 914, trailing fourth, but sailors and Marines quickly brought the blaze under control. Guns on the latter ship remained silent as a result of dispatch orders received by the captain after leaving the line of departure.[23]

Lieutenant Muetzel and his platoon were chased by LST fire from the crest of Cemetery Hill to the slope facing Inchon—where they came under fire from a Red machine gun in a building on Observatory Hill. Fortunately, a 40mm shell from one of the LSTs crashed into the building and obliterated the enemy position. There were no casualties in Muetzel's outfit, but Lieutenant Colonel Roise's 2d Battalion did not fare as luckily from the misdirected shooting by the American ships. Weapons and H&S Companies of 2/5 had landed about 1830

---

[22] Under the over-all command of LCdr James C. Wilson, who flew his broad pennant in LST 859, the eight ships were: 859 (Lt L. Tinsley); 883 (Lt C. M. Miller); 914 (Lt R. L. Holzhaus); 973 (Lt R. I. Trapp); 898 (Lt R. M. Beckley); 975 (Lt A. W. Harer); 857 (Lt D. Weidemeyer); and 799 (Lt T. E. Houston).

[23] 1st MarDiv *SAR*, Annex Queen Queen; LtGen (Ret) E. A. Craig ltr to CMC, 21 Apr 55; LCdr R. I. Trapp, USN, ltr to CMC, 18 Mar 55; and Lt (Ret) R. L. Holzhaus, USN, ltr to CMC, 14 Mar 55.

and were just proceeding inland when LST fire seared their ranks, killing one Marine and wounding 23 others. "If it hadn't been for the thick walls of the Nippon Flour Company," remarked Roise later, "the casualties might have been worse." [24]

All eight of the supply vessels were intact in their berths by 1900. Guns fell silent as soon as the LSTs touched the sea wall and contact was established with the infantry.

On the beach, meanwhile, Second Lieutenant Byron L. Magness had reorganized his 2d Platoon of Company C and, on his own initiative, attacked Observatory Hill. Second Lieutenant Max A. Merritt's 60mm mortar section followed closely behind, but the rest of the company remained fragmented in the landing area. Sparked by Technical Sergeant Max Stein, who was wounded while personally accounting for a North Korean machine gun, the provisional force advanced rapidly in the gathering darkness and at 1845 seized the saddle between Objectives A and B on Observatory Hill. This was just about the time when the LSTs stopped firing. [25]

Since their single flare misfired and they were not able to raise Lieutenant Pedersen by radio, Magness and Merritt were unable to inform the beach of their success. In the meantime, Company B, 1/5's reserve, had landed in the 2d Battalion zone, the waves having swerved to that area to avoid small-arms fire peppering their assigned approach on the left. Captain Francis I. Fenton, Jr., led the unit through a mixed group on the waterfront to an assembly area near the base of Cemetery Hill. When he discussed the beach situation by radio with the battalion commander, Lieutenant Colonel Newton ordered him to take over Charlie Company's mission and assault the northern half of Observatory Hill. [26]

Fighting on Observatory Hill

Darkness had fallen when Company B drove up the slopes of Objective A in a two-pronged attack. Six Marines were wounded in brief skirmishes with North Korean die-hards along the way. Gaining the summit at 2000, Fenton deployed three platoons on line, making con-

---

[24] LtCol H. S. Roise ltr to authors, 23 Mar 55.
[25] 1st MarDiv *SAR*, Annex Queen Queen; and Maj F. I. Fenton, Jr., ltr to authors, 21 Mar 55.
[26] *Ibid*.; Newton ltr, 8 Apr 55; and Capt B. L. Magness ltr to CMC, 29 Mar 55.

tact with the Magness-Merritt force dug in on the saddle to the right. With Objective A seized and Able Company deployed on top and to the flanks of Cemetery Hill, Newton radioed the 5th Marines at 2240 that 1/5's segment of the O–A Line was secured.[27]

In the right of the 5th Marines' zone, the 2d Battalion had also been making gains, despite the handicaps of mixed boat waves, LST fire, poor visibility, and, finally, enemy action.[28] It will be recalled that Company E suffered no casualties in landing and clearing the waterfront as far south as Objective C, the British Consulate. Next to hit the beach was First Lieutenant H. J. Smith's Company D, part of which went ashore in 1/5's zone. Assembling later near the base of Observatory Hill, the unit prepared to carry out its mission of seizing Objective B, the southern half of the big ridge.

Although 2d Battalion overlays show that Easy Company bore no responsibility for the crest of Observatory Hill, Smith's men somehow got the impression that part of Jaskilka's force was already on the summit. Its tactics based on this misunderstanding, Company D formed a simple route column, with Second Lieutenant Ray Heck's 1st Platoon leading the way, and marched up a street to the top of the hill. The vanguard troops cleared the first peak in the company zone without opposition and continued along the road to the second, expecting to meet men of Company E. They were greeted, however, by machine-gun fire from an enemy squad entrenched to the right of the street.

The Marines tumbled into positions on the left. Grenades and small-arms fire flew back and forth across the road during a brisk exchange that lasted about 15 minutes. One of Heck's men was killed and three others wounded. The company corpsmen was hit but refused evacuation until he had first administered to the other casualties and seen them off to safety. Company D's executive officer, First Lieutenant Michael J. Dunbar, went forward with Lieutenant Colonel Roise, the battalion commander, and was wounded by a ricochet.

The enemy troops were driven off just as darkness closed in, leaving the Marines to grope for night defensive positions on unfamiliar

---

[27] *Ibid.*

[28] The following narrative is derived from: 1st Mar Div *SAR*, Annex Queen Queen; Roise interv, 21 Dec 54; Roise ltr, 23 Mar 55; McNaughton interv, 7 Jan 55; and Magness ltr, 29 Mar 55.

ground. Eventually Lieutenant Smith formed a line with all three rifle platoons deployed on the forward slopes of Objective B. Out of battalion reserve came Second Lieutenant Harry J. Nolan's platoon of Company F to bridge the gap between Company D and the Magness-Merritt positions in 1/5's zone on the left.

With Cemetery and Observatory Hills secured, the only portion of the O-A Line not yet under control was the extreme right, anchored on the inner tidal basin. Since the night was pitch black, Roise felt apprehensive about sending troops any farther into the city. In answer to a query, Lieutenant Colonel Murray, whose regimental head-quarters had landed at 1830 and set up near the terminus of the Wolmi-do causeway, emphasized to Roise that where the O-A Line could not actually be defended from a suitable tactical stand-point, it must at least be outposted. The battalion commander forthwith dispatched a two-squad patrol from Fox Company to the tidal basin, and the small force returned from the 1,000-yard prowl into the city at 2300, having seen no sign of the enemy. Roise reacted by committing Company F, less its platoon on Observatory Hill, to a defensive perimeter on the right flank. Shortly after midnight, Cap-tain Uel D. Peters deployed the company next to the tidal basin as ordered; and the 5th Marines' O-A Line, though not manned in entirety, came as close to tactical reality as the tangled black depths of the seaport would allow.

1st Marines on BLUE Beach

As mentioned earlier, the overcast resulting from rain squalls and smoke had completely blotted out BLUE Beach by H-hour, 1730. This fact in itself would have sufficed to upset a precise landing pro-cedure; but at this point in the narrative, it is timely to review some of the other problems which had beset the 1st Marines since the incep-tion of the plan for the Inchon assault.[29]

In the short space of weeks, the regiment had been brought up to war strength by the rapid convergence on Camp Pendleton of Marines—in units or as individuals, both regular and reserve—from

[29] The preliminary to the landing account is derived from: 1st MarDiv *SAR*, Annex Peter; Col R. W. Rickert memo to authors, 15 Apr 55; ltr, 11 May 55; Col A. Sutter and Maj G. S. Codispoti interv, 25 Jan 55; Col A. Sutter memo to authors, 5 May 55; and Maj E. H. Simmons ltr to CMC, 28 Mar 55.

all over the United States; it had embarked at San Diego and crossed the Pacific; and it had reloaded and embarked from Japan for a combat operation designed to quench a major conflagration. There had been time for only the sketchiest training above the company level. The new 1st Marines had never operated tactically as a regiment, nor had it ever been concentrated in one place as an organizational entity up until the time it hit BLUE Beach.

During the planning phase in Kobe, battalions had to combat-load their LSTs according to an X factor, while awaiting the prescribed tactical plans that would be handed down from higher echelon at the last minute. Intelligence on the enemy and beach conditions was practically non-existent; and the speculative studies and inadequate photos available could be kept only a few hours before being passed on to the next unit in line.

Whenever Marines are given a difficult assignment, the United States Navy invariably draws its own full measure of handicaps. A typical example of the problems confronting naval planners was this case, cited by Major Edwin H. Simmons, of 3/1:

> "I was aboard LST 802, which was carrying H&S Company and elements of Weapons Company. The ship had just been recovered from the island trade. Her captain had been flown out to Sasebo from the States, given a pick-up crew and two weeks to condition the ship and crew for an amphibious landing. Despite his best efforts, the 802 had three major breakdowns and had to drop out of convoy several times. At one point it appeared as though the battalion command group would have to be taken off the 802 if they were to get to Inchon in time."

In connection with BLUE Beach itself, officers of the 1st Marines had only a vague impression of offshore conditions and the accessibility of the landing site. As already noted, the current in the channel was underestimated, and so little was known about the consistency of the mud flats that each landing craft contained planking for emergency use by the assault troops.

The sole exit from BLUE One was the dirt road already mentioned. On aerial photos the drainage ditch separating BLUE One and Two appeared to be some kind of a road over which tractors could crawl ashore. No one was certain, and "BLUE Beach Three," the cove on the right, was ruled out as a possible landing area early in the planning. At the last minute, however, recent aerial photos and studies led to the conclusion that both the inlet and the ramp at the southern tip of BLUE Two might be good approaches after all. Acting on this information while en route to the target area, Lieutenant Colonel Thomas L. Ridge, commanding officer of 3/1, decided to explore personally the right flank with his executive officer at the outset of the assault. If the ramp, BLUE Three, or both were accessible to LVTs, Ridge would divert later assault echelons on a "follow me" basis.

Thus vital questions were to remain unanswered until the officers and men of the 1st Marines got their first look at BLUE Beach. It was keenly disappointing, therefore, when they stared from the line of departure on the afternoon of 15 September and saw, instead of the distant shoreline, a murky wall rolling seaward from the blazing waterfront.

As noted previously, the line of departure was 5,500 yards—3.2 miles—from the beach, a distance requiring 45-minute trips for the slow-moving LVT waves. The ship-to-shore movement got off to a bad start owing to the current, which scattered some of the landing formations during the rendezvous phase. Other obstacles entered the picture in rapid succession, one of them best described by Lieutenant Clark, BLUE Beach Control Officer:

"At about H–50, while press boats and the initial waves of LVT(A) and LVT were milling around the BLUE Beach control vessel [*Wantuck*], mortar fire was received in the immediate vicinity. This created some confusion until a destroyer spun around on her anchor and silenced the battery. This was the beginning of the end of the well-planned ship-to-shore movement for BLUE Beach." [30]

Other shortcomings that took on special significance because of the overcast were the lack of compasses and radios in the amphibian tractors and the inexperience of many of the crews. The first wave, consisting of the Army LVT(A)s, was escorted shoreward from the line of departure by Navy guide boats, manned by UDT crews who possessed both the compasses and seamanship necessary to pierce the smoke screen and find the distant beach on time.[31] Wave number two, only a minute behind and close enough to benefit by the expert guidance, did not fare too badly. The ragged formation of number three, however, indicated mounting difficulties at the line of departure.

[30] Clark ltr, 11 Mar 55.
[31] Unless otherwise cited, the remainder of this section is derived from: ComPhibGru–1 *Opno 14–50*, Item, V–VI; 1st MarDiv *SAR*, Annex Peter Peter; 2/1 *SAR* and *OpPlan 1–50*; Sutter—Codispoti interv, 25 Jan 55; and Capt B. F. Cunliffe interv, 24 Aug 54.

From a study of numerous accounts, the experience of Major Simmons appears to have been typical:

> "Wave 5 cleared the 802 about 1630. We had been told that a wave guide would pick us up and lead us to the line of departure. . . . Time was passing and we were feeling desperate when we came alongside what was apparently the central control vessel. I asked the bridge for instructions. A naval officer with a bull horn pointed out the direction of BLUE Two, but nothing could be seen in that direction except mustard-colored haze and black smoke. We were on our way, and our path crossed that of another wave. I asked if they were headed for BLUE Two. Their wave commander answered, 'Hell no, we're the 2d Battalion headed for BLUE One.' We then veered off to the right. I broke out my map, but the LVT driver had no compass. . . . With no confidence in its accuracy within a steel hull, I got out my lensatic compass and made a best guess as to the azimuth of our approach line." [32]

The nine LVT(A)s leading off for Lieutenant Colonel Alan Sutter's 2d Battalion thrashed through the gloom and crawled ashore on BLUE One at 1730, on schedule. Meeting no opposition at the beach, they rumbled northward to the road skirting the knoll in order to penetrate the interior. The exit was blocked by an earth slide resulting from the naval bombardment of the high ground, and the column of amphibious vehicles ground to a halt.

At H-plus 1, most of the eleven LVTs of the second wave crunched ashore with elements of two assault companies. The remainder, with troops of Fox Company embarked, had grounded in mud about 300 yards offshore. The Marines had to wade to the beach, and they lost several pieces of communications gear in potholes en route. Company D, on the left, was to have remained aboard the tractors for the drive inland, while the troops of Company F debarked at the beach, cleared the knoll, and continued overland on foot. The latter scheme of maneuver unfolded as planned, and the Marines encountered no resistance when they swept to the top of the high ground. Dog Company, meanwhile, had also dismounted because of the blocked road.

The third wave groped ashore through the smoke at H-plus 4, bringing the remainder of both assault companies and raising the total strength on BLUE One to 30 tractors and over 600 men. Noting that the beach was getting crowded, Lieutenant Colonel Sutter ordered his free tractor to pull alongside the revetment of the evaporator on the left. When his battalion headquarters had debarked on the wall, he turned his attention seaward that he might signal the succeeding

---

[32] Simmons ltr, 28 Mar 55.

three waves, carrying the rest of 2/1, to do likewise. He looked and waited in vain, however, for the LVT formations did not materialize out of the offshore haze.

Meanwhile, Companies D and F reorganized quickly to continue the attack. Looking inland from the knoll, officers and NCOs could catch glimpses of the unfamiliar terrain only between billows of smoke. Several landmarks loomed ahead that were not marked on the inaccurate tactical maps. Many others that had been recorded were ablaze, and the numerous fires would make direct compass marches difficult. Moreover, since the enemy situation inland was open to conjecture, dispersed tactical formations would add to the problem of controlling the Marine advance.

Despite these disadvantages, Sutter pressed the attack. Easy Company in battalion reserve, together with part of Weapons and H&S, had not landed, nor had all of the vital signal equipment for supporting arms. But further waiting and delay was out of the question, since only about an hour of daylight remained.

Company D struck out for Regimental Objective ABLE, the junction on the left flank 1,000 yards away, and Company F drove northeast in the direction of Objective DOG, Hill 117. It was almost dark when the last of the 600 troops plunged forward into the unknown, leaving LVT crews behind to open the road with picks and shovels.

Ending the Ship-to-Shore Movement

The nine LVT(A)s comprising 3/1's first wave had closed on the sea wall of BLUE Beach Two shortly after H-hour.[33] Nosing their vehicles toward the drainage ditch on the left, the drivers apparently eyed the muck and conformation of the restricted passageway with some skepticism, for they backed off and exchanged fire with scattered enemy soldiers shooting from just beyond the waterfront.

Wave number two passed through the Army tractors and bumped the sea wall ten minutes late with the leading elements of Companies G and I, the former on the left. Since the landing echelons had

---

[33] Unless otherwise cited, this section is derived from: ComPhibGru-1 *OpnO 14-50*, Item, V-VI; 1st MarDiv *SAR*, Annexes Peter Peter and Tare Tare; LtCol R. R. Myers interv, 1 Feb 55; LtCol J. D. Trompeter interv, 31 Jan 55; Maj D. W. Bridges interv, 18 Oct 54; Maj W. L. Bates interv with MarCorps HistDiv, 27 Aug 51; Capt J. G. Costigan interv, 17 Nov 54; Capts R. W. Crowley and N. L. Adams II interv, 9 Feb 55.

intermingled in the cloudy boat lane, some LVTs of the third wave arrived with those of the second. This accounted for Lieutenant Colonel Ridge's tractor reaching the beach one increment ahead of schedule. The battalion commander and his executive officer, Major Reginald R. Myers, immediately swung their separate vehicles around to the right flank, Ridge heading toward the ramp while the other officer continued around the corner in the direction of BLUE Three.

On the left of BLUE Two, meanwhile, the amphibians carrying Captain George C. Westover's Company G formed a column and crawled into the drainage ditch.[34] Troops of First Lieutenant Joseph R. Fisher's Item Company simultaneously scrambled up their aluminum ladders and deployed just beyond the sea wall in the face of moderate small arms fire. As had been anticipated, some of the metal scaling devices bent and buckled under the strain, delaying troop debarkation from the landing craft crowding the revetment. Assault elements of Captain Lester G. Harmon's Company C, 1st Engineer Battalion, reached the beach and anchored cargo nets over the wall to speed up the landing.[35]

The lead tractor in George Company's column bellied down in the mud of the drainage ditch, blocking five other LVTs behind. Westover ordered his troops to dismount and move forward along a road near the beach. After a brief period of reorganization, Company G fanned out for the drive inland, its mission being to block a lowland corridor and secondary access road leading to BLUE Beach out of the east.[36]

Just about the time Westover's LVTs bogged down in the ditch on the left, the tractors transporting Ridge and Myers crawled ashore over the ramp and BLUE Beach Three respectively, setting a precept for the mounting number of landing craft lying off BLUE Two. A heavy volume of traffic was thus diverted to the cove, and the appreciable gain in time far outweighed the intermingling which developed by landing troops at a right angle to those scaling the sea wall.

---

[34] Maj G. C. Westover memo to CMC, 21 Apr 55.
[35] Rickert memo, 15 Apr 55. "Study of aerial photos of BLUE Beach prior to departing Kobe, Japan, convinced CO, 1st Marines, that aluminum scaling ladders might not suffice for the sea wall. Consequently, the assault companies were provided with debarkation nets, 3' steel picket pins, and sledges with which to anchor the nets on the reverse slope of the sea wall. The nets proved very valuable, not only with regard to getting personnel ashore but particularly in landing crew-served weapons, ammo, and equipment."
[36] Westover memo, 21 Apr 55.

119

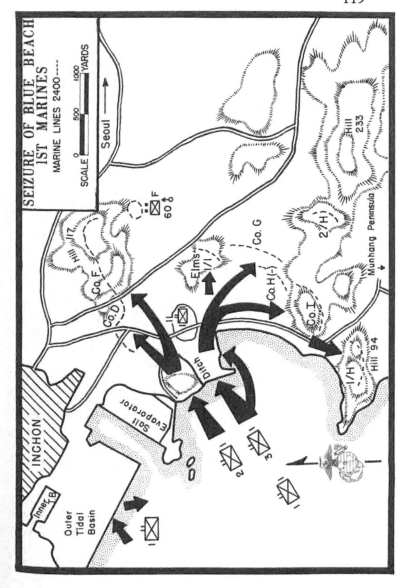

SEIZURE OF BLUE BEACH
1ST MARINES
MARINE LINES 2400----

SCALE
0   500   1000
YARDS

Seoul →

In recalling the situation ashore as of 1800 (H–plus30), Colonel Lewis B. Puller, the regimental commander, later observed:

> "I personally landed on BLUE Beach with the 3d wave. My reason for doing so was, exactly, that there was a strong possibility of confusion and disorganization under the circumstances: namely, the unavoidable necessity of landing the regiment without a rehearsal, without even a CPX . . . The reorganization of the assault battalions was accomplished with remarkable speed and effectiveness. I recall being, at the time, extremely gratified that my prior concern in this connection was not warranted." [37]

Despite the initial delays at the ditch and sea wall, Companies G and I cleared the beach rapidly. Of the few casualties taken during the first 30 minutes ashore, most were caused by an enemy machine gun in a tower about 500 yards inland. LVT fire silenced the weapon, and the Marine infantry plunged forward through a labyrinth of blazing buildings and smoke-filled streets. On the left, George Company groped almost straight ahead toward the lowland corridor as Item veered sharply southward to attack Objective CHARLIE, the seaward tip of Hill 233.

While the assault units fought inland, the gathering darkness created one more formidable handicap for the last wave serials leaving the line of departure far out in the channel. The four Navy guide boats, mentioned earlier as having escorted the first wave, were exactly 28 short of the number prescribed by amphibious doctrine for a landing of the Inchon assault's magnitude.[38] For this reason the guide boats took station on either side of the boat lanes after the initial run, since it was manifestly impossible for them to help out in any other way. The limited visibility, however, just about negated their worth as stationary markers, owing to the fact that some landing craft formations were losing their direction even before they entered the boat lanes.

In describing the situation as it developed at the line of departure Lieutenant Clark later commented:

> "The BLUE Beach Control Officer was unable to contact LVT wave commanders or wave guide officers by radio at any time during the initial assault. The control officer was aware that waves or groups of LVTs and boats were landing at the wrong places but was helpless to prevent it without communications. As a last resort, Casualty and Salvage landing craft were dis-

---

[37] MajGen L. B. Puller ltr to authors, 11 May 55.
[38] 1st MarDiv *SAR*, Annex Tare Tare, 4.

patched to assist the initial wave guides (members of UDT 1) in rounding up vehicles and leading or directing them to BLUE Beach." [39]

Since current and smoke fought relentlessly against tractors seaward of the line of departure, not all of the vehicles could find the control ship. If they did, it was next to impossible to come in close enough to get instructions shouted from the bridge. Thus many wave commanders, amtrac officers, and infantry leaders gave orders to head shoreward on their own initiative. They went in with waves and fragments of waves, displaying the kind of leadership that made the operation an overwhelming success in spite of the obstacles. This was the case with the three waves of 2/1 that failed to arrive at BLUE One. They found their way ashore, some of the LVTs landing on BLUE Two, others diverted to BLUE Three; but the important thing was that they got there. [40]

The most serious error of the day, again offset by initiative and decision, involved Lieutenant Colonel Jack Hawkins' 1st Battalion, landing in regimental reserve. [41] About H-hour, Puller radioed Hawkins and ordered him to cross the line of departure with LCVP waves 21 through 25, carrying the whole of 1/1. Had the approach to the beach gone smoothly, the battalion would have begun landing at approximately H-plus 45 (1815).

Because of conditions in the channel and boat lanes, as already described, a searchlight on the control ship now beamed the supposed course to the beach. Actually, the whole area had become so clouded that the light was mistakenly pointed toward the outer tidal basin, some 45 degrees off course to the northeast.

Moving in the designated direction, the first two of the reserve waves reached the sea wall of the basin; and the Marines, believing they were at the revetment of BLUE Two, began debarking. Hawkins, following in the third wave (wave number 23), caught the error as his boat passed within sight of two outlying islands between the basin and the salt evaporator jutting out from the left of BLUE One. About the same time, Lieutenant Colonel Robert W. Rickert, executive officer of the 1st Marines, noticed some of the errant landing

---

[39] Clark ltr, 11 Mar 55.

[40] Capt J. L. Carter ltr to CMC, 12 Apr 55.

[41] The following account of 1/1 is derived from: Rickert memo, 15 Apr 55; LtCol J. Hawkins ltr, 8 Mar 55; Bates interv, 27 Aug. 51; Bridges interv. 18 Oct. 54, and memo to CMC, 31 Mar 55; Maj R. H. Barrow memo to CMC, 25 Apr 55; and Maj R. P. Wray ltr to CMC. 23 Apr 55.

craft from his free boat between the line of departure and BLUE One. He intercepted a group of the LCVPs and reoriented them.

In the meantime, Hawkins cruised the length of the basin wall and shouted instructions to the troops of the first two waves. Most of Company B had already debarked and a few of the empty boats had left for the channel. Able Company, having just begun to land, promptly reembarked in its LCVPs. In short order, the battalion reformed at sea and headed toward BLUE Two. Owing to the lack of boats, one platoon of Baker Company remained on the tidal basin all night. Hiking to rejoin the company on the mainland next morning, this platoon rounded up an impressive bag of prisoners.

Upon reaching BLUE Two in darkness, Hawkins found Company C, which had avoided the detour owing to the sixth sense of a boat coxswain, organizing and setting up local security. The battalion commander led most of 1/1 forward to a night assembly area along the railroad tracks, half a mile inland. Major David W. Bridges, battalion S–3, was left behind to organize late-comers as they arrived from the tidal basin.

Seizure of the O–1 Line

The tactical situation ashore had meanwhile begun to crystallize for the 1st Marines. In the 2d Battalion zone, Dog Company occupied Objective A, the road intersection, at 2000. Two hours later, Fox Company reported that it occupied enough of Objective D, Hill 117, so that it could cover the Inchon-Seoul highway with fire.

The attack from the beach had cost Sutter's unit one KIA and 19 WIA as compared to enemy losses of 15 prisoners and an estimated 50 dead.

On the right of the regimental zone, Ridge's 3d Battalion was also making good progress against light resistance. Item Company reported at 1900 that it was on Objective C, the western nose of Hill 233. Half an hour later, George company began deploying in blocking positions across the corridor and road at the center of the O–1 Line. This movement was completed about 2030.[42]

The 1st Platoon of How Company passed seaward of Item at 2030 and pressed a night attack against a company of North Koreans on

---

[42] Ridge ltr, 11 May 55.

Objective B, the small cape topped by Hill 94. After a token resistance, the Reds abandoned their well-prepared entrenchments, leaving 30 dead and wounded to be counted by the Marines.

How Company (less 1st and 2d Platoons) covered the low ground between George and Item, finally occupying a blocking position about 400 yards behind the O–1 Line.

With the seizure of Hill 94, the critical portions of the O–1 Line were secured. There was, however, a good deal of activity within the perimeter for several more hours. Major Bridges of 1/1 collected about 100 late-comers at BLUE Three and led them forward in search of the battalion assembly area. Composed of men from H&S, Able and Baker Companies, the little force not only missed its destination but made one of the deepest penetrations of the day, finally halting on a hill to the left of George Company's front lines.

Shortly after Bridges set up a defensive position for the night, his position was invaded by an Easy Company contingent in search of the 2d Battalion. Reoriented to some degree, the visitors reached Dog Company's intersection much later. The 2d Battalion CP had meanwhile intercepted a group from Major Whitman S. Bartley's Weapons Company at the trail junction selected in the darkness for the initial battalion CP. At one or the other of these points, the misdirected portions of Sutter's battalion were directed to their parent units. All personnel were present or accounted for before dawn.[43]

Two other troop movements completed the tactical mosaic of the 1st Marines. The 2d Platoon of How Company was to pass through Item's lines on Objective C at 2330 and outpost the summit of Hill 233, some 2,000 yards farther along the ridge and beyond the regimental front. After setting out on schedule, the small unit covered about half of its rugged journey upon reaching Hill 180, an intermediate height. With most of the night gone and his troops wearied by the climb, the platoon leader radioed for permission to halt and his request was granted.

Another venture into the unknown was made by an even smaller unit. Second Lieutenant Bruce F. Cunliffe's 60mm section of Fox Company had somehow mingled with 3d Battalion troops during the drive inland. .When he led his men through the darkness in

---

[43] Sutter memo, May 55.

124

4 *The Inchon–Seoul Operation*

search of 2/1, the section ranged forward of friendly lines and into unexplored territory near Hill 117.

The surprise was mutual when these Marines stumbled into a small NKPA patrol. But a brief fire fight in the darkness was enough for the Red soldiers, who took to their heels and left three dead. Cunliffe's force, which had no casualties, spent the rest of the night in uneventful isolation.

CHAPTER VII

Securing the Beachhead

Supplies on RED and BLUE Beaches—Surgical Teams on the Beaches—Artillery and Tank Operations—The Attack on D-plus 1—Advance to the Force Beachhead Line—Displacement Ashore of Division CP

O F ALL THE calculated risks taken at Inchon, perhaps the most daring was the decision to ground eight LSTs abreast on RED Beach immediately after the assault troops landed. The Navy workhorses were vulnerable enough at best, and on this narrow strip of waterfront they were lined up so close to one another that shots fired by a blindfolded enemy could scarcely have missed.

Not all the NKPA shells and bullets did miss, for that matter. But fortune as usual blessed the bold, and such enemy rounds as found their targets did not touch off tons of napalm, gasoline, and ammunition.

Only with reluctance had the planners accepted the risk of landing thin-skinned supply vessels before the immediate battle area was secured. But Inchon was not a typical amphibious operation. The tremendous tidal range created an unprecedented situation; and if vital supplies were not landed on the evening high tide, the assault troops must pass a precarious first night without adequate quantities of ammunition, water, and gasoline.

Dusk had fallen, with visibility further reduced by smoke and rain squalls, when the vessels wallowed into RED Beach. The reconnaissance element of Shore Party Group Able had gone ahead with the assault troops to erect landing guides during the last moments of daylight. While the men were working under fire, one of the beach markers was riddled by enemy machine guns as it was being erected.

The H&S Company of Lieutenant Colonel Henry P. Crowe's 1st Shore Party Battalion came in with the first of the LSTs, and other elements of Groups Able and Baker followed in short order. Each of the eight vessels brought a cargo consisting of 50 tons of ammunition, 30 tons of rations, 15 tons of water, and five tons of fuel. These special loads were in addition to the normal cargo of engineer and shore party equipment and combat vehicles. Every LST was limited to 500 short tons, however, in order to insure that it could be beached without trouble.[1]

The last of the LCMs had not yet unloaded and retracted on RED Beach when the first of the LSTs appeared slightly ahead of schedule. Naval officers managed to hold the LSTs back until the beach had cleared, and the eight vessels made a successful landing in spite of treacherous currents combined with low visibility. Two of them grounded momentarily on the mud flats but butted their way through to the beach. And though the sea wall temporarily prevented several vessels from lowering bow ramps effectively, the LSTs at each end of the line were able to discharge cargo over their ramps.[2]

Bulldozers were first on the beach. They moved along the sea wall under enemy fire, pushing down sections of masonry which interfered with unloading operations.

LST 973 had no more than grated ashore when a Red Korean mortar shell exploded among the drums of motor fuel. Gasoline flooded the main deck and leaked down to the crew quarters through holes made by shell fragments. Orders were given to cut off electric motors and enforce all possible precautions, and the vessel miraculously escaped a conflagration even though it took further hits from enemy machine-gun fire.[3]

LST 857 ran into a ROK PC boat while heading in toward the beach, but no harm was done to either vessel. Hits from NKPA mortar and machine-gun fire punctured eight drums of gasoline without any of them bursting into flame. This was one of the LSTs which fired back at enemy gun flashes. During the exchange a sailor was killed and another knocked unconscious when an enemy projectile damaged one of the LST's gun mounts.

---

[1] 1st MarDiv *SAR*, Annex Dog.
[2] LCdr R. Schneelock, Jr., USN, memo to authors, 20 Apr 55.
[3] Karig, *Korea*, 236–241.

LST 859, which had a sailor wounded by enemy mortar fragments, hit RED Beach with all guns blazing away. When the vessel beached, it was immediately boarded by Marines who helped themselves to ammunition while shouting to sailors in the well deck to stop firing. The same message was slammed home more authoritatively when First Lieutenant William J. Peter, Jr., appeared on deck, as directed by Lieutenant Colonel Newton, and demanded that the LST's guns cease at once.[4]

This put an end to the bombardment of shore positions. "No LSTs fired after my ship beached," commented Lieutenant Trumond E. Houston, USN, commander of LST 799 at the extreme left of the line. "Earlier LSTs beaching had opened fire on targets unknown to me, but my command had received very firm orders not to open fire due to the danger of firing into our own forces."[5]

As dusk shaded into darkness, the Marines on and around Cemetery Hill extended their lines into the city. Even at the climax of the military drama there was an unexpected note of comedy—assault troops were to discover shortly that among the ammunition brought by the LSTs, some useless .22 caliber cartridges testified to the haste of departure from Camp Pendleton.[6] There was enough M–1 ammunition, however, so that the enemy had no cause to complain of being neglected by the Marines.

Supplies on RED and BLUE Beaches

It was absolutely essential that the LSTs unload in time to retract on the morning high tide and allow other cargo vessels to take their places. This meant an all-night job for the 1st Shore Party Battalion, which was to initiate unloading on both beaches for the organization composed also of the 1st Combat Service Group, the 7th Motor Transport Battalion, and the U. S. Army 2d Engineer Special Brigade, with the latter in control.

The vehicles came off the LSTs first—about 450 of them, all told—and darkness had fallen when the unloading of cargo got into full

---

[4] MSgt B. W. Gifford interv, 17 Nov 54; Col G. R. Newton memo to authors, 16 Apr 55; LCdr D. Weidemeyer memo to authors, 12 Apr 55.
[5] LCdr T. E. Houston ltr to authors, 8 Mar 55.
[6] SSgt H. M. Grenell interv, 15 Nov 54.

swing. Congestion on the 650-foot strip of beach did not permit normal location and employment of dumps. It was catch-as-catch-can for the shore party troops and engineers, with the cargo being off-loaded and stockpiled wherever space could be found. Later, as the tactical situation improved, designated dumps were established.

The men went about their work under the floodlights, heedless of scattered enemy small-arms fire which continued throughout the night. At a glance the unloading presented a scene of noisy chaos, yet everything was so well under control by midnight that the accomplishment of the mission within prescribed time limits was assured.

In the morning the eight LSTs were retracted according to schedule as a like number approached the beach to discharge cargo. Two of them grounded in the mud flats too far out for unloading, but the supply problem was already so well solved that this setback was not serious.

On BLUE Beach it was not the intention to develop the area beyond the needs of the initial assault, so that a comparatively small shore party element was required. Only such equipment as could be carried by hand was taken ashore in the LCVPs and LVTs.

The reconnaissance element of Shore Party Group B (–) had landed with the assault troops, followed by the rest of the group at 1930. Provisions for the use of pre-loaded LVTs having been made in the assault phase supply plan, the shore party troops set out flanking lights to mark the entire BLUE area as a single beach. This was in preparation for the arrival of the 24 LVTs bringing pre-loaded supplies to sustain the attack in the morning. Ten of these vehicles were so delayed by adverse currents that a receding tide left them high and dry. Officers of the 1st Marines decided that the supplies were not critical enough to warrant unloading by hand over the mud flats, and the job was postponed until the LVTs could be floated in on the morning high tide. While they were discharging on BLUE–3, the LCVPs came in with other gear which was unloaded and stored in the regimental dump.

Prison stockades were set up on both beaches the first night. The LSTs continued to unload most of the Division supplies on RED Beach in spite of treacherous currents, the tidal range and the mistakes made by Japanese crews. BLUE Beach was closed on D-plus 1, having served its purpose, and the shore party personnel transferred to GREEN Beach, where facilities for unloading LSTs had been improved. Supplies landed there could be trucked across the causeway, and on D-plus 2 the shore party troops on RED Beach were also relieved and sent to Wolmi-do.

The 2d Engineer Special Brigade retained control of all logistical operations in the Inchon port area on 17 September as vessels began to discharge at Pier No. 2, designated as YELLOW Beach. There were assurances by this time that the engineers would soon have the tidal basin partially operative, thus adding materially to the capacity of the harbor.[7]

The 1st Combat Service Group remained in control of consolidated dumps. This organization was the storage agency for all X Corps supplies with the exception of ammunition and engineering materials, both of which were handled by Army personnel. Owing to the shortage of trucks, the 7th Motor Transport Battalion was held in the port area under control of the engineer brigade.

The lack of enough motor trucks for port operations was alleviated by the restoration of rail transportation much sooner than had been expected. Although the planners did not count on this factor before D-plus 30, the 2d Engineer Special Brigade rounded up Korean crews and speeded up the tremendous task of putting the Inchon-Seoul line back in working order. As early as D-plus 1 a switch engine and six cars were operating in the Inchon yards. Three days later the first train, carrying 1,200 Marines, was dispatched over the 5-mile run from Inchon to Ascom City. As the ground forces advanced, the engineers followed close behind the front with rail transportation which handled a total of 350,000 rations, 315,000 gallons of fuel, 1,260 tons of ammunition, and 10,000 troops before the Division was relieved.

Surgical Teams on the Beaches

Casualties of the Landing Force on D-day amounted to 20 KIA, 1 DOW, 1 MIA, and 174 WIA in addition to 14 of non-battle classification. Medical officers regarded the operation as a landmark because of the four Navy surgical teams, each composed of three doctors and ten corpsmen, which went in behind the assault troops on the LSTs. Similar teams had been employed in the later oper-

---

[7] 1st MarDiv *SAR*, Annex Mike Mike; Costigan interv, 17 Nov 54; K. W. Condit, "Marine Supply in Korea" in *Marine Corps Gazette*, 37, no. 1:48–55 (Jan 53).

ations of World War II, but Inchon had the distinction of being the first amphibious assault in which carefully planned medical techniques were integrated with military operations.

The surgical teams had been drilled and rehearsed in Japan for their tasks. Patients requiring immediate surgery on the night of D-day were evacuated to LST(H) 898, where an improvised operating room had been installed. During the assault phase, 42 military and 32 civilian casualties were treated instead of the 300 which had been expected. Such an unqualified success was achieved that the teams were recalled to Japan afterwards to act as instructors. Within a year the numbers of Navy surgical teams had grown to a total of 22 on standby duty in the Far East.[8]

Captain Eugene R. Hering, (MC) USN, had served in the Pusan Perimeter as the Brigade Surgeon. From a study of maps and intelligence reports, he tentatively selected a site for the Division hospital on the eastern outskirts of Inchon.

The 1st Medical Battalion, commanded by Commander Howard B. Johnson, (MC) USN, consisted of an H&S Company and five letter companies. Able and Baker were hospital companies, while Charlie, Dog, and Easy functioned as collecting and clearing companies. The last was organized for attachment to the 7th Marines when that regiment landed at Inchon.

Medical planning necessarily had to be hurried. In view of the unusual landing conditions at Inchon, it was decided to revert the clearing platoons, normally attached to infantry regiments, to Division control when they reached the transport area.

Three casualty teams, each consisting of a medical officer and six hospital corpsmen—one team from Able Company, and two from Baker—landed from separate LSTs on D-day with a mission of caring for initial casualties. Supporting collection sections of Charlie and Dog Companies landed with the assault troops of the two rifle regiments.

The reconnaissance group and the two hospital companies arrived on D-plus 1, followed by the H&S Company with equipment for the hospital set up in a schoolhouse. It was opened at 1500 on D-plus 2, with 47 casualties being received the first day.

---

[8] Capt E. R. Hering, (MC) USN, memo to authors, 4 Apr 55; 1st MarDiv *SAR*, Annex How How; Lynn Montross, "They Make Men Whole Again," in *Marine Corps Gazette*, 36, no. 12:42–49 (Dec 52).

These were the forerunners of a total of 5,516 patients to be treated by the 1st Medical Battalion for all causes during the entire Inchon-Seoul operation. Most of them were WIA cases, but such ailments as acute appendicitis, hernia, piles, and sprains are also recorded.

Of the 2,484 surgical patients, only nine died after reaching the first aid station, and among them were six deaths following major surgery. The proportion of patients surviving after evacuation, therefore, reached the figure of 99.43 per cent. This meant that the chances were about 199 to 1 that a wounded Marine would live.

Artillery and Tank Operations

The planners, anticipating the need of artillery support for the assault on the mainland, had hoped that DUKWs could land two battalions of Colonel James H. Brower's 11th Marines on GREEN Beach for this mission. There was some reason to believe that these vehicles could cross the mud flats at low tide, thus enabling the 105s to get in position on Wolmi-do and registered before the Inchon landing. In the end, however, it was decided that this plan was not feasible, and the 1st and 2d Battalions of the artillery regiment landed on the evening tide while the rifle regiments were hitting the beaches at Inchon. A delay of an hour and a half occurred as a result of the confused maneuvering of ships in the inner harbor. It was not until 2150, therefore, that the 1st and 2d Battalions were prepared to deliver massed fires in support of the 5th and 1st Marines respectively.[9] Fortunately, the lack of this support at H-hour had not been a grave handicap in view of the light resistance encountered on the beaches.

Low visibility and lack of targets limited the fires to a few rounds the first night. Next day the artillery landing was completed when 4/11 went ashore on RED Beach, followed on D-plus 2 by the 96th Field Artillery Battalion, USA. Plans for the drive inland called for 1/11 and 2/11 to fire in direct support of RCT-5 and RCT-1 respectively. Support was to be provided by 4/11 for RCT-5 and by the Army battalion for RCT-1.[10]

The problems of tank support for the Inchon operation had given the planners many a headache. BLUE Beach was dismissed from

---

[9] The 3d Battalion, 11th Marines, was attached to RCT-7 and had not yet landed at Inchon.
[10] 1st MarDiv *SAR*, Annex Sugar Sugar.

consideration because of the mud flats, and the possibilities at RED Beach were not encouraging. GREEN Beach offered the best prospects for landing tanks, though it was recognized that they would be stranded if the enemy destroyed the causeway connecting Wolmi-do with the mainland.

The consequences of the hasty embarkation from Camp Pendleton had borne down heavily upon the 1st Tank Battalion, commanded by Lieutenant Colonel Harry T. Milne. Crews trained with the M–4A3 (Sherman) and 105mm howitzer were suddenly equipped with the M–26 (Pershing) and its 90mm gun. With the exception of Company A, which saw action with the Brigade, few of the men had had any experience either at driving or firing the new tanks. The flame tank platoon of Headquarters Company had received some training at Barstow, but most of the personnel of Baker, Charlie, and Dog Companies were limited to shipboard instruction.

The men of the Company A platoon which landed on GREEN Beach in support of 3/5 were veterans of several fights with NKPA tanks and infantry in the Pusan Perimeter. In the evening of D-day they supported the landing on RED Beach and moved across the causeway to the mainland at dusk. There they joined the other two platoons of Able Company and the flame tank platoon, which landed with the LSTs in support of the 5th Marines.

At 1700 on D-day a reconnaissance team went ashore on Wolmi-do to prepare for the landing of B Company, which took place late the following afternoon. YELLOW Beach, in the inner harbor, was operative for the landing of Company C on 18 September, and Company D was to arrive later with the 7th Marines.[11]

The Attack on D-plus 1

The night of 15–16 September passed quietly for both of the infantry regiments. At 2000 on D-day the 3d Battalion crossed over the causeway from Wolmi-do to rejoin RCT–5. The most dramatic action on either regimental front was an episode in the Cemetery Hill area. Two Marines mistakenly wandered out in front of the high ground and were cut down by enemy fire from a cave at the base of the hill, just below the lines of Company A, 5th Marines. Repeated attempts

---

[11] 1st MarDiv *SAR*, Annex Oboe Oboe.

to reach the fallen men were thwarted by submachine gun fire from the recess, until a ROK interpreter, threatening the use of tanks, persuaded the occupants to surrender. As a squad of North Koreans filed out in submission, troops from Able Company rushed forward to get their two comrades. One of the Marines was already dead; the other lay mortally wounded.[12]

In the middle of the night, the 1st and 5th Marines received General Smith's OpnO 3-50, directing them to attack after dawn. Murray's regiment, by previous plan, would march through the southern part of Inchon, leaving the heart of the seaport to be cleared by the KMC. About three miles inland, the 5th Marines would reach the O-2 Line coming abreast of Puller's front of the night before. (Thus, the O-1 and O-2 Lines were one and the same in the 1st Marines zone). Tied in along the Inchon-Seoul Highway at Hill 117, the two regiments would drive eastward to the O-3 Line, approximately five miles inland. This last arc was the goal specified in Smith's attack order.[13]

Murray's tactical plan was dictated by the simple necessity of getting out of Inchon as quickly as possible. The 5th Marines would therefore attack in a column of battalions, with Roise's 2d in the lead, followed by the 1st and 3d in that order. Two hills, located north of the highway on the outskirts of the city, were designated Regimental Objectives D and E. In taking this high ground, 2/5 would automatically control the 5th Marines' segment of the O-2 Line and seal off the Inchon Peninsula in conjunction with the 1st Marines. This would leave a secure pocket for the great ship-to-shore build-up commencing on the morning tide.

Following a brief orientation at dawn, Captain Jaskilka led Company E forward from the British Consulate. Unopposed, the column passed the inner tidal basin, where Fox Company fell in behind. In the meantime, Company D left its positions atop Observatory Hill and brought up the rear of the battalion formation. Inchon's streets were strangely quiet during 2/5's advance. Frightened civilians peeped from windows and alleyways, but the enemy was nowhere to be found. The sprawling seaport seemed dead.

Inconsistencies of the Oriental enemy were exposed in a striking contrast of scenes at 0700. Nearing the edge of the city, Easy Com-

[12] Muetzel interv. 6 Jan 55.
[13] 1st MarDiv *OpOrders* 2-50 and 3-50; O. P. Smith *Notes*, 346.

pany was preparing to veer off the road and attack Objective D. The troops were encountering no resistance whatsoever, and it was obvious that the North Koreans had abandoned Inchon in haste during the night. Only five miles away, however, six T–34 tanks were rumbling along the highway in broad daylight, headed toward the seaport without infantry escort.

An eight-plane strike of VMF–214 intercepted the enemy armor at the village of Kansong-ni. As the Corsairs swept down on the first pass, one of the tanks was enveloped in flaming napalm. Another was disabled when a rocket hit blew off its tracks. A third was left seemingly helpless on the road, squatting in a pool of motor fuel which poured out of its wounds.[14]

Marines of 2/1 watched the show with enthusiasm from the top of Hill 117, less than two miles away. The joy of victory went flat, however, when one of the planes failed to pull out of its dive. Captain William F. Simpson, the pilot, was killed as the F4U crashed beside the highway.[15]

A second flight of VMF–214 descended on Kansong-ni with a vengeance. Rocket fire destroyed one T–34, and a direct bomb hit knocked another off the road. It will be shown shortly that these two tanks must have been the same pair that were severely damaged by napalm and rockets during the first strike. When panicky NKPA crewmen fled to nearby thatched huts for concealment, the dwellings were promptly razed by napalm. Marine pilots, assuming incorrectly that all six tanks lay dead beneath the pall of smoke and flame, turned their attention to other targets in the area. They bombed an enemy jeep and weapons carrier standing in the open, then strafed two other motor vehicles which had been cleverly camouflaged.[16]

It would soon become more apparent why Red leaders in Seoul had sacrificed precious armor in a clearly hopeless thrust against the swelling beachhead. Communications were destroyed, so that NKPA defense forces fought or fled as isolated units. Adequate reserves were not at hand initially, with the result that stop-gap detachments were fed piecemeal into battle, only to be flattened by the Marine steamroller. In short, the North Koreans lost control. And when they attempted to regain it, time had run out.

---

[14] 1st MAW *SAR*, Annex Jig, VMF–214 rpt, 4.

[15] *Ibid.*; Cunliffe interv, 24 Aug 54.

[16] 1st MAW *SAR*, Annex Jig, VMF–214 rpt, 4.

While Marine air hammered the enemy's armored column, the 2d Battalion, 5th Marines, deployed outside Inchon. Having made sight contact with Lieutenant Colonel Sutter's troops on Hill 117 at 0730, Captain Jaskilka led Easy Company off the road and toward Objective D the left. Fox Company continued along the pavement several hundred more yards, then also veered northward in the direction of Objective E. Neither company met opposition, and both were atop their respective hills at 0930.[17]

Meanwhile, Company D had advanced eastward on the highway with a platoon of Able Company tanks. There was the occasional whine of a sniper's bullet overhead as the column moved rapidly to its junction with the 1st Marines. At 0900, while Easy and Fox Companies were climbing their objectives, Dog made contact with 2/1 at Hill 117.[18]

It was its opposite of the 1st Marines that Dog Company of 2/5 met at Hill 117. Fox Company of 2/1 had been clearing the eastern reaches of the big ridge since 0615, and Easy was to spend all morning and afternoon securing high ground and a village about a mile off on the right flank. When the attack along the highway resumed shortly after 0900, Company D of the 5th Marines and a platoon of A/Tanks took the lead. Fox and Dog Companies of 2/1 followed in trace and on the right as the formation advanced rapidly against nothing heavier than sniper fire. By 1100, elements of both battalions were deployed at Sogam-ni, just a few hundred yards short of smoking Kansong-ni. Since the former hamlet bordered the O–3 Line, the Marines held up to await further orders.[19]

To the south of the highway, the 1st Battalion, 1st Marines, reorganized in the center of Puller's zone and moved forward as regimental reserve. Simultaneously, the 3d Battalion began its sweep of the Munhang Peninsula, Companies G and I attacking generally southward from Hill 233. Since the broad front was studded with high ground and villages, Lieutenant Colonel Ridge relied on LVT transport whenever possible to regain momentum lost to hill-climbing and searching. Resistance on the peninsula proved negligible, although once again the capture of prisoners and materiel revealed

---

[17] 1st MarDiv *SAR*, Annex Queen.
[18] *Ibid.*
[19] *Ibid.*; 2/1 *SAR*, 4; Cunliffe interv, 24 Aug 54; LtGen E. A. Craig ltr to CMC, 21 Apr 55; and Capt J. L. Carter ltr to CMC, 19 Apr 55.

enemy potential unused. Among the weapons abandoned by the North Koreans were quantities of rifles and machine guns, a battery of Russian-made 120mm mortars, and four coastal guns, the latter pointing menacingly toward the ships of the Attack Force anchored in the channel.[20]

Although 1/1 and 3/1 did not reach their portion of the objective until later in the day, Division Headquarters realized by mid-morning that enemy resistance as far out as the O–3 Line could be discounted. Now that the tremendous obstacles of the actual landing had been overcome, the tactical advantage of the moment swung from the Red commander at Seoul to General Smith. Owing to the conformation of the Inchon and Munhang Peninsulas, which were linked together inland like Siamese twins, the O–3 Line formed a front three miles long with both flanks bounded by water. A glance at the map will show the beachhead thus set off as an ideal foothold. To North Koreans thinking in terms of counterattack, the vacuum rapidly being filled by the Landing Force was a defensible bottleneck. To the Marines, on the other hand, it was the gateway to freedom of maneuver for an overland offensive.

Advance to the Force Beachhead Line

Opening the gate was the subject of General Smith's OpnO 4–50, issued by dispatch at 1045, D-plus 1. He directed Puller and Murray to continue the attack from the O–3 Line, seized the Force Beachhead Line (FBHL), and thereby conclude the assault phase of the amphibious operation. The order also marked off a new Tactical Bomb Line,[21] behind which Marine Air was forbidden to strike without ground coordination.

Roughly the shape of a right angle, the FBHL corresponded to X Corps Phase Line BB. Like the O–3 arc, it was anchored on the sea at both ends. The east-west leg of the angle, five miles long, lay above and almost parallel to the Inchon-Seoul Highway. The north-south leg, about seven miles inland, added a third projection, the

---

[20] 3/1 *SAR;* Crowley-Adams interv, 9 Feb 55; Col T. L. Ridge ltr to CMC, 12 May 55; LtCol J. Hawkins ltr to CMC, 27 Apr 55; and LtCol E. H. Simmons ltr to CMC, 15 Apr 55.
[21] The first bomb line corresponded to the FBHL, and Corps Phase Line AA was the equivalent of the O–2 Line.

137

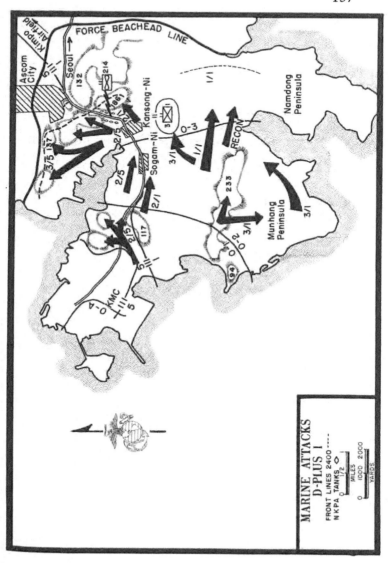

MARINE ATTACKS
D-PLUS I
FRONT LINES 2400----
NKPA TANKS
MILES
0   1/2
0   1000 2000
YARDS

Namdong Peninsula, to the beachhead. Encompassing the built-up centers of Ascom City and Mahang-ri on the main road, the apex of the FBHL pointed northeast toward Kimpo Airfield like an arrowhead.

The Inchon-Seoul Highway remained the boundary between the 1st and 5th Marines. Lieutenant Colonel Murray's order went out to the latter before noon, directing a two-pronged assault. The 2d Battalion would jump off from the O–3 Line and trace the course of the highway, clearing the hills and villages on the left. Simultaneously, the 3d was to swing sharply northward from behind 2/5 and attack high ground overlooking the east-west leg of the FBHL. The 1st Battalion would remain in regimental reserve.[22]

There were a number of reasons why Colonel Puller's scheme of maneuver was more complex. Not only was the 1st Marines' front much wider and the terrain more difficult, but the rapid advance had left troops units scattered throughout a zone of action some 15 square miles in area. There was considerable shuffling to be done before the regiment could deploy along the highway for the drive to the east.

The 2d Battalion would continue along the MSR, clearing the high ground on the right and coordinating with 2/5 on the left. To the south, the 1st Battalion would move up on the right of the 2d as quickly as the rugged terrain allowed. The 3d, after clearing the Munhang Peninsula, was to pass into regimental reserve subsequent to being relieved on the right flank by the Reconnaissance Company. Swinging around a sharp cove of salt pans and mud flats, the latter unit would patrol the Namdong Peninsula to secure the Division right.[23]

At 1335, the 5th Marines attacked against minor resistance on the north of the highway. Moving into Kansong-ni, the vanguard of 2/5 and its tank escort approached a sharp bend where the road veered northward for about a mile to avoid two large hills. Around the curve were the enemy tanks believed to have been knocked out by VMF–214 earlier in the day.

A section of Marine armor turned left off the pavement just short of the bend. The two M–26s crawled to the top of a knoll from which they could cover the infantry, as the latter advanced around the

---

[22] 1st MarDiv *SAR*, Annex Queen Queen.
[23] 1st MarDiv *SAR*, sec. 1; 2/1 *SAR*; 3/1 *SAR*; Ridge ltr, 12 May 55; and Hawkins ltr, 27 Apr 55.

corner. Looking down from their vantage point, the tank crews saw three intact T–34s parked in column on the highway, about 300 yards beyond the turn. Hatches on the Communist vehicles were buttoned, with the 85mm guns leveled at the road bend.[24]

The M–26s opened up immediately. Twenty rounds of 90mm armor-piercing (AP) ammunition crashed into the enemy armor. There was no return fire, probably because the Red crews had not time to elevate and traverse their manually-operated guns In the space of a few minutes, each of the T–34s exploded and burst into flame. The crews did not escape.[25]

The Marine attack rolled past the blazing hulks. Nearby were two other wrecked T–34s, obviously the victims of the air attack. If the pilots of VMF–214 had attacked a total of six enemy tanks, one of the vehicles must have escaped before the ground troops reached the scene.[26]

Tracing the north-south stretch of highway that led to Ascom City, Dog Company of RCT–5 marched a thousand yards beyond the bend and ascended a high hill on the west side of the road. Company F swung out to the left, crossed the railroad tracks running parallel to the highway, and seized the high ground adjacent to that held by Company D. Both assault units encountered only sniping, but it was early evening before the two hills and surrounding low ground had been searched thoroughly.[27]

Lieutenant Colonel Roise ordered 2/5 to dig in for the night. He was about 3,000 yards short of the highway's intersection with the FBHL, but his battalion held the commanding ground. Companies D and F defended the approach to Ascom City, which sprawled out on the low ground just forward of their positions. Company E, in reserve, set up a perimeter in the battalion rear.[28]

Lieutenant Sweet's five M–26s, which had supported the day-long advance from RED Beach, were relieved at dusk by the 1st Platoon of Able Company tanks. In addition to their score of three T–34s, Sweet's veterans of the Pusan Perimeter had captured an impressive

[24] 1st MarDiv *SAR*, Annex Oboe Oboe; 2dLt J. Sleger, Jr., to Dr A. D. Coox, ORO, Dept of Army, n. d. (Sleger rpt).
[25] *Ibid.*
[26] *Ibid.;* CG 1st MarDiv disp to CTF 90, 16 Sep 50.
[27] 1st MarDiv *SAR*, Annex Queen Queen; LtCol H. S. Roise interv, 24 Nov 54.
[28] Roise interv, 24 Nov 54.

tally of enemy materiel: three NKPA trucks, two 76mm AT guns, two 122mm mortars, and a pair of Russian-manufactured jeeps.[29]

. During 2/5's attack along the MSR, the 3d Battalion, 5th Marines was occupied with the hills overlooking that portion of the FBHL to the northwest. Lieutenant Colonel Taplett had launched his drive at 1330 with Companies G and I in the assault and H in reserve. On the left, George Company seized its high-ground objective at 1440, while Item took an extra hour to clear adjacent Hill 137. There were no Marine casualties during a rapid advance that netted 12 enemy prisoners.[30]

Patrols from 3/5 ranged westward to the sea, and eastward to the edge of Ascom City, where Item Company troops discovered an enemy ammunition dump and vehicle park. Location of these un-defended prizes was promptly reported to the 5th Marines CP.[31]

South of the Inchon-Seoul Highway, the 1st Marines attacked from the O–3 Line at 1600. Sutter's 2d Battalion drove forward on the right of the MSR and passed below Kansong-ni without incident. Continuing a thousand yards farther, Company D scaled the rugged slopes of Hill 186, cleared the summit, and dug in. Fox Company climbed the same high ground shortly afterwards and went into position on the left of Dog and overlooking the highway. Thus 2/1's front for the night was across the road and slightly to the rear of the high ground positions occupied by Company D of 2/5. Easy Company returned from its independent mission on the right flank and set up a reserve position in the vicinity of Kansong-ni, just rearward of Sutter's CP at the base of Hill 186.[32]

The enemy attitude in the 2d Battalion's zone gradually had de-veloped from occasional sniping early in the day to a pattern of definite light resistance as the Marines surged over Hill 186. Though most of the North Koreans fled after firing a few rounds, their token efforts cost the battalion four killed and 10 wounded. These figures are noteworthy in view of the fact that total losses for the whole Division on D-plus 1 were four KIA and 21 WIA.[33]

---

[29] 1st MarDiv *SAR*, Annex Oboe Oboe.
[30] 1st MarDiv *SAR*, Annex Queen Queen.
[21] *Ibid*.
[32] 1st MarDiv *SAR*, Annex Peter Peter; Sutter-Codispoti interv, 25 Jan 55; 2/1 *SAR*, 4; and Carter ltr, 19 Apr 55.
[33] *Ibid*.

Sutter's troops exacted a comparatively stiff price from the Reds in return, for it was estimated that 120 of the enemy were killed or wounded. Moreover, the Marines captured more than 30 prisoners, 70 rifles, 10 machine guns, and an ordnance dump loaded with small-arms ammunition.[34]

Elsewhere on the 1st Marines front there was considerably more hiking than combat. The 3d Battalion completed its sweep of the Munhang Peninsula about 1600 and assembled at the southern tip of the O-3 Line to await relief by the Reconnaissance Company.[35] In the course of rounding up NKPA prisoners and abandoned weapons, 3/1 had encountered a group of Korean villagers, headed by their schoolmaster, who called themselves the Young People's Anti-Communist Resistance League. They had armed themselves with Russian rifles and light machine guns left behind by enemy troops fleeing inland.[36]

In the center of Puller's zone, the 1st Battalion had moved rapidly to fill the gap between the 2d and 3d. Attacking into the vacuum left by the retreating enemy, Hawkins' unit drove two mountainous miles beyond the O-3 Line, finally stopping for the night on high ground about 2,500 yards south of 2/1's positions on Hill 186. The break in the regimental front was protected when 3/1 shifted northward and formed a reserve perimeter to the rear of the lines, after being relieved on the right at 1700 by Captain Kenneth J. Houghton's Reconnaissance Company. Assuming responsibility for the Division's southern flank, the Recon troops set up a night defense at the base of the Namdong Peninsula with their front linked to that of 1/1 on the left.[37]

Displacement Ashore of Division CP

The establishment of a Division CP on shore was delayed by the necessity of utilizing every minute of the limited periods of high tide for the movement of troops, supplies, and equipment. General Smith decided on D-day that it would not be advisable to displace

[34] 2/1 *SAR*, 4; and Carter ltr, 19 Apr 55.
[35] 3/1 *SAR*, 6; Ridge ltr, 12 May 55; Simmons ltr 15 Apr 55.
[36] *Ibid.*; Maj G. C. Westover ltr to authors, 1 Apr 55; and Capt J. R. Fisher ltr to authors, 18 Apr 55.
[37] Recon Co, HqBn, 1st MarDiv *Unit Rpts*, 9 Sep–11 Nov 50; and Ridge ltr, 12 May 55.

his CP ashore until General Craig and the ADC group (former head-quarters of 1st ProvMarBrig) were able to set up adequate communications. With this object in mind, the ADC group landed on the evening high tide of D-day to locate an advance echelon on Wolmi-do.

Not much could be done that evening. And in the morning Craig informed CG 1st MarDiv that the island was too crowded. He reported that he and Lieutenant Colonel Stewart had discovered a likely spot on the southeast outskirts of Inchon and recommended that the CP be moved without delay.[38] General Smith approved and the move started at once.

Meanwhile, a good deal of military housekeeping had been accomplished in the Inchon port area. Lieutenant Colonel John H. Partridge's 1st Engineer Battalion was given the task of making a survey of beach exit roads with a view to opening up an MSR between RED and BLUE Beaches.

After elements of Company A hit GREEN Beach, the remaining troops of the battalion had landed on the two beaches and assisted short party units at unloading water, ammunition, and rations. This work was so well along by the morning of D-plus 1 that the engineers opened up the MSR beteween the two beaches and assigned personnel for improvement and maintenance. A water point was established at the north end of RED Beach with 31 distillation units, and 125,000 gallons were issued during the next six days.[39]

The new Division CP on the outskirts of Inchon was ready by the afternoon of D-plus 1, and General Smith said goodbye to General MacArthur on the bridge of the *Mount McKinley*. The commander in chief wished him well and enjoined him to take Kimpo Airfield at the first opportunity.[40]

The Marine general landed at YELLOW Beach at 1730. Upon arrival at the CP, he sent a dispatch to Admiral Doyle, informing him that he was assuming responsibility for the conduct of operations ashore at 1800 on 16 September. Thus ended the amphibious assault phase, almost exactly 24 hours after the first wave of Marines set foot on RED Beach.

---

[38] BGen E. W. Snedeker ltr to authors, 5 Apr 55.

[39] 1st MarDiv *SAR*, Annex Nan Nan.

[40] O. P. Smith, *Notes*, 188–189.

CHAPTER VIII

On to Kimpo

Operations on Other Korean Fronts—Landing of RCT-7 in Japan—Destruction of NKPA Tank Column—General Mac-Arthur Visits the Front—The Drive to Kimpo Airfield—Action at 5th Marines CP—Enemy Counterattack at Kimpo

ON SUNDAY MORNING, D-plus 2, General Smith was directed as Landing Force Commander to re-establish civil government in Inchon. Although parts of the Korean seaport had been burned or battered into rubble, thousands of refugees were returning to the ruins of their homes after having fled during the bombardments. The KMC Regiment, operating under the control of RCT-5, had been given the task of screening the remaining inhabitants for their loyalty. No fault could have been found with the thoroughness of these Korean allies who were perhaps inclined to be too zealous when they suspected subversion.

General Smith concluded that the best procedure was to find loyal Korean officials and uphold their authority. He consulted Rear Admiral Sohn Won Yil, the ROK Chief of Naval Operations, and learned that the former mayor of Inchon had fled during the original NKPA invasion and never returned. Admiral Sohn vouched for the loyalty of one of the political prisoners, Pyo Yang Moon, who had been the losing candidate for the mayoralty in the last election. The Marine general decided to install him as Inchon's chief executive and issued a proclamation to that effect in Korean as well as English.

Induction ceremonies were held on the morning of 18 September on the portico of the city hall, a once imposing edifice which bore the scars of war. About 700 prominent citizens attended as the Marine interpreter led in singing the Korean national anthem. After the proclamation had been read in both languages, General Smith

143

made a few remarks and the new mayor responded.   A ROK Marine guard of honor officiated, and Admiral Sohn brought the occasion to a close with a brief address.

Steps were taken immediately to bury the civilian dead, to care for the orphans, to distribute food and clothing to the distressed, and to establish a civilian hospital and police force.[1]

Operations on Other Korean Fronts

Dispatches received from the Pusan Perimeter revealed that the Eighth Army had jumped off according to schedule on the 16th in its joint offensive.   Although gains were negligible the first day, this effort was pinning down NKPA troops who might otherwise have reinforced the defenders of Kimpo and Seoul.

Several other operations had been mounted on both coasts as diversions to keep the enemy guessing as to where the lightning would strike.   Kunsan, it may be recalled, had been briefly considered by X Corps planners as an alternate amphibious objective.   Early in September this west coast seaport was selected as the chief target of feints during the preparations for the Inchon landing.   General Stratemeyer's Fifth Air Force bombers initiated strikes on rail and highway communications within a 30-mile radius.   That same day a hit-and-run amphibious raid on Kunsan was planned at Admiral Joy's headquarters in Tokyo.   As a result, Colonel Ely sailed with his company on the British frigate *Whitesand Bay* and raided the Kunsan waterfront on the night of 12 September.   Three casualties were incurred from enemy machine-gun fire.

The Seventh Fleet added to the deception by singling out Kunsan for carrier air strikes and naval gunfire bombardments to give the impression of softening up an objective for amphibious assault. Chinnampo, the seaport of Pyongyang, also appeared to be threatened when it was bombarded by a British task force.

On the east coast the USS *Missouri,* just arrived from the United States, poured 16-inch shells into Samchok on 14 September while a Navy helicopter did the spotting.   The cruiser *Helena* and three U. S. destroyers added their metal to the bombardment.[2]

---

[1] O. P. Smith, *Notes,* 197–199.

[2] Material for this section has been derived from Karig, *Korea,* 112, 243–255.

D-day at Inchon was the date of a landing of ROK guerrillas behind the NKPA lines at Changsa-dong, a coastal town about midway between Yongdok and Pohang-dong. After the ROK merchant marine LST struck submerged rocks and grounded, it was used as an improvised fortress by the guerrillas, who retreated from the NKPA forces when their ammunition ran short. The only two Americans, an Army lieutenant and sergeant, radioed for help; and the cruiser *Helena* provided naval gunfire for the Navy relief expedition which took off the survivors.

How much these diversions on both Korean coasts may have contributed to a surprise at Inchon is a moot question. It might even be argued that the enemy was not surprised, since an intercepted NKPA radio message warned Pyongyang on 13 September that United Nations vessels were approaching Inchon and planes bombing Wolmi-do. The senders deduced that an amphibious landing was forthcoming and assured NKPA Headquarters that defensive units were being stationed where they would repulse the UN forces.[3]

This would make it appear doubtful that a surprise had been achieved. But it is the opinion of Admiral Struble that "the actual results in the Inchon-Seoul area clearly indicate surprise. . . . While the message was apparently sent, and was a good report, there is no evidence that the enemy headquarters accepted the report. It is possible that a later report that the enemy bombarding ships were retreating from Inchon may have confused the issue. In any event, only a short time was available to take advantage of strong defensive positions and certainly not enough time to mine the harbor."[4]

An excellent analysis of the outcome is to be found in Admiral Doyle's official report. After paying tribute to the pre-D-day bombardments by the cruisers and destroyers, plus the air strikes by planes of TF-77 and TG-90.5, he concluded that "the assault itself was successful only through the perfect teamwork that existed between the participating Naval and Marine elements. The successful accomplishment of the assault on Inchon demanded that an incredible number of individual and coordinated tasks be performed precisely as planned. Only the United States Marines, through their many years of special-

---

[3] Quoted in Karig, *Korea*, 202.
[4] VAdm A. D. Struble ltr to authors, 18 May 55.

ized training in amphibious warfare, in conjunction with the Navy, had the requisite know-how to formulate the plans within the limited time available and execute those plans flawlessly without additional training or rehearsal." [5]

Landing of RCT–7 in Japan

Dispatches were received on D-plus 2 at the new Division CP to the effect that the 7th Marines was preparing to embark that day from Kobe and land at Inchon on 21 September.

The 3d Battalion of this regiment, it may be recalled, had originally been a unit of the 6th Marines on FMFLant duty with the Sixth Fleet in the Mediterranean. Upon being ordered to the Far East, the unit sailed from Crete to Japan by way of the Suez Canal and Indian Ocean. Lieutenant Colonel Dowsett, the battalion commander, did not know throughout the voyage what specific mission awaited his men.

They later met at Kobe their new regimental commander, Colonel Litzenberg, who had flown to Japan ahead of the other two battalions sailing from San Diego. He informed Dowsett that his battalion was now a part of the 7th Marines and named him executive officer of the regiment. Major Maurice E. Roach succeeded to the command of the newly designated 3/7.

A formidable task awaited the 7th Marines in Japan. The officers of the staff, not having served with the Division before, were unfamiliar with references and terms in directives dealing with the Inchon landing. Problems of integrating the regiment into the operations of the division were solved only by intensive application.

A reshuffling of the regiment had to be accomplished meanwhile before embarking for Inchon. The purpose was to spread the hundreds of reservists throughout the three battalions instead of having them concentrated in several companies.[6]

It took some remarkable adjustments to get the regiment ready for embarkation from Kobe only 17 days after sailing from San Diego. But it meant that the 7th Marines would get into the fight at least a week sooner than Division planners had anticipated.

---

[5] PacFlt *Interim Rpt No. 1*, XV:Annex Able Able, 8.
[6] Dowsett interv, 2 Nov 54.

Destruction of NKPA Tank Column

The amphibious assault phase was left behind on D-plus 2 when the 1st and 5th Marines jumped off from the western outskirts of Ascom City to initiate their drive inland. With the exploitation phase coming next, command relationships would be as follows:

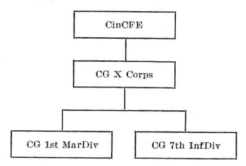

The night of 16–17 September had been quiet all along the Division front. It was so quiet, in fact, that the troops of 2/5 paid no particular heed to a truck which drove through their lines on the Inchon-Seoul Highway about midnight. Not until the vehicle penetrated a few hundred yards into Marine territory was it stopped by curious tank crews of Able/Tanks' 1st Platoon, whose M–26s were deployed across the road in deep anti-mechanized defense. The startled occupants of the stray truck turned out to be an NKPA officer and four enlisted men, but they were no more surprised than the Marines who stepped out of the darkness and took them prisoner.[1]

Apparently, neither the tank crews nor anybody else in the area attached any special importance to the strange truck incident. In a few hours, however, an epic of smoke, flame, and twisted steel would attest to the significance of this scrap of evidence. The fact of the matter was that the Red leaders in Seoul did not know the exact location of the 1st Marine Division.

It will be recalled that Dog Company of 2/5 occupied a hill on the west side of the highway as the attack on D-plus 1 ground to a halt. About 200 yards beyond the company front was a large knoll that nosed into the center of Ascom City. Observing that the highway

---

[1] 1st MarDiv *SAR*, Annex Oboe Oboe; and Capt J. E. Harrell interv, 4 Jan 55.

turned sharply to the east and passed through a cut at the base of the knoll, Lieutenant H. J. Smith decided to outpost the natural roadblock in strength. At dusk, therefore, he dispatched the 2d Platoon, under Second Lieutenant Lee R. Howard, to man the advance position along with machine-gun and rocket-launcher attachments.[8]

As the first rays of dawn creased the sky on 17 September, Howard and his troops were entrenched in a compact perimeter atop the knoll. Several hundred yards to the rear, the 1st Platoon of A/Tanks was augmented in its blocking position by 3.5-inch rocket launchers of 2/5 and the 75mm recoilless rifles of the 5th Marines. Just across the road from this formidable array were more 75s and 3.5s of the 1st Marines, emplaced with Fox Company of 2/1 on Hill 186.[9]

Records of the 5th Marines describe this bristling gauntlet as ". . . a temporary defensive position in depth . . ." It was more like a giant torpedo.

Sometime before daybreak, a North Korean column formed on the Inchon-Seoul Highway a few miles east of Ascom City.[10] In the van were six sleek T–34s of the 42d NKPA Mechanized Regiment. Perched atop the tanks and strung out for about a hundred yards were 200 Red infantrymen, comprising a mixed representation of the 18th NKPA Division in Seoul. The enemy force was on its way to block the advance of the 1st Marine Division along the highway.

It was obvious that the Communist soldiers had little or no knowledge of the situation ahead. For as they neared Ascom City at the crack of dawn, some were still sitting comfortably on the tanks and eating breakfast. Others laughed and jabbered as they trailed along the road.

Lieutenant Howard saw them approaching his Dog Company outpost on the knoll. He reported to Smith, who passed the word to Roise at 2/5's CP, first one tank, then three, and finally six. Roise took the information with the proverbial grain of salt, supposing it to be a delusion of youth and inexperience. Just as quickly as that impression formed in his mind, it was shattered by the first reverberations of the battle.

---

[8] 1st MarDiv *SAR*, Annex Queen Queen; McNaughton interv, 7 Jan 55; and Harrell interv, 4 Jan 55.

[9] 1st MarDiv *SAR*, Annexes Oboe Oboe, Peter Peter, and Queen Queen; and 2/1 *SAR*, 5.

[10] The following narrative, unless otherwise noted, is taken from: 1st MarDiv *SAR*, Annexes Baker, Oboe Oboe, Peter Peter, Queen Queen; 2/1 *SAR*; Harrell interv, 4 Jan 55; Roise interv, 21 Dec 54; and McNaughton interv, 7 Jan 55; and Statement of Capt W. D. Pomeroy enclosed in Maj G. M. English ltr to CMC, 19 Apr 55.

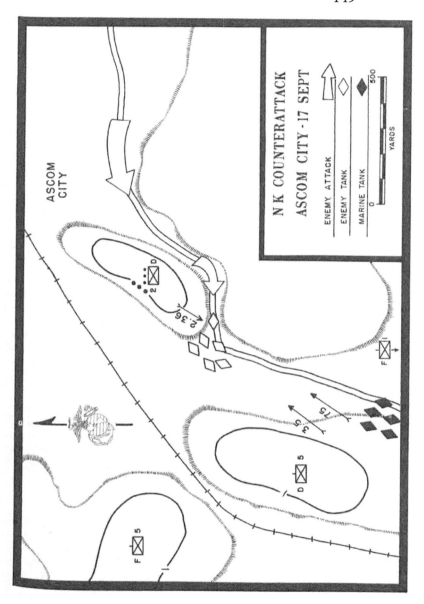

N K COUNTERATTACK
ASCOM CITY · 17 SEPT

ENEMY ATTACK

ENEMY TANK

MARINE TANK

0   500

YARDS

ASCOM
CITY

The attitude of the enemy soldiers as they neared his outpost convinced Howard that they were unaware of the proximity of Marine lines. He let the head of the column slip by on the road below, therefore, until the tanks began to round the bend leading to Dog Company's MLR. Then the platoon leader shouted the order, and his men opened up with machine guns, rifles, and BARs.[11]

The Red infantry went down under the hail of lead like wheat under the sickle. Soldiers on the tanks were knocked to the road, where many were ground under as the big vehicles lurched and roared crazily in reaction to the surprise.

Corporal Okey J. Douglas moved part way down the knoll and closed on the lead T–34 with his 2.36-inch rocket launcher. A few well-placed rounds, fired calmly at a range of 75 yards, killed the armored vehicle on the spot. Continuing the single-handed assault, Douglas damaged tank number 2 just as the main Marine position exploded into action.

Under attack by the outpost, the cripple and the four unharmed T–34s had continued around the road bend, some of them spilling off the curve in an attempt to deploy in the adjacent rice paddy. All five were taken under fire by First Lieutenant William D. Pomeroy's M–26s, about 600 yards away. Within five minutes, the Marine 90mm guns threw 45 rounds of AP at the enemy armor.

Recoilless rifles of Second Lieutenant Charles M. Jones' platoon (5th Marines AT Co) added their hot metal at a range of 500 yards, and the 75s with the 1st Marines across the road also erupted. Simultaneously, Second Lieutenant James E. Harrell ordered the 3.5-inch rocket launchers of 2/5's assault platoon into action.

The T–34's didn't have a chance. All of them exploded under the heavy fusilade; and when the smoke cleared, they were heaps of burning wreckage. Scattered around the dead tanks and along the road were the bodies of 200 Red infantrymen. So rapid and complete was the enemy's destruction that only one Marine casualty—slightly wounded—resulted from the fight.

It was only natural that conflicting claims would arise among the participants in the short, violent clash. To Pomeroy's tank crews, it appeared that the M–26s accounted for the five T–34s with little or no assistance from infantry arms. This was a reasonable conclusion on their part, owing to the limited visibility from the buttoned vehicles

---

[11] *Ibid.*

and the fact that their 90mm guns unquestionably wrought the greatest destruction on the NKPA machines. Since so many weapons were firing simultaneously from various other positions, however, and since the T–34s were wrecked so completely, kills and partial kills were also claimed by the recoilless rifles of both regiments. Moreover, the 3.5-inch rocket gunners of 2/5 and 2/1 believed that some of their rounds found the mark in the midst of the furor. It is known, for instance, that Private First Class Walter C. Monegan, Jr., rocket man in the assault squad of Fox Company, 1st Marines, closed on the enemy vehicles after they had rounded the bend and fired his weapon at point-blank ranges.

General MacArthur Visits the Front

The acrid odor of high explosives still lingered in the fresh morning air as a column of jeeps came slowly around the bend from the rear. General MacArthur was making his first visit to the front. With him and Admiral Struble were Generals Almond, Shepherd, Smith, Ruffner, Hodes, Wright, and a group of X Corps staff officers. Several jeeps filled with newspaper correspondents and photographers followed close behind the military cortege.[12]

Grimy Marines of RCT–5, their eyes dazzled by the glitter of starry insignia, gazed in wonder at this sudden revelation of the pomp and circumstance of war. The generals and admirals in their turn were equally impressed by the destruction these Marines had wrought—the warm corpses beside the road, the blazing heaps of twisted metal that had been T–34 tanks only a few minutes before.

The Marine driver parked the leading jeep on a culvert and General MacArthur leaped down to survey the spectacle. Instantly he was surrounded by cameramen snapping pictures which would soon appear on stateside front pages. All America was rejoicing at the turning tide in Korea after the humiliating weeks of delaying operations.

Early that morning CinCFE had been met by General Smith at YELLOW Beach and welcomed to the 1st Marine Division CP, a Quonset hut with a dirt floor. There the commander in chief was briefed by the Division G–2 and G–3 on the military situation.

---

[12] O. P. Smith, *Chronicle*, 17 Sep 50.

The second stop was at the 1st Marines CP. CinCFE informed Colonel Puller and Admiral Sohn that he was awarding each of them a Silver Star. Reaching into the pocket of his leather jacket, he discovered that he had no medals with him.

"Make a note of that," he enjoined an aide as the correspondents busily scribbled on their pads.

Next, the route of the procession led to the zone of RCT–5 and the scene of the Marine tank ambush. It was not exactly a happy occasion for General Smith, who felt a heavy responsibility for the lives and welfare of the 1st Marine Division's distinguished guests. Not only was the commander in chief indifferent to danger, but the Marine general had similar cause to worry about others making the tour of inspection. For instance, there was Frank Lowe, a 66-year-old retired National Guard major general visiting Korea as President Truman's personal observer. Astonishingly hardy for his age, this admirer of the Marines took personal risks which gave concern to Smith. Another source of anxiety was the attractive correspondent of a New York newspaper, Marguerite Higgins, who had hit RED Beach on the heels of the Landing Force.

Both she and Lowe were on hand when the column of jeeps stopped to survey the results of the tank ambush. Smith scanned the landscape with apprehension, devoutly hoping that some hidden foeman would not choose this moment to obliterate several visiting generals with a well-aimed mortar round. It was with relief that he departed with MacArthur for a visit to the CP of the 5th Marines. And it was just as well that he did not learn until later what happened shortly after his departure. First Lieutenant George C. McNaughton's platoon, hearing a suspicious noise, had flushed seven armed NKPA soldiers out of a culvert—the culvert on which General MacArthur's jeep had been parked! A few rifle shots persuaded them to surrender as the only survivors of the enemy expedition.[13]

The caravan of distinguished visitors proceeded meanwhile to the CP of the 5th Marines, raising a cloud of dust that could be seen for miles. Lieutenant Colonel Murray and General Craig were next to be awarded Silver Stars by General MacArthur. His tour of inspection ended with a look at the Marine stockade in Inchon, where 671 NKPA prisoners were held, and a survey of the defenses of Wolmi-do.

---

[13] McNaughton interv, 7 Jan 55.

When the Marine general returned to his CP, he found Major General James M. Gavin, USA, waiting to make a detailed study of Marine close air support and the weapons employed. The day ended with Ruffner and Hodes conferring with Smith on plans for the employment of the 32d Infantry, due to land the next day as the first unit of the 7th Infantry Division to go ashore. Plans were made for the Army unit to assume responsibility at 1200 on 19 September for the zone of action on RCT–1's right flank.[14]

The Drive to Kimpo Airfield

On the evening of D-plus 1, General Smith had issued OpnO 5–50, directing the 1st and 5th Marines to attack toward Corps Phase Line CC the next morning.[15] The actual jump-off on 17 September was delayed about an hour by the intrusion of the ill-fated Red tank column.

Both in scope and in shape, Phase Line CC was an enlargement of the FBHL. Beginning on the coast above Inchon and running parallel to the Inchon-Seoul Highway, the line extended inland about eight miles to bend around Kimpo Airfield. It then ran southward, intersecting the highway two miles east of Sosa and finally terminating at an inlet not far from the Namdong Peninsula.

The 5th Marines' tactical plan was of necessity an ambitious one, since approximately two-thirds of the Division's projected 19-mile frontage lay in Murray's zone. On the left, an attached KMC battalion would attack northward to the phase line, taking high ground Objectives One, Two, and Three en route. Roise's 2d Battalion was to advance in the center on a northeasterly course, which included Objectives ABLE, BAKER, and CHARLIE, the latter being Kimpo itself. Newton's 1st Battalion would follow the 2d initially, then take over the regimental right and seize Objectives EASY and FOX, two sprawling hills just beyond the phase line.[16]

The 3d KMC Battalion passed through 2/5's lines at 0700 for the purpose of clearing the western outskirts of Ascom City before driving toward its numbered objectives to the north. That the initial mission was accomplished only with considerable difficulty and assistance will

---

[14] MarCorps Board *Study*, II–B, 29; O. P. Smith, *Chronicle*, 18 Sep 50.
[15] 1st MarDiv *SAR*, Annex Charlie, 7.
[16] *Ibid.*, Annex Queen Queen.

154

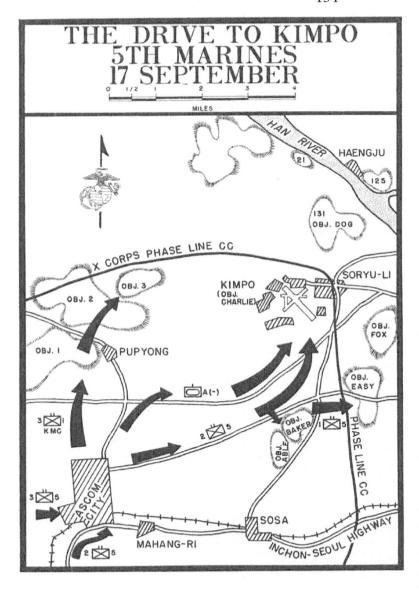

THE DRIVE TO KIMPO
5TH MARINES
17 SEPTEMBER

MILES

be shown later. Afterwards the Korean Marines made rapid progress, as they advanced over flatlands almost devoid of enemy resistance.

Lieutenant Colonel Roise launched 2/5's attack at 0900. Company E led the long route column eastward on the Inchon-Seoul Highway through the carnage left by the defeat of the Red tank thrust. Having marched about a mile, the vanguard of the battalion turned left on a secondary road that traced the eastern edge of Ascom City.[17]

This expansive urban area would prove to be a thorn in the side of the 5th Marines for the next 24 hours. Originally a large Korean village called Taejong-ni, Ascom City became the site of a huge service command of the United States Army during the occupation of South Korea after World War II. The few acres of small buildings and thatched huts had grown into almost two square miles of residential, industrial, and storage area. Caves, large warehouses, hundreds of other buildings, and a complex network of streets made it an ideal hiding place for fragments of a broken enemy, as the Marines were shortly to learn.

Marching northward through the outskirts, Easy Company of 2/5 was repeatedly held up by small pockets of resistance among the dwellings on both sides of the road. Captain Jaskilka's veteran infantry reduced the enemy positions methodically, but the whole morning was used up in the process. Simultaneously with the main advance, the 2d Platoon of Fox Company marched through the heart of Ascom City and screened 2/5's left flank. Second Lieutenant Tilton A. Anderson, the platoon leader, reported everything quiet in his zone, although his men did not have time to check all of the side streets and blocks of buildings.[18]

Having cleared the eastern fringe of the city by noon, Roise looked in vain for the branch road shown on his map as leading to Objective Able and Baker, some four miles distant. The chart was inaccurate, and only a time-consuming reconnaissance could locate the correct route. It was already 1400 by the time Company E led off on the hike.

While 2/5 was having its troubles in the eastern outskirts, Lieutenant Colonel Taplett's 3d Battalion stepped in to help the Korean Marines on the other side of Ascom City. In regimental reserve, 3/5 was scheduled to occupy a series of assembly areas throughout the day, moving forward by bounds behind the assault elements. The morning displacement, into the western edge of Ascom City, took

---

[17] *Ibid.* The word "Ascom" was formed from "Army Service Command."
[18] *Ibid.;* Capt T. A. Anderson interv, 20 Aug 54.

place before the KMC attack had cleared the suburb as planned. Using his initiative, Taplett committed his battalion against moderate resistance that was holding up the South Koreans.[19]

Company G went into action and knocked out a Communist machine-gun emplacement in the city. Next, a George Company patrol attacked a strong enemy force deployed among the buildings. The North Koreans fled after a hot fight, leaving behind 18 dead at a cost of three wounded to the Marines. Item and How Companies also spread out through the maze of streets, and there were several more skirmishes before the "assembly area" was secured. The Korean Marines then passed through and attacked to the north, as mentioned earlier.[20]

The 1st Platoon of A/Tanks, having silenced other enemy positions in the city, made contact with 3/5 at 1500. Leaving the built-up area, Lieutenant Pomeroy led his M–26s in search of 2/5, in order to support that unit's drive on Kimpo. His armor was escorted by Lieutenant Anderson's rifle platoon, which had just completed its independent mission in Ascom City without incident. Finding a road to the northeast proved as much of a headache to Pomeroy as it had to Roise, particularly since his big vehicles could not use the same route over which 2/5's infantry column had advanced an hour earlier.[21]

Extending his quest northward, the tank platoon leader found a road that not only paralleled the infantry's path but also led to within a few hundred yards of Kimpo, now about five miles distant. The M–26s proceeded approximately a mile on the new route and were stopped by a damaged bridge. First Lieutenant Wayne E. Richards rounded up a party of Korean natives to help his 2d Platoon of A/Engineers repair the span. During the layover, Pomeroy's force was beefed up by another platoon of M–26s, brought forward by Captain Gearl M. English, the company commander, and by a long column of rolling stock from 2/5's headquarters.[22]

Meanwhile, the leading elements of Roise's infantry reached the foot of Objectives Able and Baker, two large hills about 4,000 yards due south of Kimpo. There being no evidence of the enemy in the area, the battalion commander did not waste time by committing whole rifle companies to the high ground. At 1600, Lieutenant Deptula's

[19] 1st MarDiv *SAR*, Annex Queen Queen; and Maj R. A. McMullen interv. 27 Jul 54.
[20] *Ibid.*
[21] 1st MarDiv *SAR*, Annex Oboe Oboe; and Anderson interv, 20 Aug 54.
[22] 1st MarDiv *SAR*, Annexes Oboe Oboe and Queen Queen

1st Platoon of Easy Company ascended Objective Baker, while the rest of the battalion waited on the road below. The hill was laced with vacant entrenchments, and once on the summit, Deptula further observed that objective Able was unoccupied. Moreover, he reported by radio that it appeared to be clear sailing over the low ground leading to the airfield.[23]

Acting on this information, Roise promptly launched his attack on Kimpo, one of the major tactical objectives of the Inchon-Seoul operation. A left face by the roadbound column put the troops of 2/5 on line for the assault. Easy and Dog Companies, the latter on the left, advanced rapidly against only desultory sniper fire.

Captain English's tanks arrived propitiously, entering far out to the left front of the attacking infantry. At a point 1,000 yards south of the airfield, the M–26s came under moderate small-arms fire. Lieutenant Anderson's rifle platoon dismounted and engaged the small force of North Koreans, knocking out one automatic weapon with grenades. The Marine armor put down the remaining resistance with seven rounds of 90mm High Explosive (HE) followed by a thorough hosing with bow machine-gun fire.[24]

Just as this action subsided, Company D of 2/5 swept through the area, picked up a platoon of tanks, and continued toward the airfield. The other platoon of armor swung to the right to support Easy Company's attack. By 1800, the Marines were on the southern tip of Kimpo's main runway. Aside from sporadic long range fire from the east, there was no opposition worthy of note.[25]

Action at 5th Marines CP

Over a mile long and three-quarters of a mile wide, Korea's principal airdrome was no mean target to secure. Scattered around the field were more than half a dozen villages, and the runways themselves were lined by scores of plane revetments and emplacements. It was already dusk when Roise ordered his two assault companies to take

[23] 1st MarDiv *SAR*, Annex Queen Queen; and Deptula interv, 18 Jan 55.

[24] 1st MarDiv *SAR*, Annex Oboe Oboe; and Anderson interv, 20 Aug 54.

[25] 1st MarDiv *SAR*, Annex Queen Queen; Roise interv, 21 Dec 54; and Deptula interv, 18 Jan 55.

the objective "with all speed," but by nightfall the infantry and tanks had cleared only the southern portion of the runway.[26]

Rather than stretch a single defensive line to the point of diminishing returns, the battalion commander deployed his three rifle companies in separate perimeters, each one a tightly knit strong point. Easy Company dug in on the east of the main runway and Dog on the west. Company F deployed to the south of the airfield, paying particular attention to the main road and a pair of intersections that tied in secondary routes. In a central perimeter was 2/5's CP, and Able Company Tanks took up positions in Company D's area. Just before dark, Lieutenant Deptula's platoon had raced northward to outpost the village of Soryu-li, several hundred yards beyond Company E's lines.[27]

While 2/5 was investing the southern reaches of Kimpo, Lieutenant Colonel Newton's 1st Battalion, 5th Marines, pressed the attack on the regimental right. Encountering no resistance, Company A occupied the southern portion of Objective Easy at 1900. Company B ascended the northern half of the high ground without incident later in the evening. With Charlie Company on another hill to the west, 1/5 settled down for the night some 1,500 yards southeast of the 2d Battalion's lines. Two miles to the rear, 3/5 deployed in regimental reserve around a critical road junction midway between Kimpo and Ascom City.[28]

During the afternoon of 17 September, as the assault elements of the 5th Marines rolled forward over a relatively quiet front, regimental headquarters suddenly found itself in the center of an angry hornets' nest. Lieutenant Colonel Murray's CP had just displaced to the north of the railroad station in Ascom City, when Commissioned Warrant Officer Bill E. Parrish walked across the tracks to reconnoiter a site for his ordnance dump. Gaining the summit of a small knoll, the officer and his NCO assistants were met by a heavy fusilade from the orchard and rice paddy beyond. Parrish was killed instantly and two of his men seriously wounded.[29]

[26] Maj S. Jaskilka memo to authors, 13 May 55; Roise interv, 21 Dec 54. In the gathering darkness, Roise underestimated the size of the airfield and thought he controlled more than actually was the case. Thus he reported the objective "secured" at 2020, as 2/5 commenced digging in for the night.
[27] 1st MarDiv *SAR*, Annex Queen Queen; and Deptula interv, 18 Jan 55.
[28] 1st MarDiv *SAR*, Annex Queen Queen.
[29] Capt G. H. Stewart interv, 17 Nov 54.

Cries of help brought First Lieutenant Nicholas A. Canzona's 1st Platoon of A/Engineers, which had just arrived at Murray's CP. In a brief clash around the orchard, the engineers killed ten enemy die-hards. South Korean police swept through the adjoining rice paddy and came up with seven prisoners.

About the same time, Major James D. Jordan's party arrived in the area to select a position for Battery A of 1/11. Again small-arms fire crackled. Two of Jordan's NCOs, Technical Sergeants Kenneth C. Boston and Donald Comiskey, plowed through the hail of lead and killed four more North Koreans.[30]

North of the railroad, still another Marine was killed and one more wounded not far from Murray's headquarters. For obvious reasons a tight perimeter of engineers and H&S Company troops was drawn around the CP during the night. Nevertheless, a Red officer stumbled through the line in the darkness and seriously wounded Second Lieu-tenant Lawrence Hetrick of A/Engineers.

At dawn on 18 September the regimental commander and his staff were awakened by the chatter of an enemy submachine gun a few yards from the CP. Holed up in a grain field with one Communist rifleman, the officer who had shot Hetrick fought fanatically against a whole platoon of engineers. Another Marine was wounded before the suicidal stand was crushed by grenades and rifle fire.

There were no regrets when Murray's headquarters took leave of Ascom City and displaced to Kimpo.

Enemy Counterattack at Kimpo

The air at Kimpo was charged with tension during the night of 17–18 September. Troops of 2/5, manning perimeters which had been laid out on unfamiliar ground during darkness, had every reason to believe that the North Koreans would not give up the airfield without a fight.

But there were troubles enough in the North Korean camp, where confusion and panic seemed to be the order of the day. Intelligence on the enemy garrison in the Kimpo area presents a scrambled picture so characteristic of the Communist organization throughout the Inchon-Seoul operation.[31] It appears that elements of the NKPA 1st

---

[30] Maj J. D. Jordan interv, 27 Sep 54.
[31] The intelligence summary is derived from: 1st MarDiv *SAR*, Annexes Baker and Queen Queen.

Air Force Division were charged with the operation of the airfield. Under the command of 40-year-old Chinese-trained Brigadier General Wan Yong, the division was comprised of the following units or, more often than not, mere fragments thereof:

Division Headquarters
1st Co, Engineer Bn, Fighters Regt
3d Co, Engineer Bn, Fighters Regt
3d Plat, Gunners Co
2d Co, 1st Bn, 1st Regt
2d Bn, 1st Regt
Finance Co, 3d Technical Bn
Supply Co

The Kimpo force was augmented by a motley mixture of poorly trained troops from the 226th and 107th NKPA Regiments and the separate 877th Air Force Unit. In the face of the Marine advance, Colonel Han Choi Han, commander of the 107th had fled across the Han River, leaving the remnants of his regiment to an obvious fate. Major Kung Chan So, leader of the 877th AF Unit, was killed in action on 17 September. Of the 400 men originally assigned to this organization, only five remained in combat by 18 September.

Crowded into undesirable terrain between the airfield and the Han River, the Red troops were demoralized and bewildered by the rapid advance of the 5th Marines. Only the fanaticism of a few officers and NCOs prevented the complete collapse that would have resulted from the lack of tangible assistance from the North Korean leaders in Seoul. And it was no boost to sagging morale that white clothing had been issued by the Supply Company, so that the Red soldiers could quickly change to the traditional Korean garb when defeat was imminent, and dissolve in the local populace.

In the counterattack against the airfield, which was designed to uproot a full-strength Marine battalion backed by tanks and other heavy fire support, the celebrated night tactics of the Communists fizzled completely. With only a few hundred men at most, the rest having slipped away to safer parts, the North Koreans further reduced their strength by trying to develop three widely separated attacks. That they launched these assaults with only rifles and submachine guns serves to make the story more incredible.

The first move was in company strength against Lieutenant Deptula's isolated platoon outpost in Soryu-li, far to the north of Easy Company lines.[32] Deployed on both sides of a road junction in the village, the Marines heard the enemy column approaching about 0300. Deptula held fire until the Red vanguard marched into the center of his position. Sergeant Richard L. Martson then jumped to his feet, bellowed "United States Marines!" and opened up with his carbine on full automatic. A sheet of rifle and BAR fire poured into the column from the roadsides, and a dozen North Koreans went down in a heap. The remainder fled.

The Communist commander rallied his soldiers for three more thrusts against the Marine platoon. In between the attacks, his gravel-voiced exhortations ground the air. The will to fight was lacking, however, and each time, the attackers barely brushed the Marine position before darting back into the night.

A T–34 tank was finally brought up to buttress another North Korean assault. Without AT weapons to stop the armored vehicle rumbling down the road toward his platoon, Deptula retracted southward in the direction of 2/5's main positions. The outpost had suffered only one KIA and one WIA in blunting the four attacks. It was not pursued during the withdrawal.

Deptula's platoon gained Company E's lines at 0500, just before the perimeter received enemy small-arms fire from the west. Captain Jaskilka, supposing it to be coming inadvertently from Dog Company, forbade his men to reply. He stood up and yelled, "Hey! Cease fire, you guys, this is Easy Company!" Fortunately, the enemy's aim must have been disturbed by the spectacle of a Marine officer giving orders, for Jaskilka escaped without a scratch after discovering his mistake. This enemy force proved to number about two squads, and just at that moment the main NKPA force hit from the east. Easy Company was thus engaged on two fronts, with Jones' recoilless gun platoon taking on the attack from the west while the 2d Platoon bore the brunt of the assault from the east.[33]

The 2d Battalion's southernmost position, manned by Company F, had been active throughout the night. Lieutenant Harrell's assault platoon together with Richards' engineer outfit was entrenched around

---

[32] The account of the Kimpo counterattacks is taken from: 1st MarDiv *SAR*, Annex Queen Queen; Deptula interv, 18 Jan 55; and Harrell interv, 4 Jan 55.

[33] Jaskilka memo, 13 May 55.

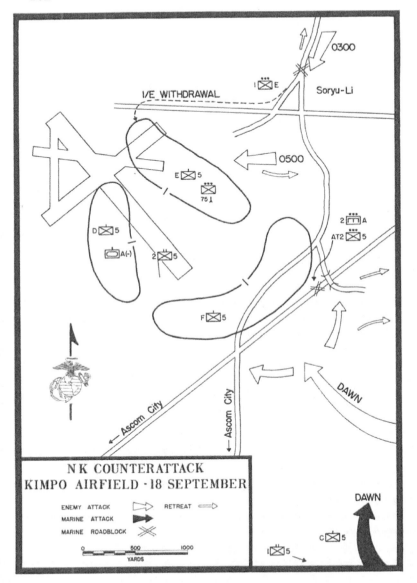

0300

I⊠E   Soryu-Li

I/E WITHDRAWAL

0500

E⊠5

75↓

2⌷A

AT2⊠5

D⊠5

A(-)

2⊠5

F⊠5

Ascom City

Ascom City

DAWN

**N K COUNTERATTACK
KIMPO AIRFIELD · 18 SEPTEMBER**

ENEMY   ATTACK   ⟹   RETREAT   ⟹
MARINE   ATTACK
MARINE   ROADBLOCK   ✕

0   500   1000
YARDS

DAWN

C⊠5

I⊠5

an overpass within the southeastern arc of the company perimeter. In the first hours of 18 September, a North Korean lieutenant and his five-man demolition team tried to reach the bridge in an apparent attempt to destroy it. Sergeant Ray D. Kearl opposed the intruders single-handedly, killing the Red officer and three of his men, and driving the remaining pair back into the night. Before daybreak, another enemy patrol approached on the road and was annihilated.

It proved that these and other scattered incidents were the prelude to the third and final attack against the airfield, which was launched from the south at dawn. This last maneuver by the Reds, however, was checked even before it began, for the 1st Battalion, 5th Marines, spotted the attackers moving across its front toward Kimpo. Baker Company took the North Koreans under fire immediately, and the battalion commander called down heavy mortar and artillery concentrations.

Most of the Communist column was disorganized and dispersed before it could reach 2/5's southern defenses. The lone platoon that did connect with Company F's perimeter engaged the Marines at the overpass. Harrell's troops and the engineers poured small-arms fire and white phosphorus rockets into the attackers. Staff Sergeant Robert J. Kikta, defying enemy bullets as he moved among his men shouting encouragement, fell mortally wounded. Sergeant David R. DeArmond, normally a bulldozer operator for A/Engineers, was killed behind his machine gun.

After the short, bitter clash, the surviving North Koreans retreated through the rice paddies and hills leading to the Han River. Companies E and F, supported by A/Tanks, fanned out from their perimeters and mopped up. In 1/5's zone, Lieutenant Colonel Newton committed Charlie Company against the withdrawing enemy and inflicted more casualties.

Kimpo and the surrounding villages were secured by 1000, 18 September. Half an hour later, Lieutenant Colonel Roise ordered Company D, supported by tanks, recoilless rifles, and heavy machine guns, to seize Regimental Objective Dog—Hill 131, which dominated the banks of the Han River north of the airfield. Advancing under cover of naval gunfire, the Marines occupied the high ground un-opposed at 1145.[34]

---

[34] 1st MarDiv *SAR*, Annex Queen Queen.

In the 24 hours since leaving Ascom City, the 2d Battalion, 5th Marines, had suffered four KIA and 19 WIA in driving over nine miles of hills and rice paddies.[35] The rapid advance cost the North Koreans 100 dead in 2/5's zone, ten prisoners, and one of the finest airdromes in the Far East.

---

[35] *Ibid.*

CHAPTER IX

Marine Air Support

Helicopters and OYs in Support—Marine Air Units at Kimpo—Progress of Eighth Army Offensive—Division CP Displaces to Oeoso-Ri—Advance of RCT-1 to Sosa—Reports of Enemy Build-up—Preparations for Crossing the Han

At 1000 on the morning of 18 September an HO3S-1 helicopter became the first American aircraft to land on Kimpo Airfield since June. Mopping up operations had scarcely been completed, following the enemy counterattack, when Captain Victor A. Armstrong of VMO-6 made a vertical approach with General Shepherd and Colonel Krulak as passengers. They were greeted by General Craig, the ADC, who had just arrived in a jeep.

The field was in surprisingly good shape, considering the fighting it had seen within the last few hours. As evidence that the enemy had been surprised, one Russian-built fighter of the Yak III type and two Stormovik type aircraft were found "relatively undamaged" and turned over to Air Force Intelligence.[1] Several other Yaks and Stormoviks had been destroyed by the enemy.

On the return trip, Armstrong was requested by his passengers to fly them across the Han for a preview of the outskirts of Seoul. Except for scattered small-arms fire, the helicopter was allowed to proceed without being molested by the enemy. There were few signs of extensive NKPA preparations to be seen at this time.[2]

---

[1] 1st MAW, Annex Able.
[2] Maj V. A. Armstrong interv, 16 Mar 55.

Helicopters and OYs in Support

VMO-6, the composite observation squadron commanded by Major Vincent J. Gottschalk, had already made a name for itself in the Pusan Perimeter actions. Consisting of eight HO3S-1 helicopters and an equal number of OY planes, this former Brigade unit came under the operational control of the 1st Marine Division and the administrative and logistical control of MAG-33. During the Inchon assault, VMO-6 was based on SCAJAP LST QO79 in the harbor except for an Oy attached to each of the two CVEs.

The first of a long sequence of helicopter rescue missions during the Inchon-Seoul operation took place on D-plus 1 when First Lieutenant Max N. Nebergall picked up a Navy pilot who had ditched in Inchon harbor. Flights carried out by other aircraft were reported as three reconnaissance, two artillery spot, three beach reconnaissance, and one utility.[3]

VMO-6 displaced ashore the next day to an airstrip improvised near the Division CP by the Marine engineers. This was the beginning of liaison, utility, reconnaissance, evacuation, and rescue flights on a dawn-to-dark basis.

Division air and naval gunfire representatives of the Fire Support Coordination Center followed VMO-6 ashore on the 16th. During the planning phase they had worked with their opposite numbers of PhibGru One and with the 11th Marines after the Division landed at Kobe. Although some of the officers and men embarked for Inchon in the *Mount McKinley*, the materiel and 90 percent of the personnel arrived in the *President Jackson*. At 1400 on D-plus 2 the FSCC became operational after all elements and their equipment reported to the Division CP. Responsibility for the coordination of supporting arms ashore was assumed at 0630 on 16 September for air, at 1500 on the 17th for artillery, and at 1800 on the 18th for naval gunfire.[4]

The rapid advance of Marine ground forces during the first three days meant that Major Robert L. Schreier's 1st Signal Battalion had a job on its hands. The main body reached the objective area on board the *President Jackson*, and the first units ashore were the battalion and regimental ANGLICO teams, most of which had embarked

---

[3] 1st MarDiv *SAR*, Annex Oboe.
[4] *Ibid.*, Annexes Baker Baker, Charlie Charlie, and Dog Dog.

in LSTs.   When the ADC group displaced from Wolmi-do to Inchon, radio facilities were maintained without a hitch.

Radio and message center facilities met all requirements during the night of 16–17 September.   Teletype (through radio carrier) was initiated between the Division CP and Corps, afloat on the *Mount Mc-Kinley*.   And by the morning of D-plus 2, such progress had been made that wire communication was established not only with both advancing infantry regiments but also with most of the battalions.[5]

Enemy resistance was so ineffectual from 16 to 18 September that the Marine infantry regiments were able to advance without much flank protection.   The three battalions of the 11th Marines did more displacing than firing in their efforts to keep pace, and men and vehicles of the Signal Battalion were kept busy at laying wire.

Security was provided for the left, or northern, Division flank by the attack of the KMC Regiment (less the 2d Battalion, left behind for police duties in Inchon) under the control of the 5th Marines.   Attached to the regiment for possible use in calling down naval gunfire were two Shore Fire Control Parties.   Objectives on Corps Phase Line CC were reached without much difficulty after the initial KMC setbacks described in the previous chapter.[6]

Marine Air Units at Kimpo

There had been little or no urgent need for close air support until 18 September, when RCT–1 met stubborn opposition in the Sosa area. Thus the capture of Kimpo in comparatively good condition was a timely boon, since it meant that land-based Marine tactical air support could be initiated as soon as Captain George W. King's Able Company Engineers made the field operative with temporary repairs.

This was the conclusion of Generals Harris and Cushman, commanding the 1st MAW and TAC X Corps, when they visited Kimpo by helicopter on the afternoon of the 18th.   They advised CG X Corps accordingly, and that evening he ordered the deployment of MAG–33 to the captured airfield with its headquarters and service squadrons.

The tactical squadrons figured in an administrative switch that has sometimes puzzled chroniclers of Marine air operations.   By order

[5] 1st MarDiv *SAR*, Annex George George.
[6] *Ibid.*, basic rpt, and Annex Queen Queen.

of General Harris, the following reassignments were directed to take effect on 21 September 1950:

From MAG–33 to MAG–12—VMF–214, VMF–323, and VMF (N)–513;

From MAG–12 to MAG–33—VMF–212, VMF–312, and VMF (N)–542.[7]

Both MGCIS–1 and MTACS–2 were already ashore at Inchon under the operational control of the 1st Marine Division. Aircraft and flight echelons of the tactical squadrons were to be flown to Kimpo on the 19th from Itazuke and Itami airfields in Japan, with the remaining elements following by surface shipping. Thus MAG–33 would consist of these units:

Organization	Officers	Enlisted	Total
HqSq–33	74	177	251
SMS–33	29	538	567
VMF–212	32	154	186
VMF–312	53	221	274
VMF(N)–542	54	291	345
MTACS–2	34	190	224
MGCIS–1	19	185	204
Total	295	1,756	[8] 2,051

VMFs–214 and 323 would continue to operate from the carriers *Sicily* and *Badoeng Strait,* with the night-fighters, VMF(N)–513 being based as usual at Itazuke AFB in Japan. The only difference was that a scratch of the pen had transferred these units from MAG–33 to MAG–12. It was their responsibility to support the advancing ground forces during the critical period while the other three tactical squadrons were making the move from Japan to Kimpo.

Control of tactical air support had passed from the TADC on the *Mount McKinley* to the Air Support Section of MTACS–2 on D-plus 2, after the Landing Force Commander signified his readiness to assume it. Calls for close air support were increasing as the enemy recovered from the first shock of invasion. On the 18th and 19th, the three fighter squadrons of MAG–12 flew a total of nearly 50 close

[7] CG 1st MAW speedltr, 20 Sep 50.

[8] 1st MAW *SAR,* Annex Item.

support sorties controlled by the Air Support Section of MTACS–2. Napalm, 20mm ammunition, rockets, and 500-pound bombs were used to blast NKPA troop concentrations in the zone of the 1st Marines.[9]

Logistical as well as tactical and administrative problems had to be solved. During the planning phase, it may be recalled, Colonel Kenneth H. Weir (C/S TAC X corps) had learned that X corps would not have enough trucks to support air operations at Kimpo by transporting aviation gasoline and aircraft munitions from Inchon. As a solution, arrangements were made to accept the offer of FEAF Combat Cargo Command to provide logistical support; and these totals in tonnage were flown in from Japan during the first week:

Date	Ammo	Avgas	Oil
18 Sep	16	8	0
19 Sep	73	28	5
20 Sep	151	86	0
21 Sep	219	88	11
22 Sep	268	153	5
23 Sep	139	80	0
24 Sep	118	81	[10] 16

This proved to be the largest total for a single week during the Inchon-Seoul operation. In addition, about 1,025 tons of POL and 425 tons of ammunition were trucked from Inchon to Kimpo during the entire period, and the forward echelon of VMR–152 flew in spare parts and items of urgently needed equipment.

Headquarters of the 1st MAW remained at Itami AFB in Japan, though General Harris made frequent trips to Kimpo. The chief task of the Wing during the Kimpo air operations was furnishing administrative and logistical support to TAC X Corps and MAG–33.

TAC X Corps set up its headquarters at Kimpo Airfield on 19 September, followed by MTACS–2, MGCIS–1, and VMO–6. The first fighter squadron of MAG–33 to arrive at the new base was VMF(N)–542. Lieutenant Colonel Max J. Volcansek, Jr., the commanding officer, and five pilots landed their F7F–3Ns at 1830 on the 19th after a flight from Itami AFB. This was the baptism of fire for

[9] MarCorps Board *Study*, IV–B, 16, 17; 1st MAW *SAR*, basic rpt, and Annex Jig.
[10] 1st MAW *SAR*, basic rpt.

a majority of the squadron's pilots. Numbering 54 officers and 274 enlisted men when it left El Toro, VMF(N)–542 had only 20 trained night fighter pilots. The remainder were volunteer reservists qualified by "a good experience level and a desire to become night fighters." [11]

The squadron claimed the distinction of flying the first Marine combat mission from Kimpo at 0735 on the 20th when four of the F7F–3N aircraft destroyed two enemy locomotives after expending some 3,000 rounds of 20mm ammunition. The Corsairs of Lieutenant Colonel Richard W. Wyczawski's VMF–212 and two aircraft of Lieutenant Colonel J. Frank Cole's VMF–312 also landed at Kimpo on the 19th and got into action the following day. Conditions were primitive at the outset. In the lack of refueling facilities, the first strikes had to be flown on fuel remaining in the aircraft, and bombs were loaded by hand.[12]

It had been an achievement to have two tactical squadrons of MAG–33 in action less than 48 hours after the reconnaissance landing by Generals Harris and Cushman. This accomplishment owed a great deal to the care shown by the 5th Marines to keep damage at a minimum. Lieutenant General George E. Stratemeyer, CG FEAF, expressed his appreciation of this factor in a letter to General Smith:

"I want to take this opportunity of expressing my admiration and gratification for the manner in which elements of your Division recently captured Kimpo Airfield and so secured it as to make it available for use by Far East Air Forces and Marine Corps aircraft in the shortest possible time." [13]

Progress of Eighth Army Offensive

General MacArthur had intended the Eighth Army to be the hammer and X Corps the anvil of a great joint operation. During the first few days, however, it sometimes appeared as if these roles were reversed. On 18 September, after a penetration of 16 miles on the X Corps front, the attacking forces in the Pusan Perimeter had just begun to inch ahead against desperate NKPA resistance. In some sectors,

[11] 1st MAW *SAR*, Annex Item, VMF(N)–542 rpt.
[12] 1st MAW *SAR*, Annex Item VMF–212 rpt.
[13] O. P. Smith, *Notes*, 212–213.

indeed, the enemy not only put up a stubborn defense but counter-attacked vigorously. (See map in end papers.)

The Eighth Army now consisted of the U. S. I Corps (IX Corps did not become operational until 23 September) and the ROK I and II Corps. General Walker's command was already on the way to becoming the most cosmopolitan army in which Americans have ever served. Contingents of British ground forces had reached the front; and before the end of the year, 40 countries of the United Nations would have offered assistance, either military or economic, to the fight against Communism.

Most of this aid had not yet materialized on 16 September, but the Eighth Army had overcome its disadvantage in numbers of trained troops, thanks to NKPA losses, when it jumped off all along the line in southeast Korea. In the north the 1st Cavalry Division, 24th Infantry Division, ROK 1st Division, and British 27th Brigade launched a determined attack along the Taegu-Waegwon axis to win a bridge-head across the Naktong. It was nip-and-tuck for the first three days, and not until the 19th did the UN forces fight their way across the river against the last-ditch opposition of the 1st, 3d, 10th, and 13th NKPA Divisions.[14]

Still farther north, the enemy relinquished little ground until the 18th. On that date the ROK 3d Division recaptured the east coast port of Pohang-dong, which the invaders had taken in their drive during the first week of September.

In the south, the U. S. 2d and 25th Infantry Divisions and attached ROK units were held up for three days by the NKPA 6th and 7th Divisions. The deadlock lasted until 19 September, when the enemy fell back in the Masan area along the southern coast.[15]

Major Joseph H. Reinburg's VMF(N)-513, operating out of its Itazuke base, played a conspicuous role in the first days of Walker's offensive. Although specialists in night-fighting, the Marine pilots flew 15 daylight close support missions for Army units from 17 to 19 September. Enemy troops, tanks, vehicles, and artillery were scored during every strike, as the planes ranged the entire extent of the Pusan Perimeter.[16]

---

[14] Almond, *UN Mil Ops*, 13.
[15] *Ibid.*
[16] 1st MAW *SAR*, Annex Item, VMF(N)-513 rpt.

Division CP Displaces to Oeoso-ri

So much progress had been made by this date on the X Corps front that General Smith displaced the 1st Marine Division CP from the eastern outskirts of Inchon to Oeoso-ri, about a mile and a half southeast of Kimpo Airfield. This forward location was selected by General Craig with a view to preliminary Division planning for the crossing of the Han, which would entail a reshuffling of units.

Oeoso-ri having been an American housing area during the post-World War II occupation, duplex houses and Quonset huts were available. General Smith arrived by helicopter on the afternoon of the 19th, and the new CP opened at 1645. During the next few days the area was treated to intermittent artillery fire, apparently from a single well-hidden gun somewhere in the Seoul area. It was an embarrassment to Marine artillery officers, who were never able to locate the offending weapon, but no great harm was done.

By this time General Smith could look forward to the arrival of more units at the front. On D-day the strength of X Corps on paper had been 69,450 ground force troops. In addition to the 1st Marine Division and 7th Infantry Division, there were such major units as the 93d and 96th Field Artillery Battalions, the 73d Tank Battalion, 56th Amphibian Tank and Tractor Battalion, the 2d Engineer Combat Group. In GHQ UNC Reserve were the 3d Infantry Division and the 187th Airborne RCT.[17]

The 3d Division had not sailed for the Far East in time to take part in the Inchon-Seoul operation. The 187th Airborne RCT, due to land at Inchon on 23 September, had been the answer to General MacArthur's requests in July for paratroops to land behind the enemy's lines in conjunction with the amphibious assault planned as Operation BLUEHEARTS. Although the Joint Chiefs of Staff decided against flying an airborne RCT to Japan at the time, the 11th Airborne Division was later directed to organize and train such a unit for service in the Far East. On account of the large proportion of new troops filling out a skeleton unit, General Collins stipulated that the 187th was not to be committed for an airdrop before 29 September. It was decided, therefore, that the RCT would be given an initial mission of protecting the left flank of the 1st Marine Division.

---

[17] GHQ UNC *OpnO No. 1*, 30 Aug 50.

Advance of RCT–1 to Sosa

Preliminary planning for the crossing of the river Han began as soon as the Division staff settled down in the new CP. The reshuffling of various units had to wait, however, until both Marine regiments took their assigned objectives of 18 and 19 September. Throughout the 17th, while Murray's regiment drove northeastward toward Kimpo, the 1st Marines had continued the attack from Ascom City along the Inchon-Seoul Highway. As mentioned previously, Monegan's rocket launcher and the 75mm recoilless rifles, emplaced in 2/1's positions on Hill 186, helped smash the North Korean tank-infantry column at dawn. It appeared that a second enemy force was supposed to have closed on Marine lines by taking a parallel course through the hills south of the highway. The Red infantry, in about company strength, was spotted moving along the high ground toward Company D's front on Hill 186. Fox Company dispersed the column with mortar fire and then notified Dog to be on the alert.[18]

Though the North Koreans were stopped cold, they did not flee with the usual rapidity. Their base of operations seemed to be Hill 208, a land mass that began near Mahang-ri on the highway and spread southward across most of the 2d Battalion front. Lieutenant Colonel Sutter's attack plan committed Easy Company on the left of the road, Fox on the right, and Dog in the high ground to the south. No sooner had the companies jumped off than they became involved in scattered, stubborn fighting with Red soldiers on and around Hill 208.[19]

Howitzers of the 11th Marines raked the high ground ahead of the attackers, and Sutter's troops measured off slow but steady progress. In the low ground bordering the highway, enemy troops had taken cover in the fields on both sides of a road block about 500 yards from Mahang-ri. Second Lieutenant Robert C. Hanlon's 2d Platoon of Easy Company was pinned down by fire from three sides. Second Lieutenants Johnny L. Carter and George E. McAlee started forward with reinforcements, but McAlee was wounded by several bullets. After summoning a corpsman, Carter got through to Hanlon, and they called for 3.5-inch rockets and 75mm recoilless fire on huts sheltering enemy soldiers. The two officers then led an advance which took the platoon to a small hill on the right of the road block, where

[18] 2/1 *SAR*, 5; and Cunliffe interv, 24 Aug 54.
[19] *Ibid.*.

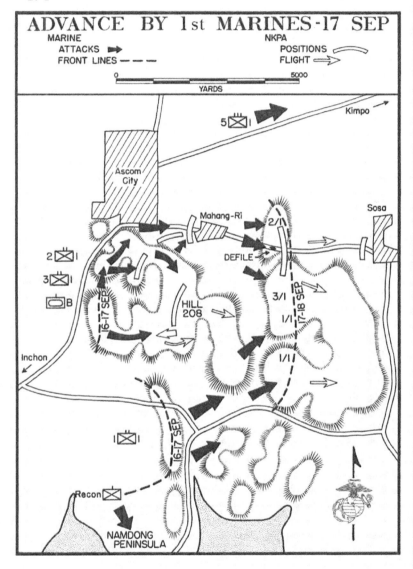

ADVANCE BY 1st MARINES·17 SEP

MARINE
  ATTACKS ➡
  FRONT LINES – – –

NKPA
  POSITIONS
  FLIGHT ⟹

0   5000
YARDS

Kimpo

5 ⊠ 1

Ascom
City

Sosa

Mahang-Ri

2/1

DEFILE

2 ⊠ 1

3 ⊠ 1

☐ B

16-17 SEP

HILL
208

3/1

1/1

17-18 SEP

1/1

Inchon

1 ⊠ 1

16-17 SEP

Recon ⊠

NAMDONG
PENINSULA

the other two platoons moved up abreast. About 20 NKPA troops were estimated to have been killed.[20]

At noon, Companies F and D had secured Hill 208 overlooking the FBHL, but it remained for E to break into Mahang-ri on the highway. By this time 3/1 had entered the fight with an armored column. Company G, led by First Lieutenant Robert L. Gover's 1st Platoon of Baker Company Tanks, punched down the road in an attempt to pierce the screen of Red resistance with the rest of 3/1 in column close behind. The M–26 crews spotted an 85mm gun protruding from a thatched hut and destroyed the camouflaged T–34 before it could fire a shot. An infantry platoon riding the Marine tanks was forced to dismount at Mahang-ri and deploy, while the armor fired from the road at numerous targets of opportunity. The village was finally secured shortly before 1600, and small bands of enemy were seen darting eastward to take up new positions along the highway.[21]

The advance to Mahang-ri and the FBHL had carried the 1st Marines 3,000 yards from its starting point at Ascom City. As the attack continued late in the afternoon, the next objective was Corps Phase Line CC, whose boundaries were defined in the previous chapter. Midway between Mahang-ri and the phase line was the town of Sosa, and it was from this locale that North Korean soldiers were pouring westward to delay the Marine advance on the highway.

Since the 5th Marines had veered to the northeast to attack Kimpo, its boundary with the 1st had moved well to the left of the highway. Henceforth, Puller's regiment would have to go it alone on the main road. This was the case as the 2d and 3d Battalions butted against enemy delaying forces between Ascom City and Mahang-ri, and the isolation became more pronounced as they attacked toward Sosa late on the 17th.

Sutter's unit advanced on the left of the highway with Companies E and F in assault. George Company of 3/1, transported in LVTs and followed by the rest of the battalion, moved along the road behind the 2d Platoon, Baker Company Tanks. There is a defile halfway between Mahang-ri and Sosa, and at this spot the North Koreans chose to make a determined stand. Second Lieutenant Bryan J. Cummings nosed his lead M–26 into the pass, while infantry moved to the shoulders

[20] Capt J. L. Carter ltr to authors, 9 May 55.

[21] 1st MarDiv *SAR*, Annex Oboe Oboe; 2/1 *SAR*; 3/1 *SAR*; and Capt B. J. Cummings interv, 12 Oct 54. Col T. L. Ridge, memo to authors, 13 May 55.

on either side against light opposition. Suddenly the troops and lone
tank were hit from the front by a heavy volume of small-arms, antitank, and mortar fire.[22]

The Marine infantry was thrown back by the intensity of the outburst, the most severe they had yet encountered. As luck would have
it, the engine of Cummings' tank went dead at this inopportune
moment, and the big vehicle stalled. Remembering that infantry had
been riding on top of his M-26, the platoon leader opened the hatch
to make a quick check. He yanked a lone rifleman inside and buttoned
up just as Red soldiers scrambled down the embankment.

Fumes from the 90mm gun choked the Marines in the vehicle as
they listened to the clamor of North Koreans on the hull. The in-
fantryman who had been pulled to safety by Cummings suddenly went
berserk and had to be knocked out. Then the officer was forced to
choose between two evils: either his crew must succumb to the acrid
fumes or take its chances on opening the pistol port for ventilation. He
opened the port. A grenade bounced inside, and the ear-shattering
explosion within the steel enclosure wounded Cummings, the rifleman,
and one of the tank gunners. At this moment the semi-conscious
Marines resigned themselves to the worst.[23]

Help was on the way, however, and it was timed to the split second.
Just as the grenade exploded, Sergeant Marion C. Altaire's M-26
moved to the mouth of the defile and "scratched the back" of the
beleaguered vehicle with bow machine-gun fire. Riddled Red soldiers
were swept from the top of Cummings' tank and piled up alongside.
Within a few minutes, a VMF-214 flight appeared over the pass, and
the planes peeled off to bomb, rocket, and strafe the high ground.[24]

As the tide of battle swept past, Cummings and his men opened the
hatch, coughing and choking, and drank in long breaths of fresh air.
It took them a moment to realize that they were back again in the land
of the living after one of the closest calls that Marines have ever
experienced.

Company G of 3/1 fought back on the right of the MSR and gained
the high ground above the pass. Simultaneously, Staff Sergeant Arthur
J. MacDonald led the second section of Cummings' tank platoon into

[22] 2/1 *SAR;* 3/1 *SAR;* and Cummings interv, 24 Aug 54.
[23] Cummings interv, 24 Aug 54.
[24] *Ibid.;* and 1st MAW *SAR,* Annex Jig, VMF-214 rpt, 5.

the defile, and the M–26s laid down heavy 90mm and machine-gun fire on the crescent of North Korean emplacements ahead. A total of six enemy AT guns was destroyed, but not before the weapons had knocked a track off Cummings' vehicle and damaged two others to a lesser extent.[25]

The 2d Battalion drove to the top of the high ground on the left of the road, and the Marines enjoyed a small-scale "turkey shoot" as the North Koreans pulled out and pelted toward Sosa. While the assault units consolidated their holdings, the remainder of the 2d and 3d Battalions moved into the area around the defile and dug in for the night.

The 1st Marines' attack along the highway had netted 4,800 yards. Despite repeated clashes in the course of the day, 2/1 lost only one killed and 28 wounded, and Company G of the 3d Battalion suffered six WIA. Enemy losses included 250 killed and wounded, 70 prisoners, one T–34 tank, several AT guns, and large quantities of small arms and ammunition.[26]

Action on the Division's southern flank involved little more than hill climbing and foot races for the 1st Battalion, 1st Marines, and the Division Reconnaissance Company. After jumping off in the morning of D-plus 2, Lieutenant Colonel Hawkins' infantry fanned out through a maze of twisting valleys and ridges. The battalion encountered only light resistance, which invariably evaporated under pressure, and by dark the assault elements had gained 4,000 yards. Hawkins then deployed his troops for night defense on the high ground south of 3/1's positions overlooking the highway defile.[27]

On the right of the 1st Battalion, Captain Houghton's Reconnaissance Company reached the tip of the Namdong Peninsula. The Recon troops spent two days, the 17th and 18th, patrolling this spacious tactical vacuum. A number of dispirited prisoners were collected and

---

[25] *Ibid.;* 3/1 *SAR;* and Cunliffe interv, 24 Aug 54.

[26] 1st MarDiv *SAR,* Annex Oboe Oboe; 2/1 *SAR;* and 3/1 *SAR.* In its account of NKPA losses for 17 September, 2/1 lists four other enemy tanks destroyed. These vehicles were among the six knocked out jointly by the 1st and 5th Marines and Able Company Tanks at the dawn ambuscade near Ascom City. 1st MarDiv G-2 reports of 14 NKPA tanks destroyed this date cannot be supported by the records of subordinate units. In addition to the six T–34s destroyed in the morning and the single vehicle knocked out by our tanks near Mahang-ri, one other kill was recorded by Marine air.

[27] McGee-Carlon interv, 9 Feb 55.

caches of arms and munitions uncovered. One of the more significant discoveries was a small arsenal in which Russian-type wooden box mines were being manufactured and stored in quantity. First encountered by Able Company engineers in the Pusan Perimeter, these crude but effective explosives would become serious obstacles to the Marine advance in the days ahead.[28]

The night of 17–18 September passed quietly for the 1st Marines. During the hours of darkness, Ridge requested intermittent naval gunfire to interdict Sosa and Hill 123, where he believed enemy defenses to be located. Jump-off fires were also planned for the morning in addition to air strikes. Captain P. W. Brock's HMS *Kenya* poured in more than 300 6-inch rounds with good results. "Our Royal Navy ally not only supported the battalion to the maximum of its naval gunfire desires," said Ridge, "but volunteered to render more than was requested." [29]

Shortly after first light on D-plus 3, the 2d Battalion attacked along the highway with Easy Company on the left of the road and Dog on the right. Premature air bursts from an artillery preparation resulted in two KIA and three WIA among the troops of Company E.[30]

Ridge's 3d Battalion boarded a column of LVTs, DUKWs, and jeeps, then rumbled down the highway through 2/1's assault companies. In striking contrast to the previous day's advance, there was a conspicuous absence of NKPA infantry along the way. The Marines brushed aside light opposition, including an antitank roadblock at Sosa's outskirts, and captured the town at noon. Covered by Baker Company Tanks, 2/1 moved into defensive positions on the right side of the railroad about a mile beyond the built-up area, and the 3d Battalion deployed on Hill 123 just across the tracks.[31]

On the Division's right, 1/1 gained another 4,000 yards in the course of 18 September. In its third consecutive day of attack, the battalion had yet to encounter anything more formidable than steep hills and vapid enemy bands. Hawkins built his night defenses along a mountainous two-mile front south of 2/1's position overlooking the highway.

[28] HqBn, 1st MarDiv *Unit Rpts,* 9 Sep–11 Nov 50; and Houghton interv, 3 Aug 54. See also this series, 1:225.
[29] Ridge memo, 13 May 55.
[30] 2/1 *SAR,* 6; Cunliffe interv, 24 Aug 54; Carter ltr, 9 May 55.
[31] *Ibid.;* and 3/1 SAR, 7.

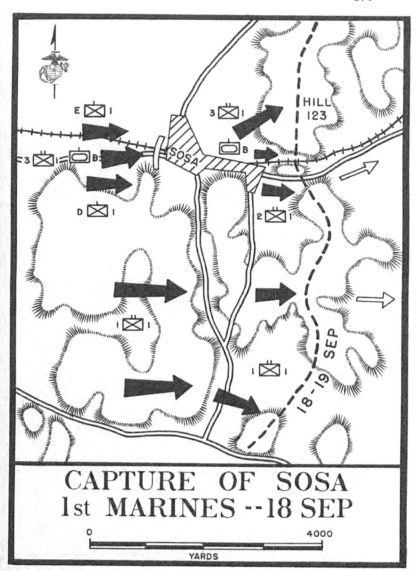

E ☒ 1

3 ☒ 1

HILL
123

3 ☒ 1 ☐ B

☐ B

SOSA

D ☒ 1

2 ☒ 1

1 ☒ 1

1 ☒ 1

18 - 19 SEP

CAPTURE OF SOSA
1st MARINES --18 SEP

0   4000

YARDS

Reports of Enemy Build-up

There was little activity in the 5th Marines' zone of action during the 1st Regiment's drive on Sosa. After helping 2/5 smash the dawn counterattack at Kimpo, Company C, 1st Battalion, attacked Objective Fox under cover of an artillery preparation. Lieutenant Pedersen's unit seized the high ground against light opposition at 0930, while the remainder of 1/5 remained entrenched at Objective Easy, captured the previous day.[32]

Murray's CP displaced to Kimpo at 1245 on the 18th, and the regiment spent the rest of the day patrolling from its positions which ringed the airfield. On the 5th Marines' left, the 3d Battalion of the KMC was joined by 1/KMC in searching out the base of the Kumpo Peninsula. A new security force was added to the Division sector when the 17th ROK Regiment landed at Inchon and fanned out to comb the troublesome area between Ascom City and the sea.[33]

The General Situation Map gives the disposition of friendly and suspected enemy elements as of late afternoon on 18 September. This date is particularly important in that the Marine division, regimental, and battalion headquarters were swamped by a torrent of intelligence which indicated for the first time the future patterns of organized NKPA resistance.

Beginning on the left of the broad arc of the 1st Marine Division's front, repeated reports told of enemy concentrations north and south of the Han River in the area of the Kumpo Peninsula.[34] Upwards of 1,000 troops were sighted by natives and air observers, and it was believed that the North Koreans were organizing for an attempt against Kimpo. A strike by four Navy Skyraiders caught part of the Red force exposed on both banks of the Han northeast of the airfield. After killing an estimated 50 of the enemy and dispersing the remainder, the Navy pilots reported the area "still active."

Marine Air in turn warned of a build-up of Communist troops and equipment in the vicinity of Haengju and Hill 125, directly across the Han from 2/5's position north of Kimpo. East of the airfield, the enemy was withdrawing from the 5th Marines' zone toward Yong-

---

[32] 1st MarDiv *SAR*, Annex Queen Queen.

[33] *Ibid.*; and 1st MarDiv *Chief of Staff* (C/S) *Journal*, 15–20 Sep 50.

[34] The following narrative, unless otherwise noted, is derived from: 1st MarDiv *C/S Journal*, 15–20 Sep 50; 1st MarDiv *SAR*, Annex Queen Queen; and 1st Marines *PIR No. 3*.

Hail to the Chief—General Smith welcomes General MacArthur ashore, on D-plus 2, for his first trip of inspection (U. S. Army Photo). B1

Drive to Kimpo—Above, Marines pass burning enemy tank with bodies of NKPA soldiers on top; and, below, enemy transport knocked out by Marine planes (Marine Corps Photos).

Advance to Yongdungpo—Above, an enemy ammunition dump goes up in smoke (U. S. Army Photo); and, below, RCT–1 Marines march prisoners back through a rice paddy (Marine Corps Photo).

B3

Kimpo Airfield Secured—Above, correspondents examine captured Yak fighter (U. S. Army Photo); and, below, First Lieutenant J. V. Hanes of VMF–214 shows Lieutenant Colonel Walter Lischeid the flak scars on his Corsair (U. S. Navy Photo). B4

Marine Aircraft—Above, Corsair fighter-bombers on Kimpo Airfield; and, below, the F7F Tigercat used as a night fighter and intruder.

B5

Crossing the Han—Above, Marine amtracs take Marines and KMCs across river, with Hill 125 on far shore; and, below, troops of 32d Infantry, USA, cross in Marine amtracs (U. S. Army Photos).

B6

Approach to Seoul—Above, the rugged terrain northwest of Seoul as seen by Marine from ridge on south bank of Han; and, below, Marine fire team fighting in this terrain (U. S. Navy Photos).

B7

Regimental Commanders—Above, Lieutenant Colonel Raymond L. Murray, commanding officer of RCT-5, in his CP; and, below, General Smith being greeted by Colonel Homer L. Litzenberg, commanding officer of RCT-7 (Marine Corps Photos). B8

Command Conferences—Above (left to right) Colonel Lewis B. Puller, commanding officer of RCT-1, General MacArthur and General Smith; and, below (left to right), Colonel Charles E. Beauchamp, commanding officer of 32d Infantry, General Barr, General Almond and General Craig (U. S. Army Photos). **B9**

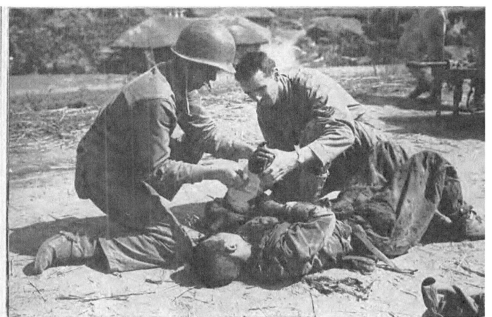

Battle Casualties—Above, Navy Hospitalmen R. E. Rosegoom and Frank J. Yasso give first aid to wounded NKPA prisoner; and, below, Marines carry wounded comrade back from firing line (U. S. Army Photos). B10

Northwest of Seoul—Above, the KMCs move up in amtracs; and, below, Korean refugees return to ruined homes on outskirts of Seoul (U. S. Army Photos).

The Fight for Seoul—Above, Marine tank and infantry close in on northwest approaches; and, below, Marines pass refugees in battered streets (U. S. Army Photos).

B12

Return of Refugees—Displaced residents of Seoul come back to find railway station (above) and Hotel Banta (below) scarred by artillery fire (U. S. Army Photos). B13

Ceremonies—Above, former Marine cemetery at Inchon is dedicated as United Nations Cemetery; and, below, President Syngman Rhee and General MacArthur at liberation ceremony in Seoul (U. S. Army Photos).   B14

Marine Artillery—Two views of 105mm howitzers of 11th Marines in Korea (Marine Corps Photos).

Marine Air Commanders—Above, Major General Field Harris, commanding the 1st Marine Aircraft Wing, holding a captured Russian burp gun; and, below, facing camera from left to right, General Harris and Brigadier General Thomas J. Cushman, commanding TAC X Corps.   B16

dungpo, using the Hill 118 area as an intermediate rallying point. Moreover, interrogation of two NKPA officers captured near Kimpo disclosed that a Communist regiment was already committed to the defense of Yongdungpo. Since this large industrial suburb of Seoul rambled across the 1st Marines' path to the Han, Colonel Puller knew well in advance that trouble lay ahead of his regiment.

Further evidence that storm clouds were gathering over the highway came from a number of sources in Sosa. Informants were almost unanimous in their predictions that the approaches to Yongdungpo would be sown liberally with land mines.

VMF–214, which provided effective close air support for the 1st Marines' attack through Sosa, reported destroying huge enemy stockpiles hidden in and around buildings on the sand spit between Yongdungpo and Seoul. The squadron also sighted six enemy tanks far beyond Marine lines and killed two of them with direct napalm hits. Its sister unit, VMF–323, likewise scoured the Division front and radioed similar findings to Tactical Air Control.

Other reports from scattered sources placed approximately 3,000 North Koreans in Seoul—with more on the way. Air spotters noted heavy traffic south from the 38th Parallel and north from the Suwon area. Tanks, troops, and vehicles from the latter not only were heading for the capital but also were veering off toward Yongdungpo and the Division right flank.

Thus, the Marines faced the possibility of major interference from: (1) the Kumpo Peninsula; (2) the Haengju locale on the north bank of the Han; (3) the area around Hill 118 between Kimpo Airfield and Yongdungpo; (4) Yongdungpo itself; (5) Seoul; and (6) the direction of the Division's right (southeastern) flank. Strangely enough for an enemy who was at his best with the artful dodge, only the two flank threats failed to measure up to expectations.

The North Koreans gave a preview of the changing picture on the afternoon of 18 September when, at 1415, the first shells of a sustained mortar barrage crashed into 3/1's positions on Hill 123. During the next hour, 120mm eruptions traced accurate paths back and forth along the ridge, and 30 Marines were cut down by the whirring fragments. Moving through the explosions with near-miraculous immunity, the 3d Battalion's senior medical officer, Lieutenant Robert J. Fleischaker, (MC) USN, remained fully exposed to the barrage while administering

182

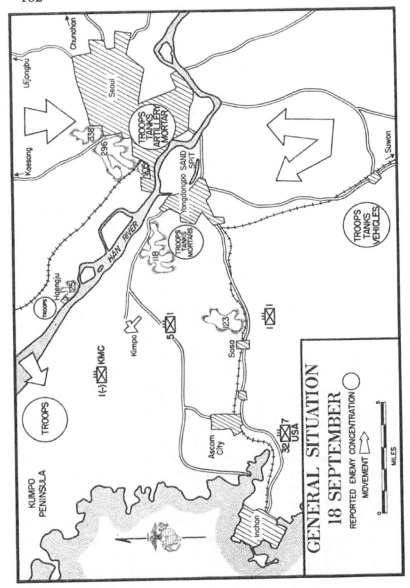

GENERAL SITUATION
18 SEPTEMBER

REPORTED ENEMY CONCENTRATION ◯
MOVEMENT ⟶

MILES
0   5

KUMPO
PENINSULA

TROOPS

HAN RIVER

Hoengju

I 25

troops

Kimpo

I(-) KMC

Ascom
City

32 7
USA

Sosa

5 I

I23

I II

IIB

TROOPS
TANKS
MORTARS

Yongdongpo SAND
SPIT

TROOPS
TANKS
VEHICLES

Seoul

TROOPS
TANKS
ARTILLERY
MORTAR

KG

296

338

Uijongbu

Koesong

Chunchon

Suwon

Inchon

to the wounded. "He never thought of his own safety when men needed his services," commented Lieutenant Colonel Ridge.[35]

South of the highway, enemy gunners ranged in on 2/1's lines at 1800, adding 14 more Marines to the casualty rolls. Lieutenant Colonel Sutter and his S-3, Captain Gildo S. Codispoti, narrowly escaped injury when two mortar rounds hit the battalion CP. The explosions wounded Captain Albert L. Williams, commander of Company E, and Warrant Officer Bartley D. Kent, the battalion supply officer.[36]

Orders for Crossing the Han

Late in the afternoon of the 18th, both Corps and Division issued orders within a period of two hours for crossing the Han. In OpnO 6-50, the Commanding General of the 1st Marine Division directed RCT-5 to seize crossing sites along the south bank the next day and be prepared to cross on order while RCT-1 continued its attack along the highway toward Yongdungpo.

Much more territory was taken in by X Corps Operational Instructions No. 1, which ordered the 1st Marine Division to reconnoiter the river on the 19th and cross the next day. Then, after enveloping enemy positions on the north bank in the vicinity of Seoul, the Marines were to seize and secure both the city and the high ground to the north.

Since the Corps did not concern itself much with ways and means, General Smith asked for a conference at 0930 the next morning with General Almond. He informed the X Corps commander that he and his staff had already given considerable thought to the question of a crossing site. A preliminary Marine study had disclosed that three abandoned ferry crossings met military requirements: one downstream from Kimpo Airfield; one at Yongdungpo in the zone of the 1st Marines; and one opposite Kimpo near the village of Haengju. The first was too far from Seoul, and the second too near; but the Haengju site seemed to satisfy all conditions, subject to General Craig's verification by helicopter reconnaissance.[37]

Next to be discussed was the problem of bridging material. The X Corps engineer officer, Lieutenant Colonel Edward L. Rowny, reported

---

[35] Myers interv, 1 Feb 55; Ridge memo, 13 May 55.
[36] Cunliffe interv, 24 Aug 54.
[37] O. P. Smith, *Notes*, 218–219.

that Corps had no material other than that brought by the 1st Engineer Battalion of the Marines.   Fortunately, that unit's commanding officer, Lieutenant Colonel Partridge, was prepared to meet the emergency. Although he did not have enough floating bridge material to span such a wide stream, he reported to General Smith that he could have one 50-ton raft in operation to support the assault of troops crossing in LVTs, and another shortly afterwards.   These rafts would take the tanks and vehicles across, and Partridge added that later his engineers might be able to put together an actual bridge by combining floating and Bailey components.[38]

   The two Marine regiments had been in effect the infantry of X Corps up to this time.   But Almond promised the Marine general that the 32d Infantry of the 7th Infantry Division would be moved up on the right flank of RCT–1.   This Army unit, it may be recalled, had made an administrative landing at Inchon on the 18th and gone into an assembly area under 1st Marine Division control.   The other two regiments of the 7th Division were the 31st Infantry, due to arrive on the 20th, and the 17th Infantry, still attached to the Eighth Army.

   The X Corps commander lost no time at ordering the 32d to move up on the right, after reverting to the control of the 7th Division, to relieve the 1st Battalion, 1st Marines.   This was the first of a series of maneuvers carried out on the 19th in preparation for the river crossing. On the left, the 2d Battalion of the KMCs advanced against negligible opposition to occupy the high ground south of the Han and provide flank protection for the crossing.

   A more intricate maneuver was carried out when 1st Battalion of the 5th Marines was relieved west of Yongdungpo by its opposite of RCT–1, which had sideslipped to the left after the 32d Infantry moved up in protection of the regiment's right flank.   This shift was not accomplished without some fighting, the account of which belongs in a forthcoming chapter dealing with the battle for Yongdungpo.

   Another preliminary step was taken on the 19th when the 1st Amphibian Tractor Battalion was relieved of its mission of supporting the 1st Marines.   All LVTs were withdrawn as the unit displaced by motor march to the vicinity of Kimpo Airfield, a distance of about 18 miles.[39]

---

[38] LtCol J. H. Partridge interv, 23 Nov 54.
[39] 1st MarDiv *SAR*, Annex Tare Tare.

The 1st Shore Party Battalion was also concerned in planning for the river crossing. On the 19th this unit reverted to Division control and displaced to the vicinity of Oeoso-ri. Meanwhile, a reconnaissance detail reported to the CP of the 5th Marines with a mission of selecting DUKW, LVT, and ferry sites. The shore party battalion was also to have the responsibility of establishing evacuation stations and supply dumps on both banks after the crossing while exerting LVT and DUKW traffic control.[40]

Except for the 1st Battalion, the 5th Marines had no trouble on the 19th while advancing to its assigned positions on the south bank of the Han. All objectives were occupied against little or no opposition, placing the regiment in position for the crossing.

---

[40] 1st MarDiv *SAR*, Annex Mike Mike.

CHAPTER X

Crossing the Han

Swimming Team Leads the Way—Marine LVTs Grounded in Mud—Daylight Assault Crossing by 3/5—Departure of General MacArthur—Supporting Arms of Bridgehead—Command Ashore Assumed by X Corps

THE CP OF the 5th Marines had a holiday atmosphere during the afternoon of 19 September. An already large group of newspaper and magazine correspondents had been reinforced by new arrivals flown in from Tokyo to report the crossing of the Han. The gathering might have been mistaken for a journalistic convention, and Lieutenant Colonel Murray and his regimental planners could scarcely make themselves heard. Finally it became necessary to request the gentlemen of the press to leave, so that the battalion and company commanders could be summoned for briefing and orders.

The CP was located in a basement room of the Kimpo Airfield administration building. Coleman lanterns lighted the scene as Murray gave a brief talk to his officers, seated about him on boxes and bedrolls. There had been little time for planning, said the regimental commander, but he was confident of success. General Craig, who made a helicopter reconnaissance of the river and roads leading to Seoul, had recommended the old ferry crossing to Haengju. The river was about 400 yards wide at this site, which was about a mile from the Kaesong-Seoul railroad and main highway to Seoul. Hill 125, as the principal terrain feature, was an isolated knob rising nearly 500 feet and located on the right of the landing point. To the left was the village of Haengju, bordered by dikes and rice paddies.

Regimental planning, said Murray, had been conducted in compliance with 1st MarDiv OpnO 7-50, issued at 1430 that afternoon. The 5th Marines was directed to cross the Han in the vicinity of Haengju seize Hill 125 and advance southeast along the railroad to the high ground dominating the Seoul highway. The units attached for the operation were the 2d Battalion, KMC Regiment, the Division Reconnaissance Company, Company A of the 1st Tank Battalion, and Company A of the 56th Amphibian Tractor Battalion, USA. In addition, the 11th Marines had been directed to give priority in artillery fires to the 5th Marines, while the 1st Engineer Battalion, 1st Shore Party Battalion and 1st Amphibian Tractor Battalion were in direct support.

Swimming Team Leads the Way

Major William C. Esterline, the S–2 of the 5th Marines admitted that intelligence as to conditions on the north bank left much to be desired. He mentioned the reports of an enemy build-up on the other side of the river, and he added that a POW had told of enemy mining activities along the road to Haengju. But in spite of these warning notes, his listeners got the impression that 5th Marines' planning was based on assumptions of light resistance.

Major Charles H. Brush, Jr., the S–3, announced the hastily formulated regimental plan. Houghton's Recon Company was to lead the advance by sending a swimming team across shortly after nightfall. If the swimmers found the other bank clear of the enemy, they were to signal for the rest of the men to follow in LVTs. Recon Company then had the mission of seizing a bridgehead consisting roughly of the triangle formed by Hills 95, 125, and 51. After securing these objectives, about 1,500 yards apart, Recon was to defend until Taplett's 3d Battalion crossed at 0400, with Bohn's and McMullen's companies in assault and Wildman's in reserve. While they passed through Recon and attacked toward Seoul, Roise's 2d Battalion would follow in column two hours later, with Newton's 1st Battalion remaining in reserve and crossing on order as the KMC battalion protected the regiment's left flank. Tanks and vehicles would be ferried across on 50-ton floating bridge sections.[1]

No alternate plan was provided. After the briefing ended at 1700, Houghton and Lieutenant Colonel Lawrence C. Hays, Jr., executive officer of RCT–5, climbed a hill on the south bank and inspected the

---

[1] 1st MarDiv *SAR*, Annex Queen Queen, 19 Sep 50; Capt R. B. Crossman ltr to authors, 23 Nov 54.

189

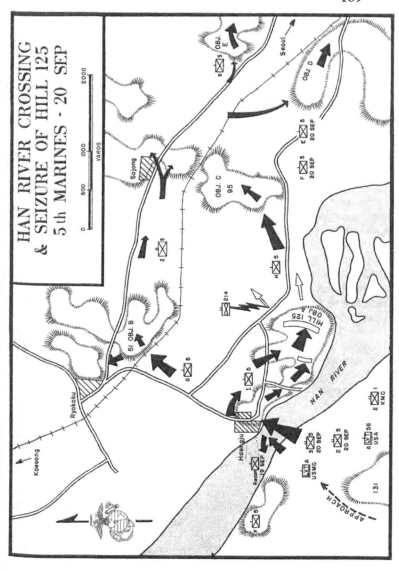

HAN RIVER CROSSING
& SEIZURE OF HILL 125
5th MARINES - 20 SEP

old ferry crossing and the opposite shore. They saw no enemy activity. Houghton was so optimistic that he asked permission to swim across at dusk but Murray denied the request.[2]

The swimming team consisted of Houghton, Second Lieutenant Dana M. Cashion, and ten enlisted men, accompanied by two Navy reserve officers, Lieutenant Horace Underwood and Ensign John Seigle. The first went along as interpreter, and the other as public information officer with a tape recorder. General Lowe had asked permission to cross in the LVTs; and when the Division commander refused, the 66-year old observer showed a card signed by President Truman, requesting that he be allowed to go anywhere. Even this passport did not swerve General Smith, who decided that Lowe must wait to accompany the reserve battalion.[3]

It was a dark and moonless night when the swimmers trudged through the muddy grain fields to the river bank, carrying two small rubber boats in which to tow the arms and equipment. After checking the current and making allowances for drift, they stripped to their skivvies and slipped into the tepid water shortly after 2000. Only two or three sets of rubber fins were available, but speed was not expected of men using a slow breast stroke to avoid making noise or ripples. These precautions became all the more necessary after a Marine shell or aerial bomb set fire to a native house on the far bank and the flames cast a lurid glow over the water. Apparently the swimmers had not been observed when they scrambled ashore, dripping, about 2040. They encountered two Koreans at the water's edge and overpowered them without much difficulty. Lieutenant Underwood questioned the captives in their native tongue and reported that they were escaping from Seoul.[4]

Houghton ordered Lieutenant Cashion and four enlisted men out on patrol duty with a mission of reconnoitering Hill 125 and the Haengju area. The Recon commander remained at the beach, where Gunnery Sergeant Ernest L. DeFazio and the other members of the swimming team guarded the prisoners and prowled the immediate area without encountering enemy. There were so few signs of NKPA activity that Houghton decided even before the return of Cashion's patrol to give the signal for the rest of the company to cross.

[2] Maj K. J. Houghton interv, 3 Aug 54.
[3] O. P. Smith, *Notes*, 227.
[4] 1stLt E. L. DeFazio ltr to authors, 11 Dec 54.

And it was when the LVTs revved up on the south bank, shattering the night's stillness, that hell broke loose.[5]

Marine LVTs Grounded in Mud

The men in the amtracs had the problem of advancing five miles by road from Kimpo to an embarkation site they had never seen, crossing a river in the darkness, and seizing three objectives on a basis of map reconnaissance. First Lieutenant Ralph B. Crossman, executive officer of Recon Company, had received oral orders without an overlay or an opportunity to take notes during the briefing at the Fifth Marines CP. His first message by SCR–300 from Houghton came about 2000, warning that the swimming team was taking to the water. This was the signal for the amtracs to start their road trip. They were on the way when Houghton prematurely radioed the familiar words:

"The Marines have landed and the situation is well in hand." [6]

An hour later the Recon commander came in again with a message that no enemy had been encountered. He directed his executive officer to cross in LVTs with the three platoons of Recon Company and the attached platoon of Company A, 1st Engineer Battalion, which had a mission of mining road blocks after the objectives were secured.

Crossman acknowledged this message but replied that he could not reach the river bank for nearly an hour. He had assigned the three objectives to his platoon commanders, directing that they take their orders from Houghton upon reaching the other bank. SCR–300 communications were frequently blurred, however, or blasted off the air altogether by the more powerful radios of the tractors. Thus the possibilities for confusion were multiplied as the nine amtracs proceeded in column to the embarkation point, clanking and revving up thunderously in preparation for the crossing.[7]

The din was deafening enough to arouse even an enemy who had not shown much fight so far in the zone of RCT–5. Hill 125 suddenly came to life as NKPA bullets whipped the water and mortar

[5] *Ibid.*; Houghton interv, 3 Aug 54.
[6] Houghton interv, 3 Aug 54; Crossman ltr, 23 Nov 54.
[7] Crossman ltr, 23 Nov 54.

shells exploded among the LVTs or along the beach occupied by Houghton's swimmers. Although Cashion's patrol reported no enemy encountered on Hill 125, his men came under fire from that quarter on their return to the beach. One of them, Private First Class Alphonse O. Ledet, Jr., was reported as missing in action, and it was assumed that Communists bullets had cut him down.[8]

The embarkation area was so cramped that Crossman had found it necessary to send the LVTs across the river in column, with First Lieutenant Francis R. Kraince's 1st Platoon in the lead, followed by Second Lieutenant Philip D. Shutler's 2d Platoon and the 3d commanded by Second Lieutenant Charles Puckett. Kraince was to seize Hill 125 while Shutler attacked Hill 51 and Puckett went up against Hill 95.

The three platoons were accompanied by a 4.2-inch mortar forward observer team, two 105mm FO teams from the 11th Marines, and a squad of engineers. Communications on the SCR-300 net were so badly jammed, however, that Houghton and Crossman were figuratively as well as literally in the dark on opposite sides of the river. Crossman's final messages from Kraince and Shutler reported that four of their amtracs had drifted from the course and grounded in the mud. He ordered both officers to extricate themselves while Puckett, who had not yet left the south bank, covered them with fire. Just then DeFazio radioed that Houghton and his team were planning to swim to the LVTs. This was the last word from the north bank received by Crossman, who lost all radio contact afterwards with anyone except the 5th Marines.[9]

At the height of the pandemonium on the north bank, the two Korean prisoners attempted to escape. Both were killed by Marines of the swimming team.[10]

Houghton's first thought had been to swim out and guide the LVTs to the north bank. But the enemy had shown such unexpected resistance as to justify the withdrawal of the swimming team. The rubber boats and excess equipment were hidden along the shore and some of the weapons thrown in the river to prevent capture.[11] Then

---

[8] Houghton interv, 3 Aug 54; DeFazio ltr, 11 Dec 54.

[9] Crossman ltr, 23 Nov 54.

[10] Houghton interv, 3 Aug 54; DeFazio ltr, 11 Dec 54.

[11] Ensign Seigle found it hard to part with his tape recorder containing an account of the venture. He hid it near the water, but the record had been erased by subsequent sounds when he retrieved it the next day.

the swimmers started their return trip through water churned by mortar shells, chiefly Marine 4.2-inch bursts falling short. One of these projectiles exploded so near to Houghton as to knock him out momentarily, and he was assisted to a grounded LVT by Corporal James Morgan. The Recon commander suffered a sprained back and double vision from the concussion, and two men of the team were slightly wounded. DeFazio led the remaining swimmers to the south bank.

There he learned that all the amtracs had returned except the four reported grounded. Most of the Recon troops on these stranded vehicles had chosen to swim or wade back to the south bank. These stragglers were collected on the northern tip of Hill 131 by Captain John F. Paul and Corporal James P. Harney of the amtracs and shuttled to Kimpo as fast as they returned.[12]

DeFazio took care of his casualties, then set out with eight men in search of Houghton. It was low tide by this time, but wading through the mud proved to be more tiring than swimming. After finding Houghton in a dazed condition on one of the grounded LVTs, the sergeant agreed with Kraince and Shutler that the approach of dawn made it necessary to abandon the two amtracs which were still stuck. They returned on the two that the officers had succeeded in extricating. Thus at daybreak the swimming expedition ended in the CP of the 5th Marines, with DeFazio reporting to Murray and Brush after seeing his commanding officer on the way to a field hospital.[13]

The crews and troops on the LVTs retained a confused impression of the night's events. Master Sergeant Edwin L. Knox, who crossed with the engineers in the second amtrac, could not understand why the column withdrew. The vehicles were dispersed in every direction after some became stuck, and it was on his LVT that Captain Houghton received first aid.[14]

It was not officially established who gave the order for the return of the LVTs when they neared the north bank, if indeed such an order was ever given. But all participants agreed that it was for the best. Events had proved that too much dependence was placed in assumptions of little or no resistance, despite G–2 warnings of an

---

[12] 1stLt J. P. Harney interv, 17 Nov 54.
[13] DeFazio ltr, 11 Dec 54.
[14] MSgt E. L. Knox, ltr to authors, 13 May 55.

enemy build-up in the Haengju area. And even if Recon Company had landed, the task of taking three hills in a night attack without previous reconnaissance would probably have been too much for a unit of 126 men against an enemy estimated by Houghton at a battalion.

Daylight Assault Crossing by 3/5

At dawn on the 20th the command and staff of the 5th Marines rebounded from this preliminary reverse with vigor and firmness. General Craig, the ADC, summed up the viewpoint of Murray and his officers when he commented:

"The eyes of the world were upon us. It would have looked bad for the Marines, of all people, to reach a river and not be able to cross." [15]

It was decided at 0430 that the 3d Battalion would make a daylight assault crossing just two hours later. The revised plan called for LVTs to cross at the Haengju site in waves of two to six vehicles. Troop units would be organized into boat teams, and the plan provided for a 15-minute artillery preparation by the 1st and 4th Battalions of the 11th Marines.[16]

Many of the Marine shells fell short, so that little benefit was derived from the barrage by the assault troops. On the other hand, enemy fire from Hill 125 was only too well placed. About 200 hits were taken by the first wave of amtracs from 14.5mm antitank projectiles and small caliber high explosive shells as well as machine-gun bullets. The armor plate prevented any infantry losses, and only four casualties were suffered by the crews.

Battalion objectives, according to the revised plan, were designated ABLE, BAKER, and CHARLIE—Hills 125, 51, and 95. Captain McMullen's Item Company landed at 0650 in the first wave, followed by How and George. While discharging troops, the LVTs were exposed to more machine-gun and antitank fire, resulting in several infantry casualties.[17]

---

[15] LtGen (Ret) E. A. Craig ltr to authors, 25 Aug 54.
[16] MarCorps Board *Study*, II–B, 27, 28.
[17] This section is based upon: McMullen interv, 27 Jul 54; Maj J. N. Irick interv, 16 Nov 54; 1st MarDiv *SAR*, Annexes Peter Peter and Queen Queen.

Item Company, it may be recalled, consisted of newcomers who had arrived at Pusan to make up third infantry companies just before the Brigade embarked for Inchon. Barring a few World War II men, these troops had known no combat experience before they hit GREEN Beach at Wolmi-do. They acquitted themselves like veterans in the Han crossing, however, as platoon leaders organized them under fire after they piled out of the amtracs.

The only covering fires at first were provided by the 50-caliber machine guns of First Lieutenant Stanley H. Carpenter's platoon of amtracs, which had taken the first wave across. Then four Corsairs of VMF–214 struck the enemy on Hill 125 while Captain Joseph N. Irick of the amtracs led four of his vehicles eastward to a position where they could direct 50 caliber fire on the NKPA positions.

Item Company's plan of attack called for a two-pronged assault on Hill 125 (Objective ABLE) from the northwest by First Lieutenant William F. Sparks' 3d Platoon on the right, attacking up the main spur paralleling the river, while First Lieutenant Elmer G. Peterson's 2d Platoon attacked on the left after riding a few hundred yards inland on LVTs. Second Lieutenant Roy E. Krieger's 1st Platoon was to remain on call in reserve.

Item Company had it hot and heavy from the beginning. The two assault platoons overcame such difficulties as bogged-down amtracs, intermingled units, and bullet-swept open areas before getting in position to return the Communist fire. The first phase ended on a plateau about halfway up the hill when enemy machine guns cut down most of the mortar section before the Marines could gain a foothold.

At this point is became necessary for the 3d Platoon to fall back and redeploy. Contact had been lost momentarily with Peterson's men; but after he appeared on the left, McMullen called up his reserve unit to pass through the 3d Platoon. Sparks having been wounded, First Lieutenant Wallace Williamson took command of his men, now reinforced by an engineer squad and troops from company headquarters. The revamped 3d Platoon was sent out to envelop the enemy left while Krieger hit the center and Peterson worked his way around the NKPA right.

This time the plateau was carried in a single rush. But casualties had reduced the company to the point where another reorganization was necessary before attacking the military crest. Although Captain

McMullen had been wounded, he remained in action to lead the final assault.

The 1st and 3d Platoons were clawing their way upward when Peterson radioed from the left that he could see enemy soldiers in flight from the peak to the low ground north of the hill mass. One of the VMF–214 Corsairs also reported Communists streaming down the eastern slopes with Marine planes in hot pursuit. Thanks to their efforts, not many Korean Reds were left on the crest when the panting Marines arrived to finish the job. More lucrative targets were presented by the foes racing down the eastern slopes. Marine rifles and BARs cut down many of these fugitives when they attempted to change into civilian clothes to avoid capture.

It was estimated that the enemy had 200 killed on Objective ABLE. The other two battalion objectives offered little or no resistance to troops who rode in column from the beaches on LVTs—How Company to seize Hill 95, and George Company attacking Hill 51. Thus at a total cost of 43 casualties—most of them in Item Company—the 3d Battalion had secured its three objectives by 0940.

Among the other results of the successful assault crossing was the salvaging of the two grounded LVTs, both of which had been in the enemy's field of fire. The equipment left on the north bank by the swimming team was also recovered, and PFC Ledet showed up unharmed. After being assigned to an observation post, he had inadvertently been left behind as missing in action when the Reds opened fire. But he kept his head throughout his lonely night's vigil and was able to give a good report of enemy numbers and activities.

At 1000 on the 20th the first wave of amtracs crossed the river with troops of 2/5. This battalion had orders to remain in the LVTs while passing through 3/5 and continuing the attack. The scheme of maneuver called for a sharp turn to the right at Hill 51, and the next objectives, DOG and EASY, consisted of the high ground on either side of the Kaesong-Seoul Railroad about three miles east of Haengju.

Company A of the 56th Amphibian Tractor Battalion, USA, was to follow with the 2d Battalion of the KMC regiment in DUKWs. These troops had a mission of providing security for the rear of the 5th Marines.

The 1st Battalion of that regiment was alerted to be ready to cross the Han at 1330 and move into an assembly area near Hill 95, prepared to continue the attack toward Seoul.

Once the plan has been told, it would be repetitive to describe a performance which put it into effect without incident. At 1400 the regimental CP displaced across the river to the vicinity of Sojong, about two miles northeast of the Haengju crossing site. Fifteen minutes later the 2d Battalion reported that it had secured Objectives DOG and EASY. Troops of that unit had ridden the LVTs as far as Sojong, where they encountered a swamp and a bridge too small for anything larger than a jeep. The infantry proceeded on foot while a few LVTs and a platoon of tanks crossed over a railroad bridge. About 30 prisoners, believed to be the remnants of enemy forces on Hill 125, were taken on Objective EASY. They were hiding in a cave and surrendered after a couple of warning rounds fired by a platoon of the Army amtrac troops supporting the battalion. Company D dug in on Objective EASY and Company E on Objective DOG while Company F covered the gap between.[18]

The 3d Battalion went into an assembly area a mile north of Hill 95. And after 1/5 moved a company to Hill 125 to secure the landing area for the night, the 1st Marine Division had a firm bridgehead on the north bank of the Han.

Departure of General MacArthur

General Shepherd and Admiral Struble witnessed the crossing from a vantage point on the south bank, where they had a good view of the fight for Hill 125.[19] Both accompanied General MacArthur that afternoon, when he made a final tour of the front before his departure for Tokyo.

The caravan of jeep-borne officers and reporters stopped first at the crossing area, then proceeded to the zone of the 1st Marines, where the battle for Yongdungpo was going on full blast. General MacArthur got out of his jeep and continued on foot along rice paddies where Marines were still flushing out snipers. This meant a period of anxiety for General Smith which lasted until the responsibility for the safety of the commander-in-chief passed to General Barr in the zone of the 7th Infantry Division.

[18] Roise memo to authors, 13 May 55.
[19] Col V. H. Krulak interv, 27 Jun 55.

On the afternoon of the 21st the Marine general saw MacArthur off at Kimpo on his plane for Tokyo. Never had the old warrior worn his famous "scrambled egg" cap with more verve. Barely a week had gone by since the Marines scrambled ashore on RED and BLUE Beaches, yet most of the major objectives had already been taken— Inchon, Kimpo, Yongdungpo, the north bank of the Han, and the approaches to Seoul. In the Pusan Perimeter meanwhile, the Eighth Army had been hitting the enemy hard in its joint offensive.

This was the score on D-plus 7. But perhaps the famous septuagenarian recalled with pardonable complacency that as late as D-minus 7, the Joint Chiefs of Staff had reiterated doubts of the Inchon landing which they had expressed on several previous occasions. MacArthur was warned that if the operation failed, the entire United Nations cause in Korea might be plunged into serious difficulties. The commander in chief replied with superb assurance, "I and all of my commanders and staff officers, without exception, are enthusiastic and confident of the success of the enveloping operation." [20]

Such confidence could not be withstood. But it was not until 8 September 1950 that the Joint Chiefs of Staff finally acquiesced in an operation they had never entirely approved—an operation scheduled to take place in just one week.

It may be that Douglas MacArthur was recalling this exchange of views as he stood in the sunlight of Kimpo Airfield, his eyes flashing and his chin outthrust. There is no tonic like victory, and he looked 20 years younger than his actual years as he decorated General Smith with a Silver Star just before the plane took off.

"To the gallant commander of a gallant division!" said the commander in chief by way of citation.

Supporting Arms of Bridgehead

Even success did not alter the conviction of Navy and Marine amphibious specialists that risks had been assumed in the Inchon landing which might have resulted in disaster. It was taking no credit away from General MacArthur for his unshakeable faith in victory to con-

---

[20] CinCFE radio to JCS, 8 Sep 50, quoted in OCMH (Schnabel), *Korean Conflict* (MS), v. I, ch. I.

clude that fortune had smiled in some instances when a frown would have been costly.

The teamwork of Marine supporting arms was never shown to better effect than in the establishment of a bridgehead over the Han. Lieutenant Colonel Partridge's engineers, of course, were on the job from the beginning. It was up to them to get the tanks across the river as soon as possible, in case the infantry needed the support of armor. Approaches and ferry landings had to be constructed for this purpose; and just six hours after the initial infantry crossing, the engineers had their first six-float M4A2 raft in operation. It had taken them four hours to build.[21]

The 2d Platoon of Able Company, 1st Tank Battalion, crossed the river at 1410 on 20 September and moved up in support of 3/5. The 1st Platoon followed at 1600 and the 3d Platoon late that afternoon, after the engineers completed a second raft.

When the KMCs attempted to cross in DUKWs, the clumsy vehicles bogged down several yards from the river on the south bank. Partridge suggested to the KMC commander that his troops build a makeshift corduroy approach off the main route which Marine engineers were constructing to the embarkation point. The Korean officer agreed with Partridge that this was a sensible solution and soon had his men gathering logs.

Neither of them dreamed that they had stirred up an international incident which called for a decision on the division level. American policy makers had felt it necessary to lean backwards to avoid giving Communist propagandists any excuse to charge us with recruiting Koreans for "slave labor." It was an extremely sensitive subject, and Partridge was astonished at the repercussions. At last General Craig visited the ferry site and ruled that it was a closed incident after finding all explanations satisfactory. It was further decided—for mechanical rather than political reasons—to take the KMCs across in amtracs rather than waste any more time on DUKWs.[22]

On the night of the 20th, Partridge and Colonel McAlister, the Division G–4, interviewed a captured NKPA engineer major at Kimpo Airfield. The prisoner informed them that the bombed highway bridge between Yongdungpo and Seoul had been damaged beyond repair with the means at hand. This agreed with the conclusions of

---

[21] 1st MarDiv *SAR*, Annex Nan Nan; Partridge interv, 23 Nov 54.
[22] Partridge interv, 23 Nov 54.

the Marine officers on the basis of aerial observation. Prospects for a span over the Han seemed dim as Partridge was leaving McAlister's quarters. That very evening, however, Lieutenant Colonel Rowny, chief of the X Corps engineers, telephoned to announce that materials for a floating bridge unit had been accumulated by the Army in Japan and would be flown to Korea shortly. Up to this time, with rafts the only solution, the Marine engineers had supplied all the materials. But Rowny announced that Corps would assume the responsibility after the arrival of enough materials for a floating bridge unit.[23]

Military operations could not wait a week or ten days for the new span, and the Marine ferry plus amtracs and DUKWs[24] had to nourish the assault on Seoul. With this end in view, the 1st Shore Party Battalion reverted to Division control on the 19th and displaced from Inchon to Oeoso-ri. By nightfall the entire battalion was bivouacked in this area.

On the 20th, after establishing a forward CP at Kimpo Airfield, the shore party troops of Baker Company moved up to the Han in support of the 5th Marines, followed by two teams from Able Company. Evacuation stations and supply dumps were set up on both banks. Other shore party missions were maintaining LVT and DUKW traffic control, providing guides for the amtracs, posting security at the crossing sites on both banks, and effecting unit distribution of supplies upon request by the DUKWs and LVTs.

Control of the ferry site, known as BAKER Ferry, became the responsibility of Baker Company of the 1st Shore Party Battalion. Teams 1 and 2 were employed on the south bank, and Team 3 plus headquarters troops on the other shore. Traffic control was of the utmost importance, since ferry operation had to be limited to periods of low tide, and during idle intervals a long line of vehicles accumulated. Most of them were trucks containing cargo to be reloaded in LVTs and taken across the river. The shore party men had the duty of keeping the traffic flowing as smoothly as possible, both on land and water, and special regulations were enforced to prevent the LVTs from colliding with the ferries. With the establishment of a third ferry, the problem of supplying the troops across the river was pretty well solved.[25]

[23] *Ibid.*
[24] MajGen E. W. Snedeker ltr to authors, 29 Apr 55.
[25] 1st Mar Div *SAR*, Annex Mike Mike.

Command Ashore Assumed by X Corps

A military ceremony was held on 21 September when the commanding general of X Corps established his CP in Inchon and assumed command at 1700 of all forces ashore. It was stated in some reports that command had been transferred from the commander of JTF–7 to the commander of X Corps. But officers familiar with amphibious doctrine pointed out that at no time prior to landing did CG X Corps relinquish command; and only through him did the commander of JTF–7 exercise command.[26]

The date was also significant for the 1st Marine Division in that its third rifle regiment, the 7th Marines, landed at Inchon with Major Francis F. Parry's 3d Battalion of the 11th Marines attached. Before the ships reached the inner harbor, Colonel Litzenberg went ashore and reported at the Division CP. Informing General Smith that troop units in the convoy had been vertically loaded for maximum flexibility, he asked what troops the Division commander desired to have unloaded first.

"An infantry battalion," said General Smith.

"And what next?"

"Another infantry battalion," said the commanding general.

Colonel Litzenberg began unloading at once, and by 2200 his CP had opened at Wonjong-ni, two miles south of Kimpo Airfield, while H&S Company and the 3d Battalion (Major Maurice E. Roach) occupied near-by assembly areas. The 2d Battalion (Lieutenant Colonel Thornton M. Hinkle) had reached an assembly area at Hill 131, a mile north of Kimpo, by 0100 on 22 September with a mission of providing security for the airfield and a river crossing site. The 1st Battalion (Lieutenant Colonel Raymond G. Davis) was given the duty of unloading the ships of the convoy.[27]

It appeared for a few hours on 21 September that the enemy might be planning to retake Kimpo Airfield. At 0730 a report came to the 3d Battalion, KMC Regiment, warning of an attempted NKPA crossing of the Han in the area about seven miles northwest of the field. Air strikes were called immediately with the result of dispersing the enemy. At 1310, however, an estimated two NKPA battalions were reported in front of KMC positions by the air liaison officer attached

[26] MarCorps Board *Study*, II–B, 32.
[27] MajGen H. L. Litzenberg memo to authors, 11 May 55.

to the battalion.   All units in the Kimpo area were alerted to the possibility of attack.   The CO of the 1st Shore Party Battalion was designated as coordinator of defensive forces consisting of his unit, and elements of the 1st Engineer Battalion, 1st Tank Battalion, 1st Ordnance Battalion, and 1st Amphibian Tractor Battalion.   Army troops of the 56th Amphibian Tractor Battalion were also ordered to Kimpo.

With an NKPA attack threatening, some concern was felt about an enemy Yak type aircraft—fueled, armed, and ready for flight—which had been discovered in a revetment on the edge of the airfield by First Lieutenant Edward E. Collins of the Ordnance Battalion and later of the 5th Marines.   The plane was hastily disarmed and painted with U. S. markings, so that it could be flown to Japan in case the enemy overran Kimpo.[28]

Although the NKPA threat did not materialize, there could be no doubt of an enemy build-up within striking distance.   And it was on this sensitive left flank that the support of naval gunfire was most effective.

As early as 19 September the 1st and 5th Marines had advanced beyond the range of the light cruisers and destroyers.   The battleship *Missouri* was made available the next day, but targets in Seoul proved to be too distant for her maximum range, and no further efforts were made to call upon the battleship's 16-inch rifles.   In the Kimpo area, however, naval gunfire was at its best, and a total of 535 8-inch shells were fired from 21 to 24 September by the *Toledo* and *Rochester*. These fires were requested by Lieutenant Wayerski in support of patrol actions by the 3d KMC Battalion.   One of the KMC attacks wiped out a company-size pocket of Red Korean resistance in the vicinity of Chongdong—about three miles northwest of the airfield on the south bank of the Han—with a loss to the enemy of 40 counted dead and some 150 prisoners.[29]

After the Han crossing, the 1st Marine Division found itself in the position of advancing astride an unbridged tidal river with the northern flank wide open.   Generals Smith and Craig depended on VMO–6 helicopters for their visits to the 5th Marines front.   Those rotary-winged aircraft were in increasing demand for evacuating serious casualties; and the commanding general directed that such missions

---

[28] Capt E. E. Collins ltr to authors, 6 May 55.
[29] Capt J. R. Wayerski, interv, of 28 Sep 54.

be given priority over command and liaison flights. This meant that Smith and Craig were occasionally "bumped." In such instances they crossed the river by LVT or waited until their helicopter could return.

At the time of the Han crossing, the general plan of the 1st Marine Division had been for RCT-5 to clear the north bank and open up crossing sites for RCT-1 in the Yongdungpo area. That regiment would then cross to seize South Mountain, just north of the crossing site, thus forming an enclave in Seoul proper. Further objectives were to be seized by RCT-1 to the north and east while the KMC Regiment passed through RCT-5 to attack the center of the city. Here a political motive entered the picture, since it was desired to have Koreans take a prominent part in the liberation of the former ROK capital. To the north, on the left flank of the Division, it was planned for RCT-7 to seize objectives to protect the flank and cut off the escape of the enemy. Meanwhile, RCT-5 would revert to Division reserve as soon as the tactical situation made it possible.

So much for the plan. Before it could be put into execution, stiffening NKPA resistance made it necessary to consider revisions.[36] Not only was the hilly terrain northwest of Seoul well suited to defensive operations, but it had been a training area as far back as the Japanese overlordship, with fields of fire accurately charted. Moreover, it had become evident by the 21st that the enemy was about to exchange a strategy of delaying operations for one of defending to the last ditch. The 1st Marines had already experienced the new NKPA spirit at Yongdungpo, and on the 21st the 5th Marines contented itself with limited advances for the purpose of seizing high ground from which to launch the assault on Seoul.

The attack on the 21st was launched astride the railroad by the 3d Battalion to the north and the 1st Battalion between the railroad and the river. After passing through the 2d Battalion, Taplett's men seized three hills and by dusk were digging in on Hill 216, about six miles east of Hill 125 and the ferry landing site.

The 1st Battalion had meanwhile advanced to Hill 96, about 3,000 yards southeast of yesterday's Objective DOG, now occupied by the 2d Battalion in reserve. Further gains of some 2,500 yards to the southeast took the battalion to Hill 68, between the railroad and river, which was seized and held for the night.

---

[36] O. P. Smith, *Notes*, 253–255.

Enemy resistance ranged from light to moderate in both battalion zones. Between them, the 1st Battalion of the KMCs moved up to Hill 104, just north of the railroad and south of Sachon Creek.[31]

This was the situation across the river at nightfall on the 21st. The 5th Marines was in position to grapple with the enemy for possession of Seoul. Hill 104, in the center of the 5th Marines front, was only 5,000 yards west of the Government Palace in the northwest section of the city. Less than three miles, yet officers and men alike realized that they would have to fight for every inch of the way. If anyone had any doubts, he had only to watch the flashes of gunfire stabbing the night sky to the southeast, and he had only to listen to the unremitting roar of gunfire. For at Yongdungpo the 1st Marines had been slugging it out with the enemy for the last three days in a battle for the rambling industrial suburb.

---

[31] 1st MarDiv, *SAR*, Annex Queen Queen; O. P. Smith, *Notes*, 255–256.

CHAPTER XI

The Fight for Yongdungpo

*Three Hills Taken by 1/5—Enemy Minefields Encountered—
NKPA Counterattacks of 20 September—Recapture of Hills
80 and 85—1st Marines in Position—Assault of Yongdungpo—
Able Company on a Limb—Yongdungpo Secured*

"I F YONGDUNGPO is lost, Seoul also will fall." This was the warning
note sounded during the conferences of the Red Korean military
leaders in Seoul. So important did they consider the industrial suburb
that a regiment of the 18th NKPA Division was assigned to the
defense of the built-up area on the south bank of the Han.[1]

Slogans of this sort were a favorite form of Communist inspirational
literature, and they may have served to buck up the defenders. From
the tactical standpoint, however, the quoted catch phrase was illogi-
cal. Yongdungpo was untenable. Squatting on the low ground at
the confluence of the Kalchon and Han Rivers, the town was an
isolated landmark of only symbolic significance. It was separated
from Seoul by two miles of sand and water, and the only connecting
links, the old railroad and highway bridges, had long since been
destroyed. Thus, what had once been a vital communications hub
south of the Han was now a veritable dead end.

While the Reds in Seoul were able to ferry troops and materiel
across the exposed river and sand spit by night, they could not hope
by this primitive method to meet the logistical requirements of a
regimental garrison confronted by a modern juggernaut of combined
arms. Nevertheless, the North Koreans chose to make a fight of it,
and in addition to the hundreds of troops in Yongdungpo, they sent
over considerable artillery and armor that could have been put to
better use in the defensible terrain around Seoul.

---

[1] 1st MarDiv C/S Journal, 15-20 Sep 50.

Three Hills Taken by 1/5

Hill 118 was the principal terrain feature between Kimpo Airfield and Yongdungpo, the dominating peak being about three miles from the former and two from the latter. Giant spurs from the main ridge extended northward toward the Han and eastward to the bed of the Kalchon, beyond which lay Yongdungpo. At the end of one easterly projection were the twin caps, Hills 80 and 85. Paralleling the Han River, a modern highway led from Kimpo, passed north of Hill 118, skirted 80 and 85, then bridged the Kalchon to enter Yongdungpo from the northwest.

It will be recalled that the 1st Battalion, 5th Marines, occupied high ground generally east of Kimpo Airfield at the close of 18 September. During the night, Lieutenant Colonel Murray ordered the unit to seize Hills 80 and 85 the next day. To gain these gates to Yongdungpo, it would be necessary to take Hill 118; and the battalion commander, Lieutenant Colonel Newton, formulated his plan accordingly.[2] Company B would leave its positions on old Objective EASY at dawn and envelop Hill 118 from the south. Company C would attack frontally from Objective FOX, assist the enveloping force by taking one of 118's spurs, then continue eastward to seize 80 and 85. Company A was to remain behind an Objective EASY for the purpose of guarding the approaches to the airfield.

At dawn of 19 September, Company C atop Objective FOX was greeted by a hail of mortar and small-arms fire. Under this shield part of a 500-man enemy force attacked the Marine position from the east, while the remainder attempted to move along the Yongdungpo-Kimpo Highway, obviously bent on reaching the airfield. Other large NKPA concentrations were spotted at the base of Hill 118.

Charlie Company's organic weapons roared into action along with the battalion 81s. While the Marine fire cut swaths through the exposed enemy ranks, Baker Company lunged forward to envelop Hill 118 according to plan. Air and artillery paved the way so effectively that Captain Fenton's unit gained the commanding peak about 1100 without suffering a casualty. This left the North Korean attackers, who had been contained by Charlie Company, trapped between Objective Fox and Hill 118. After losses of 300 dead and 100 prisoners,

---

[2] Unless otherwise noted, the story of 1/5's fight is derived from 1st MarDiv *SAR*, Annex Queen Queen.

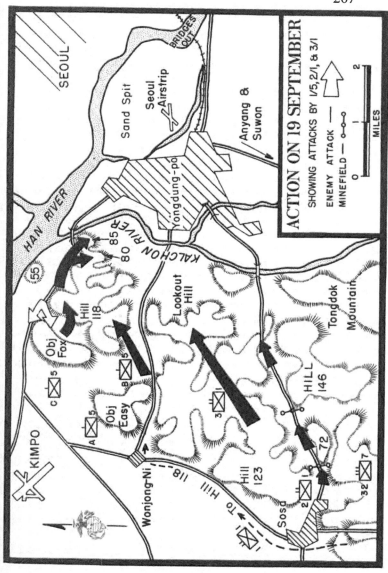

SEOUL

Sand Spit

Seoul
Airstrip

BRIDGES
OUT

HAN RIVER

Yongdung-po

Anyang &
Suwon

KALCHON RIVER

55

80

85

Hill
118

Obj
Fox

Lookout
Hill

Tongdok
Mountain

KIMPO

C☒5

A☒5

Obj
Easy

2/5

3/1

HILL
146

HILL
72

Wonjong-Ni

Hill
811

To Hill
811

Hill
123

Soso

3/2

32/7

ACTION ON 19 SEPTEMBER

SHOWING ATTACKS BY I/5, 2/1, & 3/1

ENEMY ATTACK —

MINEFIELD — o-o-o

0   1   2

MILES

the Red Force broke into a few small bands that fled across the high-way to the fields and villages bordering the Han. Company C's casualties in stopping the attack and moving forward to its spur on Hill 118 were two killed and six wounded.[3]

As the two assault companies reorganized on the newly won ridge, Fenton spotted a large number of Red troops on Hill 80, now about 1,000 yards away. He directed an air strike from his advance position, and the Corsairs not only cut down many of the North Koreans but completely routed the survivors. While the planes worked over the enemy positions on the high ground, the Marines of Company B observed a growing throng of NKPA soldiers in the vicinity of the Kalchon Bridge leading to Yongdungpo. Some of the Reds were milling around, but others were filing across the undamaged span and disappearing into a knot of warehouses and huts at the far end. Fenton radioed for artillery fire just as Communist machine guns and an AT weapon opened up on Baker Company from positions across the bridge. Four times firing for effect with "battery four rounds," the Marine howitzers sent a total of 96 shells crashing into the enemy positions within the space of a few minutes. The explosions neutralized the bridge area, but the span itself was badly damaged in the process.[4]

First Lieutenant Pedersen led Company C along the highway toward Hills 80 and 85 at 1430. Owing to the press of time, the area between the road and the Han River was not cleared, with the result that small bands of enemy were left free to roam the fields and make their presence felt later. The 3d Platoon, under Second Lieutenant Harold L. Dawe, Jr., peeled off the column and attacked Hill 80 shortly after 1500. Following at an interval of 500 yards, Second Lieutenant Robert H. Corbet's 1st Platoon continued along the pavement toward Hill 85. A platoon of A/Tanks supported the two-pronged assault along with Charlie Company's mortars and machine guns, and by 1650 the two heights were secured. In the wake of the air strike called down by Fenton, the attacking infantry had encountered practically no opposition.

Yongdungpo, bristling with Communist armament, rumbled its challenge from the low ground 500 yards east of Hill 85. Taken

---

[3] *Ibid.;* and Capt. P. F. Pedersen memo to authors, 30 May 55.
[4] Maj F. I. Fenton, Jr., memo to authors, 1 Jun 55.

under heavy fire by artillery, mortars, and small arms, Company C was forced to dig in on the reverse slopes of its high ground, there to await the expected counterattack after nightfall.

Enemy Minefields Encountered

As noted previously, the 2d and 3d Battalions, 1st Marines, spent the night of 18–19 September astride the Inchon-Seoul Highway a mile east of Sosa. The 1st Battalion, deployed over a broad front in the hills south of the road, was to be relieved in the morning by the 32d Infantry, so that Colonel Puller could shift his regiment to the left. Since the relief did not take place as early as expected, Puller ordered his 2d and 3d Battalions to attack at 1030, leaving 1/1 in position to await replacement by the Army unit.[5]

On the left of the highway, 3/1 jumped off from Hill 123 with Companies H and I in the assault. The battalion's mission was to clear a rambling ridge complex that extended more than three miles before stopping short of Hill 118. Assigned as a final objective was the terminal height, Lookout Hill, facing western Yongdungpo across the wide bottomland of the Kalchon.[6]

Considering the formidable cross-compartment approach, the assault companies led by the battalion S–3, Major Joseph D. Trompeter, made good progress against enemy resistance described as "light but stubborn." At a cost of two killed and 15 wounded, the Marines combed the vertical wilderness and seized Lookout Hill late in the evening. The attack was almost too successful, for the battalion was now out on a limb. The closest friendly forces were on Hill 118, several hundred yards to the north, and along the Inchon-Seoul Highway, about a mile to the south, as will be shown.[7]

The 2d Battalion could boast comparable success along the highway in the course of 19 September, but gains were made under far different circumstances. Spearheaded by Charlie Company Tanks commanded by Captain Richard M. Taylor, the battalion had advanced only 500 yards in the morning when the lead M–26 was enveloped in a violent explosion. With one track and two road wheels destroyed, the steel

---

[5] 1st MarDiv *SAR*, Annex Peter Peter.
[6] *Ibid.;* and 1st MarDiv *C/S Journal, 15–20 Sep 50.*
[7] *Ibid.;* and Myers interv, 1 Feb 55.

monster settled into the crater left by the detonation of a wooden box mine.[8]

Simultaneously, the infantrymen of Company F came under heavy small-arms fire from Hill 72 to the right front. In an attempt to sight in on the enemy positions, other tanks tried to bypass the mine field in the highway, only to discover that explosives were concealed in both road shoulders as well. Howitzers of the 11th Marines registered on Hill 72, and during the ensuing bombardment a VMF–214 flight appeared overhead to lend further assistance.[9]

Despite his generous use of supporting arms, Lieutenant Colonel Sutter was forced to commit all three rifle companies to the fight. Tank gunners tried to detonate mines embedded in the road with machine-gun fire, but without success.[10] It remained for First Lieutenant George A. Babe's 2d Platoon, Charlie Company Engineers, to remove the obstacles under fire. Darting forward on the bullet-swept highway, the engineers placed "snowball" charges of C–3 on the wooden boxes, then took cover while the mines exploded.[11]

After 2/1 had driven the enemy from the area with the assistance of Marine air and artillery, the job of clearing the 250-yard mine field proceeded under less hair-raising conditions. To get the armor back into the fight as soon as possible, Babe ignored the explosives embedded in the highway shoulders. Word was passed back to this effect, but several jeeps and trucks were lost later when drivers failed to heed the warning.[12]

While the tanks remained on the sideline, Companies D and F punched about a mile down the highway against continuing resistance, which gradually solidified at Hill 146. Like 72, this ridge was on the right side of the road, in the 32d Infantry's zone of action. Since the Army unit had yet to enter the picture, the Marine flank was becoming more and more exposed with each forward bound by 2/1.[13]

Sutter had no choice but to commit troops beyond his zone. Not only were the Reds entrenched on Hill 146 with machine guns and field pieces, but they had blocked the highway with trees and other

[8] 1st MarDiv *SAR*, Annex Oboe Oboe.

[9] 2/1 *SAR;* 1st MAW *SAR*, Annex Jig; Easy; and Cunliffe interv, 24 Aug 54.

[10] Owing to the crude design, the top of the wooden box mine must protrude above the road for best effect. Although the Communists sometimes concealed the projections with debris, Marines usually had no difficulty in spotting them.

[11] Capt G. A. Babe—1stLt P. Paolino interv, 15 Nov 54.

[12] *Ibid.;* 1st MarDiv *SAR*, Annex Peter Peter.

[13] 2/1 *SAR*, and Sutter-Codispoti interv, 25 Jan 55

encumbrances. Thus, while Fox Company seized a knoll on the left, Dog Company invaded Army territory and battled its way to the top of Hill 146's western spur. VMF–214 plastered the peak itself, and the 11th Marines shelled enemy positions across the whole battalion front.[14]

It was 1300 when the mine field to the rear was finally cleared, enabling Charlie Company Tanks to move forward in an attempt to overtake Sutter's infantry. Within sight of the fighting around Hill 146, the armor ground to a halt before the roadblock of trees, rice bags, and other debris.[15] A dozer tank rumbled ahead, smashed through the first obstruction, then went up in a cloud of smoke. Under the litter on the road lay a second mine field, 75 yards long.[16]

Again the tank men watched from behind as engineers cleared the highway and 2/1 drove forward out of sight. By 1730, the Marine infantry had completely smashed the main enemy concentration on the highway. When the surviving Reds fled, they exhibited the same determination that had characterized their stand throughout the day. Weapons and equipment were strewn along the road, and the Marines captured a truck loaded with mines as further evidence of the hasty retreat.[17]

Sutter ordered 2/1 to hold up at 1900 and dig in astride the highway. The 4,800-yard advance had cost the Marine unit four killed and 18 wounded, against 350 casualties and five prisoners for the North Koreans. Since all written and personal accounts agree that 19 September amounted to almost one continuous fire fight for the 2d Battalion, the amazing contrast in friendly-enemy loss figures must be attributed to the sound employment of Marine supporting arms.[18]

As mentioned earlier, 2/1's positions for the night were a mile southeast of the 3d Battalion on Lookout Hill. Company E entrenched on high ground to the left of the highway—4,000 yards from Yongdungpo—while D and F manned a long, low hill on the right. Because the latter height ran parallel to the road, the line formed by Dog and Fox was at a right angle to that held by Easy. Sutter's choice of this L-shaped defense would shortly prove to be an extremely wise one.

[14] *Ibid.;* and Cunliffe interv, 24 Aug 54.
[15] Rice bags filled with dirt commonly were used by the NKPA for barriers in place of sandbags.
[16] 1st MarDiv *SAR,* Annex Oboe Oboe.
[17] *Ibid.;* and 2/1 *SAR.*
[18] 2/1 *SAR;* Sutter-Codispoti interv, 25 Jan 55; and Cunliffe interv, 24 Aug 54.

NKPA Counterattacks of 20 September

The right flank of the 1st Marines was bare. Not until 1200, 19 September, did the 32d Infantry begin relieving 1/1 in its old positions southeast of Sosa. Liaison between the Marine and Army units at this time was weak. Apparently many of the Marines were unaware that General Barr's OpnO No. 2,[19] for the 7th Infantry Division did not call for a jump-off by the 32d until 0630 on the 20th. At that time the Army regiment would attack a series of objectives which included Hill 146 and other high ground above the road.[20] Thus, the schedules north and south of the highway were running one day apart, and it would take the enemy himself to straighten the line when he slammed the gates of Yongdungpo.

Meanwhile, the 1st Battalion, 1st Marines, entrucked below Sosa for its circuitous journey from the right flank of the regiment to the left, where it was to relieve the 1st Battalion, 5th Marines, on Hills 118, 80, and 85. The 11-mile trip via Sosa and Wonjong-ni was uneventful, except that the troops had to dismount at the latter village and proceed on foot over the primitive road. With the first increment to arrive at Wonjong-ni, Captain Robert H. Barrow, commanding Company A of 1/1, set a rugged pace to get his troops on top of Hill 118 before dark. Relieving Company B of 1/5, he expected Charlie Company to pass through and replace its opposite of the 5th Marines on Hills 80 and 85.

It was dusk, and Companies B and C were still on the move when Hawkins of 1/1 met Newton of 1/5. They briefly discussed the lay of the land, the latter's tactical disposition, and the requirement that 1/5 assemble at Kimpo within a matter of hours to prepare for the river-crossing next day. Time, space, and terrain factors were too great, Hawkins concluded, for his battalion to assume all positions then occupied by the other. To facilitate the rest of the relief, which now would take place in darkness, he ordered Charlie Company to occupy Hill 118 with Able and directed Baker to dig in on a southern extension of the big ridge.[21]

---

[19] Issued at 2000, 19 September.
[20] 7th InfDiv (USA) *Opn Rpt*, in Inclusions to 7th InfDiv War Diary for Sep 50.
[21] 1st MarDiv *SAR*, Annex Peter Peter; Maj R. H. Barrow interv, 17 Aug 54; and LtCol J. Hawkins ltr to CMC, 21 May 55.

Having relieved Fenton on Hill 118 before nightfall, Barrow enjoyed the opportunity to reconnoiter 1/5's area and to realize the tactical significance of Hills 80 and 85. When it became apparent that Company C would not arrive before dark, he radioed the battalion S-3 for permission to move his company to the twin peaks immediately, explaining that Charlie Company of 1/5 could remain in position no later than 2100. Since Hawkins had already decided against taking over too much unfamiliar ground after daylight, Major Bridges turned down the request. Thus, at 2100, with no relief in sight, the 5th Marines' unit withdrew from the two heights as ordered. Company C of 1/1 reached Hill 118 at 2200 and went into position with Barrow's outfit for the night. Unknown to the enemy, Hills 80 and 85 had become a no-man's-land.[22]

While the battalions of the 1st Marines settled down for the night in a three-mile arc facing western Yongdungpo, the North Korean commander within the town organized part of his garrison for two separate thrusts against the closing vise. In one case he would win by default; in the other he would see more of his limited resources go down the drain.

Just before dawn of 20 September, the Marines on Hill 118 were alerted by a furious clatter of small arms and automatic weapons far out to the east. Daylight disclosed that the enemy was "assaulting" Hills 80 and 85. When the North Koreans finally discovered that their objectives were unoccupied, they abruptly ceased firing, surged over both crests, and entrenched in about company strength. An attempt was made to extend the counterattack to Hill 118, but Companies A and C, backed by a flight of VMF–323, threw the Reds back with ease.[23]

During the early morning blackness which found the enemy filling the vacuum on Hills 80 and 85, a stronger North Korean force—estimated at a battalion—marched out of Yongdungpo toward 2/1's positions astride the Inchon-Seoul Highway.[24] In the van of the Red column were five T-34 tanks preceded, oddly enough, by a truck loaded with ammunition. Other vehicles, laden with less sensitive supplies, were safely interspersed among the infantry in the long file.

---

[22] *Ibid.;* and Fenton ltr, 1 Jun 55.
[23] *Ibid.;* and Bates interv, 27 Aug 51.
[24] The account of this counterattack is taken from: 1st MarDiv *SAR,* Annex Peter Peter; 2/1 *SAR;* Sutter-Codispoti interv, 25 Jan 55; Cunliffe interv, 24 Aug 54; and CMH Citation for PFC W. C. Monegan, Jr.

It will be remembered that Companies D and F, the latter in the fore, occupied high ground positions parallel to and south of the highway. Farther back, Easy Company's line tied in at a right angle and extended to the north of the road. The troops of Fox Company, tense with anticipation in their advance deployment, heard the first distant sounds of clanking armor and racing engines sometime before 0400. The noise grew steadily louder until, at 0430, the shadows of the ammunition truck and T-34s passed beneath the Marine defenses and continued along the road toward Easy Company's lines. At the latter, Private Oliver O'Neil, Jr., rose from behind his machine gun and shouted a challenge to the truck, which by this time was well out in front of the enemy tanks. O'Neil was cut down by automatic fire in answer, and pandemonium broke out on the highway.

Obviously the North Koreans had stumbled into it again, just as they had done at Ascom City. Two T-34s stopped short of Easy Company's front and opened up wildly. Companies D and F in turn exploded with machine guns, small arms, grenades, and mortars against the flank of the enemy column, while E fought to deny further passage along the road. Under the hail of fire from above, the Red soldiers milled about in panic and were slaughtered. Some flung themselves into roadside ditches, where the crowding only increased the odds of destruction. Others sought escape by scrambling up the slopes—into the very muzzles of Dog and Fox Company weapons.

The T-34s began to lurch back and forth like trapped animals. Owing either to mines laid by Marine engineers or a grenade thrown from above, the ammunition truck exploded in a brillant spectacle of pyrotechnics. In the midst of the furor, Private First Class Monegan moved across the hillside from Company F's front with his rocket launcher. Observing his progress against the backdrop of flames from the truck, his comrades either held or shifted their fire to protect him.

Monegan closed on the lead tank and wrecked it with one 3.5-inch projectile. Approaching the second T-34 under intense fire, he paused and took aim with imperturbability. Again his rocket connected with a roar, and the black hulk on the road turned into a blazing furnace. Silhouetted against the hillside, the Marine leveled his weapon at a third armored vehicle just as it was pivoting around to retreat. But at this moment an enemy machine gun found the mark, and Monegan—killer of tanks—fell dead.

Although the North Korean attack was thus smashed at the outset, fighting along the highway continued until daylight. In addition to the two T-34s destroyed, another was captured intact with its crew. The 11th Marines closed the "back door" of the highway with a curtain of high explosive, thereby sealing the fate of the Red battalion.

Dawn of 20 September revealed a scene of utter ruin across the Marine front. The highway was littered with burnt NKPA trucks, tanks, and equipment. Heaped on the road, in ditches, and along hillsides were 300 enemy dead.[25]

Recapture of Hills 80 and 85

For the most part, fighting around Yongdungpo on 20 September was a contest of the giants. Supporting arms of both sides exchanged heavy blows, and the 1st Marines reported with business-like frankness that it was ". . . leveling the southern part of Yongdungpo, which is infested with enemy." North Korean mortars, tanks, and field pieces pumped hundreds of rounds out of positions in the center of town and the eastern outskirts. Marine planes and howitzers replied by smothering Red concentrations and emplacements with literally thousands of missiles of all types.

The 4th Battalion, 11th Marines, commanded by Major William McReynolds, fired 28 concentrations in the course of the day; and Lieutenant Colonel Merritt Adelman's 2d Battalion expended 1,656 rounds in 21 missions. It was the precision firing of these two units which had supported 2/1 so effectively during the pre-dawn counterattack.[26]

Battery C, 1st 4.5-inch Rocket Battalion, FMF, moved to advance positions in the morning to increase the pressure on the Yongdungpo garrison. Land counterpart of the LSMRs which rocked the Inchon waterfront on D-day, this unit had seen little action to date, owing to the lack of M48 fuses for its missiles. Banking on substitute detonating devices (M51 for 105mm and 155mm Howitzer shells), First Lieutenant Eugene A. Bushe ordered his gunners to fire a test salvo of 24 rockets. No visible effect being noticeable from his OP, the

---

[25] Marine losses were surprisingly small, although the exact number cannot be determined. In the whole course of 20 September, 2/1 sustained four KIA and 32 WIA, but these figures included losses during the Marine advance after the NKPA counterattack.

[26] 1st MarDiv *SAR*, Annex Sugar Sugar.

battery commander then called for a full ripple of 144—enough high explosive to flatten a good portion of the town.   Again the big missiles plowed into the target area with a dull thud, and Bushe withdrew his battery to the rear.   The M48 fuses did not arrive until 28 September, with the result that the potent Marine rocket artillery was sidelined until the closing days of the operation.[27]

Colonel Puller's tactics during the bombardment on 20 September were designed to align the 1st Marines for the actual assault of Yong-dungpo, planned for the next day.   It was necessary to occupy in strength all the final approaches to the town, so that the full weight of the regiment could be brought to bear against the defending garrison.   From left to right, therefore, the schedule of operations on the 20th was as follows: (1) 1st Battalion to seize Hills 80 and 85; (2) 3d Battalion to remain in position on Lookout Hill; and (3) 2d Battalion to advance to the first of two highway bridges which spanned branches of the Kalchon just outside of Yongdungpo.

These limited attacks would also provide time for the 32d Infantry to catch up on the right.   The day's mission for the Army unit was to attack over a six-mile front and secure, among other objectives, towering Tongdok Mountain south of the MSR and two miles from Yongdungpo.[28]

Shortly after first light, Lieutenant Colonel Hawkins reached the crest of Hill 118 and established his OP.   He was in time to see Able and Charlie Companies repulse disconnected Red elements moving on the Marine lines from Hills 80 and 85.   While the battalion commander issued his order for the attack, Major William L. Bates, Jr., commander of 1/1's Weapons Company, set up his "supporting arms center" to cover the impending assault.[29]

Hawkins gave Company C the mission of taking Hills 80 and 85.[30]   Deciding on a southerly approach, the company commander Captain Robert P. Wray ordered his 2d Platoon to lead off by clearing a village sprawled across the route to the lower peak.   Second Lieutenant John N. Guild moved out at the head of the skirmishers

[27] *Ibid.;* and Capt D. A. Rapp interv, 18 Nov 54, with comments by Capt E. A. Bushe.

[28] 1st MarDiv *SAR*, Annex Peter Peter; and 7th InfDiv *OpnO* 2.

[29] Though not provided for in Fleet Marine Force T/O, the "supporting arms center," a provisional facility for coordination modeled after the regimental SAC, was a favorite with many battalion commanders in the field.

[30] The following narrative is taken from: Bates interv, 27 Aug 51; Barrow interv, 17 Aug 54; and Captains F. B. Carlon and J. M. McGee interv, 9 Feb 55; Hawkins ltr 21 May 55; and Maj R. P. Wray ltr to CMC, 30 May 55.

and led them over 500 yards of intervening low ground. Nearing a knoll which topped the clump of thatched huts, the platoon came under heavy small-arms fire and was stalled.

Wray immediately committed the rest of his company in a two-pronged attack which wrapped around the flanks of Guild's line and smashed through the North Korean resistance. After a hot fire fight, the surviving Reds fled to Hill 80, and Company C occupied the village and knoll by early afternoon. The executive officer, First Lieutenant James M. McGee, led a six-man patrol eastward to clean out a small nest of holdouts, while Wray reorganized the company for the assault on the twin caps.

Charlie Company's tactics in advancing on the enemy's southern flank were ideal from the standpoint of Weapons and Able Companies, which supported the attack from Hill 118. The two units could actually witness the progress of the assault troops across the 1st Battalion's front, so that mortars and machine guns at the base of fire had only to shift gradually leftward to support the Marine advance.

Late in the afternoon, Wray launched a double envelopment of Hill 80. Second Lieutenant Henry A. Commiskey led his 3d Platoon around to the right, and Second Lieutenant William A. Craven's 1st swung through the low ground on the left. A few huts concealing snipers were demolished by 3.5-inch rockets, but otherwise the Marines met little resistance as they moved over the crest of the objective early in the evening. With the first signs of darkness already in the sky, Wray lost no time in preparing for his third double envelopment of the day.

The remnants of the North Korean company were entrenched on the crest and forward slopes (facing the Marine attack) of Hill 85, obviously intent on making a determined stand. Anticipating Charlie Company's tactics, the Red leader had bent back both flanks to prevent encroachments on the sides or rear. Thus, though both Marine assault platoons swung out to stab at the enemy flanks, the Communist disposition actually relegated each maneuver to a separate frontal attack.

Craven's platoon and Charlie Company machine guns, under First Lieutenant Francis B. Carlon, covered the attackers from a base of fire on the northern slopes of Hill 80. Moving aggressively through a hail of bullets, the 2d Platoon on the left crossed the low ground

218

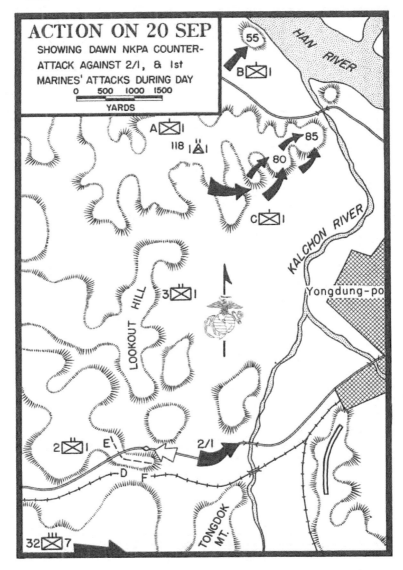

ACTION ON 20 SEP

SHOWING DAWN NKPA COUNTER-
ATTACK AGAINST 2/1, & 1st
MARINES' ATTACKS DURING DAY

0   500   1000   1500
YARDS

and drove up the western incline of the objective. Almost to the top, Guild was grievously wounded by a machine-gun burst.

On the right, Lieutenant Commiskey paved the way in the face of heavy resistance. Nearing the crest of Hill 85, the officer abruptly bounded ahead of his platoon and went over the top. He jumped into a machine-gun emplacement and was dispatching the last of five occupants when his lead skirmishers caught up with him. He ran forward again to clean out another North Korean position in a single-handed attack. By this time, the Reds on the eastern side of the hill had had enough. Those who still had hides to save pelted down the northern slopes in the direction of the mouth of the Kalchon River, where the stream was spanned by the now damaged bridge.

Guild's platoon, inspired by its leader who remained in action despite a mortal wound, gained the summit shortly after Commiskey's unit. Captain Wray, following closely behind, later described his meeting with Guild on the slope as follows:

"He stayed on his feet and turned toward where I was climbing 20 yards behind him. He dropped at my feet and made every effort to remain conscious long enough to tell me how his squads were attacking and pleading with me to keep them attacking. I called for a corpsman; he tried to refuse, saying that he had a wounded man who needed one more than he did."

Lieutenant Guild died shortly afterwards.

1st Marines in Position

During the morning phase of Charlie Company's attack, Hawkins and the others on Hill 118 were racked by frustration of a type seldom experienced by Marines in the history of the Corps. It will be recalled that the ground between the Kimpo-Yongdungpo Highway and the Han River was not cleared in the course of 1/5's attack on Hills 80 and 85 on 19 September. Since the 5th Marines' unit had withdrawn to cross the Han at Haengju, and since Charlie Company of 1/1 had chosen a southern route in recapturing the twin heights, enemy bands in hiding along the river bank were unmolested. The potential danger in the area was not realized, however, until too late.

From Kimpo came a "weasel" of the 1st Signal Battalion, the crew calmly stringing wire into the 1st Marines' zone as the vehicle rattled along the highway.   Just short of the Kalchon bridge, the little tractor struck a mine and was ambushed by a party of North Koreans.   The power-packed Marine infantry on Hill 118, less than a thousand yards away, watched helplessly as the communications men were either killed or captured.   No sooner had the Reds disappeared into the brush with two prisoners than a Marine truck, belonging to A/Engineers, cruised down the highway with four unsuspecting passengers.   Captain Barrow ordered his troops to fire over the vehicle, hoping that the driver would hear the bullets in the air and turn back. But the truck continued on into the ambuscade, where it was stopped by an enemy fusilade.[31]

The engineers piled out and plunged into a rice paddy in an attempt to escape.   Three of them made it.   The fourth, Private First Class Clayton O. Edwards, was tracked down and captured.   Although the Marine was out of ammunition and already wounded, one heroic warrior of the NKPA stepped forward and bayoneted him in the shoulder after he had surrendered.   Edwards later escaped from a POW train fleeing before the UN drive into North Korea.

Not long after these incidents, Captain Richard F. Bland led Baker Company of 1/1 through the area and secured Hill 55 and the nearby villages on the bank of the Han.   The North Koreans pulled out and crossed the Kalchon to join the Yongdungpo garrison.

With fighting going on to the right and left, 3/1 sat quietly on Lookout Hill during 20 September without suffering a casualty.   An occasional break in the orange and black pall over Yongdungpo allowed the Marines a glimpse of the wrecked railroad and highway spans which once had bridged the Han to Seoul.

The ROK capital was still a long way off for the 1st Marines; and the 2d Battalion, now on the regimental right and in its sixth straight day of the assault, was more concerned with the immediate foreground.   After smashing the Red attack in the morning of the 20th, Sutter's unit jumped off at 0645 against scattered resistance along the Inchon-Seoul Highway.   The assault elements reached the bridge spanning the western branch of the Kalchon at 1230, and the battalion commander immediately ordered engineers to inspect the long concrete structure.   It was reported to be in good enough condition to support M-26 tanks for the attack on Yongdungpo the next day.[32]

[31] Barrow interv, 17 Aug 54; and SSgt C. O. Edwards interv, 12 May 54.
[32] 2/1 *SAR*.

While the battalion dug in on the west side of the stream, the Marines eyed the 2,000-yard stretch of highway leading ahead to a second span, bridging the Kalchon's eastern branch at the very edge of the blazing town. A high ridge on the right of the road—technically in the 32d Infantry's zone of action—was a beehive of North Korean activity. Anticipating the effect of this commanding position on his attack the following day, Sutter contacted Lieutenant Colonel Charles M. Mount, USA, commanding the 2d Battalion of the 32d, for permission to shell the height. The Army officer approved the request at 1300, but more than *seven hours* elapsed before the necessary clearance filtered through 7th Division, X Corps, and 1st Marine Division to reach the 11th Marines. When the howitzers finally opened up, darkness prevented effective observed fire from being delivered on the enemy strong point.[33]

Out of sight and earshot of 2/1 during 20 September, Colonel Charles E. Beauchamp's 32d Regiment, in its first day of actual combat, paid with seven killed and 36 wounded in taking Tongdok Mountain and part of "Copper Mine Hill." Using the Inchon-Anyang road as an MSR, the Army unit lost three tanks in a field of over 150 wooden box mines. Beauchamp himself narrowly escaped death or serious injury when his jeep struck one of the explosives, killing the driver and wounding a radio operator. By nightfall, the 32d was deployed far out on the right of the Marines on the Inchon-Seoul Highway; and the 31st Infantry, having landed at Inchon earlier in the day, went into position even farther southward.[34]

Assault of Yongdungpo

There was no infantry action during the night of 20–21 September. Both sides were steeling themselves for the ordeal each knew would commence at dawn. The Red commander in Yongdungpo threw up formidable earthworks to block the approach over the Kalchon from Hills 80 and 85 in the northwest; and he concentrated a strong force between the two tributaries in the southwest. That edge of town facing due west, though most defensible, he left unguarded, with the result that a single Marine rifle company would hasten his demise.

---

[33] *Ibid.;* and Sutter-Codispoti interv, 25 Jan 55.
[34] 32d InfRegt *War Diary,* 18–30 Sep 50.

Marine artillery thundered all night long, and the glare from flaming Yongdungpo rolled back the darkness in an ever broadening arc. Shortly after dawn, the Marines of Company B, 1st Battalion, threaded across the wreckage of the Kalchon bridge under cover of machine-gun, mortar, and tank fire from Hill 85. Reaching the eastern bank, the attackers swept over a knoll over-looking the Han on the left, which the North Koreans had left undefended. The assault inched forward toward the town, first through sporadic small arms resistance, then into a deadly cross-fire from several automatic weapons.[35]

Baker Company was now confronted by two dikes which the Reds had converted into a main line of resistance. One of the barriers paralleled the Han River north of Yongdungpo; the other ran the entire length of the western edge of town. Where they met to form a point facing the Kalchon bridge and the Marine advance, a rein-forced company of North Koreans was deployed across each levee in strong, mutually supporting positions.

Captain Bland chose wisely in directing his attack against the northern dike alone. By this decision he not only kept his left flank and rear protected by the Han, but also maintained local superiority in numbers over the Reds immediately confronting him. Grinding slowly forward with heavy casualties, Company B rolled up the length of enemy entrenchments on the levee and pushed eastward 2,000 yards by afternoon. The Marines then formed a line with their backs to the Han and shot it out with the Communists on the second dike at a range of 500 yards. At this point the attack stalled, and the fight settled down to one of attrition. Casualties on both sides mounted rapidly under the ceaseless exchange of machine-gun, mortar, and tank fire.[36]

Part of Bland's difficulty owed to the random deployment of all opposing forces at this time, as indicated on the charts of the 11th Marines. Noting that Company B's positions were along the Han north of Yongdungpo, the artillerymen expressed reluctance to fire on the enemy-held dike to the "rear" in answer to Lieutenant Colonel Hawkins' repeated requests from his OP on Hill 85. It was a matter of the howitzers pointing generally north toward Seoul, while Bland's outfit, at the moment, was trying to head south. The mis-

---

[35] 1st MarDiv *SAR*, Annex Peter Peter; and Bates interv, 27 Aug 51.
[36] *Ibid.*

understanding was finally cleared up late in the afternoon, and Marine air joined the artillery in pounding the southern barrier. The Reds held stubbornly under the battering, and at darkness Hawkins sent Charlie and Weapons Companies across the bridge to form a perimeter with Baker for the night.[37]

The narrative will now switch to the action in the 2d Battalion zone, leaving the separate attack of Company A to be taken up in detail later.

Sutter's unit jumped off at 0630 on the 21st with Companies D and E in the assault. The infantry crossed the first bridge without incident, then fanned out to move on the second. It was no surprise when the North Koreans on the intermediate ridge to the right of the highway suddenly threw heavy fire across the Marine front, but it was disconcerting to Sutter that his calls for artillery fire met with the same delay as on the previous day. He therefore shelled the high ground with attached 4.2-inch mortars on his own initiative, before ordering Companies E and F to attack the enemy bastion.[38]

Meanwhile, Captain Welby Cronk led Company D forward on the left of the highway against a strongly defended dike fronting the Kalchon's western branch. Progress was slow and casualties severe, but the Marines closed to within 100 yards of the barrier by noon. There they dug in and slugged it out, while the 2d and 3d Platoons of Charlie Company tanks alternated in ripping the Communist trenches with 90mm, delayed-action shells.

Heavy fighting continued on the right side of the road until evening. Companies E and F fought part way up the slopes of the ridge and suffered heavily during the close exchange with the Reds on the crest. Since the enemy was still in control of most of the high ground at dusk, Sutter ordered the assault units to withdraw into 2/1's zone and dig in with Dog Company. VMF–214 covered the hot disengagement—one of the most difficult of all tactics—under a masterful job of forward air controlling by First Lieutenant Norman Vining, Sutter's FAC. After bombing and rocketing from 75 to 100 yards beyond the Marine front, the Corsairs closed to within 30 yards for strafing runs to shield the retracting line of infantry.[39]

[37] *Ibid.*
[38] 2/1 *SAR;* and Sutter-Codispoti interv, 25 Jan 55.
[39] *Ibid.;* and E. H. Giusti and K. W. Condit, "Marine Air Over Inchon-Seoul," *Marine Corps Gazette*, 36, no. 6 (Jun 52).

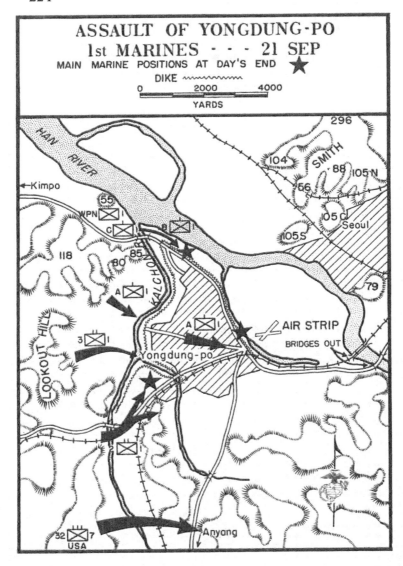

ASSAULT OF YONGDUNG-PO
1st MARINES - - - 21 SEP
MAIN MARINE POSITIONS AT DAY'S END ★
DIKE 〰〰〰〰
0   2000   4000
YARDS

The seventh straight day in the assault had cost the 2d Battalion 11 killed and 74 wounded, bringing its total casualties since D-Day to 28 KIA and 226 WIA. Partially because of these crippling statistics, Colonel Puller, at 1530 on the 21st, had committed 3/1 to the relief of the battle-weary outfit. The reserve battalion swung northeast from Lookout Hill to flank the enemy dike positions facing Company D from the eastern tributary. Crossing the Kalchon against light resistance, the attackers ran into trouble at the fortified levees fronting southwestern Yongdongpo.

After heavy machine guns of 3/1 bested a battery of Communist automatic weapons, Companies G and I, the latter on the right, attacked astride the stream branch. Progress was slow, but at a cost of 11 killed and 18 wounded, the Marines rolled up the heavily defended dike and reached the bridge entering the city. Darkness fell with the 3d Battalion entrenching to the north of the 2d, both units along the left side of the Inchon-Seoul Highway.[40]

To the south of the 1st Marines, the 32d Infantry met with considerable success during its attack over a mountainous nine-mile front. The 1st Battalion on the right mopped up Copper Mine Hill, then seized the high ground around Anyang against "light sniper fire." In the left of the Army zone and adjacent to the Marines, 2/32 took its objective south of Yongdungpo against light-to-moderate resistance. Thus, at a cost of two KIA, 28 WIA, and one MIA, the regiment succeeded in cutting the railroad and highway leading from Suwon to Seoul via Anyang and Yongdungpo. Difficulties in Marine-Army liaison and coordination throughout 21 September stemmed from the fact that neither realized the size of the gap between them. The map will show that the 32d's route of advance was planned to miss Yongdungpo by two miles, not even coming close to the NKPA strong point which gave the 2d Battalion, 1st Marines, so much trouble.[41]

Able Company on a Limb

With the coming of night on 21 September, there was grave apprehension in the 1st Marines over the fate of one rifle company. In the

---

[40] 2/1 *SAR;* 3/1 *SAR;* LtCol T. L. Ridge ltr to CMC, 20 May 55; and LtCol E. H. Simmons ltr to CMC, 19 May 55.
[41] 32d InfRegt *War Diary,* 18-30 Sep 50.

course of the day, the Reds had staved off major penetrations by two Marine battalions in the southwest and the better part of another in the northwest. Incredibly enough, one Marine unit of some 200 men had swept through the space in between and cleared the very heart of Yongdungpo; so that when darkness fell, the isolated force was anchored in the rear of the enemy, a good mile and a half beyond the closest friendly units.

Company A of the 1st Battalion had jumped off from below Hill 80 on the morning of the 21st, after Baker Company was slowed by the dike positions east of the Kalchon bridge. In committing the unit to an attack through a mile of open rice paddies, Lieutenant Colonel Hawkins was gambling with high stakes for surprise.[42]

Captain Barrow employed the classic approach-march formation. Forward on the left was Second Lieutenant John J. Swords' 3d Platoon; on the right front was the 2d, under Second Lieutenant Donald R. Jones. To the left rear was First Lieutenant William A. McClelland's 1st Platoon, with the dual mission of company reserve and flank guard. In the right rear were the 60mm mortars, a section of heavy machine guns of Weapons Company, and the assault squad. Light machine gun sections were attached to each rifle platoon, so that they could be employed to the front or flanks on a moment's notice. Barrow's six-foot, four-inch frame loomed between the two assault platoons.

To say that these Marines were tense and expectant as they plodded across the broad, flat expanse would be an understatement. Far off on the left and right, small arms crackled continuously at the bridge entrances to Yongdungpo. Marine planes were swooping down in the distance, the hollow eruptions of their ordnance adding to the incessant rumbling of artillery and mortars.

Almost hidden from view by the high grain stalks, Company A swept through the rice paddies against no opposition whatever. Its advance was rapid until the 3d Platoon was slowed by muck which marked the beginning of the Kalchon's bed. Heads craned eagerly to the front and flanks as progress dropped to a snail's pace for several minutes.

The crucial moment seemed certainly at hand when the assault line stepped forward from the concealment of the rice and waded

---

[42] The following narrative is derived from: 1st MarDiv *SAR*, Annex Peter Peter; Bates interv, 27 Aug 51; Maj R. H. Barrow intervs, 8 Oct 51 and 17 Aug 54; and Bridges interv, 18 Oct 54.

into the stream, completely exposed to the wide bank and parallel dike beyond. Still, not an enemy shot was fired. Dripping mud and water, the green-clad figures in the van surged ashore and over the dike. The rest of the men followed, unbelieving, close behind.

Retaining the same tactical formation, ready to engage in any or all directions, Company A marched into Yongdungpo. The first buildings were 100 yards ahead of the levee. Barrow channeled his advance astride the main east-west street. Although buildings and dwellings were many, the layout was not dense; and the Marines were able to keep their ranks open and enjoy good all-around observation.

The place seemed empty and dead. By noon Able Company was several hundred yards within the town, its careful search of buildings and side streets having failed to uncover a flicker of enemy resistance. Barrow could tell from the din far out on either flank that he was well ahead (eastward) of Baker Company and the 2d Battalion. He radioed for instructions, and Hawkins told him to keep going.

Halfway through town, Barrow noted on his map that the Inchon-Seoul Highway was now converging on his right, so that it would meet the company's attack route just east of Yongdungpo. Because of the furious clatter along the stretch of highway out of sight on the southwest (2/1's fight), he ordered the reserve platoon to shift from the left side to the right. No sooner had McClelland completed the move than his men spotted an enemy column advancing down the highway in the direction of 2/1's front. The Reds were chanting a spirited military air when the 3d Platoon opened up and cut the formation to ribbons.

Simultaneously, the two lead platoons began firing on individuals and small groups in the streets of eastern Yongdungpo. Astonished at the sight of a large Marine force in the very heart of their bastion, most of the North Koreans took to their heels. But there were other Reds "in the rear with the gear" who obviously did not recognize the attackers. After glancing curiously from distant streets, they went calmly about their business.

Swords' 3d Platoon barreled through town on the left of the street and broke into the open. A dike topped by a road lay across the Marine front, and the platoon leader led his men into a hasty defense on top. From this position they could cover the vast sand spit with its airfield and approaches to Seoul. Looking north, they observed a large body of enemy soldiers withdrawing from Baker Company's zone onto the spit. Light machine guns took the North Koreans under fire immediately, and the section of heavies sent forward by Barrow joined in shortly afterwards. Caught by surprise in the open, the Red outfit suffered heavy casualties before the survivors could fan out and disappear.

The rest of Company A moved up on the right of the 3d Platoon, occupying more of the dike and the junction with the Inchon–Seoul Highway. It was at this point that Company A—if it could hold the ground—had an opportunity to deal the Yongdungpo garrison a mortal blow. For the road junction turned out to be the enemy's supply center.

Across the intersection lay what appeared at first glance to be a huge coal pile. Actually it was a camouflaged mountain of ammunition. During a fire fight with a small group of North Koreans taking cover behind the explosives, one Marine set off the dump with a grenade. The whole countryside shook with the detonation, and the great cloud of smoke that shot into the air marked Able Company's isolated position for the rest of the 1st Marines on the outskirts of town.

While part of the unit dug in on the dike, the remainder inspected and cleared the area around the intersection. A five-story building on the near corner was jammed with captured U. S. Army medical supplies, field equipment, ammunition, and enemy ordnance. The Marines could not use the heavy caliber ammo but they did help themselves to blood plasma for their wounded.

Throughout the afternoon, the Reds made repeated attempts to regain the vital area by throwing small assault parties against Able Company from the south. Each attack was smashed, and darkness found the Marines firmly entrenched on the dike, hoping only that their limited supply of ammunition would last throughout the night. A weak SCR300 battery prevented further communications with the battalion CP.

Yongdungpo Secured

If the Marine Corps Schools ever enlarges its varied curriculum to include "The Defense of a Dike," Captain Barrow's tactical disposition on the night of 21–22 September 1950 can be taken as a unique precedent. Able Company's commander chose to defend a 100-yard stretch of the levee just north of the intersection. Here the macadam road ran about 25 feet above ground level, and the incline on either side sloped gently. The Marines staggered their foxholes alongside, some high on the slope, others low. Machine guns and BARs were emplaced along the shoulders at the top, so that automatic fire could be directed in volume in any direction. Since all of their ammunition had been fired during the afternoon counterattacks, the 60mm mortar crews laid aside their tubes and went into the line as infantry.[43]

Company A's perimeter for the night thus had the shape of a long sausage, with the 3d Platoon in an arc at the northern end, the 1st defending the west side, and the 2d in position on the east. From their foxholes on the top and sides of the levee, the Marines commanded the sand spit, the road on the dike, Yongdungpo's eastern exits, and the vital intersection with the Inchon-Seoul Highway.

Fortunately, they had dug their holes deep. At dusk came the telltale rattling, revving, and clanking from the direction of 2/1's front; and five unescorted T–34s loomed on the Inchon-Seoul Highway, headed toward the intersection. They turned left just short of the crossroads and proceeded in column along a street that paralleled Company A's dike.

The Marines on the levee crouched low in their holes. Cruising majestically like a file of battleships, the tank column cut loose with a hail of machine-gun fire and salvoes of 85mm shells at a range of 30 yards. Able Company's rocket gunners, whose total experience with the 3.5-inch launcher was limited to the firing of a few practice rounds, popped up from their holes and let fly. One of the tanks exploded in a convulsion of flame and smoke, its turret twisted askew as though some giant hand had torn the steel cap from the body.

The other four tanks continued to the end of the perimeter, then reversed course past the Marine line a second time, pumping a steady stream of steel into the western slope of the dike. Reaching their starting point at the Inchon-Seoul Highway, they turned back and made another round trip, with Marine rocket fire damaging two more vehicles and sending them limping off the field. The remaining pair, upon completing the second circuit, again reversed course and made a final pass—the fifth—on the Marine lines. Clearing the perimeter, they rumbled into town and disappeared.

⁴³ *Ibid*.

230

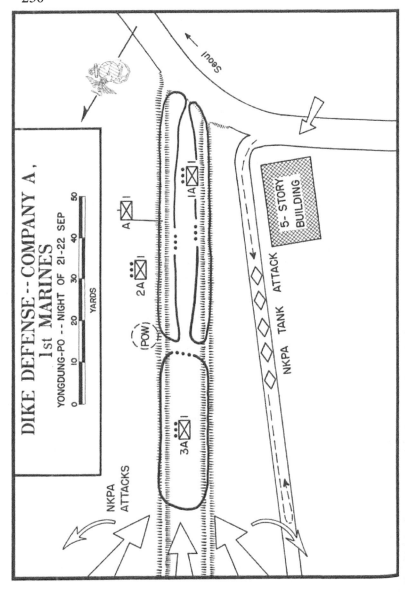

DIKE DEFENSE -- COMPANY A, 1st MARINES

YONGDUNG-PO -- NIGHT OF 21-22 SEP

YARDS

0 10 20 30 40 50

Seoul

5- STORY BUILDING

NKPA TANK ATTACK

NKPA ATTACKS

(POW)

A

2A

3A

1A

Fantastic as it may seem, Company A sustained a single casualty, a concussion case, during the half hour of sustained heavy caliber pounding at pistol ranges. Tremendous muzzle velocity had embedded the 85mm, armor-piercing shells deep in the slope of the dike in the split second before each explosion; and Marine foxholes proved to be sufficient protection against the raking machine-gun fire.

Between 1900 and 2100 it was relatively quiet. McClelland's platoon, facing town, killed a few Reds attempting to remove stores from the five-story building. Then the long expected report reached Barrow by sound-power telephone: Swords' platoon, manning the northern arc of the perimeter, could hear a large enemy force approaching its front.

The counterattack hit shortly after 2100. Transmitting a running account of the sharp fire fight by phone, Swords assured his company commander that he was "having no trouble." After 15 minutes of failure, the Reds withdrew for a breather. They struck in the same place half an hour later and were thrown back again, despite any inspiration derived from a display of multi-colored flares and wild cries of "banzai."

By midnight, the 3d Platoon had withstood five such onslaughts, each appearing to be in about company strength. Before the last attack, a captive Red officer escaped from Company A's POW "compound" east of the dike and ran northward into the blackness, shouting repeatedly, according to Barrow's ROK interpreter, "Don't attack any more! They're too strong for you!"

Apparently his advice was heeded, much to the relief of the Marines, whose ammunition supply was becoming dangerously low. At midnight, following the enemy's fifth unsuccessful attempt against Swords' position, the fight for Yongdungpo came to an end for the 1st Marines. There was scattered firing throughout the night, but the North Koreans, denied access to their vital supplies, quickly withered on the vine.

At dawn, Company A counted 275 dead and 50 automatic weapons around its perimeter, principally in front of the 3d Platoon. The four T-34 tanks which had withdrawn into town were found abandoned.

The 1st and 3d Battalions attacked at 0800 against negligible resistance and converged on the isolated unit, making the historic link-up in short order. The enemy was gone, except for the hundreds of dead that littered the borders of the city. He had left behind practically all of his heavy armament, equipment, and supplies.

Continuing the advance on the 22d, the 1st Marines surged eastward beyond Yongdungpo, then spent the remainder of the day reorganizing and patrolling. On the 23d, the regiment moved almost unopposed to the bank of the Han, 3/1 seizing Hill 108 which dominated the battered bridges. Late that night Puller received orders to effect the river-crossing early next morning.

CHAPTER XII

Main Line of Resistance

*Three Hills Designated 105—RCT-7 North of the Han—
Attack Continued by RCT-5—Modified Plan of Corps At-
tack—Climax of the Marine Assault—The Epic of Dog
Company—River Crossing of RCT-1*

DURING THE NIGHT of 21–22 September an NKPA shell crashed
through the roof of the native house serving as CP of the 5th
Marines northwest of Seoul. The explosion wounded Lieutenant
Colonel Hays so severely that the regimental executive officer required
immediate evacuation. Lieutenant Colonel Murray, who escaped
with a slight cut, directed that the CP be moved to a cave on the reverse
slope of a hill.

Thus did the enemy serve notice that henceforward the battle for
the northwest approaches to Seoul would be furiously contested.
Yongdungpo had been taken by the 1st Marines only after a grim,
three-day struggle in which the Korean Reds made their first real
stand as distinguished from delaying operations. And now it was
the turn of the 5th Marines to meet opposition such as that regiment
had not encountered since D-day.

Two new NKPA units had much to do with the sudden stiffening of
resistance. One was the 78th Independent Regiment, commanded by
Colonel Pak Han Lin. This unit, numbering about 2,000 recruits in
July, was organized into three battalions of infantry supported by
medical, motorcycle, weapons, reconnaissance, mortar and 76mm gun
companies, and an engineer platoon.

Another recent arrival which won the respect of the Marines for
rugged fighting qualities was the 25th Brigade of 4,000 to 5,000
troops. Commanded by Major General Wol Ki Chan, who had re-
portedly studied in Russia in 1947, the unit was made up of four heavy

233

weapons battalions and an infantry battalion in addition to engineer, 120mm mortar, heavy artillery, and brigade artillery battalions.[1]

It was literally a fight to the death for these two NKPA outfits, which were all but wiped out of existence by the Marines of RCT–5 during the battle for Seoul. But while they lasted, the 78th Regiment and 25th Brigade put up a determined and at times desperate resistance in hill country well adapted to defense.

Three Hills Designated 105

The grapple for the northwest approaches to Seoul began in deadly earnest at 0700 on the morning of 22 September. From north to south, the three assault battalions of the reinforced 5th Marines were the 3d on the left, the 1st KMC in the center, and the 1st on the right. They were jumping off from the high ground about three miles southeast of Haengju along a line bounded by Hill 216 on the north, 104 in the center, and 68 on the south.

Misunderstandings in regard to routes and unit boundaries were made inevitable by maps disagreeing as to place names and heights of ridges. Added to the confusion was the fact that each battalion zone had a Hill 105 as one of its final objectives. (Staff officers played safe by designating them 105–N, 105–C, and 105–S to indicate north, central and south.)

Ahead of the Marines lay a hill complex which constituted a great natural bastion of interlocking heights and fields of fire. Spurs and defiles leading from one ridge to another enabled NKPA troops to move up in concealment and launch counterattacks in the most unexpected quarters.

Casualties of the next three days were the heaviest for a comparable period that RCT–5 had suffered in Korea. Added to previous totals, it meant that 17 of the original 18 platoon leaders were killed or wounded in a 50-day period, and five of the six company commanders who landed with the Brigade.[2]

Grim as the outlook was, the Marines of the 2d Battalion enjoyed a sideshow on the eve of battle when Sergeant James I. Higgins and a companion made a prize of an enemy locomotive. Knowing

---

[1] 1st MarDiv *SAR*, Annex Baker, and Queen Queen:Baker, app. 1.
[2] Geer, *The New Breed*, 163.

nothing about operating it, they found a simple but effective solution by firing up and opening throttles or depressing levers until the gauges were at the halfway mark. This policy of moderation led to success. The locomotive took off with ponderous docility, and Higgins managed to bring it to a safe stop near the regimental CP. His exploit was not applauded, however, by supply officers taking alarm from the dense clouds pouring out of the smokestack. They did not relish the idea of providing enemy artillery with a target marker, visible for miles, in an area full of exposed Marine ammunition. As a result of their anxiety, Higgins was promptly invited to keep rolling until he reached the rear.[3]

The 2d Battalion remained in reserve while the 1st KMC Battalion jumped off in the center from Hill 104. Heavy resistance was met immediately. In fact, NKPA detachments infiltrated all the way to Hill 104 itself, though it had been secured by 3/5 the previous afternoon. They poured small-arms fire into KMCs already taking a pounding from mortar and artillery fire, and the battalion was held up until the high ground to the front could be cleared by artillery and air strikes.[4]

On the left, 3/5 also ran into trouble after deceptively easy progress at first. At 0700 all three companies jumped off from Hill 216, secured by Item Company the day before. The new objective, as directed by 5th Marines' Operations Order 24-50, was Hill 296.

This height was reported by How Company as taken at 0945. It was not realized at the time that Hill 296 was actually the bastion of the Red Korean defense complex northwest of Seoul if its three southern spurs were considered. Attached to the main land mass like the roots of an ulcerated molar were Hills 56, 88, and 105-N, with 105-C, 72, and 105-S describing an arc to the southward. Nearly all of these positions would have to be reduced before the road could be opened to Seoul.

Only long-range small-arms fire from Hill 338 was encountered by How Company at the outset, but enemy pressure steadily increased from the southern spurs of 296. An NKPA counterattack in estimated company strength was repulsed with heavy enemy losses, including some 40 prisoners, by Marine riflemen supported by tanks.

---

[3] Capt G. H. Stewart interv, 17 Nov 54.
[4] 1st MarDiv *SAR*, Annex Queen Queen.

Communist pressure was soon renewed, however, with How Company receiving heavy small-arms, automatic, AT, and mortar fire.

Patrols from the other two companies, ranging to the northeast of Hill 216 in the early afternoon, met determined opposition. A reinforced rifle platoon of Item Company encountered an NKPA force, in estimated company strength, defending the village of Nokpon-ni. During the ensuing fight the Marines lost two men killed and 11 wounded. Action was broken off at dusk, when the 3d Battalion received oral orders to defend against an enemy infiltrating from the south, southeast, and northeast in attempts to regain lost ground.

The fight for Hill 296 had only begun.[5]

South of the railroad, 1/5 had about 2,000 yards to cover to its objective, Hill 105–S. The battalion plan of maneuver called for Baker Company to deliver fire support while Able passed through Charlie and advanced to the base of the hill. Meanwhile, Charlie was to envelop the objective from the right. When the three Able platoons moved into position, they were pinned down by enemy automatic fire from the forward slope of 105–S. First Lieutenant Joseph A. Schimmenti of 3/A and his men had a grim reminder of American reverses earlier in the war when they found a 50-caliber machine gun and ammunition of U. S. manufacture which the enemy had abandoned.[6]

Schimmenti was severely wounded and First Lieutenant Nathaniel F. Mann, Jr., killed before Able Company won a foothold on the lower slopes of 105–S. It took until 1500 for Charlie Company, supported by a machine gun section, to complete its wide swing and close in on the right of the enemy's positions. Baker Company passed through Able meanwhile and attacked the forward slopes. At 1720, after an intense mortar, air, and artillery preparation, the 1st Battalion needed only 15 minutes in which to secure the objective. The three companies had taken losses of 12 killed and 31 wounded during the day.[7]

Close air support was provided for RCT–5 by the MAG–33 squadrons which had begun tactical operations at Kimpo on the 20th. Although they were still in process of moving to the airfield from Japanese bases, VMF–212 and VMF(N)–542 flew strikes in support of all three assault battalions. Of the two carrier-based squadrons,

---

[5] 1st MarDiv *SAR*, Annex Queen Queen:Peter.
[6] Capt J. A. Schimmenti interv, 4 Jan 55.
[7] 1st MarDiv *SAR*, Annex Queen Queen:Nan.

237

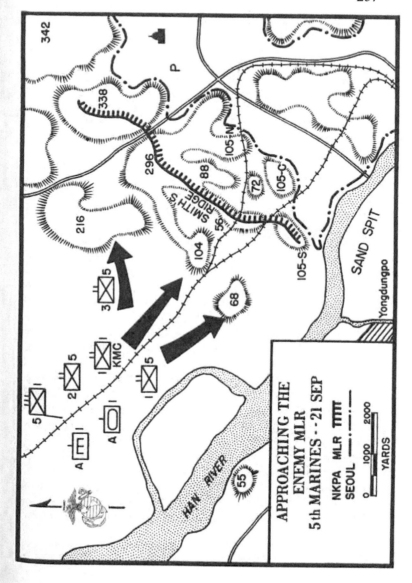

APPROACHING THE
ENEMY MLR
5th MARINES - - 21 SEP

NKPA MLR ······
SEOUL ─ · · ─

0   1000   2000
YARDS

342

P

338

296

316

216

105-N

88

105-C

72

SMITH'S RIDGE

56

104

105-S

68

SAND SPIT

Yongdungpo

3 5

KMC

2 5

5

A 5

A

55

HAN RIVER

VMF–323 almost doubled its usual number of daily missions on 22 September.[8]

Just before nightfall, Lieutenant Colonel Murray directed 1/5 to pull back to Hill 68 with one company while holding Hill 105–S with the other two. This shift was made necessary by the fact that the KMCs had been compelled to withdraw to Hill 104, their starting point. As a consequence, the center of the line was more than 1,000 yards in the rear of the battalions on the right and left. The company on Hill 68 was to provide covering fires in the morning, therefore, when the KMC battalion would renew its attack in an effort to regain lost ground.

RCT–7 North of the Han

On D-plus 8 the 1st Marine Division had its third rifle regiment in line for the first time. OpnO 9–50, issued at 1200 on 23 September, directed the 7th Marines (less 2d Battalion) to cross the Han into a zone of action in the rear of the 5th Marines.

In response to verbal instructions and a fragmentary warning order the day before, the regimental headquarters and 3d Battalion crossed late on the morning of the 23d. Colonel Litzenberg set up his CP on the north bank at 1710, and his men had their first contact with the enemy the following morning. A 3d Battalion patrol ranging to the north of the battalion zone of action encountered an estimated 200 NKPA troops, and Marine air and artillery supported a successful attack.[9]

Division orders called for the relief of 2/7 on the 24th in the area northwest of Kimpo by the 2d Battalion of the 187th Airborne RCT, USA. The Marine unit was directed to cross the Han that afternoon, followed by the 1st Battalion, which had completed unloading at Inchon.

It had been decided by the Division command and staff to give the 7th Marines time for shaking down instead of committing the newcomers immediately to the attack on Seoul. The regiment was assigned a series of five objectives along a ridgeline extending from the ferry crossing at Haengju on a gentle arc to a point north of the city.

---

[8] 1st MAW *SAR*, Annex Jig: Appendix Fox; Annex Item: Roger, Sugar.
[9] 1st MarDiv *SAR*, Annex Roger Roger.

Protecting the north flank and rear of the 5th Marines was a primary mission, and Colonel Litzenberg was also directed to prevent the escape of the enemy to the northward.[10]

Attack Continued by RCT-5

On the morning of the 23d the 1st KMC Battalion was directed to attack from Hill 104 at 0700 to straighten out the line. The 1st and 3d Battalions of the 5th Marines were to remain in position and assist the advance by fire.

Heavy and immediate resistance was encountered from NKPA troops dug in on Hill 56. Although the KMCs made a valiant effort, they were soon stopped cold. Only slight gains resulted at an excessive cost in casualties from artillery, mortar, and automatic weapons fire.[11]

Lieutenant Colonel Roise moved his CP forward at 1300 to the western base of Hill 104. While his 2d Battalion assembled under cover of that height, he conferred with Lieutenant Colonel Murray after receiving orders to pass through the KMCs and continue the attack on Hill 56. Both officers realized the advantages of swinging around to hit the enemy from the left after approaching along the low ground. But it was already midafternoon and this movement could not be completed before darkness. The only alternative was a line-buck in the center if Hill 56 was to be taken that day. And since the line had to be stabilized and the KMCs pulled back in reserve to give the regimental defense some depth, Murray and Roise agreed that the situation called for a frontal assault without delay.[12]

At this stage the Marine officers did not realize that Hill 56 was part of the enemy's main line of resistance. It seemed logical to them that he would make his final stand on the next ridgeline, crowned with Hills 105–C and 105–N. As for the repulses suffered by the KMCs, it was a logical assumption that their inexperience had been a contributing factor. In view of these circumstances, a brief artillery preparation and the support of a platoon of tanks seemed sufficient when Com-

[10] O. P. Smith, *Notes*, 251–252.
[11] 1st MarDiv *SAR*, Annex Queen Queen.
[12] LtCol H. S. Roise interv, 9 Nov 54.

panies D and F attacked and E contributed fires from the eastern slopes of Hill 104.[13]

Captain Peters' Fox Company was to lead off on the right, south of the railroad, and seize the portion of the objective below the railroad tunnel. From this high ground, his men could then support First Lieutenant H. J. Smith's Dog Company, moving forward under cover of a sunken road, to assault Hill 56 north of the tunnel. About 1,000 yards of rice paddies had to be crossed at the outset, and the expected support of the tanks in this low ground failed to materialize. The leading M–26 bogged down in a wide ditch which prevented the advance of the other four. One of them remained in the paddies to give supporting fires while three took a new route along the railroad tracks. Fox Company received increasingly heavy casualties meanwhile on the way across the low ground.

Peters ordered Second Lieutenant S. E. Sansing's mortar section forward, but the officer reported afterwards that his radio did not pick up the message. This left the three assault platoons without 60mm support as they climbed the lower slopes of Hill 56 and became heavily engaged with NKPA troops just below the railway tunnel.[14]

Apparently the Reds so overrated the weight of Company F's assault that they lost the topographical peak of Hill 56 by default. Whether their timely withdrawal from Dog Company's initial objective was meant to be permanent is not known, for they might have been caught flatfooted while shifting troops against Fox. Nevertheless, Company D emerged from the sunken road in a column of platoons and moved onto the high ground in its zone against negligible opposition.

Lieutenant Heck's 1st Platoon, according to plan, then pivoted leftward to spearhead the attack on the final objective, Smith's Ridge— named by the men after their company commander. Halfway into the connecting saddle, the Marines were caught in the open by a heavy burst of fire from a large knoll on the southern tip of the wooded ridge. Heck fell mortally wounded, and his senior NCO, Staff Sergeant T. Albert Crowson, went down with a shattered leg. In the space of a few minutes, more than half of the exposed platoon became casualties.[15]

---

[13] *Ibid*.
[14] Anderson interv, 20 Aug 54.
[15] 1st MarDiv *SAR*, Annex Queen Queen; McNaughton interv, 7 Jan 55.

Startled by the intensity of enemy reaction from this unexpected quarter, Smith personally retrieved the battered 1st Platoon, while the 2d and 3d were clearing the northeastern slopes of Hill 56. Then, owing to the lateness of the hour, he deployed Company D defensively on that high ground for the night. There was no contact with Fox Company or any other friendly unit. This fact, coupled with the evidence of strong enemy positions on Smith's Ridge, led the company commander to reconsider carefully his plans for the postponed attack.[16]

Fox Company had meanwhile been heavily engaged along the eastern slopes of Hill 56 in the vicinity of the railway tunnel. Peters ordered Lieutenant Anderson to lead his 2d Platoon against the strong NKPA positions just beyond the tunnel. Only 27 men were left to fight it out at close quarters with an entrenched enemy estimated by the platoon leader at company strength. The Communist force was wiped out in exchanges of small-arms fire and grenades at murderous ranges, but the effort took a frightful toll of the 1st Platoon in KIA and WIA casualties. Only seven able-bodied men were left when Peters ordered a withdrawal to the company position south of the tunnel.[17]

All of Anderson's wounded and most of his dead were brought back, and he combined his remnants with the survivors of Lieutenant Nolan's 2d Platoon. A gap of about 50 yards separated their position from First Lieutenant Albert F. Belbusti's isolated 3d Platoon as Fox Company dug in for the night.[18]

No fault could be found with the over-all plan of attack, providing as it did for each assault company to seize ground from which it could support the advance of the other. But as darkness approached, it became evident that the 2d Battalion had bargained for more North Korean real estate than it could handle. The two isolated companies had no choice but to cling desperately to their scorched holdings while organizing to meet an expected NKPA counterattack.

Although the other two battalions of the 5th Marines had defensive missions on 23 September, enemy threats and encroachments kept them occupied. On Hill 296, in the zone of 3/5, Weapons Company took a good deal of satisfaction in firing a captured NKPA howitzer to break up hostile troop concentrations in the vicinity of Nokpon-ni.

---

[16] *Ibid.*
[17] Anderson interv, 20 Aug 54.
[18] *Ibid.*

242

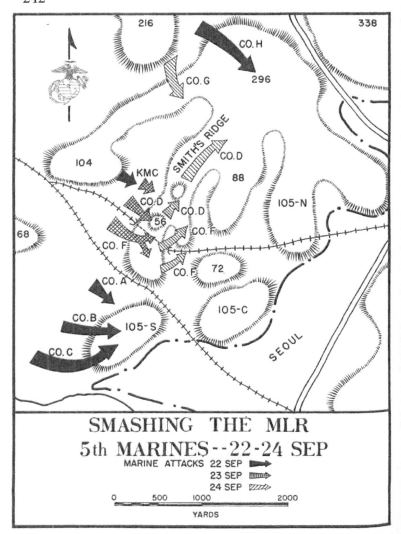

216
338
CO. H
296
CO. G
SMITH'S RIDGE
CO. D
104
KMC
88
CO. D
CO. D
105-N
56
68
CO. F
CO. F
CO. F
72
CO. A
105-C
CO. B
105-S
SEOUL
CO. C

SMASHING THE MLR
5th MARINES --22-24 SEP

MARINE ATTACKS 22 SEP
23 SEP
24 SEP

0   500   1000   2000

YARDS

How Company remained in contact with the enemy all day, supported by 50-caliber and 90mm fires from Marine tanks.[19]

It was in the How Company zone that Taplett's men first made the acquaintance of "Fireproof Phil." This was the name applied to a gigantic NKPA officer, towering head and shoulders over his troops, who exposed himself with contempt for Marine bullets. Not only his burly build but his light complexion gave some of the Marines the conviction that he was Russian. At any rate, Fireproof Phil was both fearless and lucky. Machine gun bullets and mortar rounds seemed to bounce off his frame. Finally, the tanks paid the honor of making him the special target of 90mm ammunition, and still Fireproof Phil always had the benefit of a minor miracle at the last moment.[20]

Combat leadership by enemy officers and NCOs was outstanding in the operations north of Seoul. On Hill 105-S the 1st Battalion came under pressure all day on 23 September. Movement was impossible for the men of Baker and Charlie Companies, and supplies of water, food, and ammunition had to wait for darkness. Enemy smoke pots created a haze restricting air activities, but it did not prevent a timely strike flown by Lieutenant Colonel Lischeid and five planes of VMF–214 to break up a threatened enemy counterattack on Hill 105–S. This was one of six close support missions completed on the 23d by that squadron in the zone of RCT–5.[21]

Why the enemy did not launch a counterattack that night against the hard-hit assault companies of the 2d Battalion is one of the mysteries of the war. But the weary Marines on the slope of Hill 56 attributed their respite to effective and unremitting artillery support. All night long the howitzers of the 11th Marines lit up the night sky like heat lightning in the rear and crashed like thunder in front as they scourged the NKPA positions.

Modified Plan of Corps Attack

Up to this time the Corps plan of attack had called for the 1st Marines to clear the south bank of the Han and cross in the vicinity of Yong-

[19] 1st MarDiv *SAR*, Annex Queen Queen:Peter.
[20] LtCol R. D. Taplett interv, 19 Apr 55.
[21] 1st MarDiv *SAR*, Annex Queen Queen:Nan; 1st MAW *SAR*, Annex Jig:Easy.

dungpo to join the 5th Marines in an assault on Seoul from the west and southwest. In view of the location of the boundary between the 1st Marines and the 7th Infantry Division, this meant that the Army troops would not participate in the attack on the city.

General Almond had already made it plain in conversations with General Smith that it was highly desirable to take Seoul by 25 September as GHQ wished to announce the liberation just three months to the day after the NKPA invasion.

The subject came up again during a conference at Corps Head-quarters on 23 September. Almond proposed that Smith send RCT–1 around to attack Seoul from the southeast while RCT–5 continued its assault from the northwest. This plan struck the Corps commander as promising to maneuver the enemy out of the city sooner than the attack as formerly conceived.

Smith replied that the NKPA forces defending Seoul had proved to be much stronger than had been expected. He said he was con-vinced that the enemy would put up a fight from street to street regard-less of any flanking maneuvers. The Marine general added that the fierce opposition met by RCT–5 had demonstrated that the western approaches to Seoul were too much for one regiment to handle, and he urged that no change be made in the original plan of crossing RCT–1 northwest of Yongdungpo to aid the attack. This plan, Smith asserted, would offer the advantage of keeping the 1st Marine Division together; for when the 1st and 5th Marines had penetrated well into the city, the 7th Marines could be brought around from the northwest to deliver the *coup de grace*.[22]

Differences between commanders are not remarkable, and it is note-worthy that Corps and Division usually managed in the Inchon-Seoul operation to reach an acceptable solution. Such was the case when General Almond reconsidered on the 23d and agreed to allow the 1st Marines to cross northwest of Yongdungpo, as originally planned, and take part in a two-regiment attack on Seoul from the west and south-west. In place of the 1st Marines, the 32d Regiment of the 7th Infantry Division was to cross the Han and enter Seoul from the southeast. Amphibian tractors for the operation would be furnished by the 1st Marine Division.

---

[22] This section has been derived from: 1st MarDiv *SAR*, sec. 1; O. P. Smith, *Notes*, 252–253, 262–265, and *Chronicle*, 23–24 Sep 50.

Revised 1st Marine Division plans called for RCT–1 to take position on the right flank of RCT–5 after the crossing, then pivot to the northeast and continue the attack through the heart of the city. RCT–7 (less one battalion in Division reserve) would have the mission of advancing across the northern approaches to protect the left flank and prevent the enemy from escaping while RCT–5 sliced through the western edge of the built-up area. Thus the burden of capturing Seoul fell chiefly upon Colonel Puller's regiment.

Climax of the Marine Assault

As the eastern sky turned gray on the Saturday morning of 24 September, the men on the firing line northwest of Seoul knew that the time had come. They knew with the instinct of battle-wise troops that supporting arms had done all they could. Now it was up to the infantry to come to grips with the enemy. Supporting arms could only sue for victory and it was up to the infantry to collect.

The two companies of 2/5 were still clinging by their eyelashes to the scarred slopes of Hill 56. All three of the Company F platoon leaders, Nolan, Anderson, and Belbusti were carrying on in spite of wounds. Corporal Welden D. Harris, who had killed three Red Koreans in hand-to-hand combat the day before, refused to be evacuated after a second wound.[23]

The survivors of Captain Peters' outfit could not say too much in praise of the support given continuously throughout the night by Captain Arnold C. Hofstetter's Baker Battery of the 11th Marines. There were indications that several incipient NKPA counterattacks had been broken up during the night by the bombardment.

In the Dog Company zone the night had been relatively uneventful except for sniping, though the enemy could be heard digging new positions and bringing up ammunition.

The regimental scheme of maneuver, as outlined in OpnO 26–50, called for the 2d Battalion to continue the attack, with Hill 105–N as a final objective. This meant going up against practically the entire Hill 296 defense system, since Smith's Ridge and all of Hill 88 also remained to be seized. An estimated 2,500 enemy troops, well supported by automatic weapons, mortars, and artillery were defending

[23] Anderson interv, 20 Aug 54.

every foot of defensible ground in front of the two thinned companies of 2/5.

It was intended that 3/5 should assist by attacking down the principal eastern spur of 296 to outflank the enemy and contribute supporting fires. Taplett's men were to be relieved in gradual stages on Hills 216 and 296 by elements of the 1st Battalion. As a preliminary, Newton was to send out a patrol to secure a portion of the river bank on the right flank of Hill 105–S in preparation for the crossing of the Han by the 1st Marines that morning. The reserve company of 1/5 would then commence the relief of the 3d Battalion while the 1st Battalion of the KMC Regiment remained in an assembly area in the rear of the 5th Marines and elements of the 7th Marines protected the left flank. Units of 1/5 were to continue to defend 105–S—seized and held at a total cost of 27 KIA and 72 WIA—until the crossing of the 1st Marines and the relief of 3/5 had been completed.[24]

Two small enemy counterattacks were repulsed without much trouble by elements of 3/5 on Hill 296 before dawn. Company H remained in contact with the enemy on the eastern slopes until 1550, when Company G moved around the right flank and a coordinated attack was launched against moderate NKPA artillery, mortar, and AT fires. Relief of Item Company and other 3/5 troops remaining on Hill 216 was completed by the 1st Battalion at 2000. Casualties of the 3d Battalion for the day were five killed and 33 wounded.[25]

The movements of these two battalions were subsidiary to the main attack launched by 2/5 on 24 September. H-hour at 0630 was preceded by a 20-minute artillery preparation and an air strike by VMF–323 planes. Lieutenant Colonel Roise planned to bring up Easy Company from reserve on Hill 104 and push it forward between Dog and Fox while those companies completed the seizure of Hill 56 and cleared the heavily wooded spur to the north known as Smith's Ridge, linking up with the main land mass of Hill 296. Easy Company would then take the lead in a battalion attack aimed at Hills 88 and 105–N as the final objectives.

Fox Company jumped off on the eastern slope of Hill 56. Nolan having been evacuated, Anderson led what was left of the 2d and 3d Platoons—a total of some 20 riflemen. Belbusti commanded about the same number in the combined assault on the heavily defended finger

---

[24] 1st MarDiv OpnO 10–50, 24 Sep 50.
[25] 1st MarDiv *SAR*, Annex Queen Queen:Peter.

of high ground east of the tunnel. Counting machine gunners, mortar-men, and troops bringing up ammunition, Fox Company had been reduced to fewer than 90 effectives, including wounded men refusing evacuation.

Corsairs of VMF–323 swooped down to drop 500-pound bombs less than a hundred yards in front of the attackers. Thanks to such close air support, Fox Company soon seized high ground which enabled the men to gain fire superiority.[26] At this point they took cover to make use of their advantage in an exchange of small-arms and automatic fire.

Dog Company, with two platoons still almost at full strength, had at least a dozen walking wounded who elected to keep on fighting. Ground mist and smoke from burning huts made for low visibility when the men jumped off in a column of platoons. The enemy opened up from Smith's Ridge as the Marines came within close range, pinning them down for two hours by concentrated and accurate artillery, mor-tar, AT, and automatic fire. One of the Marine tanks moving up the road in support was disabled by a mine and another became inoperative after a direct hit by an NKPA mortar shell on the motor hatch.[27]

The Epic of Dog Company

The large knob across the sunken road from Hill 56 remained to be taken before Dog Company completed its mission by advancing north-ward to clear the enemy from the wooded spine of Smith's Ridge. After the attack stalled with heavy casualties Lieutenant H. J. Smith ordered every available man into line, including personnel of company headquarters. Two Marine machine guns were kept in action at a cost of repeated casualties as First Lieutenant Karle Seydel made five consecutive trips under fire to bring up ammunition.

At some points the opposing forces were within long grenade-throw-ing distance. In these exchanges the Marines had a pronounced ad-vantage because of stronger arms and the control developed by baseball.

Both sides attempted without success to break the deadlock by send-ing out detachments for flanking movements. Sergeant Robert Smith of McNaughton's platoon led a squad in a wide end sweep to the north, only to meet such fierce NKPA opposition that Smith and

[26] Anderson interv, 20 Aug 54; 1st MarDiv *SAR*, Annex Queen Queen:Oboe.
[27] McNaughton interv, 7 Jan 55; 1st MarDiv *SAR*, Annex Queen Queen.

eight of his men were killed, including a corpsman. Only three wounded Marines ever got back.[28]

At 1000 the company commander sent the first of three messages to inform the battalion CP of his situation and request reinforcements. Roise could only reply that Easy Company, his reserve unit, was irrevocably committed to the attack on the final objectives. During the course of the battle the battalion commander himself was wounded by a mortar fragment but returned to the CP after having his arm dressed.[29]

When Second Lieutenant George Grimes' 60mm mortar section ran out of ammunition, the survivors fought as riflemen. Two platoon leaders, McNaughton and Lieutenant Howard, were wounded but continued in action.

About 1030, as the smoke and mist cleared, the howitzers of the 11th Marines and the 81mm mortars of 2/5 poured it into the enemy positions along the wooded ridge. The men on the firing line had another welcome assist when four Corsairs of VMF–323 roared in to make passes with bombs, rockets, and napalm.

Lieutenant Smith had 44 effectives left as he alerted his men for the assault. McNaughton, Seydel, Grimes, and First Lieutenant Karl Wirth were the other officers still on their feet. Platoons, sections, and squads had ceased to exist as units when the 44 men of Dog Company moved out of their foxholes and swarmed over the high ground that had held them up for more than two hours.

First impressions under more normal circumstances would have been shocking, for the position held more enemy dead and dying than the Marines had ever seen before in Korea. The entire area was honeycombed with foxholes, trenches, and bunkers, which had become the graves of Red Koreans cut down by Marine air and artillery. There they had died at their posts, crowded together so closely that every shell, bomb, or rocket had caused frightful carnage. The dead outnumbered the living, in fact, for the men of Dog Company met unexpectedly weak resistance from the few NKPA effectives who trusted to their weapons instead of their feet.[30]

Lieutenant Smith paused to regroup in a skirmish line for the final attack to clear the remainder of the ridge. Again the Marines seemed

[28] McNaughton interv, 7 Jan 55.
[29] 1st MarDiv *SAR*, Annex Queen Queen:Oboe.
[30] McNaughton interv, 7 Jan 55.

to prevail by sheer moral ascendancy as the assault went forward by leaps and bounds. But the victory was bought at the cost of the company commander's life, for Smith was killed at the head of his men.

Only five additional casualties were taken in this phase, but Marines dropped from exhaustion until McNaughton, as acting commander, had just 26 able-bodied men left at the finish. They were greeted by the strange spectacle of three enemy officers exhorting about 150 Red Koreans to retreat. No second invitation was needed, and the Marines had a "turkey shoot" at the expense of foemen scurrying down the eastern and northern slopes in the direction of Seoul.[31]

Seydel was the only officer left unwounded when Dog Company notified the Battalion CP at 1300 that objectives had been secured. Fox Company reported about two hours later that it also had seized all assigned ground and was digging in after a mopping-up period.[32]

Casualties had not been heavy on the east side of the ridge as compared to the day before. The Company F attack consisted of two prolonged fire fights in which the Marines seized better positions and made good use of their advantage. After reaching the objective, they took cover and proceeded systematically to cut the enemy down to size with the support of VMF–214 planes. Captain Peters then sent both platoons forward to eliminate an NKPA force firing on them from a distance. Anderson's men passed through a small built-up area and took cover behind a stone wall on the enemy's flank. Opening fire on Communists about 300 yards away in an open field, they made short work of the opposition.[33]

Second Lieutenant Wiley J. Grigsby, the machine gun platoon leader, was killed in the day's final Fox Company attack. Anderson's composite platoon had three men killed and three wounded. Among the casualties was Corporal Harris, who received a mortal wound after twice refusing evacuation. He was posthumously awarded the Navy Cross.[34]

The attack of Easy Company on Hill 105–N was delayed until after the other two companies took their objectives. At 1500, after moving up from battalion reserve, Jaskilka's men ran into heavy enemy mortar and automatic fire soon after passing Hill 56. Two tanks of the 1st Platoon, Company B, 1st Tank Battalion were knocked out, one by

[31] *Ibid.*
[32] 1st MarDiv *SAR*, Annex Queen Queen:basic rpt and Oboe.
[33] Anderson interv, 20 Aug 54.
[34] *Ibid.*

an AT mine and the other by a direct hit of a mortar shell. The remaining three tanks could not have continued in action except for the efforts of Staff Sergeant Stanley B. McPherson of Company A, 1st Engineer Battalion, who went ahead and cleared a path through the enemy mine field. By some miracle he survived the hail of NKPA fire unhurt, and the tanks went on to destroy two enemy AT guns and several machine gun emplacements.

The main enemy stronghold appeared to be Hill 72, a conical height located between Hills 105–N and 105–C and enfilading both of them. Not enough daylight remained on 24 September to mount an assault on this position, and the effort was put off until the following morning.[35]

Marine air had a busy day. Lieutenant Colonel Lischeid's VMF–214, repeating the pattern of the day before, launched strikes of five aircraft every two hours in support of 2/5 attacks northwest of Seoul— a total of six missions. Not only was the city a flak-trap, but Marine pilots were flying Corsairs from which the armor around the air-cooler system had been removed by order of BuAer as a peacetime economy measure and never restored. As a consequence, NKPA small-arms fire was likely to hit the oil lines and send a machine down in flames.[36]

A 1st MAW record for combat sorties flown in a day by a single squadron was set on the 24th by VMF–212 with 12 flights and 46 sorties. Close support missions were about equally represented along with search and attack.[37]

Nightfall of this eventful day found 2/5 in possession of ground containing the most enemy dead in a small area ever seen in the Inchon-Seoul operation. Lieutenant Colonel Roise estimated that 1,500 NKPA bodies were left on Hill 56 and Smith's Ridge, and the command of the 1st Marine Division put the figure at 1,750 enemy killed in the Hill 296 defenses.[38]

Survivors of Dog Company agreed that in spite of such frightful losses, the Red Koreans had enough able-bodied men left at the finish to make mincemeat of the 26 attackers who took Smith's Ridge. But this Marine effort seemed to break the heart of enemy resistance in the Hill 296 defense complex, thus giving fresh proof of Napoleon's famous dictum, "The moral is to the material in war as three to one."

[35] 1st MarDiv *SAR*, Annex Queen Queen:Oboe; Deptula interv. 18 Jan 55.
[40] Cushman interv, 26 Jul 54.
[37] 1st MAW *SAR*. Annex Item:Roger.
[38] Roise interv, 9 Nov 54; and O. P. Smith, *Notes*, 286.

River Crossing of RCT-1

The battle for Seoul entered its final stage on the 24th with the river crossing of the 1st Marines. At first light a site about 2,000 yards southwest of Hill 105–S was cleared by Charlie Company of the 1st Engineer Battalion. Extensive mine-clearing operations at the crossing site area caused delays, and it was 0800 when reconnaissance and assault elements of 2/1 embarked in the LVTs of Company A, 1st Amphibian Tractor Battalion. Sutter's troops completed their crossing at 0945 against scattered and ineffectual fire, and made contact that afternoon on the north bank with elements of Company C, 5th Marines.[39]

For lack of a ferry, the 1st Marines had no tank support at the crossing site. Plans had been made to send Baker Company, 1st Tank Battalion, around by the Haengju ferry to join the infantry north of the river. As it worked out, however, the armor was delayed by a fight on the north bank which will be discussed in the next chapter.

Hill 79, about 4,000 yards from the crossing site, had been assigned to the 1st Marines by Division OpnO 10–50 as an objective. The 2d Battalion began a rapid advance toward this point after moving into position on the north bank abreast of the 5th Marines on a 1,500-yard front.

The 1st Battalion and Regimental Headquarters were next to cross. Puller ordered Hawkins and his men to drive eastward along the river and pass through the 2d Battalion. Since that unit was rapidly advancing at the time, one of the 1/1 staff officers looked dubious.

"You'll just have to advance a little faster," explained the veteran regimental commander.[40]

This proved to be a practical even if not exactly a school solution. On the march the 1st Battalion had the same experience as the 2d when small-arms and automatic fire came from Hill 105–S, supposedly secured by 1/5. Again the enemy was demonstrating his ability to hide out behind the Marine lines and make the most of his nuisance value. The 2d Battalion had two men killed and nine wounded by harassing fires, and the 1st suffered four casualties while passing through at 1300 to continue the attack.

Effective Marine artillery and 4.2-inch mortar fire supported the advance. After drawing out of range of Hill 105–S, Hawkins and

---

[39] 2/1 *SAR*; and O. P. Smith, *Notes*, 268.
[40] Bridges interv, 18 Oct 54.

his men encountered long-range small-arms fire, and roads into the city were mined. Hill 79 was located in the southwest section of Seoul itself, commanding a good view of the railroad marshaling yards and industrial area. After seizing the objective at 1500, the men celebrated by raising an American flag, thus precipitating a friendly race with the 5th Marines in exuberant ceremonies of this sort.

At 1515 the 3d Battalion was relieved by the Division of its mission of defending Hill 108, south of the wrecked Han bridges, and reverted to regimental control for a river crossing completed at 2000. On the north bank Ridge's outfit was thought to have pulled the last fangs of enemy resistance on Hill 105–S after his men in their turn came under fire from hidden opponents. Since this height dominated the new regimental CP, Company I was given the mission of outposting the height. A small but lively fire fight took place at dusk, and the Marines bagged ten prisoners at a cost of one man killed and two wounded.[41]

The 3d Battalion went into an assembly area near the crossing site for the night. Hawkins set up a perimeter defense on the objective, and the 2d Battalion occupied positions about 2,000 yards in the rear. A few probing attacks were received from enemy patrols on Hill 79, but Marine artillery and 4.2-inch mortars made short work of these attempts.

---

[41] 3/1 *SAR.*

CHAPTER XIII

Seoul as a Battlefield

Two More River Crossings—Division Attack of 25 September—Night Pursuit Ordered by Corps—Renewal of Drive Through Seoul—Entrapment of Dog Company, RCT–7—Last Fight on Hill 296—1st Marines in the Heart of Seoul—Objective Secured

O N THE MORNING of 25 September 1950, with RCT–1 across the river, the 1st Marine Division was in a position for the first time since D-day to launch an attack of all three regiments abreast.

This was but one of the portents indicating that the days of the North Korean People's Army were numbered. Exactly three months had passed since the invasion of the Republic of Korea, and now the forces of the Communist puppet state were reeling under blows from two directions. While X Corps pounded inland to seize the NKPA main communications hub, the Eighth Army had smashed through the Pusan Perimeter and was driving northward to place the enemy between two fires.

The big break in South Korea came on 23 September. Up to that time, the NKPA 5th, 8th, 12th, and 15th Divisions had put up a stubborn resistance on the northern front of the Pusan Perimeter against six ROK divisions. Then the enemy crumpled and the ROKs began an advance (see map in end papers) that would take them 70 miles during the ensuing week.[1]

It was much the same story along the Kumchon-Taejon axis of the central front. There the U. S. I Corps, comprising the U. S. 24th Infantry and 1st Cavalry Divisions, the 1st ROK Division, and the British 27th Brigade, drove a deep salient into the line of the 1st, 3d,

---

[1] Almond, *UN MilOps*, 13.

13th, 10th, and 2d NKPA Divisions. UN gains of 35 miles were made from the 22d to the 25th.

In the south the U. S. 2d and 25th Divisions had hurled the NKPA 6th, 4th, 9th, and 7th Divisions back from the vicinity of Masan to the Chinju area. This gain of about 15 miles from 21 to 23 September was only a prelude as the two U. S. divisions pressed their advantage against a retreating enemy.[2]

The ultimate purpose of the joint Eighth Army and X Corps offensive must already have been made alarmingly apparent to NKPA generals. Not only was the Eighth Army salient along the Kumchon-Taejon axis being extended northwest, but a X Corps regiment was driving southeast toward a junction. This was the 31st Infantry of the 7th Infantry Division, which had been given the mission of following in the trace of the 32d, then wheeling southward toward the Suwon area to meet the elements of the 1st Cavalry Division spearheading the Eighth Army advance. Thus was the drawstring being rapidly pulled on the remnants of the invading NKPA army, soon to have its main routes of escape cut off by UN forces.

Two More River Crossings

After nearly a week of commanding a division in combat on both sides of an unbridged tidal river, Generals Smith and Craig now had a consolidated front north of the Han, with RCT–1 on the right, RCT–5 in the center, and RCT–7 on the left. The 11th Marines was in position on the south bank. The 1st, 3d, and 4th Battalions lined up northwest of Yongdungpo, while the 2d Battalion and the U. S. Army 96th Field Artillery emplaced to the east of that shattered suburb.[3]

Two more river crossings took place on 25 September. First, the 32d Infantry of the 7th Infantry Division moved to the north bank in accordance with the revised Corps plan. The Marine 1st Amphibian Tractor Battalion (less Company B) and the Army's Company A, 56th Amphibian Tractor Battalion had to make a 25-mile round trip that night to bring the troops to an embarkation point about 5,000 yards east of the railroad bridge at Yongdungpo. Scattered enemy small-arms and artillery fire was received during the crossing, resulting in

---

[2] *Ibid.*
[3] MarCorps Board *Study,* II–B, 37.

a few casualties among crews and soldiers. The LVTs took the troops about 200 yards inland, where they advanced on foot to their objectives on South Mountain without encountering any opposition other than long-range harassing fires.[4]

Later that same day the 17th ROK Regiment, under the control of the 7th Infantry Division, crossed in the LVTs. It was hoped by United Nations leaders that this unit, known as the Seoul Regiment, could take part in the liberation of the ROK capital. Apparently the second river crossing of the day alarmed the enemy, for it drew mortar and artillery fire in greater volume and accuracy than had been encountered before.

The support given to the two crossings by the 1st Amphibian Tractor Battalion was commended by General Barr in a letter to General Smith. "Despite long hours, loss of sleep, maintenance difficulties, and exposure to fire," said the commanding general of the 7th Infantry Division, "the personnel of your battalion performed so magnificently that I have nothing but praise to offer. If at any time in the future elements of this Division are called upon to cross a river, it is my sincere wish that they may be supported by the 1st Amphibian Tractor Battalion." [5]

From South Mountain the troops of the 32d Infantry looked down upon the city. They could not enter as yet because of the danger of interfering with the fires of the 1st and 5th Marines. But the 32d and the ROK unit were assigned a zone of action by Corps for an advance on the right of the Marines when the time came for a concerted effort.

Division Attack of 25 September

At 0700 on the 25th the 1st Marine Division launched the final phase of its attack on Seoul. The following objectives were assigned by Division OpnO 11–50:

RCT–1, with the 2d KMC Battalion attached, was to seize the part of Seoul within its zone of action and Objective ABLE, consisting of the high ground beyond the northeastern outskirts and about six miles from the jump-off positions. The zone of action, ranging from a mile to a mile and a half wide, carried the attack through the heart of the city, with South Mountain on the right and Ducksoo Palace on the

[4] MarCorps Board *Study*, II–B, 37; Irick interv, 16 Nov 54.
[5] MajGen D. G. Barr (USA) ltr to MajGen O. P. Smith, 5 Oct 50.

left. Mopping-up operations were assigned to the KMCs, who would revert to their own regimental control afterwards.

RCT–5, with the Division Reconnaissance Company and 1st KMC Battalion attached, was to seize that part of Seoul within its zone of action and Objective BAKER, comprising the high ground overlooking the Seoul-Uijongbu road six miles from the line of departure. About a mile and a half wide, this zone included the northwest section of the city and the Government Palace, though the regiment would be operating in open country after an advance of about two miles. The KMCs were to be used for mopping up after RCT–5.

RCT–7 had the mission of protecting the left flank of the Division and seizing Objective CHARLIE—the high ground astride the Seoul-Kaesong road about six miles northwest of the center of Seoul in the vicinity of Chonsong-ni.

The KMC Regiment (less the 1st and 2d Battalions) was designated the division reserve. It was to be prepared to resume control of detached battalions and occupy Seoul.

The 3d Battalion, 187th Airborne RCT, with Special Operations Company attached, was to continue under operational control of the 1st Marine Division and protect the Corps left flank west and south of the river Han.[6]

Following the artillery and air preparation, 3/5 and 2/5 jumped off abreast from left to right in an attack on the remaining defenses of the Hill 296 complex. Roise's objective was Hill 105–N. He was to be supported by fires from Taplett's men, attacking down the slopes of Hill 296 in an advance that would eventually pinch out the 2d Battalion, which would go into reserve. The 1st Battalion had completed its relief of 3d Battalion elements on Hills 216 and 296, thus placing it in position to move up on the left of the 3d.[7]

During the air strikes, VMF–214 had its second pilot fatality in two days when Lieutenant Colonel Lischeid was shot down in flames over the western edge of the city. His death brought to light a curious train of circumstances. It was recalled that the squadron had lost its first pilot on D-plus 2 when enemy fire killed Captain Simpson in plane No. 17. Two days later, while inspecting the new No. 17 on the flight deck of the *Sicily*, Technical Sergeant George C. Underwood received a mortal wound from an accidental discharge of the guns. Major

[6] O. P. Smith, *Notes*, 133–135.
[7] 1st MarDiv *SAR*, Annex Queen Queen.

Robert Floeck was flying this Corsair when he met his death on 23 September, but the machine was saved. And it was in plane No. 17 that the squadron commander crashed on the 25th. This was enough for Captain John H. Thach of the *Sicily,* and he issued an order banning the number forever on the carrier.[8]

Within two hours of Lischeid's death, two other squadron commanders were shot down, Lieutenant Colonel Wyczawski of VMF–212 and Lieutenant Colonel Volcansek of VMF(N)–542. Both escaped with moderate injuries, but in the space of a few minutes Volcansek had pressed his luck within a hair's breadth of the point of no return. Wounded, his plane badly damaged by enemy fire from Seoul, the squadron commander stubbornly led his flight in two more passes on Red positions. Approaching Kimpo, he was forced to keep the battered F7F–3N at almost 200 knots—twice the landing speed—to prevent its stalling.

There was no alternative but to bail out. When he jettisoned the canopy, his altimeter needle wavered around the 1,000-foot mark. Slipstreams from the twin engines pinned him to the cockpit as the plane continued losing altitude. In desperation he kicked violently at the stick with both feet. The aircraft lurched downward and Volcansek was thrown clear, the big tail of the machine missing him by inches as both plummeted earthward. A few seconds after the officer's chute opened and broke the fall, his feet touched earth a few miles northwest of Kimpo. Within 45 minutes he was aboard a helicopter rattling back to the airfield.[9]

It was the last day for the *Sicily* and VMF–214 in the Inchon-Seoul operation. That evening the CVE left the area for maintenance work, and the *Badoeng Strait* took over with VMF–323.

Easy Company led the attack of 2/5 on the 25th, with Dog on the left and Fox in reserve. The advance was supported by a platoon of tanks as well as fires from 3/5 on Hill 296. An effective artillery preparation aided the advance, but Captain Jaskilka's men were enfiladed by enemy mortar and automatic fire from Hill 72. Lieutenant Deptula's platoon led the assault and seized this position by 1335 after suffering heavily along the way. Lieutenant Seydel commanded the remnants of Dog Company which jumped off from Smith's Ridge and took Hill 88 at 1320.[10]

[8] 1st MAW *SAR*, Annex Jig:Easy; Karig, *Korea,* 259.
[9] *Ibid.,* Annex Item:Sugar; Col M. I. Volcansek, Jr. interv, 15 Mar 55.
[10] 1st MarDiv *SAR,* Annex Queen Queen:basic rpt and Oboe.

While Fox Company moved up to occupy Hill 72, an airstrike was called on Hill 105–N at 1310, and the artillery bombardment began 15 minutes later in preparation for the final assault by Easy Company. Second Lieutenants James W. Epley and Samuel L. Eddy, Jr., led the advance with their platoons, and Hill 105–N was reported as secured at 1545.

The 2d Battalion, with the exception of Deptula's platoon had met moderate opposition as compared with the last two days. It was in the zone of the 3d that the enemy put up his most stubborn resistance on 25 September. George and How Companies, the latter on the exposed left flank, led the attack on the remaining NKPA positions along the two southeastern spurs of Hill 296. Initial progress was slow, the attackers being harassed by long range fires from Hill 338 on the left and 105–N on the right. Lieutenant Colonel Murray directed the battalion to hold up until the situation around 105–N clarified. Resuming the attack against mounting resistance on the left, at 1435, the two companies reached their objectives two hours later and made contact with 2/5 on the right.[11]

Since 105–N capped the terminus of the lower of 3/5's two spurs, the whole length of the 1,000-yard projection was tagged with that number. This fact accounts for both Roise and Taplett reporting that they were in possession of the height. Actually, 2/5 was on 105–N, and George Company of 3/5 held an unnumbered peak to the north on the same ridge.[12]

Company H, in moving down the huge spur on the open left flank, had taken heavy casualties before reaching its objective, an intermediate peak. Just as Item Company was passing through to continue the attack at about 1700, the Marines were hit hard by a force of 200 Reds, who advanced under cover of accurate supporting fire. The close-in fire fight raged until after nightfall, and both depleted companies were hard-pressed to hold their own. Weakened by the loss of 100 dead, the enemy finally withdrew, thereby allowing Item Company to take over the front line while How reverted to battalion reserve.[13]

Thus, the 3d Battalion was now in position to pinch out the 2d on the morrow and to trace Item Company's spur into the very heart of Seoul. In preparation for the assault of Hill 338, Newton's 1st Battalion had

---

[11] 1st MarDiv *SAR*, Annex Queen Queen:Peter.
[12] LtCol R. D. Taplett interv, 11 May 55; and LtCol H. S. Roise interv, 11 May 55.
[13] 1st MarDiv *SAR*, Annex Queen Queen; Taplett interv, 11 May 55; and Maj R. A. McMullen interv, 25 Aug 54.

shifted to the regimental left, where, with the Division Recon Company and the 1st KMC Battalion, it blocked the precipitous approaches to 216 and 296.

In the zone of the 7th Marines, the 2d Battalion had jumped off at 0630 and occupied Objective CHARLIE at 1215 without meeting resistance. Patrols of the 1st Battalion devoted the day to reconnoitering the area between RCT-7 and RCT-5, maintaining contact with both. The 3d Battalion was employed defensively along roads and trails in an arc around the ferry crossing site at Haengju.[14]

Tank Victory on Hill 105–S

In preparation for the attack of the 1st Marines, the 3d Battalion moved forward before daybreak in a column of companies. Passing eastward through the 2d Battalion, Ridge's men began a sharp wheel to the north. The 1st Battalion, on Hill 79, withdrew slightly, pivoting on its left flank in order to reorient its direction of attack and tie in with the 3d Battalion on the left.

Thus did RCT-1 carry out the Corps plan of maneuver on the morning of the 25th by making a 90-degree change of direction, after advancing eastward to Hill 79, and driving straight northward toward the heart of Seoul. It was necessary to jump off without tank support, however, since the assigned armor had been delayed by a fight on the way.

The 2d and 3d Platoons of Captain Bruce F. Williams' Baker Company, 1st Tank Battalion, had crossed the river at the Haengju ferry on the 24th. Reports of enemy mines along the railroad leading into Seoul caused Lieutenant Babe's 2d Platoon of Company C Engineers to be attached to the tanks. And since the column was to pass through the zone of the 2d Battalion, 5th Marines, a depleted infantry platoon of Company F was attached under the command of Staff Sergeant Arthur Farrington.

Owing to the shift of 1/5, a gap existed at this time between the zones of the 1st and 5th Marines; and the little task force entered this area with the infantry at the point and the engineers sandwiched between the tanks—a total of some 50 men supporting the armor. About half of the gap between the regiments had been safely traversed when the

---

[14] O. P. Smith, *Notes*, 286–287.

head of the column received a few scattered shots from the slope of Hill 105–S.

After being supposedly secured by 1/5, with a final mopping up by 3/1, this troublesome position now erupted into enemy small-arms fire that could only have come from at least a company-size pocket of resistance. Lieutenant Babe was severely wounded before he could carry out his plan of sending Farrington's platoon around to envelop the left flank of the NKPA troops entrenched on the slope. After Technical Sergeant Pasquale Paolino took command of the engineers, his men and the infantry platoon were so badly outnumbered that Captain Williams considered pulling them inside the tanks and withdrawing. Then it occurred to him to send a flame-thrower tank, escorted by Staff Sergeant Altaire's M–26, around the enemy's left flank by way of a primitive trail leading southward from the railway tracks.[15]

This maneuver had a spectacular success. The flame tank moved into a position enabling it to sear the length of the NKPA trenches with bursts of napalm. When the terrified Red Koreans fled down the slope, they became targets for the machine guns of Lieutenant Cummings' platoon of tanks.

Sergeants Paolino and Farrington had meanwhile been organizing an infantry and engineer base of small-arms fire from men taking cover along the railroad embankment and the lower slopes of the hill. The engineer NCO noticed that enemy grenades were being lobbed from three thatched huts below the NKPA trenches on the left flank. Closer inspection revealed the mouth of a cave, concealed by the third house and extending back into Hill 105–S.

Paolino, after getting Williams' permission to direct tank fire, banged on the hull of Cummings' M–26 and indicated the huts and mouth of the cave as targets. A few 90mm rounds destroyed the huts; but before Cummings could fire into the cave, eight or ten NKPA soldiers came out with upraised hands. When they were allowed to surrender unharmed, the example had an amazing effect as a seemingly endless file of enemy troops poured out of the cave. Altogether, 131 prisoners were taken, in addition to an estimated 150 killed, on a hill first reported secured two days before. Apparently the undiscovered cave had provided a refuge for nearly 300 Red Koreans.

---

[15] The description of this fight is based upon the following sources: 1st MarDiv *SAR*, Annex Peter Peter; Cummings interv, 12 Oct 54; and Babe-Paolino interv, 15 Nov 54.

Among the captives, as the Marines discovered later were two women in uniform who had evidently been armed. Because of the NKPA reputation for treachery, it was considered necessary to search them; but they were treated with respect and provided with garments more appropriate to their sex. In spite of the consideration shown them, the incident resulted in sensational articles in stateside publications after the women reached the rear and claimed mistreatment on the grounds that they were nurses.

Two wounded engineers and an infantry casualty were the price of the Marine success after a surprise encounter had been turned to the disadvantage of the enemy. Since the NKPA prisoners were more than double the numbers of the engineers and infantry, they were placed between two M–26s when the column resumed the march.

It was 1200 when Cummings reported to Colonel Puller at the intersection of the railroad and a boulevard with street car tracks leading into the heart of the city. The tanks took the lead, joining 3/1 in its fighting advance up both sides of the north-south boulevard. Enemy mines knocked out two of the M–26s, one of them being Cummings' tank, but both were retrieved in spite of heavy NKPA fire.

Successive road blocks consisting of earth-filled rice bags were stubbornly defended by enemy infantry supported by NKPA automatic, AT, and mortar fire from the roof tops. The Marines pressed forward methodically and by evening the 3d Battalion had penetrated about 2,000 yards into the city to occupy positions astride the streetcar line and on the western slopes of Hill 97. The 1st Battalion, on the high ground to the right, had advanced about 2,000 yards when both assault units tied in for the night with defensive positions on Hill 82. The 2d Battalion, as regimental reserve, deployed in the rear of the 1st to protect the right flank and rear.[16]

Night Attack Ordered by Corps

The battle for Seoul took a sudden and unexpected new turn at 2009 on the night of 25 September 1950 when the following X Corps flash (plain) message was received at the CP of the 1st Marine Division:

"Info addressee (X Corps TacAir Commander) reports enemy fleeing city of Seoul on road north of Uijongbu. . . . He [TacAir] is

---

[16] 1st MarDiv *SAR*, Annex Peter Peter; O. P. Smith, *Notes*, 284–285.

conducting heavy air attack and will continue same. You will push attack now to the limit of your objectives in order to insure maximum destruction of enemy forces. Signed Almond."[17]

The Division G–3 immediately called the Corps G–3 for corroboration. Colonel Bowser questioned the ability of night air observation to determine whether the movement out of the city consisted of urban refugees or enemy troops. He was informed, however, that the intention of Corps was for the attack to begin at once.

General Smith then called the X Corps chief of staff for confirmation, pointing out the inadvisability of attacking at night in an unfamiliar Oriental city of the size and complexity of Seoul, particularly as there was no indication of the enemy fleeing from the Division front. But General Ruffner replied that General Almond himself had dictated the message and it was to be executed without delay.[18]

General Smith gave the attack order to the commanding officers of the 1st and 5th Marines, directing them to coordinate their efforts and confine them to avenues of advance which could be identified at night. His order was receipted by the 1st Marines at 2205 and the 5th Marines at 2215 just a few hours after the NKPA counterattack hit the 3d Battalion of Murray's regiment.

While the two rifle regiments made preparations to jump off, the order was relayed to the 7th and 11th Marines. Colonel Puller coordinated hastily with the 5th Marines and supporting arms for an attack scheduled to begin at 0145 on 26 September, following a 15-minute artillery preparation.[19]

At 0138, deciding that the preparation was inadequate, he notified the assault battalions to "stand fast, preparatory fires to be repeated." A new jump-off time of 0200 was set, but at 0153 a dramatic interruption came in the form of a flash message from the 3d Battalion of the 1st Marines. Lieutenant Colonel Ridge reported that a heavy enemy attack, supported by tanks and self-propelled guns, was moving down the main avenue leading from the center of the city to the southwest in the zone of the 1st Marines.[20]

It was the enemy's misfortune that 3/1 had sent out a patrol of eight Marines and three natives under Corporal Charles E. Collins to make

[17] O. P. Smith, *Notes*, 288–289.
[18] *Ibid.*
[19] 1st MarDiv *SAR*, Annex Peter Peter, Queen Queen; MarCorps Board *Study*, II–B, 38–39.
[20] 1st MarDiv *SAR*, Annex Peter Peter.

contact with a similar patrol from the 5th Marines. But at 0130 the clamor of a fire fight about 400 yards in front of 3/1 was followed by the return of members of the patrol who gave the alarm. Corporal Collins was still missing when Major Simmons heard the sound of tracked vehicles and was warned that two enemy tanks were approaching the George Company roadblock defended by heavy machine guns, 3.5-inch rocket launchers and 75mm recoilless guns.[21]

These weapons accounted for the destruction of one enemy tank and the hasty retreat of the other. The Division attack scheduled for 0200 was indefinitely postponed, of course, until 3/1, astride the principal avenue of approach, could deal with a large-scale enemy counterattack launched by an estimated battalion of infantry and about 12 tanks supported by self-propelled guns and mortars. A terrific concentration of Marine artillery was called down upon an NKPA effort that reached its peak about 0230. High-angle Marine howitzer and 81mm mortar fire almost literally blasted the attacking column out of existence, and enemy infantry action was negligible afterwards.[22]

At 0315 the artillery liaison officer informed Puller that the three battalions of the 11th Marines must cease barrage fire at the penalty of burning out the tubes of their howitzers. During the comparative lull the T–34s continued to attack at intervals until daybreak, and the last two tanks were killed at 0630.[23] About that time Corporal Collins returned safely after having been given up as dead. Exposed to friendly as well as enemy fire all night, he had made his way back through enemy-held areas in a disguise of Korean civilian garments.

POW interrogation and examination of the ground revealed that seven enemy tanks and two self-propelled guns were destroyed or disabled by Marine mines, rockets, mortars, or artillery. An estimated 475 to 500 infantry of the NKPA 25th Brigade had been killed and many more wounded, and the Marines took 83 prisoners at a relatively light cost in casualties.[24]

At 0500, as 3/1's fight in the city was tapering off, another Red force of battalion strength hit the 2d Battalion, 32d Infantry, on South Mountain. A section of the Army unit's front was overrun, but a counterattack restored the line by 0700. Finally driven from the ridge, the North Koreans left behind 394 dead and 174 prisoners, according to the regimental report.[25]

Entrapment of Dog Company, RCT-7

On the morning of 26 September it may have occurred to some of the Marines that yesterday's announcement by X Corps of the capture of Seoul was a bit premature. The lines of the Division remained where they were the night before, with only the difference that hundreds of enemy dead gave testimony of a busy night.

Division OpnO 12–50, issued at 1230 on the 26th, directed a continuation of the attack on Seoul, the principal change from the last order being the commitment of the 7th Marines. This regiment, augmented by the Division Recon Company and 5th KMC battalion, was given the mission of pinching out the 5th Marines about 1200 yards beyond the Government Palace and attacking abreast of the 1st Marines toward the northeast. In the 7th's zone of advance north of the city lay Objectives DOG (northern half of Hill 338), EASY (Hill 342), FOX (Hill 133), GEORGE (Hill 343), and BAKER (Hill 171)—as rugged an order of terrain as any outfit could be served. Puller's regiment, with the 2d KMC Battalion attached, would drive northward from Hills 97 and 82 in lower Seoul, clear the center of the city, then wheel to the right to take Objective ABLE, Hill 133 in the northeastern outskirts.

The 5th Marines, with the 1st KMC Battalion attached, was to support Litzenberg's attack until being pinched out, whereupon it had orders to assemble in Division reserve and relieve elements of the 7th Marines. The KMC Regiment was still under orders to resume control of its detached battalions for the occupation of Seoul. The 3d Battalion, however, was detached from the 1st Marine Division and ordered to report to the 3d Battalion, 187th Airborne RCT, for operational control in Kumpo Peninsula operations. Responsibility for the security of Kimpo Airfield now rested upon X Corps.[26]

Thus, the Marine front prior to the assault formed a semicircle extending from the Kaesong Highway in the northwest to Hill 82 in

---

[25] 32d Inf *War Diary*, 18–30 Sep 50.
[26] O. P. Smith, *Notes*, 294–295.

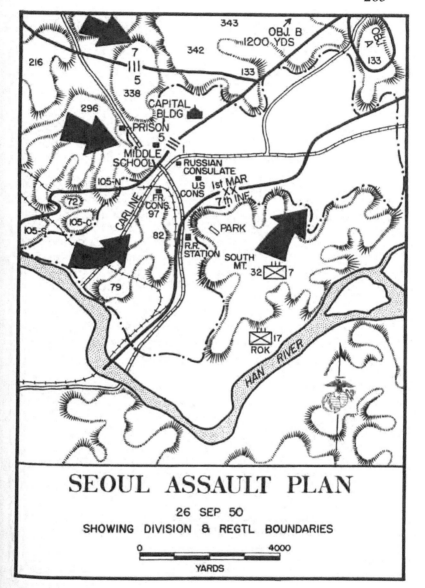

SEOUL ASSAULT PLAN

26 SEP 50

SHOWING DIVISION & REGTL BOUNDARIES

0   4000

YARDS

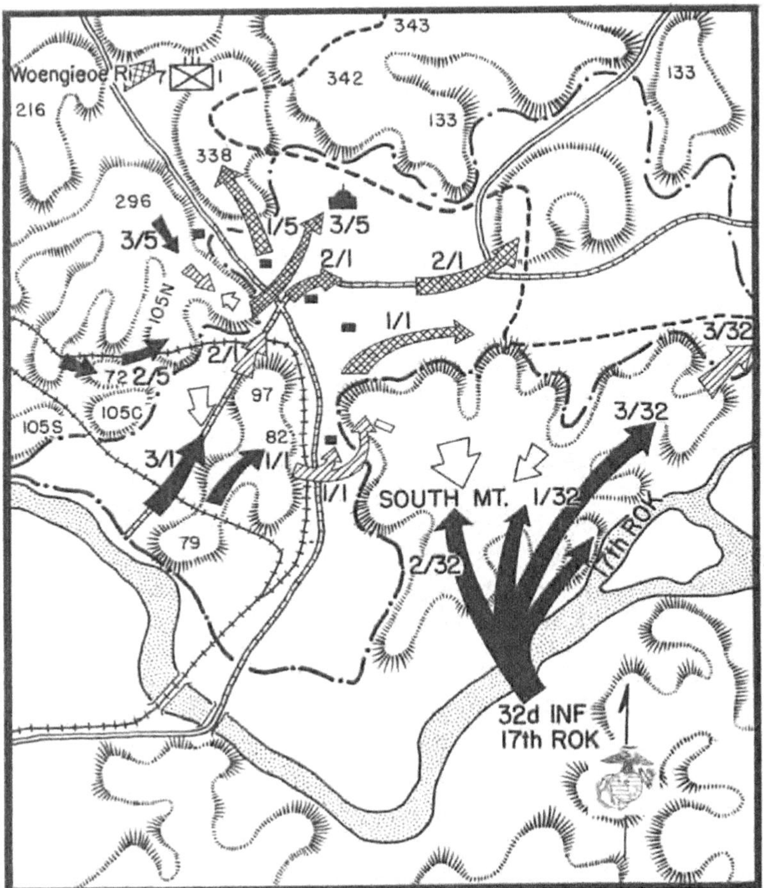

THE BATTLE OF SEOUL

SHOWING ATTACKS BY 5th MARINES, 1st MARINES, & 32d INF

25 SEP 26 SEP 27 SEP

NK COUNTERATTACKS OF 25 & 26 SEP

APPROXIMATE X CORPS FRONT, 2400 27 SEP

0 4000

YARDS

the south, and the concave side faced Seoul like a giant scythe poised to mow down the last remnants of NKPA resistance.

Colonel Litzenberg dispatched Dog Company of the 7th Marines southwest along the Kaesong Highway at 0630 on 26 September. The mission of the unit was to approach Seoul and make contact with the 5th Marines on the right. In the van of the column was the company machine gun officer, First Lieutenant William F. Goggin. For a while it seemed as though this untried unit was reaping the laurels earned by its battle-weary relatives of the 1st and 5th Marines, since hundreds of Koreans lined the highway to welcome the "victors" with resounding cheers.[27]

Progress was marked off rapidly in the absence of enemy resistance. The Marines passed through Hoengjeoe-ri, and by 0900 the great slopes of Hill 296 loomed up on the right and those of 338 on the left. Tracing the road through the narrow valley between, the company approached the Sodaemun Prison at the northwest corner of Seoul. Suddenly the column came under machine-gun fire from a high tower about 400 yards down the road. The initial burst caused several casualties, including Lieutenant Goggin, and the Marines quickly deployed on both sides of the road. Several more enemy machine-guns and rifles opened up from hillside positions only a hundred yards away. Since the throngs of well-wishers along the highway had prevented the use of flank guards, Company D was caught flatfooted in the low ground by the hail of lead.

After a few minutes, other Red weapons began firing from the lower slopes of Hills 296 and 338, directly to the flanks, and encirclement seemed imminent. Dog Company's commander, Captain Richard R. Breen, reacted by ordering the 2d Platoon to attack the high ground around the prison. Simultaneously, First Lieutenant Paul P. Sartwell set up two 60mm mortars on the road and silenced one of the North Korean emplacements. Directing his crews from an exposed position, the young officer was wounded three times before finally being put out of action.

First Lieutenant Edward H. Seeburger closed on the prison with his 2d Platoon, while First Lieutenant Paul V. Mullaney's 1st ascended

---

[27] The following narrative is derived from: 1st MarDiv *SAR*, Annex Roger Roger; and Maj J. D. Hammond interv, 17 Aug 54.

the slopes of Hill 338 on the left. The 3d, under First Lieutenant James D. Hammond, Jr., remained in position along the road. When the assault platoons were stopped on the high ground by stiffening resistance, Company D settled down in an elongated perimeter for a battle of survival. There was no artillery support, but Marine air assisted by pounding the crescent of Red positions.

The S–3 of the 7th Marines, Major Raymond V. Fridrich, radioed Captain Breen and asked about the situation. Though now wounded himself, Breen stated that he could hold his ground. A small tank-infantry column was dispatched from regiment to reach the beleaguered force with ammunition and supplies. By this time, however, the Reds had set up in the rear of Dog Company, and the relief force was turned back.

Faced with the bleak fact that it was now surrounded, Company D withdrew 1000 yards to a defensible road cut between Hills 296 and 338. The Marines completed the move with their wounded and dead at 1600. After being resupplied by air drop in their tight perimeter, they prepared grimly for an all-night stand.

Elsewhere in the 7th Marines' zone, 26 September would be remembered as much for exhausting marches and climbs as for enemy contacts. In the morning the 1st Battalion, under Lieutenant Colonel Davis, had taken over flank responsibility far to the northeast along the Kaesong highway, thereby relieving the 2d (less Company D) and 3d for the advance on Seoul. The 2d Battalion then moved out in trace of Dog Company, but according to plan veered leftward into the hills at Hoengjeoe-ri, one mile short of the ambuscade. While 2/7 reconnoitered the high ground above the village, Major Roach's 3d Battalion completed an eight-and-a-half-mile forced march to gain an assembly area in preparation for the assault of northern Hill 338.

At 1400 Fox and Easy Companies of 2/7 attacked eastward from the height above Hoengjeoe-ri to seize Hill 343. After an advance of 1000 yards, they were stopped cold by heavy fire from the direction of Hill 338 to the south. Lieutenant Colonel Hinkle ordered 2/7 to dig in short of the objective, since any further progress would only make his right more vulnerable to the enemy guns on the flank.

Captain Thomas E. Cooney led Company G of 3/7 through Hoeng-jeoe-ri about 1700, circled the northern half of Hill 338, then launched a two-platoon assault on the crest. His Marines gained the north summit against no opposition, but Company H, led by Captain Nicholas

269

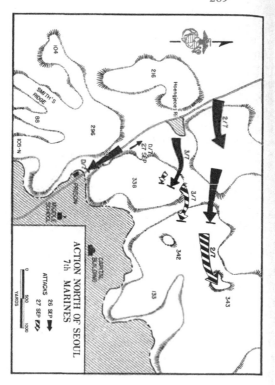

ACTION NORTH OF SEOUL
7th MARINES

ATTACKS   26 SEP
          27 SEP

YARDS
0   500   1000

L. Shields, was taken under fire in a draw to the right and held up on the slopes for the night.[28]

Last Fight on Hill 296

While the 7th Marines were fighting uphill on 26 September, the 3d Battalion, 5th Marines, punched downward in a bitter contest to clear the last NKPA resistance from the Hill 296 complex. The attack was launched early in the morning after preparatory fires by artillery and 81mm mortars. Item Company on the left was to sweep the remainder of the giant spur which descended into the very heart of Seoul. George, upon jumping off from the ridge above Hill 105–N, would clear the low ground on Item's right.

Dissatisfied with the accuracy of the preparatory barrages, and underestimating the enemy's strength and determination, Captain McMullen called off supporting arms and based the success of his two-platoon assault on organic company weapons alone. No sooner had the Marines lunged downhill than great gaps were torn in the skirmish line by fire from swarms of North Koreans on the lower slopes. Both assault platoon leaders were wounded before an intermediate knoll was taken, and McMullen was forced to commit his reserve to bolster the hard-hit 3d Platoon on the right.

Continuing the attack under the personal leadership of its commander, the entire company waded into a maze of entrenchments manned by 200 enemy soldiers. In the close-in fighting that followed, the Reds were driven from their emplacements to seek cover farther down the spur. The depleted ranks of Item Company ground to a halt.

There followed a brief calm—abruptly shattered when the North Koreans rallied and counterattacked uphill against the company center. A wild melee enveloped the ridgeline, and the tactical situation gradually became a blur. Just as it seemed the Marines' hold on the lower spur would be pried loose, Lieutenant Williamson plowed into the tumult at the head of a small supply party. Ammunition distributed in the heat of the fighting tipped the scales in favor of the Marines, but not before McMullen was carried from the field as a result of his seventh battle wound in two wars.

---

[28] *Ibid.;* and Capt H. H. Harris—Capt R. R. Van Cleve interv, 10 Aug 54.

The heavy fighting finally eased toward the close of the day. Although the last organized defenses of the enemy were smashed, Company I was too badly battered to seize the tip of the spur before nightfall. Abreast on the right, First Lieutenant Charles D. Mize led Company G into defensive positions after a day of inching forward against stubborn opposition in the low ground.[29]

Other units of the 5th Marines experienced little action during 3/5's day-long engagement. While the 2d Battalion mopped up in its zone south of the 3d, the 1st KMC Battalion moved into position between the latter and the Reconnaissance Company, now manning the topographical peak of Hill 296 in the northwest. To the rear of 3/5, the 1st Battalion enjoyed a quiet interlude in regimental reserve.

1st Marines in the Heart of Seoul

Early in the morning of 26 September, the 2d Battalion, 1st Marines, moved out of reserve to pass through the 3d on the streetcar line and continue the attack northward into the center of Seoul. On the right of Puller's zone, 1/1 prepared to descend Hill 82 and clear the main railroad station and adjoining slopes of South Mountain, where increasing enemy activity had been noted below the positions of the 32d Infantry.[30]

Sutter's unit completed the passage of lines at 0900 and attacked along the boulevard with Fox and Easy Companies in the assault. Leading the advance up the street were the tanks of Baker Company, Cummings' M–26 in the van. The young officer's machine had proceeded only a few yards when it struck an American M6 mine, overlooked by Marine engineers while they were removing their hasty field of the previous night. Not only did the explosion wreck the tank, but it also caused several casualties among the infantry on either side.

The attack edged forward in the second day of the "Battle of the Barricades." Every 200–300 yards, fanatical Red detachments manned rice-bag barriers about eight feet high and five feet thick, stretching

[29] As is frequently the case after heavy fighting, 3/5's *SAR* contains inaccuracies in its account covering 24–27 September, leaving the reader with the impression that the entire spur leading into the city was secured on the 26th. In retracing the progress of the attack during interviews with the authors, both Lieutenant Colonel Taplett and Captain (now Major) McMullen agree that the foregoing account is correct.

[30] The following narrative is derived from: 1st MarDiv *SAR*, Annexes Oboe Oboe and Peter Peter; 2/1 *SAR*; Sutter—Codispoti interv, 25 Jan 55; and Cummings interv, 12 Oct. 54.

the whole width of the street. It fell to the M–26s to smash the emplacements and silence the NKPA antitank guns behind each one. Marine tank action in turn hinged on mine clearance by supporting engineers, who looked to flanking infantry for covering fire. Thus was a system of three-party teamwork developed and perfected during the roar of battle.

Aiding the Communists behind the barricades were other North Koreans who fired their rifles and submachine guns from roof tops, windows, and side streets. The Marine infantry, therefore, had to defend in every direction as it attacked to the front. Intense heat from burning buildings along the street added to the handicaps, and the constant discovery of South Korean civilians, including women and children, huddled in the rubble further strained the taut nerves of men who looked for trouble from every quarter.

It was a dirty, frustrating fight every yard of the way, perhaps best described by Puller himself, who reported that "progress was agonizingly slow." A principal deterrent to speed was the fact that all supporting tanks simultaneously expended their ammunition and fuel, so that all had to return to the rear for replenishment at the same time. During their absences from the fight, the infantry understandably chose to await their return rather than pay heavily in casualties by assaulting barricades with small arms alone.

At one point in the street battle, an enemy soldier darted from behind a building and charged a flame tank advancing behind two lead M–26s. Ignoring the Marine infantrymen, who gaped in disbelief, the North Korean hurled a huge satchel charge over the engine compartment of the armored vehicle, then escaped unharmed as the explosion rocked the area. The flame tank was wrecked, but the crew escaped serious injury with the assistance of supporting infantry. Apparently a suicide squad of NKPA demolitions men had been assigned the mission of destroying Marine armor in this fashion, for several other Red soldiers tried single-handed assaults shortly afterwards. The riflemen of 2/1 were alert for the later attempts, however, and the enemy fanatics were cut down before inflicting further damage.

The crucial period in the 2d Battalion's day-long fire fight came as Captain Goodwin C. Groff's Fox Company approached a street junction below Hill 97. It had been planned that this unit would advance through the intersection and continue along the streetcar line, while Company E, moving behind in column, veered off on the right branch.

Enemy resistance against Fox's advance proved so fierce that Captain Norman R. Stanford by-passed the fork and threw Easy Company's weight in support of the other unit. The North Korean strong point crumbled under the two-company onslaught, but not before Stanford and several others were added to the casualty rolls. 81

By dark, 2/1 had measured off a hard-won gain of 1200 yards. Lieutenant Colonel Sutter ordered the battalion into defensive positions astride the boulevard a scant 100 yards from the tip of the ridge spur which was costing Item Company, 5th Marines, so dearly.

In the right half of Puller's zone on 26 September, the 1st Battalion stamped out a hornets' nest around the main railroad station, nestled at the foot of South Mountain.82 Charlie Company had led off the early morning attack in the wake of a preparation by air, artillery, and mortars. After descending Hill 82 in a column of platoons, the com-pany formed on line along a stream paralleling the rail yard. Then, at a signal from Captain Wray, the platoons crossed over, wheeled to the north, and advanced up the tracks by leaps and bounds.

Though the over-all intensity of enemy resistance in this quarter could be termed only moderate, the random deployment of the Reds among buildings and train cars made the going slow and costly for the Marines. After clearing out the yard, the attackers converged on the station house itself and drove the last North Koreans from the building during a sharp exchange. The interior of the bullet-pocked structure produced only a handful of enemy dead, but in one corner were heaped the bodies of several South Korean women and children. It was obvious that the latter had been gunned by Communist execu-tioners, since their sheltered location within the building was ample protection against the small arms of the advancing Marines.

By darkness, Company C was in undisputed control of the railroad terminal, a patrol led by Lieutenant Carlon having mopped up the fringe area. To the right, Company A had secured the park promon-tory on the northwestern tip of South Mountain in conjunction with Baker Company's drive which included the nose jutting out below. East of the 1st Marines, the 32d Infantry's zone was the scene of con-siderable activity throughout 26 September. After the 2d Battalion repulsed the enemy's pre-dawn counterattack, the 3d jumped off at

"Capt N. R. Stanford, "Road Junction," Marine Corps Gazette, 35 no. 9 (Sep 51) :16-21.
"The following narrative is derived from: 1st Mar Div SAR, Annex Peter Peter; Bridges interv, 18 Oct 54; and Capt F. B. Carlon interv, I Mar 55.

0800 from positions a mile and a half east of South Mountain. Its objective, Hill 106, lay more than 3000 yards away, just south of the highway leading eastward out of Seoul. Approaching the base of the ridge, Company L surprised and destroyed a strong NKPA position, while Company I swept up the objective itself against light opposition.

Reaching the summit, the company commander called an air strike on an enemy column marching out of Seoul on the highway. As the planes broke up the Red formation, Company L, reinforced with tanks and additional infantry, drove down the road to mop up and block the escape route.[33]

In the day-long attack, 3/32 and its supporting armament accounted for 500 enemy dead, five tanks, 45 vehicles, three artillery pieces, and two ammunition dumps, according to regimental reports. The remainder of the 32d, now augmented by the 2d Battalion, 17th Infantry, in addition to the 17th ROK, saw spots of heavy fighting during the mop-up and consolidation on and around South Mountain. Casualties for the 32d, as reported on 26 September, were six KIA, 92 WIA, and three MIA. Most of those reported the following day—32 KIA, 33 WIA, and nine MIA—could also be traced to action on the 26th.[34]

Thus the Army regiment, having been impressively blooded in its eight days of action, could lay claim to clearing both South Mountain and that 15 per cent of Seoul's built-up area east of the great height.[35]

In the course of the day, the 1st Marines had made patrol contact with the 5th Marines in the left rear and with Army elements atop South Mountain on the right flank. Prospects for the morrow appeared much brighter at Division and Corps levels, where there must have existed some apprehension over the complicated maneuvering which had denied the attackers a solid front until they were in the heart of the sprawling capital.

Objective Secured

The twenty-seventh of September dawned as the day of reckoning. Applicable to the tactical situation in Seoul was the old law of physics, that two bodies cannot occupy the same space at the same time. With

---

[33] 32d Inf *War Diary*, 18–30 Sep 50.
[34] *Ibid*.
[35] MarCorps Board *Study*, II–B, 42.

X Corps troops pouring into the city and environs to share them with the Communist garrison, it was axiomatical that one side or the other would shortly have to go.

Oddly enough, despite the electrified atmosphere, the night of 26–27 September had passed quietly, even for Dog Company, 7th Marines, isolated in the road cut between Hills 296 and 338.[36] At dawn a tank-infantry team supported by engineers of Company D, 1st Engineer Battalion, advanced down the Kaesong Highway against negligible resistance and escorted the beleaguered rifle company back to the 7th Marines CP at Hoengjeoe-ri.

While the anticlimatical "rescue" was taking place, the 3d Battalion jumped off in the attack, supported by fire from the 2d on the left, to clear the northern reaches of Hill 338. How Company pressed forward up the draw on George's right but was stalled by heavy fire which suddenly erupted on the slopes above. The 3d Platoon, under Second Lieutenant Paul E. Denny, broke through in its zone, only to be recalled by Shields when the rest of the company failed to regain the lost momentum. Captain Richard H. Sengewald's Item Company, en route to take positions on the left of George, paused to assist Shields' outfit for a short time. After further attempts by Company H to gain the summit were unsuccessful, Sengewald led his unit to the north and attacked the right flank of the NKPA elements scattered indiscriminately over the remote humps of Hill 338. The situation on the northern half of the towering objective did not change appreciably in the course of the day.

Colonel Litzenberg developed further pressure against the enemy's right by ordering 2/7 to continue the attack against Hill 343 in mid-morning. On the right of the battalion zone, Captain Walter D. Phillips, Jr., led Company E forward in the face of stubborn enemy resistance from the crest. Owing to steady North Korean fire and the rugged terrain, gains were measured off by the yard, both for Phillips' unit and for Captain Elmer J. Zorn's Fox Company on the left. By nightfall, nevertheless, the Marines had mastered the situation to the extent that Company E sat firmly entrenched atop Hill 343—2500 yards from its starting point.

---

[36] The following narrative is derived from: 1st MarDiv *SAR*, Annex Roger Roger; Hammond interv, 17 Aug 54; Harris—Van Cleve interv, 10 Aug 54; and Maj W. R. Earney, *Notes on Operations of 3d Bn, 7th Mar, in South Korea* (Earney Notes), MS.

More force was applied to Litzenberg's flanking lever north of Seoul when Company G was withdrawn from its ridgeline on Hill 338 and ordered to attack eastward to seize Hill 342, which loomed above the capital building in the northern tip of Seoul. Circling through the low ground north of Hill 338, the company passed safely through an extensive minefield that had been conveniently marked off by friendly South Koreans. As the Marines approached the base of their objective and came under heavy sniper fire, Captain Cooney ordered the 1st Platoon, under Second Lieutenant Arthur R. Mooney, to set up a base of fire on intermediate high ground in order to support an assault by the 2d and 3d.

The plan backfired, for the 1st Platoon became engaged in a hot fire fight as it moved toward the designated position. The two assault units fared no better when, without the expected covering fire, they were hit by a hail of lead on the lower slopes of Hill 342. Several officers and NCOs were killed or wounded within a matter of minutes, and the scattered fighting that continued until nightfall brought about no significant change in the local situation.

Thus, the day ended on Litzenberg's "Seoul Front" with the 7th Marines in control of Hill 343 but sharing parts of 338 and 342 with the NKPA. The story would not be complete, however, without a brief visit to the regiment's "Haengju Front," several miles to the west, which had crackled with activity during the early afternoon. About 1200, a company of North Koreans emerged from the northern hills and attacked toward the old ferry crossing at Hill 125. On the way the Reds had the misfortune to stumble into Captain David W. Banks' Able Company of 1/7, manning a blocking position at Ryokoku. (See map of Han River crossing). To avoid the danger of infiltration in the bustling bridgehead, Lieutenant Colonel Davis promptly committed Company C, under Captain Richard F. Delamar, III.

Despite their disadvantages in numbers and fire power, the dogged Reds extended the fight sufficiently to involve even a platoon of Captain Myron E. Wilcox's Baker Company. After a prolonged clatter, the engagement ended almost as abruptly as it had begun; and the immediate result was that all Communist troops above the ferry site withdrew to Kaesong.

The 7th Marines claimed 375 enemy killed and 34 taken prisoner in the fighting which ranged its vast front from 23 to 27 September. The spoils of war included the strangely unbalanced assortment of four machine guns, six rifles and 600 bayonets.

While the 2d and 3d Battalions of Litzenberg's regiment struggled among the massive ridges north of Seoul on the 27th, the 1st and 5th Marines struck at the vital nerve center of the ROK capital. The regimental attacks through the center of the city began as separate thrusts in the morning, but as the day wore on they took on aspects of a coordinated foot race. It could even be said, finally, that the battle became a flag-raising contest between the two Marine units, as the last NKPA resistance died in heaps of rubble and torn rice bags.

At 0645, the 3d Battalion, 5th Marines, jumped off to clear the tip of Hill 296's troublesome eastern spur. For the first time in longer than they cared to remember, the infantrymen were greeted not by a sheet of small-arms and machine-gun fire, but by occasional, erratic pops from the rifles of dispirited snipers. Groping through the smoke and haze boiling up from the shattered city, Companies G and I swept the high ground by 0730 and—at long last—slowly filtered through the first streets of western Seoul. In short order they were encountering the expected barricades and minefields. There was a hint of stiffening opposition, but it quickly dissolved as the riflemen, backed by supporting tanks and engineers, ground forward relentlessly.[37]

By 0930, George Company made contact with the 1st Marines on the right.[38] Less than an hour later, after wheeling northward 3/5 controlled Middle School and adjacent high ground—the springboard for the assault on the capital building 1000 yards away. At 1200, Lieutenant Colonel Taplett ordered Companies G and I to continue the attack, guiding on the two Red flags which whipped the wind defiantly on both sides of the great dome ahead. Meanwhile, the 1st Battalion moved up behind and prepared to advance on the left of the 3d. Its mission in the final assault was to seize the craggy peak of Hill 338, which reared upward on the left of the capital building like a grim fortress.[39]

On the right of the 5th Regiment, the 2d Battalion, 1st Marines had smashed through another series of rice-bag barriers on the boulevard

---

[37] 1st MarDiv *SAR*, Annex Queen Queen.
[38] Contact on 26 September was between rearward elements of the 1st and 5th Marines, not between assault units.
[39] *Ibid.*

and at 1057, the United States colors unfurled above the French Consulate. A furious fight exploded around the city's main intersection,
where the principal streetcar lines crossed to form an X not far from
Middle School. Company D, spearheading 2/1's drive, waded into the
fray with determination. Lieutenant Cummings, who by this time
appeared to have a remarkable affinity for heavy trouble, again lost
his tank to enemy mines, but not before he had knocked out two
Russian 76mm self-propelled guns emplaced in the middle of the
intersection. Staff Sergeant MacDonald's M–26 obliterated an NKPA
truck with two 90mm rounds when the vehicle tried to escape with a
howitzer and its crew.[40]

The afternoon of 27 September was a time of climax as the 1st Marine
Division front surged forward of Middle School and the central intersection. Though beaten and faltering, the North Koreans still managed to fight stubbornly here and there; but their over-all deployment
no longer bore any semblance of tactical integrity.

By early afternoon the Reds facing the 5th Marines broke and fled.
Troops of 3/5 poured into the government compound, their final
objective, and secured it at 1508. The North Korean flags were struck,
and in their place rose the United States colors. Somewhat awed by
the historic import of their accomplishment, young Marine riflemen
wonderingly probed the spacious halls and chambers of the huge
building that shortly would be reoccupied by the government of the
Korean Republic.[41]

On the left of the 3d Battalion, Company A of 1/5 had launched
its attack on Hill 338 at 1300 in the wake of devastating preparations by
air, artillery, and mortars. Second Lieutenant Nicholas M. Trapnell
led off with the 1st Platoon, which seized an intermediate piece of
high ground against moderate resistance. The 2d Platoon, under
Second Lieutenant Edward E. Collins, then drove forward on the left
of the ancient wall leading to the crest of the objective; but the attack
was stopped by heavy mortar and small-arms fire. Marine air thundered down to rake the target with machine guns and rockets. The
ground troops followed up with heavy concentrations of 60mm and
81mm mortars. Moving closely behind the supporting fire, the 1st
Platoon overran a knob situated below the dominating peak. The 2d
Platoon then resumed its advance on the left of the wall, and the 3d,

[40] 2/1 *SAR*; and Cummings interv, 12 Oct 54.
[41] 1st MarDiv *SAR*, Annex Queen Queen.

under Technical Sergeant George W. Bolkow, took the lead on the right. It was the latter unit that smashed through the last resistance and secured the cliffs at the summit of Hill 338 at 1850.[42]

While the 5th Marines completed its final mission in Seoul, 2/1 on the right continued along the streetcar line which curved below the government buildings to run eastward to the far edge of the city. Since the 7th Marines had been slowed in the hills north of the capital, the expected tie-in on the left flank did not occur, and Puller's troops had to go it alone through the dense maze of streets in eastern Seoul. At 1530 infantrymen of 2/1 raised the American flag over the Russian Consulate, just to the right of the curve in the boulevard. Seven minutes later the flag also waved above the United States Consulate, about 350 yards farther off on the flank.[43]

To the right of 2/1, the 1st Battalion was making good progress after a slow start against stiff opposition. Charlie Company had been held up at the outset in the neighborhood of the railroad station, but supporting tanks, including flame throwers, had paved the way by blasting and burning a formidable nest of NKPA automatic weapons and AT guns. One armored vehicle was disabled by a mine and another by antitank fire before the Marines finally broke through. As the battalion pivoted eastward in accordance with the general plan, both Charlie Company and Able on the right hammered through the usual barricades and suicide detachments.[44]

The 32d Infantry and elements of the 17th enjoyed a relatively quiet day on and around South Mountain, for these units had only to hold firm in their positions until the 1st Marines could complete its wheeling movement and come abreast, facing east.[45]

Shortly before 1630, 2/1 was pounding eastward through a stretch of the streetcar line south of the government compound. Fire poured into the ranks of Dog Company from three sides, and Marines sweltered in the heat of burning buildings that offered dubious protection. Corsairs screamed down to plaster enemy positions only a block ahead of the foremost infantry. Immediately after each pass by the gull-winged planes, Second Lieutenant Carl B. Thompson, Jr., led his 1st Platoon in the assault with covering fire provided by supporting tanks.[46]

[42] *Ibid.*
[43] 2/1 *SAR.*
[44] Bridges interv, 18 Oct 54; and Carlon interv, 1 Mar 55.
[45] 32d Inf *War Diary,* 18–30 Sep 50.
[46] 2/1 *SAR;* and Capt T. Culpepper interv, 9 Feb 55.

There was a final surge up the street by the green-clad riflemen and BAR-men, and then it was all over. At 1630 enemy resistance across the 1st Regiment's front abruptly collapsed, with the result that the Battle of Seoul came to an end. Snipers and bypassed pockets remained to be mopped up by the Marines, KMC units, and South Korean Police; but the NKPA had clearly quit the fight and abandoned the city. The 1st and 2d Battalions of the 1st Marines marched rapidly through desultory sniper fire to the eastern part of town, where they dug in for the night.[47]

---

[47] *Ibid.;* Bridges interv, 18 Oct 54; and Carlon interv, 1 Mar 55.

CHAPTER XIV

The Drive to Uijongbu

Operations of 28 September—Liberation Ceremony at Seoul— Crumbling of NKPA Resistance—RCT–7 and the Battle for Uijongbu—Last Days of Inchon-Seoul Operation—Summaries and Conclusions—MacArthur's Report to United Nations

As RAPIDLY as the advance of the troops permitted, preparations were made for the restoration of civil government to Seoul. A group of former city officials had arrived by plane from Pusan; and on 26 September, Mayor Lee opened a temporary office in Yongdungpo. The police chief, construction engineer, and the health and welfare officials also resumed their old duties.

Collecting points were set up for handling the civilian wounded. The following statistics, comprising the patients treated for all causes by the 1st Medical Battalion of the 1st Marine Division, show that Korean civilians were second in numbers only to the Marines themselves:

U. S. Marine	2,811
Korean civilian	1,908
U. S. Army	358
KMC and ROK	322
U. S. Navy	78
POW	[1] 39

The problem of food for a city with a pre-war population of a million and a half was met during the advance when stores of rice and other supplies were turned over to Seoul officials by the Marines. Medical supplies found in the city were redistributed for use in Seoul and Inchon hospitals as well as the hospital established at Yongdungpo

---

[1] 1st MarDiv *SAR*, Annex How How.

by Captain Hering, the Division Surgeon, expressly for the treatment of civilian wounded.

A shipment of some 50 tons of rice through X Corps, plus large amounts located in Seoul by the Marines, enabled the officials to take over without critical food shortages.   On the 28th, Mayor Lee moved into the city hall at Seoul and acted immediately to re-establish police authority, clear destroyed areas and provide for the restoration of such public utilities as water and electricity.[2]   These prompt measures did much to ease the hardships of thousands of returning refugees.

Operations of 28 September

The 5th Marines passed an uneventful day on 28 September, having taken its assigned objectives and been pinched out by the 1st Marines on the right and the 7th Marines on the left, as planned.   An assembly area was established in the vicinity of the Women's University, and though the regiment sent out patrols, no enemy were encountered.[3]

The 7th Marines put in a busy day at seizing objectives which consisted of the high ground north of Seoul on both sides of the main highway from the capital to Uijongbu.   Opposition was light to moderate, with the stiffest resistance occurring in areas which indicated that the enemy intended to put up a fight to protect his escape route to Uijongbu.   Seventy-five tons of American-made dynamite and explosives, captured by the 7th Marines, were believed to have been originally supplied to the ROK forces before the war and abandoned during the NKPA invasion.[4]   Total advances for the day ranged from 1,500 yards in the zone of the 3d Battalion to 2,600 yards in the zone of the 2d Battalion.

When the 1st Marines jumped off at 0645 on the 28th, the 1st and 2d Battalions were in assault.   The 3d Battalion remained in an assembly area in the rear and continued mopping up along with the 2d KMC Battalion.   Although organized resistance in the city had been broken, the 1st Battalion met stubborn resistance from enemy groups and encountered many mines.   The 2d Battalion, on the left, made headway against light opposition.

---

[2] O. P. Smith, *Notes,* 312–313.
[3] 1st MarDiv *SAR,* Annex Queen Queen.
[4] *Ibid.,* Annex Roger Roger.

These attacks cleared the remainder of Seoul and took the assault battalions to Hill 133 (Objective ABLE) commanding the city on the northeast.[5]

General Smith visited the CPs of all three regiments on the 28th by helicopter. He found Colonel Puller at the Ducksoo Palace, near the intersection of the streetcar lines. Colonel Litzenberg's CP was located a short distance to the west, and Lieutenant Colonel Murray had established his headquarters in the Women's University on the northwest outskirts of the city.

Later that day Generals Smith and Craig displaced the Division CP from Oeoso-ri to a barracks area in Seoul, southwest of South Mountain. The two Marine generals took over a former infirmary, but they decided that the mortuary slab was too depressing and had that fixture removed.[6]

Liberation Ceremonies at Seoul

Planning for impressive liberation ceremonies at Seoul had begun while the street fighting was at its height. The 1st Marine Division was requested by Corps to furnish two honor guards and a band. Musical instruments having been left behind in Japan, air shipment was prescribed.[7]

General MacArthur had hoped to hold the liberation ceremony at Seoul on 25 September, just three months to the day after the launching of the NKPA invasion. The enemy, however, was not co-operative with respect to this date; and even on the morning of the 29th, three NKPA counterattacks were repulsed on the outskirts of the city. As it proved, General MacArthur vetoed plans for a ceremony with band music. "I will personally conduct the proceedings without being introduced," said his message to X Corps, and he specified that there be no honor guard.[8]

Two pre-dawn counterattacks on the 2d Battalion, 1st Marines, were not auspicious beginnings for the day of the liberation exer-

[5] *Ibid.*, Annex Peter Peter.
[6] O. P. Smith, *Notes,* 308, 338–339.
[7] O. P. Smith, *Chronicle,* 27 Sep 50, *Notes,* 313–315.
[8] CinCFE msg to CG X Corps, 28 Sep 50.

cises. The first occurred at 0445 on 29 September, when the OP, located on a spur projecting forward of the MLR and defended by a rifle platoon, was infiltrated by an estimated 70 to 100 NKPA troops. A second enemy attack hit the left flank of the battalion shortly afterwards. Both attempts were repulsed with total losses of 48 to the Communists, and the Marines had casualties of 4 KIA and 28 WIA, most of them resulting from hand grenades."

Another assault, launched by the enemy at 0600 in the zone of action of the 7th Marines, was repulsed without trouble. Most of the fighting on 29 September was done by this regiment, which pushed forward to gain all the rest of its objectives before nightfall.

At dawn, in preparation for the liberation ceremony, Marine guards were unobtrusively stationed along the route of approach from the new floating bridge to the Government Palace. This duty fell chiefly on 3/1, with elements of the 5th Marines being responsible for security in the western part of the city.

General MacArthur and President Syngman Rhee drove directly to the Palace after separate arrivals at Kimpo Airfield. The guests included Korean dignitaries and United Nations officials in addition to high-ranking representatives of military organizations.

The commander in chief opened the ceremony with a moving five-minute address ending with the Lord's Prayer. The rumble of artillery could be heard at times, and some of the guests glanced up apprehensively at the shattered skylight overhead.

"Occasional falls of glass from the dome and drifting smoke and ashes were part of the scene," commented a Marine officer. "Unheeded noise of rifle shots punctuated the talks. Grim Marines from Puller's regiment surrounded the seated audience. . . . The youth of the guards was offset by the tall, gray-haired figures of Generals Smith and Barr at the front of the audience. They were patently the men who had borne precisely and capably the load of decision." [10]

With the 1st Marine Division still responsible for security, it was a relief to General Smith when the distinguished visitors departed unharmed. Not all the mines had been removed from the streets as yet, and it was suspected that snipers might still be lurking in the ruins. [11]

[9] 1st MarDiv *SAR*, Annex Peter Peter.
[10] Col E. H. Forney memo to authors, Dec 54.
[11] O. P. Smith, *Chronicle*, 29 Sep 50.

Crumbling of NKPA Resistance

Although more hard fighting lay ahead in the Inchon-Seoul operation, X Corps alerted its major units on 29 September to the possibility of a new amphibious landing on the east coast of Korea. This was one of the earliest announcements of the planning which led to the Wonsan landing and the advance to the Chosin Reservoir, but the history of those events belongs in the next volume of this series.

The new operation was suggested by the rapid disintegration of the main body of the NKPA invasion forces. In a single day, 26 September, elements of the 1st Cavalry Division had advanced more than 100 miles; and a total of about 23,600 prisoners were taken by the Eighth Army before the end of the month. Enemy resistance was still encountered, to be sure, and sometimes it was of a desperate nature as Red Korean troops fought to escape encirclement. But all hope and heart had gone out of the Communist cause. One Eighth Army column sliced across the peninsula to Kunsan while other spearheads drove northward and ROK units pushed up the east coast nearly to Samchok. NKPA opposition was crumbling everywhere as demoralized invasion troops threw away their weapons and changed to civilian clothes in the hope of making their way to North Korea through the ever tightening Eighth Army cordon.[12]

The X Corps troops in the Seoul area had enough on their hands to finish the old operation before starting a new one. 1st Marine Division OpnO 13–50, issued at 2000 on 29 September, provided for the securing of the captured city by these means:

(1) a continuation of the attack to the east;
(2) the conduct of reconnaissances in force to the north and northwest;
(3) the relief of elements of the 7th Infantry Division north of the river Han;
(4) the seizure of prescribed blocking positions.[13]

The Division plan of maneuver called for the three Marine rifle regiments to take blocking positions forming a rough semi-circle defending Seoul from three sides—the 5th Marines to the northwest, the 7th Marines to the north, and the 1st Marines to the northeast. Responsibility for the area north of the Han river and west of the Pukhan

---

[12] U. S. MilAcad, *Operations in Korea*, 18–19.
[13] O. P. Smith, *Notes*, 318.

River had passed to the 1st Marine Division, and at 1500 on 30 September the following missions were assigned by OpnO 14–50:

RCT–1—To protect the right flank of the Division and be prepared to assemble in Division reserve by battalions for a motor lift. Blocking positions, as assigned by OpnO 13–50, consisted of high ground from two to five miles northeast of Seoul.

RCT–5—To continue reconnaissance in force with minimum of a reinforced battalion to Suyuhyon and establish a blocking position; to protect the left flank of the Division; and to be prepared to provide a reinforced rifle company for Task Force Kumpo, on order. These attachments to be made: 1st Battalion, 11th Marines, and one battery of 50th AAA Battalion, USA; Company A, 1st Tank Battalion; Company A, 1st Engineer Battalion; and a company from the 1st Motor Transport Battalion.

RCT–7—To advance rapidly and seize blocking positions in the vicinity of Uijongbu. These attachments to be made: 3d Battalion, 11th Marines, and one battery of 50th AAA Battalion, USA; Company D, 1st Tank Battalion; and one company of the KMC Regiment.

The KMC Regiment (less the 1st and 3d Battalions and one company of the 5th Battalion, with a detachment of ANGLICO attached) was meanwhile to advance to the east and seize blocking positions at the junctiton of the Han and Pukhan rivers where the road leading northeast from Seoul reaches that point. The 1st KMC Battalion had been attached to the 7th Infantry Division, and the 3d Battalion was operating on the Kumpo Peninsula.

Task Force Kumpo, when activated on Division order, was to consist of the 3d KMC Battalion and Battery C, 50th AAA Battalion, USA, plus a 5th Marines rifle company and a tank detachment, if required. As it proved, however, X Corps held responsibility for the defense of this area until 2 October, when the 187th Airborne RCT was relieved by Task Force Kumpo.[14]

Two more small fire fights awaited the 5th Marines in carrying out the missions assigned by Division OpnO 14–50. At 1030 on 1 October, while patrolling the extensive area of regimental responsibility, a detachment of 2/5 made contact with an NKPA force estimated at 150 to 200 men. Air strikes and mortar fire soon took the fight out of the enemy, who left 30 dead behind.

At 0600 on 1 October the 3d Battalion, reinforced with a battery of artillery and a platoon of tanks and engineers, moved out toward Suyuhyon. Charlie Company of 1/5 followed in trace to protect the battalion rear and provide security for returning motor transport.

---

[14] *Ibid.*, 318–319, 336–337. Both "Kimpo" and "Kumpo" are used in reports to designate the same area—the peninsula formed by the mouth of the Han. The first name was derived from the airfield, of course, and the second from the principal town of the peninsula.

Two road blocks were cleared before the battalion tied in for the night on high ground just short of the objective. Then, at 0230 the next morning, the enemy struck in estimated company strength. The attempt was repulsed by machine-gun fire, and 67 Red Korean bodies were found at daybreak in the attack area. At 0700 the column resumed the march to Suyuhyon, which was occupied without further incident.[15]

The 1st Marines found little difficulty in carrying out all missions assigned by Division OpnO 14–50. In fact, the regiment had only a few minor patrol actions after taking blocking positions northeast of Seoul.

Colonel Litzenberg's men were now making the main effort of the 1st Marine Division. Preparations for the drive to Uijongbu began with every indication that the enemy was bent upon flight. A patrol from the 3d Battalion found 30 Korean bodies beside a wall, including several women and a child, whose hands had been bound behind them before they were shot. The victims, according to a POW, were members of the families of ROK soldiers.[16]

Positions had been consolidated by the late afternoon of 30 September in readiness for the jump-off in the morning. The 7th Marines might well have been called Task Force Litzenberg at this stage for it was reinforced by Major Parry's 3d Battalion of the 11th Marines, Captain Lester T. Chase's Company D of the 1st Tank Battalion, Captain Byron C. Turner's Company D of the 1st Engineer Battalion, and Captain Kim's Company C of the 5th KMC Battalion.

The drive to the new objective began at 0630 on 1 October in a column of battalions. Air reconnaissance had made it appear likely that any NKPA resistance would probably take advantage of a tactical bottleneck, about halfway to Uijongbu, where steep and rocky ridges overlooked a narrow defile through which the road passed. Colonel Litzenberg and his staff decided to maneuver by sending the 1st Battalion to make a broad feint to cover the entry of the 3d Battalion into the defile with tank support while the 2d Battalion followed in reserve.

Lieutenant Colonel Davis secured his preliminary objectives, then swiftly spread out on both sides of the defile for his feint. Unfortunately, Major Roach was delayed by an enemy mine field, which brought the 3d Battalion and the tanks to a halt while the engineers

---

[15] 1st MarDiv *SAR*, Annex Queen Queen :basic rpt and Peter.
[16] *Ibid.*, Annex Roger Roger.

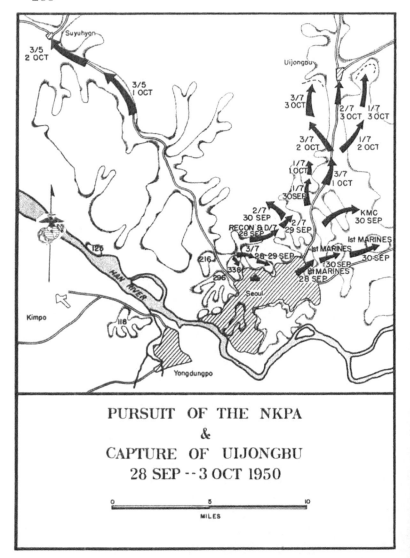

**PURSUIT OF THE NKPA
&
CAPTURE OF UIJONGBU
28 SEP -- 3 OCT 1950**

0   5   10
MILES

cleared the way. Davis' simulated attack had meanwhile disclosed that the enemy was entrenched in depth along the high ground on each side of the defile. Both Marine battalions took heavy NKPA artillery and mortar fire before halting for the night.[17]

At least the day's attacks had unmasked the enemy's positions and exposed them to savage attacks by the Corsairs of VMF–312. RCT–7 continued the attack at 0630 on the 2d, with Roach on the left of the road and Davis on the right. About halfway through the defile the 3d Battalion was pinned down by a concentration of NKPA artillery, mortar, and small-arms fire. Again the tanks were held up while the engineers cleared away mines, working in a hail of bullets. The tanks of the 1st Platoon repaid the favor by closing in on two huts sheltering NKPA troops and killing an estimated 35. Here an attached dozer tank, without blade, had a freakish accident when two men in the turret were wounded by enemy fire down a 105mm gun tube while the breech was open.

The 1st Battalion managed to cross the stream east of the defile and seize the high ground just beyond. But the day ended with gains of only 300 yards in the defile.

Roach's men returned to the attack in the morning, supported by the tanks of the 2d Platoon. Again VMF–312 flew one close air support sortie after another. Major Charles E. McLean was hit by enemy AA fire but crash-landed his plane in friendly territory. First Lieutenant Robert O. Crocker was killed in action shortly after being brought down by NKPA small-arms fire.

VMF–312 fliers intercepted an enemy convoy and First Lieutenant Franklin Stratton reported the destruction of seven out of eight trucks. The tanks also gave the infantry helpful support, firing 167 90mm rounds during the day and an estimated 20,000 machine gun rounds at enemy troops along the ridge.

While 1/7 cleared the high ground on the east side of the road and 3/7 on the west side, Colonel Litzenberg directed Major Webb D. Sawyer [18] to pass between them with 2/7 and drive directly along the highway. Progress was satisfactory from the start. When Sawyer's men began to overrun abandoned NKPA artillery pieces and supply

---

[17] This section is derived from: 1st MarDiv *SAR*, Annexes Oboe Oboe and Roger Roger; 1st MAW *SAR*, Annex Item:Queen; Col H. L. Litzenberg interv with HistDiv, 22 Apr 51; Hammond interv, 17 Aug 54; and Capt R. T. Bey interv, 17 Nov 54.

[18] Lieutenant Colonel Hinkle, the former 2/7 commander, had been wounded and evacuated on 28 September.

dumps, they pounded ahead with the realization that enemy resistance was broken.

At five that afternoon the 2d Battalion entered the ruins of Uijongbu, evacuated by the enemy. The last large-scale fight of the Inchon-Seoul operation had ended in a smashing victory for the Division's youngest regiment.

Identifications showed that the Marines had been opposed by three battalions of the 31st Regiment of the 31st NKPA Division. Elements of the 17th and Seoul Divisions and of an artillery battalion were also encountered. These troops had been supported by 13 tanks, of which four were killed by Marine air attacks and two captured in a damaged condition by 2/7 after the others escaped.

The three-mile advance of RCT-7 on 3 October had resulted in the cutting of lateral communications to the east and west of Uijongbu and the securing of an important blocking position on the X Corps final phase line. Losses of 13 killed and 111 wounded were suffered by the regiment in the three-day fight.

Last Days of Inchon-Seoul Operation

The climax of the battle was witnessed by General Cates, who visited the front on 3 October, accompanied by Major Generals Edwin A. Pollock and Clayton C. Jerome. After being briefed at the Division CP by the G-1, G-2, G-3, and G-4, the Commandant inspected the positions of RCT-1 and RCT-5 by helicopter before taking a jeep tour along the road to Uijongbu to watch Colonel Litzenberg's men slug their way forward into the battered town.[19]

That evening the fighting virtually came to an end, for the 1st Marine Division had a total of only seven casualties during the last four days of the Inchon-Seoul operation. The rifle regiments had only to maintain their blocking positions while patrolling to front and flank.

Operations on the Kumpo Peninsula, which had been sputtering intermittently ever since the occupation of the airfield, also drew to a close.[20] Responsibility for the area having passed from Corps back to Division on 2 October, elements of the 187th Airborne RCT were relieved by Task Force Kumpo, consisting of the 3d KMC Battalion,

---

[19] O. P. Smith, *Chronicle*, 2–3 Oct 50.
[20] Capt J. E. Dolan memo to authors, 24 Nov 54.

a detachment from the 1st Signal Battalion, and Battery C of the 50th AAA Battalion, USA.

Naval gunfire had found its greatest mission of the exploitation phase in support of the widely assorted units which protected the left flank of X Corps at various times. The 187th, being short on artillery, had relied on the naval gunfire and spot teams commanded by Lieutenant (jg) Leo D. McMillan, USN, and First Lieutenant J. E. Dolan, of the 2d Battalion, 7th Marines. These officers and their men remained with Task Force Kumpo after it relieved the 187th, but patrols reported no enemy contacts after 2 October. The chief activity on the peninsula was listening to the baseball games of the World Series, which came in clearly over the radios of the naval gunfire teams.[21]

As directed on 5 October by OpnO 15–50, the last to be issued by the Division in the Inchon-Seoul Operation, the major Marine units were scheduled to close into staging areas in Inchon as follows:

5th Marines	1800 on 5 October;
11th Marines	1700 on 6 October;
1st Marines	Prior to darkness, 6 October;
7th Marines	Midafternoon, 7 October;
KMC Regiment	Prior to darkness, 7 October.

An impressive ceremony was held on the 6th, when the cemetery established by the Marines on the outskirts of Inchon was taken over by the United Nations. After an invocation by Chaplain R. M. Schwyhart of the 1st Marine Division, General Almond made a few remarks and laid a wreath on the grave of an unknown soldier. Then General Smith, General Barr, and Colonel Lee performed the same ceremony over Marine, Army, and ROK graves. Volleys were fired, taps were sounded, and the dedication ended with the national anthems of the United States and Korea.[22]

There could be no doubt, as the Marines prepared to mount out for a new amphibious operation, that the NKPA invaders had been knocked out of the war by the combined X Corps and Eighth Army offensives. The Red Korean retreat had become a rout, and Marine staff officers considered it doubtful whether the enemy could hold the

---

[21] *Ibid.*
[22] O. P. Smith, *Notes*, 342; 1st MarDiv *SAR*, Annex George, 7.

east coast port of Wonsan long enough to defend it against the proposed new Marine assault landing.[23]

It was apparent, in fact, that only the active intervention of Red China or the Soviet Union could save the North Korean People's Republic from imminent collapse. At this time, however, it did not seem likely that any such attempt would be made.

And so it was that one of the most remarkable amphibious operations in Marine Corps annals came uneventfully to an end on 7 October 1950. Early in the morning the Division CP displaced from Seoul to a housing area just north of Ascom City. At 0935, in accordance with X Corps OpnO 5, General Smith reported to Admiral Doyle, ComPhibGru One, for duty as commander of the landing force for the proposed Wonsan assault. And at 1200 the Inchon-Seoul operation passed into history when the last troops of the 7th Marines were relieved in the Uijongbu area by elements of the Eighth Army.

Summaries and Conclusions

At this stage the men of the 1st Marine Division and 1st Marine Aircraft Wing were still too close to the operation to see it clearly in detail. If there was any one overwhelming impression they all had in common, it was a sense of the speed with which events had raced toward a climax.

This was by no means an illusion. Hundreds of Marine reservists had watched baseball games or enjoyed picnics with their families on the Fourth of July, never dreaming that shortly after Labor Day they would be scrambling out of landing boats to assault a flaming Asiatic seaport on the other side of the earth!

Speed was an essential if the assault landing were to be completed on the prescribed D-day. But there was no place for the proverbial haste that leads to waste. It had to be the speed of precision—an acceleration of men and events made possible by the amphibious know-how of a Navy-Marine Corps team that had worked together throughout the Pacific operations of World War II.

Sometimes this acceleration was so unobtrusive as to pass almost unnoticed. Shipping does not grow on trees, particularly the enormous

---

[23] Wonsan fell without a fight on 10 October, before the Marines embarked, to ROK units advancing up the coastal route.

amounts of shipping required for a major amphibious operation. Yet the U. S. Navy made it appear a simple and routine matter to assemble from all the seven seas an invasion fleet made up of craft ranging from cruisers to rowboats.

The Marines, as the Landing Force, worked hand-in-hand with the Attack Force commanded by Rear Admiral James H. Doyle, who had no superior in the world of 1950 as an amphibious specialist. From preliminary planning to final execution, Doyle and his staff officers of PhibGru One supplied a precision which had much to do with the success of an operation holding so many potentialties of disaster.

Looking back, some of the Marine participants could hardly recall a full night's sleep from 25 July 1950, the date of the order directing that the 1st Marine Division be brought up to full war strength, until 7 October 1950, when the operation came to a victorious end. From the mobilization at Camp Pendleton to the street fighting in Seoul, it was often necessary to utilize the hours of darkness ordinarily devoted to rest. At Kobe, for instance, there were so few copies of the plans for the Inchon landing that they were circulated on a 24-hour schedule for study by Marine officers who took turns.

The acceleration of the 1st Marine Division in 64 days from a peace-time basis to the capture of Seoul has been summarized as follows:

(a) Expansion from a reduced peace strength (less the !st Provisional Ma-rine Brigade) to a reinforced war strength, less one RCT, was completed in a period of approximately 15 days.

(b) Administrative sea lift and movement of over 15,000 personnel, organic equipment, and partial resupply from San Diego to the Far East Command commenced in less than three weeks after expansion was ordered.

(c) Debarkation and unloading from administrative shipping, and re-embarkation and reloading at Kobe, Japan for the assault landing at Inchon were done in a period averaging about seven days per unit, two days of which were lost due to a heavy typhoon in the Kobe area.

(d) Completed planning and the issuance of the complete operation order for the amphibious landing at Inchon were accomplished 17 days after the receipt of the initial directive.

(e) The !st Provisional Marine Brigade was disengaged from active combat with the enemy on the South Korean front at midnight on 5 September, moved to Pusan, and outloaded in combat shipping in less than 7 days.

(f) A successful assault landing was executed at Inchon, Korea, on 15 September under some of the most adverse landing conditions in the history of amphibious operations.

(g) The Force Beachhead Line approximately six miles from landing beaches was seized within 24 hours after the main landing on Beaches RED and BLUE.

(h) Kimpo Airfield, a primary objective of the operation in the 1st Marine Division's zone of action, was captured 50 hours and 35 minutes after H-Hour, D-Day.

(i) The first assault crossing of the Han River (400 yards wide at the crossing site) was executed by RCT-5, employing LVTs, DUKWs, and pontoon ferries, less than five days after landing at Inchon.

(j) The remainder of the Division crossed the Han River without bridging, and after intense fighting completed the seizure of Seoul 12 days after landing at Inchon.

(k) The effectiveness of the Marine air-ground team and close air support doctrine were reaffirmed with outstanding success.

(l) The ability of Marine units to participate in extended land operations, provided additional transportation requirements are met during the emergency, was demonstrated in the Inchon-Seoul operation.[24]

In any such summary, it is understood that credit for the accomplishments of the 1st Marine Division was shared by the 1st Marine Aircraft Wing. Two more days of fighting remained for the squadrons at Kimpo after the relief of the ground forces, since Marine air operations cover the period from 7 September to 9 October 1950. Altogether, 2,774 combat sorties were flown by the five Marine squadrons during this 33-day period, most of them in close support of infantry units. Following are the totals:

Squadron	Days in action	Combat sorties
VMF-214	16	484
VMF-323	22	784
VMF-212	19	607
VMF-312	10	288
VMF(N)-542	19	573
Total		[25] 2, 774

[24] O. P. Smith, *Notes*, 365–366.

[25] Summaries and statistics for Marine air have been derived from: 1st MAW *SAR*, Annexes Able, Item, Jig, Queen, and Sugar; also E. H. Giusti and K. W. Condit, "Marine Air over Inchon-Seoul," *Marine Corps Gazette*, 36, no. 6 (Jun 52): 19-27.

Note that the total of 2,774 combat sorties includes 38 flown by two aircraft of VMF-312, which began operating from Kimpo nine days before the rest of the squadron arrived.

"No enemy air operations of any significance were encountered," stated the TAC X Corps report. "Some enemy antiaircraft fire from light to moderate was encountered. Most of this AA fire was of small caliber."

Eleven Marine planes (not counting VMO-6 aircraft) were shot down by NKPA ground forces. Six pilots and a crewman were killed in action and two pilots wounded.

As an example of the types of missions, the 326 combat sorties flown by VMF-322 fell into these categories: close air support, 163; reconnaissance, 99; rescue cover, 18; deep support, 17; helicopter escort, 8; photo escort, 6; combat air patrol, 6; tactical air control, 4; leaflet, 2; R4D escort, 2; message drop, 2. In addition, the squadron was credited with 151 noncombat sorties.

There could be no question that Marine close air support had won the esteem of Army infantry units. Generals Harris and Cushman were the recipients of many spontaneous comments of appreciation from individuals as well as formal endorsements. (See Appendix L for the record.)

On the other hand, the Marines had cause to be grateful for the deep support and interdiction strikes provided by the Naval fast carrier planes of JTF-7 in combination with the Fifth Air Force, which was committed primarily to the support of the Eighth Army in South Korea. During the first two weeks of September, JTF-7 had responsibility for the gradual isolation of the Inchon target area by means of air operations conducted as far as 150 miles north of the objective and 100 miles to the south.

The air defense of our forces at sea and in the Inchon area, and the air interdiction operations of the first five or six days of the landing— these were carried out largely by Naval air effort under Commander JTF-7. Mutual assistance between JTF-7 and the Fifth Air Force was provided for, with coordination being achieved by the delineation of areas for each.[26]

VMO-6, under the control of the 1st Marine Division and administration control of MAG-33, completed a total of 643 helicopter and OY flights in 515 hours. Of the 139 seriously wounded men evacuated by helicopter from the firing line, a large proportion owed their lives to the speed and ease with which they were transported to the hospital. The

---

[26] VAdm A. D. Struble ltr to authors, 3 May 55.

helicopters also were credited with twelve rescue missions of friendly pilots shot down behind the enemy lines.[27]

In the long run, of course, it took the co-ordinated efforts of ground, air, and sea forces to win the final victory in one of the most unusual and difficult amphibious operations of all time. And though this book is limited to an account of Marine activities primarily, the Marines who took part would be first to acknowledge how much the final victory owed to the efforts of other ground forces—the U. S. Army units, the KMC Regiment, and the ROK contingents.

Many of these units, like the Marines, had been handicapped by a hasty build-up which allowed little or no time for special training and rehearsals. No greater feat of organization was recorded in 1950 than the creation of a new 7th Infantry Division from the bare bones of the old in only a few weeks. The Marines saw more of the 32d Infantry than General Barr's other units, for it was this regiment which protected the right flank during critical periods of the advance on Seoul while elements of the 187th Airborne RCT were responsible for the security of the left flank.

The Army artillery units, amphibian tractor troops, and AAA companies also deserve their full share of credit for the victory. And though the Marines were not often in contact with the ROKs, they realized how much these allies had contributed, often under the most adverse circumstances.

Naturally, the Marines felt a special interest in the KMC Regiment, which they had trained and equipped. The KMCs repaid this feeling by the valor with which they fought in every phase of the operation from the mopping up of Inchon to the battle for Seoul.

The Inchon landing and its exploitation have been made the subject of a study by officers of the Marine Corps Schools at Quantico, who summed up the over-all effects as follows:

(a) The amphibious envelopment at Inchon produced a decisive threat to the North Korean forces which led directly to the rapid disintegration of their front on the Pusan Perimeter. The 1st Marine Division was the landing force in this amphibious envelopment.

(b) It completed the dislocation of the enemy's entire logistical system by the capture of Seoul, which, together with the combat action of other UN forces, shattered the enemy in all of South Korea, causing the complete rout

---

[27] 1st MarDiv *SAR*, Annex William William.

of the North Korean forces. The 1st Marine Division played a principal role in the capture of Seoul.

(c) The successful completion of the campaign made available to UN forces the port facilities of Inchon and the extensive Seoul communications complex for carrying offensive action into North Korea.

(d) By the direct action of the 1st Marine Division, the enemy's potential was reduced by the capture of 4,692 POWs, by inflicting 13,666 casualties on the enemy, by destroying 44 tanks, and by destroying or capturing much other material.[28]

In view of such far-reaching results, total casualties for the 1st Marine Division of 366 KIA, 49 DOW, 6 MIA, and 2,029 WIA cannot be considered excessive for an operation fraught with so many calculated risks. No man's life was given in vain, for the Communist challenge to the free nations was met in Korea and the aggressors beaten so decisively that the world would soon have had peace except for the intervention of Red China.

MacArthur's Report to United Nations

Again it is worthy of emphasis that the victory was not won by any one nation or any one branch of the military service. As far as this country is concerned, the Inchon-Seoul operation was conducted jointly by the United States Army, Navy, Air Force, and Marine Corps. General Douglas MacArthur was spokesman for all of them late in September 1950, in these extracts from the Sixth Report of the Commander in Chief, United Nations Command, to the Security Council of the United Nations:

"Events of the past two weeks have been decisive. The strategic concepts designed to win the war are rapidly proving their soundness through aggressive application by our ground, sea, and air forces.

"The seizure of the heart of the enemy's distributing system in the Seoul area has completely dislocated his logistical supply to his forces in South Korea and has quickly resulted in their disintegration. Caught between our northern and southern forces, both of which are completely self-sustaining because of our absolute air and naval supremacy, the enemy is thoroughly shattered

---

[28] MarCorps Board *Study*, II–B, 45–46. Here again it may be noted that later reports, not available when this study was made, indicate that duplicate claims were entered for four of these 44 tanks, with two others unaccounted for in records. The actual total, therefore, is 38.

through disruption of his logistical support and our combined combat activities.

"The prompt junction of our two forces is dramatically symbolic of this collapse.

"The obstacles to this wide envelopment were not only the enemy opposition, but also the natural obstacles of poor beaches fronted by miles of mud flats, a narrow channel and an extraordinary tidal range of over 29 feet. The success demonstrated a complete mastery of the technique of amphibious warfare, clockwork coordination, and cooperation between the units and services participating. There was nothing noteworthy about the North Korean opposition, but there could have been. The potential was there. The North Koreans were proceeding with the construction of coastal fortifications, dug-in tanks and guns of all calibers, beach defenses and mining operations. Had this development been delayed for as much as a month, the enemy would have been ready and the assault, if possible, would have been more costly to United Nations forces."

At no time, not even when the United Nations forces were fighting with their backs to the wall at Pusan, did the commander in chief ever have any doubts as to the outcome. It was fitting, therefore, that he should have summed up the results of the combined Eighth Army and X Corps offensives in this conclusion written after the securing of Seoul:

"A successful frontal attack and envelopment has completely changed the tide of battle in South Korea. The backbone of the North Korean army has been broken and their scattered forces are being liquidated or driven north with material losses in equipment and men captured."

APPENDIX A

Glossary of Technical Terms and Abbreviations

AAA(AW)Bn—Antiaircraft Artillery (Automatic Weapons) Battalion (USA).

AD—Destroyer Tender.

AE—Ammunition Ship.

AerialDelPlat—Aerial Delivery Platoon.

AF—Air Force; Store Ship.

AGC—Amphibious Force Flagship.

AH—Hospital Ship.

AK—Cargo Ship.

AKA—Assault Cargo Ship.

AKL—Cargo Ship—Light.

AKS—Stores Issue Ship.

AM—Minesweeper.

AmphTracBn—Amphibious Tractor Battalion.

AmphTrkBn—Amphibious Truck Battalion.

AMS—Auxiliary Motor Minesweeper.

ANGLICO—Air and Naval Gunfire Liaison Company.

AO—Oiler.

AOG—Gasoline Tanker.

AP—Transport.

APA—Assault Transport.

APD—High Speed Transport.

ARG—Repair Ship—Internal Combustion Engines.

ARH—Repair Ship—Heavy Hull Damage.

ARL—Repair Ship—Landing Craft.

ArmdAmphBn—Armored Amphibian Battalion.

ARS—Salvage Vessel.

AT—Antitank.

ATF—Ocean Tug—Fleet.

AV—Seaplane Tender.

AVP—Seaplane Tender, Small.

Bchmstr Unit—Beachmaster Unit.

BLT—Battalion Landing Team.

Bn—Battalion.

CA—Heavy Cruiser.

CG—Commanding General.

CICDet—Counter-Intelligence Corps Detachment (USA).

CinCFE—Commander in Chief, Far East.

CinCPacFlt—Commander in Chief, Pacific Fleet.

CL—Light Cruiser.

CMC—Commandant of the Marine Corps.

CNO—Chief of Naval Operations.

CO—Commanding Officer.

Co—Company.

ComAirSupGrp—Commander Air Support Group.

ComCarDiv—Commander Carrier Division.

ComNavFE—Commander Navy Far East.

ComPhibGruOne—Commander Amphibious Group One.

CP—Command Post.

C/S—Chief of Staff.

CSG—Combat Service Group.

CTF—Commander Task Force.

CV—Aircraft Carrier.

CVE—Aircraft Carrier—Escort.

CVL—Aircraft Carrier—Light.
DD—Destroyer.
DDE—Escort Destroyer.
DDR—Radar Picket Destroyer.
DOW—Died of wounds.
DUKW—Amphibious Truck.
Emb Off—Embarkation Officer.
EngrBn—Engineer Battalion.
EngrPortConstCo—Engineer Port Construction Company (USA).
EngrSpecBrig—Engineer Special Brigade (USA).
ETO—European Theater of Operations.
EUSAK—Eighth United States Army in Korea.
FABn—Field Artillery Battalion (USA).
FAC—Forward Air Controller.
FBHL—Force Beachhead Line.
FEAF—Far East Air Force.
FECOM—Far East Command.
F4U—Vought "Corsair" Fighter.
FMF—Fleet Marine Force (Pac-Pacific; Lant-Atlantic).
FO—Forward Observer.
FSA—Fire Support Area.
FSCC—Fire Support Coordination Center.
F7F–3—Grumman "Tigercat" Night Fighter.
Fum & Bath Plat—Fumigation and Bath Platoon.
GCI—Ground Control Intercept.
GHQ—General Headquarters.
H & S Co—Headquarters and Service Company.
HO3S–1—Sikorsky Helicopter.
HqBn—Headquarters Battalion.
HqCo—Headquarters Company.
HqSq—Headquarters Squadron.
InfDiv—Infantry Division (USA).

interv—Interview.
JANIS—Joint Army-Navy Intelligence Studies.
JCS—Joint Chiefs of Staff.
JSPOG—Joint Strategic Planning and Operations Group.
JTF—Joint Task Force.
KIA—Killed in Action.
KMC—Korean Marine Corps.
LCM—Landing Craft, Mechanized.
LCVP—Landing Craft, Vehicle and Personnel.
LSD—Landing Ship, Dock.
LSM—Landing Ship, Medium.
LSMR—Landing Ship, Medium-Rocket.
LST—Landing Ship, Tank.
LSU—Landing Ship, Utility.
LVT—Landing Vehicle, Tracked.
LVT(A)—Landing Vehicle, Tracked (Armored).
MAG—Marine Air Group.
MAW—Marine Air Wing.
MedBn—Medical Battalion.
MGCIS—Marine Ground Control Intercept Squadron.
MIA—Missing in action.
MOS—Military Occupational Specialty.
MPCo—Military Police Company.
MTACS—Marine Tactical Air Control Squadron.
MTBn—Motor Transport Battalion.
NCO—Noncommissioned Officer.
NGF—Naval Gunfire.
NK—North Korea(n).
NKPA—North Korean Peoples Army.
OCMH—Office of the Chief of Military History (USA).
Off—Officer.
OP—Observation Post.
OpnO—Operation Order.

OrdAmmCo—Ordnance Ammunition Company (USA).

OrdBn—Ordnance Battalion.

OY—Consolidated-Vultee light observation plane.

PC—Submarine Chaser.

PCEC—Escort Amphibious Control Vessel.

PF—Frigate.

PhibGru—Amphibious Group.

PhibTraPac—Training Command, Amphibious Forces, Pacific Fleet.

PIR—Periodic Intelligence Report.

Plat—Platoon.

POL—Petroleum, Oil, Lubricants.

POW—Prisoner of War.

RAF—Royal Air Force.

RcnCo—Reconnaissance Company.

RCT—Regimental Combat Team.

RktBn—Rocket Battalion.

ROK—Republic of Korea.

SAC—Supporting Arms Center.

SAR—Special Action Report.

SCAJAP—Supreme Commander Allied Powers, Japan.

ServBn—Service Battalion.

SigBn—Signal Battalion.

SigRepCo—Signal Repair Company (USA).

SPBn—Shore Party Battalion.

SpOpnsCo—Special Operations Company (USA).

TAC—Tactical Air Coordinator.

TAC X Corps—Tactical Air Command, X Corps.

TacAir—Tactical Air.

TADC—Tactical Air Direction Center.

T-AP—Transport Operated by MSTS.

T/E—Table of Equipment.

TF—Task Force.

TG—Task Group.

T/O—Table of Organization.

UDT — Underwater Demolitions Team.

UF—Unit of fire.

UN—United Nations.

UNC—United Nations Command.

USA—United States Army.

USAF—United States Air Force.

USMC—United States Marine Corps.

USN—United States Navy.

VMF—Marine fighter type aircraft (squadron).

VMF (N)—Marine night fighter type aircraft, all-weather (squadron).

VMO—Marine observation type aircraft (squadron).

VMR—Marine transport type aircraft (squadron).

WIA—Wounded in action.

WP—White phosphorous.

YMS—Motor Minesweeper.

YTB—Harbor Tug, Big.

YW—District Barge, Water (self-propelled).

Build-Up of 1st Marine Division (Reinf)

(Figures include Marine Corps and Navy, both officer and enlisted)

Units	Strength (Authorized by CMC ltr conf. Ser. 03C20550 of 25Jul54 and CMC ltr conf. Ser. 03A21250 of 4 Aug 50)	1st Prov Marine Brigade (sailed San Diego 14Jul50 arrived Pusan, Korea 2Aug50)	Main body (sailed San Diego 10–22Aug 50, arrived Kobe Japan 28Aug to 10Sep50)	7th RCT (sailed from Mediterranean 16Aug50 and San Diego 28 Aug-2Sep50 arrived Inchon on 21Sep50)[1]	Total in Inchon-Seoul area on 23Sep50 [2]
DIVISION	22,343	4,770	12,195	5,336	20,218
Hq Bn	923	259	725	....	860
Hq Co	(656)	(182)	....		
MP Co	(140)	(38)	....		
RcnCo	(127)	(39)	....		
1st Serv Bn	827	173	656	....	785
1st Sig Bn	960	249	591	116	661
1st MT Bn	783	118	582	89	761
1st Ord Bn	558	124	438	....	518
1st Med Bn	636	99	432	107	667
1st Tank Bn	907	181	677	132	921
1st SP Bn	755	188	357	196	836
1st Engr Bn	1,180	218	815	163	969
11th Marines	3,108	518	1,845	697	3,009
1st Marines	3,902	....	3,942	....	3,395
5th Marines	3,902	2,643	[3]1,135	....	3,170
7th Marines	3,902	....	....	3,836	3,666
FMF TROOPS	3,969	554	3,167	....	2,973
1st ArmdAmphBn	526	....	490	....	....
1st AmphTracBn	944	256	720	....	[4]842
1st AmphTrkCo	245	77	166	....	236
BtryC, 1st4.5"RktBn	90	....	89	....	77
Carrier Plat FMF	94	....	84	....	86
1stCombServGp	1,434	109	1,120	....	1,167
7th MT Bn	431	....	418	....	410
1stAirDeliveryPlat	63	....	62	....	63
1stFum & BathPlat	30	....	18	....	30
VMO 6	112	112	....	....	62
Total reinforced division	26,312	5,324	15,362	5,336	23,191

See footnotes on p. 304.

[1] Activated 17 Aug 50. The 3d Bn 6th Marines, in the Mediterranean, was assigned to the 7th Marines and, upon arrival in Kobe, Japan, on 3 Sept 50, was redesignated the 3d Bn 7th Marines. Augmentation personnel for this battalion arrived in Kobe, Japan, on 14 Sept 50 on the USS *Thomas Jefferson*. The regimental commander and his staff arrived by air at Kobe on 6 Sept 50.

[2] Based on Division Personnel Periodic Report No. 1 covering the period 15–23 Sept 50. The following losses and gains during the period are reflected in this report:

Losses		*Gains*		*Net Loss*
KIA	118	Replacements	28	
WIA	845	Returned to duty	160	
MIA	14			
Non-battle Cas	286		188	1,075
	1,263			

[3] Augmentation personnel for the 5th Marines (Reinf) already in Korea. The CO, 1st Marines was charged with the assembly and organization of the augmentation units for the 5th Marines (Reinf). Augmentation personnel were organized into three reinforced rifle companies. (The battalions of the 5th Marines in Korea contained only two rifle companies each.) The reinforced rifle companies were embarked together on one ship. Augmentation personnel for units of the Brigade, other than the 5th Marines, were attached to the reinforced rifle companies.

[4] The 1st Armored Amphibian Tractor Battalion was left in Kobe. In addition, at Kobe, were the Division Administrative Center and some 500 17-year olds, who, by order of SecNav, were removed from the troop list just before sailing for Inchon. As of 15 Sept 50 there were the following personnel of the 1st Marine Division (Reinf) at Kobe:

Marine Corps		*Navy*		*Total*	
Officers	*Enlisted*	*Officers*	*Enlisted*	*Officers*	*Enlisted*
59	1,268	3	14	62	1,282

APPENDIX C

Task Organization of Marine Division for Inchon Landing

In order to present a concise picture of the Task Organization of the 1st Marine Division (Reinf), FMF, for the period of 1 August–7 October 1950, task organizations are presented for the following five conditions:

(1) Completion of mobilization of the Division (less 1st Provisional Marine Brigade and RCT–7) at Camp Pendleton, Oceanside, California, 12 August.

(2) Organization for landing at INCHON, KOREA, 15 September.

(3) RCT–7 task organization on arrival INCHON, KOREA, 21 September.

(4) Intermediate temporary attachments and detachments during the period 15 September–7 October.

(5) Completion of INCHON-KIMPO-SEOUL operation on 7 October.

The detailed Task Organizations are as follows:

(1) Completion of Mobilization on WAR "K" series T/O, 12 August.

1st Marine Division, (Reinf) FMF	MajGen O. P. SMITH
HqBn, 1stMarDiv, less Brig Det	LtCol M. T. STARR
1st SigBn, less Brig Det, 2 SP Comm Sects & Det Anglico Carrier Plat, FMF	Maj R. L. SCHREIER
1st ServBn, less Brig Det	LtCol C. L. BANKS
1st OrdBn, less Brig Det	Maj L. O. WILLIAMS
1st MT Bn, less Cos A and D; 1st Amph Trk Co, FMF, less 1 Plat	LtCol O. L. BEALL
1st Med Bn, less Cos A and E	Comdr H. B. JOHNSON, USN
1st EngrBn, less Cos A and D	LtCol J. H. PARTRIDGE
1st SP Bn, less Cos A and C	LtCol H. P. CROWE
1st Tk Bn, less Cos A and D; Tk Plat AT Co, 1st Mar Tk Plat AT Co, 5th Mar	LtCol H. T. MILNE
1st Amph Trac Bn, FMF, less Cos A and D	LtCol E. F. WANN
1st Armd Amph Bn, FMF, less 1st Plat Co A and Cos C and D	LtCol F. H. COOPER

1st Marine Division—Continued

1st CSG, SC, FMF, less BrigDet;	
1st Fum & Bath Plat, SC, FMF	
1st Aerial Del Plat, SC, FMF	Col J. S. COOK
7th MT Bn, SC, FMF	Maj J. F. STEPKA
1st Mar, less Tk Plat, AT Co; Cos	
C, F, and I, Reinf, 5th Mar	Col L. B. PULLER
11th Mar, less 1st and 3rd Bns;	
Btry C, 1st 4.5″ Rkt Bn, FMF	Col J. H. BROWER

(2) Organization for landing at INCHON, KOREA (1st Prov Mar Brig disbanded 13 September, units and detachments reverted control parent organizations of division). Task Organization from Annex "A", 1st Mar Div Op Order 2–50 as derived from X Corps Op Order No. 1.

1st Marine Division (Reinf) FMF   MajGen O. P. SMITH

HqBn, Reinf, 1stMarDiv, less dets
  163rd Mil Int Service Det
  441st CIC Det
1st Sig Bn, Reinf, less dets;
  Det, 205th Sig Rep Co USA
  Carrier Plat, FMF
  Det, 4th Sig Bn, USA
1st Serv Bn, less Dets
1st MT Bn
1st Ord Bn, less dets
Det, MTACS–2

Blt–3, RCT–5   LtCol R. D. TAPLETT

3dBn, 5th Mar
Det, ANGLICO, 1st Sig Bn
Det, Co A, 1st Tk Bn
Recon Det, 11th Mar
Team 1, SP Gp A
  1stPlat, Co A, 1st SP Bn
  SP Comm Sqd, 1st Sig Bn
  Amm Sqd, 1st Ord Bn
  Det, Rat Sec, 1st Ser Bn
  Det, 1st CSG, (SP Aug)
  Det, Bchmstr Unit, USN

RCT–5   LtCol R. L. MURRAY

5th Mar, less 3dBn & Tk Plat, AT
  Co
Co A, 1st Engr Bn
Co C, 1st Med Bn
Det Anglico, 1st Sig Bn
ROK Marine Bn
SP GP A, less Team 1;
  Co, A, 1st SP Bn, less 1 Plat
  Evac Sec, 1st SP Bn
  Det, Ord Sup Plat, CSG
  Det, Auto Sup Plat, CSG
  Det, Engr Sup Plat, CSG
  Det, CS Plat, CSG
  Det, Sig Sup Plat, CSG
  SP Comm Sec, 1st Sig Bn
  Det, 1st CSG (SP Aug)
  Det, Bchmstr Unit, USN
1st Traffic Plat, MP Co
  Police Sqd, MP Co
FO & Ln Sec, 1st Bn, 11th Mar
Co A, 1st Tk Bn, less det
Det, Sig Co, 1st Sig Bn

RCT–1   Col L. B. PULLER

1st Mar, less Tk Plat, AT Co
Co A, Reinf, 56th Amph Trac Bn,
  USA
Btry C, 1st 4.5″ Rkt Bn, FMF
Co C, Reinf, 1st Engr Bn, less det;
  Water Sup Sec
Co D, 1st Med Bn, less det
Det ANGLICO, 1st Sig Bn
SP Gp B, less Team 3;
  Co B, 1st SP Bn, less 1 Plat &
    Equip Sec
  Evac Sec, 1st SP Bn
  Amm Plat, less 1 Sqd, 1st Ord
    Bn
  Rat Sec, 1st Ser Bn
  Fuel Sec, 1st Ser Bn
  SP Comm Sec, 1st Sig Bn

RCT–1—Continued

Det, Bchmstr Unit, USN
Det, 1st CSG (SP Aug)
2d Traffic Plat, MP Co
Police Sqd, MP Co
FO & Ln Secs, 2d Bn, 11th Mar

11th Mar, less 3d Bn, reinf   Col J. H. BROWER

96th FA Bn, USA
Det, Co B, 1st Engr Bn
1st Amph Trk Co, FMF

1st Tk Bn, less dets, reinf   LtCol H. T. MILNE

Tk Plat, AT Co, 1st Mar
Tk Plat, AT Co, 5th Mar

1st Engr Bn, less dets   LtCol J. H. PARTRIDGE

1st SP Bn, less dets   LtCol H. P. CROWE

H&S Co, 1st SP Bn, less dets
SP Comm Sec, 1st Sig Bn
Team 3, SP Gp B
  3d Plat, Co B, 1st SP Bn
  Equip Sec, Co B, 1st SP Bn
  SP Comm Sec, 1st Sig Bn
  Det, Ord Sup Plat, CSG
  Det, Auto Sup Plat, CSG
  Det, Engr Sup Plat, CSG
  Det, Sig Sup Plat, CSG
  Det, GS Plat, CSG
  Det, Depot Plat, CSG

Rcn Co, 1st MAR Div   Capt K. J. HOUGHTON

1st Amph Trac Bn, FMF   LtCol E. F. WANN

VMO–6   Maj V. J. GOTTSCHALK

ROK Marine Regt (–)   Col SHIN, KMC

2d Engr Spec Brig reinf   Col J. TWITTY, USA

1st CSG, SC, FMF, less dets
1st Fum & Bath Plat
1st Aerial Del Plat

2d Engr Spec Brig reinf—Continued
Naval Beach Gp 1, less dets
7th MT Bn, SC, FMF
73d Engr (C) Bn, USA
50th Engr Port Const Co, USA
65th Ord Amm Co, USA

(3) RCT–7 Task Organization on landing at INCHON, KOREA, 21 September. Attachments reverted to parent control on arrival assembly areas.

RCT-7   Col H. L. LITZENBERG

    7th Mar
    3d Bn, 11th Mar
    Co D, 1st MT Bn
    Co D, 1st Tk Bn
    Co D, 1st Engr Bn
    Co E, 1st Med Bn
    Co C, 1st SP Bn
    Det, 1st Sig Bn (ANGLICO
      & 2 SP Comm Sec)

(4) Intermediate temporary attachments and detachments during the period 15 September–7 October.

18 Sept–32nd RCT USA attached 1st Mar Div
19 Sep–SpOpnsCo USA attchd 1st Mar Div
    32nd RCT detached 1st MarDiv reverted to 7th Inf Div
23 Sep–17th ROK Regt attchd 1st Mar Div
    17th ROK Regt detached 1st Mar Div
24 Sep–3d Bn, 187th Airborne RCT USA Attchd 1st Mar Div
    3d Bn, KMC Regt detached 1st Mar Div attached 3d Bn, 187th AB RCT
    1st Amph Trac Bn, FMF, less 3 Cos, detached 1st Mar Div attchd 7th Inf Div
    Co A, 1st Amph Tk and Trac Bn, USA, detached 1st Mar Div attchd 7th Inf Div
25 Sept–3d Bn, 187th AB RCT detached 1st Mar Div, attchd X Corps
    3d Bn, KMC Regt det 3d Bn, 187th AB RCT attchd 1st MarDiv
    161st KMC Bn (redesignated 5th KMC Bn) attchd 1st Mar Div
    Sp Opns Co, USA detached 1st Mar Div, attchd 3d Bn, 187th AB RCT
26 Sep–3d Bn KMC Regt detached 1st Mar Div, attchd 187th AB RCT (TF ABLE)

29 Sep–1st Amph Trac Bn, less 3d Cos, detached 7th Inf Div attchd 1st
  Mar Div
    96th FA Bn, USA detached 1st Mar Div
30 Sep–50th AAA(AW)Bn attached 1st Mar Div
3 Oct–50th AAA(AW)Bn detached 1st Mar Div

(5) Completion of INCHON-SEOUL operation, 7 October, and prior to
mounting out at INCHON.

1st Marine Division Reinf, FMF	MajGen O. P. SMITH
HqBn, 1st MarDiv	
163d MISD	
441st CIC	
Civ Asst Team	LtCol M. T. STARR
1st Sig Bn	
Carrier Plat, FMF	Maj R. L. SCHREIER
1st Serv Bn	LtCol C. L. BANKS
1st Ord Bn	Maj L. O. WILLIAMS
1st MT Bn	
1st Amph Trk Co, FMF	LtCol O. L. BEALL
1st Tk Bn	LtCol H. T. MILNE
1st Med Bn	Comdr H. B. JOHNSON, USN
1st SP Bn	LtCol H. P. CROWE
1st Engr Bn	LtCol J. H. PARTRIDGE
1st Mar	Col L. B. PULLER
5th Mar	LtCol R. L. MURRAY
7th Mar	Col H. L. LITZENBERG
11th Mar	
Btry C, 1st 4.5″ Rkt Bn, FMF	Col J. H. BROWER
1st Amph Trac Bn, FMF	
less Co D	LtCol E. F. WANN
1st Armd Amph Bn, FMF	
less Cos C & D	LtCol F. H. COOPER
7th MT Bn, SC, FMF	Maj J. F. STEPKA
1st CSG, SC, FMF less dets;	
1st Fum & Bath Plat	
1st Aerial Del Plat	Col J. S. COOK

APPENDIX D

Supplies and Equipment for Inchon

1st Marine Division Embarkation Order 1–50 of 31 August 1950 provided that the following supplies and equipment would be embarked in assigned shipping:

a. Class I

    (1) Rations: 30 days as follows:

    For attached Army units and 5th Marines (Reinf)

Individual Assault Type C		5 days
(Combat Unit Loaded)	(5 days)	
Operational Type B		25 days
(Unit Loaded)	(25 days)	
PX Accessories Pack		30 days
(Combat Unit Loaded)	(5 days)	
(Unit Loaded)	(10 days)	
(Convoy Loaded)	(15 days)	

    For 1st Marine Division (Reinf) (Less Army elements

and 5th Marines (Reinf))		5 days
Operational Type B		
(Convoy Loaded)		
Food Packet, Individual Assault 1A1		2 days
(In hands of individuals)	(1 day)	
Individual Combat, Type C		10 days
(Combat Unit Loaded)	(5 days)	
(Unit Loaded)	(5 days)	
PX Accessories Pack		30 days
(Combat Unit Loaded)	(5 days)	
(Unit Loaded)	(10 days)	
(Convoy Loaded)	(15 days)	
Small Detachment 5 in 1 Type		5 days
(Unit Loaded)	(5 days)	
Individual Combat Type C		
(Convoy Loaded-Corps Reserve)		150,000 Rations
(In hands of 1st Serv Bn)		

    (2) Water

        (a) All water containers filled, not less than 5 gallons per man combat loaded; 5 gallons per man to be unit loaded.

        (b) Assault Elements: 2 filled canteens per individual.

        (c) Others: 1 filled canteen.

b. Class II

    (1) Essential Class II items as determined by unit commanders. Vehicles to be loaded on priority basis within available space.

    (2) Initial (less chemical warfare) in hands of units.

    (3) Chemical warfare in hands of 1st Serv Bn.

    (4) 30 day replenishment in hands of appropriate service units.

    (5) All distillation units to have high priority for unloading.

    (6) No special services gear to be lifted in assault shipping.

    (7) Tentage: not to exceed 10% of T/E allowance.

    (8) Other Class II in accordance AdOrder 2–50.

c. Class III

    (1) Vehicle tanks ¾ full. Jeeps–1 filled expeditionary can (5 gal); all other vehicles: 2 filled cans (5 gal each).

    (2) Replenishment   30 days

Assault units:	
(Combat Unit Load)	(15 days)
(Unit Load)	(15 days)
Other Units:	
(Combat Unit Load)	(5 days)
(Unit Load)	(25 days)

d. Class IV

    (1) In accordance with AdOrder 2–50.

e. Class V—5 units of fire

(1) Assault Units		
(Combat Unit Load)	(2 U/F)	
(Unit Load)	(3 U/F)	
(2) Other than Assault Units		
(Combat Unit Load)	(1 U/F)	
(Unit Load)	(4 U/F)	
(3) Flame thrower fuel		15 U/F
(Combat Unit Load)	(5 U/F)	
(Unit Load)	(10 U/F)	

Task Organization
Joint Task Force Seven

JOINT TASK FORCE SEVEN	VAdm Arthur D. Struble
Task Force 90–Attack Force	RAdm James H. Doyle
92.1 Landing Force	MajGen Oliver P. Smith
1st Marine Division (Reinforced)	
92.11 Regimental Combat Team 1	Col Lewis B. Puller
92.11.1 Battalion Landing Team 1, 1st Marines	LtCol Jack Hawkins
92.11.2 Battalion Landing Team 2, 1st Marines	LtCol Alan Sutter
92.11.3 Battalion Landing Team 3, 1st Marines	LtCol Thomas L. Ridge
92.12 Regimental Combat Team 5	LtCol Raymond L. Murray
92.12.1 Battalion Landing Team 1, 5th Marines	LtCol George R. Newton
92.12.2 Battalion Landing Team 2, 5th Marines	LtCol Harold R. Roise
90.00 Flagship Element	
Mount McKinley AGC	Capt Carter A. Printup
Eldorado (RAdm Lyman K. Thackrey embarked) AGC	Capt Joseph B. Stefanac
90.01 Tactical Air Control Element	Cdr Theophilus H. Moore
Tactical Air Squadron 1	
90.02 Naval Beach Group Element	Capt Watson T. Singer
90.02.1 Headquarters Unit	
90.02.2 Beachmaster Unit	LCdr Martin C. Sibitzky
90.02.3 Boat Unit 1	LCdr Herman E. Hock
90.02.4 Amphibious Construction Battalion	LCdr M. Ted Jacobs, Jr.
90.02.5 Underwater Demolition Team Unit	LCdr David F. Welch

Task Force 90–Attack Force—Continued

90.03 Control Element		LCdr Clyde Allmon
Diachenko	APD	LCdr James R. Wilson
90.03.1 Control Unit Red		LCdr Ralph H. Schneeloch, Jr.
Horace A. Bass	APD	LCdr Alan Ray
90.03.2 Control Unit Green		Lt Reuben W. Berry
PCEC 896	PCEC	Lt Reuben W. Berry
90.03.3 Control Unit Blue		Lt Theodore B. Clark
Wantuck	APD	LCdr John B. Thro
90.04 Administrative Element		Capt Virginius R. Roane
90.04.1 Service Unit		
Consolation	AH	Capt Charles M. Ryan
12 LSU (plus additional LSUs on arrival)	12–20 LSU	
90.04.2 Repair and Salvage Unit		Cdr Emmanuel T. Goyette
Lipan		LCdr Howard K. Smith
Cree		Lt George E. Poore
Arikara	3 ATF	LCdr Kenneth A. Mundy
Conserver	ARS	Lt James L. Thompson
Askari	ARL	LCdr Robert J. Siegelman
YTB 406	YTB	
Gunston Hall		Cdr Charles W. Musgrave
Fort Marion		Cdr Noah Adair, Jr.
Comstock	3 LSD	Cdr Emmanuel T. Goyette
90.1 Advance Attack Group		Capt Norman W. Sears
92.12.3 Advance Landing Force Unit		
Battalion Landing Team 3 5th Marines		LtCol Robert D. Taplett
90.11 Transport Element		Capt Norman W. Sears
Fort Marion		Cdr Noah Adair, Jr.
3 LSU embarked		
90.11.1 Transport Unit		Cdr Selden C. Small
Horace A. Bess		LCdr Alan Ray
Diachenko		LCdr James R. Wilson
Wantuck		LCdr John B. Thro
90.2 Transport Group		Capt Virginius R. Roane
George Clymer		Capt Raymond S. Lamb
Cavalier		Capt Daniel J. Sweeney
Pickaway		Capt Samuel H. Crittenden, Jr.
Henrico		Capt John E. Fradd

Task Force 90–Attack Force—Continued
  90.2   Transport Group—Continued

Noble	5 APA	Capt Michael F. D. Flaherty
Union		Capt Gerald D. Zurmuchlen
Alshain		Capt Robert N. S. Clark
Achernar		Capt Crutchfield Adair
Oglethorpe		Capt Paul F. Heerbrandt
Seminole		Capt Henry Farrow
Thuban		Cdr Erle V. Dennett
Whiteside		Capt Eugene L. Lugibihl
Washburn	8 AKA	Capt James A. Prichard
President Jackson	AP	Capt Charles A. Ferriter
*Gunston Hall**		Cdr Charles W. Musgrave
*Comstock**		Cdr Emmanuel T. Goyette

  *3 LSU embarked

  90.3   Tractor Group   Capt Robert C. Peden

LST 611		Lt Delmar E. Blevins
LST 715		Lt Willie J. Gros
LST 742		Lt Robert B. Leonnig
LST 802		Lt Vladimir Fedorowicz
LST 845		Lt John F. Butler
LST 1048		Lt Rayburn M. Quinn
LST 1123		Lt Charles L. Wall
LST 1134		Lt William B. Faris
LST 1138		Lt Mike Stapleton
LST 857		Lt Dick Weidemeyer
LST 859		Lt Leland Tinsley
LST 898		Lt Robert M. Beckley
LST 914		Lt Ralph L. Holzhaus
LST 973		Lt Robert I. Trapp
LST 799		Lt Trumond E. Houston
LST 883		Lt Charles M. Miller
LST 975	17 LST	Lt Arnold W. Harer
SCAJAP LSTs	30 LST	
LSM 419	LSM	Lt John R. Bradley

  90.4   Transport Division 14   Capt Samuel G. Kelly
         (7th RCT U. S. Marines and MAG
           33 embarked; did not arrive
           Inchon until 21 Sept.)

Bayfield		Capt William E. Ferrall
Okanogan		Capt Timothy F. Donohue
Bexar		Capt Clarence E. Coffin, Jr.
Thomas Jefferson	4 APA	Capt Tyrrell D. Jacobs

Task Force 90–Attack Force—Continued
  90.4 Transport Division 14—Continued

Algol		Capt John A. Edwards
Winston		Capt Jack Maginnis
Montague	3 AKA	Capt Henry P. Wright, Jr.
Catamount		Cdr Kenneth Loveland
Colonial	2 LSD	Cdr Thomas J. Greene
90.5 Air Support Group		RAdm Richard W. Ruble
90.51 CVE Element		RAdm Richard W. Ruble
Badoeng Strait		Capt Arnold W. McKechnie
Sicily	2 CVE	Capt John S. Thach
90.52 CVE Screen		Cdr Byron L. Gurnette
Hanson	DDR	Cdr Cecil R. Welte
Taussig		Cdr William C. Meyer
George K. MacKenzie		Cdr William R. Laird, Jr.
Ernest G. Small	3 DD	Cdr Franklin C. Snow
90.6 Gunfire Support Group		RAdm John M. Higgins
90.61 Cruiser Element		RAdm John M. Higgins
90.6.2 Fire Support Unit 1		RAdm John M. Higgins
Toledo		Capt Richard F. Stout
Rochester		Capt Edward L. Woodyard
HMS Kenya		Capt P. W. Brock, RN
HMS Jamaica		Capt J. S. C. Salter, D. S. O., O. B. E., RN
90.62 Destroyer Element		Capt Halle C. Allan, Jr.
90.6.2 Fire Support Unit 2		Capt Halle C. Allan, Jr.
Mansfield		Cdr Edwin H. Headland
De Haven		Cdr Oscar B. Lungren
Lyman K. Swenson	3 DD	Cdr Robert A. Schelling
90.6.3 Fire Support Unit 3		Cdr Robert H. Close
Collett		Cdr Robert H. Close
Gurke		Cdr Frederick M. Radel
Henderson		Cdr William S. Stewart
90.63 LSMR Element		Cdr Clarence T. Doss, Jr.
90.6.4 Fire Support Unit 4		Cdr Clarence T. Doss, Jr.
LSMR 401		LCdr Melvin E. Bustard, Jr.
LSMR 403		Lt Frank G. Schettino
LSMR 404	3 LSMR	Lt George M. Wrocklage
90.7 Screening and Protective Group		Capt Richard T. Spofford
Rowan	DD	Cdr Alan R. Josephson
Southerland	DDR	Cdr Homer E. Conrad
Bayonne		LCdr Harry A. Clark
Newport		LCdr Percy A. Lilly, Jr.

Task Force 90–Attack Force—Continued
  90.7 Screening and Protective Group—Continued

Evansville		LCdr Elliot V. Converse, Jr.
HMS Mounts Bay		Capt J. H. Unwin, D. S. C., RN
HMS Whitesand Bay		LCdr J. V. Brothers, RN
HMNZS Tutira		LCdr P. J. H. Hoare, RNZN
HMNZS Pukaki	7 PF	LCdr L. E. Herrick, D. S. C., RNZN
RFS La Grandiere	8 PF	Cdr Urbain E. Cabanie
Pledge	AM	Lt Richard Young
Partridge		Lt(jg) Robert C. Fuller, Jr.
Mockingbird		Lt(jg) Stanley P. Gary
Kite		Lt(jg) Nicholas Grkovic
Osprey		Lt(jg) Philip Levin
Redhead		Lt(jg) T. R. Howard
Chatterer	6 AMS	Lt(jg) James P. McMahon

  90.8 Second Echelon Movement Group   Capt Louis D. Sharp, Jr.
      92.2 7th Infantry Division
      (Reinforced)

General G. M. Randall		Capt Alexander C. Thorington
General J. C. Breckinridge		Capt Fremont B. Eggers
General H. W. Butner	3 AP	Capt Dale E. Collins
Fred C. Ainsworth		
General Leroy Eltinge		
Aiken Victory		
Private Sadao S. Munemori		
	4 T-AP	
SS African Rainbow		
SS African Pilot		
SS Robin Kirk		
SS Helen Lykes		
SS Meredith Victory		
SS Empire Marshall		
SS Mormacport		
SS Lawrence Victory		
SS Southwind		
SS Beaver Victory		
SS Robin Goodfellow		
SS California Bear		

  90.9 Third Echelon Movement Group   Capt Albert E. Jarrell
      X Corps troops

General William A. Mann	AP	Capt Charles H. Walker
General William Weigel		

Task Force 90–Attack Force—Continued

  90.9 Third Echelon Movement Group—Continued

Marine Phoenix	2 T–AP	
SS Robin Trent		
SS Dolly Turman		
SS Charles Lykes		
SS Twin Falls Victory		
SS American Veteran		
SS American Attorney		
SS Empire Wallace		
SS Green Bay Victory		
SS P. & T. Navigator		
SS Luxembourg Victory		
SS Belgium Victory		
SS Bessemer Victory		
SS Cotton State		

91   Blockade and Covering Force   RAdm Sir William G. Andrewes, K. B. E., C. B., D. S. O., RN

HMS Triumph	CVL	Capt A. D. Torlesse, D. S. O., RN
HMS Ceylon	CL	Capt C. F. J. L. Davies, D. S. C., RN
HMS Cockade		LtCdr H. J. Lee, D. S. C., RN
HMS Charity		LtCdr P. R. G. Worth, D. S. C., RN
HMCS Cayuga		Capt Jeffry V. Brock, D. S. C., RCN
HMCS Sioux		Cdr P. D. Taylor, RCN
HMCS Athabaskan		Cdr R. T. Welland, D. S. C., RCN
HMAS Bataan		Cdr W. B. M. Marks, RAN
HMAS Warramunga		Cdr O. H. Becher, D. S. C., RAN
HNethMS Evertsen	8 DD	LtCdr D. J. Van Doorninck

ROK NAVAL FORCES   Cdr Michael J. Luosey, USN

Paik Doo San (PC 701)		Cdr Chai Yong Nam, ROKN
Kum Kang San (PC 702)		Cdr Lee Hi Jong, ROKN
Chi Ri San (PC 704)	4 PC	LCdr Hyun Sibak, ROKN
YMS 302		
YMS 303		
YMS 306		
YMS 307		
YMS 501		
YMS 502		
YMS 503		
YMS 510		

ROK NAVAL FORCES—Continued
    YMS 512
    YMS 515
    YMS 518   11 YMS

TASK FORCE 77–FAST CARRIER GROUP		RAdm Edward C. Ewen (in *Philippine Sea*)
Carrier Division 1		RAdm Edward C. Ewen
Philippine Sea	CV	Capt Willard K. Goodney
Carrier Division 3		RAdm John M. Hoskins
Valley Forge	CV	Capt Lester K. Rice
Carrier Division 5		
Boxer	CV	Capt Cameron Briggs
77.1 Support Group		Capt Harry H. Henderson
Worcester		Capt Harry H. Henderson
77.2 Screen Group		Capt Charles W. Parker
DesDiv 31		Capt Charles W. Parker
Shelton		Cdr Charles B. Jackson, Jr.
James E. Kyes		Cdr Fran M. Christiansen
Eversole	3 DD	Cdr Charles E. Phillips
Higbee	DDR	Cdr Elmer Moore
DesDiv 111		Capt Jeane R. Clark
Wiltsie		Cdr Carrol W. Brigham
Theodore E. Chandler		Cdr William J. Collum, Jr.
Hamner	3 DD	Cdr Jack J. Hughes
Chevalier	DDR	Cdr Blake B. Booth
DesDiv 112		Capt Bernard F. Roeder
Ozbourn		Cdr Charles O. Akers
Mc Kean		Cdr Harry L. Reiter, Jr.
Hollister	3 DD	Cdr Hugh W. Howard
Frank Knox	DDR	Cdr Sam J. Caldwell, Jr.
CortRon 1		
Fletcher		Cdr W. M. Lowry
Radford	2 DDE	Cdr Elvin C. Ogle
TASK FORCE 79—COMMANDER SERVICE SQUADRON 3		Capt Bernard L. Austin
79.1 Mobile Logistic Service Group		Capt John G. McClaughry
Cacapon (Initially)		Capt John G. McClaughry
Passumpsic (Initially)	2 AO	Capt Frank I. Winant, Jr.
Mount Katmai	AE	Capt Albert S. Carter
Graffias	AF	Capt William W. Fitts

TASK FORCE 79—COMMANDER
  SERVICE SQUADRON 3—Continued

79.2 Objective Area Logistic Group		Capt Philip H. Ross
Navasota (Initially)	AO	Capt Robert O. Strange
Virgo	AKA	Capt Philip H. Ross
Grainger	AK	Cdr Horace C. Laird, Jr.
Hewell		Lt Stanley Jaworski
Ryer		Lt Gurley P. Chatelain
Estero	3 AKL	Lt Tom Watson
79.3 Logistic Support Group		Capt Bernard L. Austin
Piedmont		Capt James R. Topper
Dixie	2 AD	Capt Jose M. Cabanillas
Kermit Roosevelt	ARG	Cdr Lester C. Conwell
Jason	ARH	Capt William B. Epps
Cimarron	AO	Capt Stanley G. Nichols
Warrick		Capt George Fritschmann
Uvalde	2 AKA	Capt Louis F. Teuscher
Nemasket	AOG	Lt Harry F. Dixon
Karin	AF	LCdr Berley L. Maddox
79.4 Salvage and Maintenance Group		
Mataco	ATF	Lt Frank P. Wilson
Bolster	ARS	Lt Billis L. Whitworth

TASK FORCE 99—PATROL AND RE- CONNAISSANCE FORCE		RAdm George R. Henderson
Curtiss	AV	Capt Anson C. Perkins
Gardiners Bay	AVP	Capt Frank G. Raysbrook
Salisbury Sound	AV	Capt Francis R. Jones
99.1 Search and Reconnaissance Group		Capt Joseph M. Carson
99.11 Patrol Squadron 6		Cdr Arthur F. Farwell, Jr.
99.12 88th Squadron RAF		Squadron Leader P. Helme
99.13 209th Squadron RAF		Squadron Leader P. Le Cheminant
99.2 Patrol and Escort Group		Capt Joseph M. Carson
99.21 Patrol Squadron 42		Cdr Gordon F. Smale
99.22 Patrol Squadron 47		Cdr Joe H. Arnold

Final Troop List of Division for the Inchon Landing

Below, as nearly as can be determined, is the troop list of the 1st Marine Division (Reinf) for the Inchon Landing. The list is correct as to units included, but it has been difficult to reconcile the totals given for units.

Unit	Actual Strength
Headquarters Bn	916
1st Serv Bn	873
1st Sig Bn	[1] 652
1st MT Bn	686
1st Med Bn	566
1st Am Trk Co	244
1st Ord Bn	533
1st Shore Party Bn	[2] 648
1st Engr Bn	1,038
1st Tank Bn	[3] 811
11th Marines	[4] 2,360
1st Marines	3,850
5th Marines	3,611
7th Marines	0
1st Am Trac Bn	868
1st CSG	[5] 1,291
7th MT Bn	430
Det MTACS-2	55
VMO-6	62
Total Marine Corps and Navy	19,494
Korean MC Regt	2 786

[1] Includes Carrier Platoon, FMF.
[2] Includes Detachments of Naval Beach Group 1.
[3] Includes Anti-tank Platoons of the Anti-tank Companies of the 1st and 5th Marines.
[4] Includes Battery C, 1st 4.5" Rocket Bn, FMF.
[5] Includes 1st Fumigation and Bath Plat., FMF; 1st Aerial Delivery Plat., FMF; and Naval Beach Group 1 (less dets. with the 1st Shore Party Bn).

Unit	Actual Strength
Co A, 56th Am Trac Bn, USA	151
Hq Det, USA	38
Sig Det, USA	37
96th FA Bn, USA	388
2d Engr Spec Brig, USA	952
73d Engr (c) Bn, USA	724
50th Engr Port Const Co., USA	214
65th Ord Amm Co., USA	256
Total U. S. Army	2,760
Grand Total	25,040

Distribution of Units of the Division Not Participating in the Inchon Landing

The following units of the Division, distributed as indicated, did not participate in the Inchon Landing:

	Marine Corps		Navy		Total	
	Officers	Enlisted	Officers	Enlisted	Officers	Enlisted
RCT–7, en route to the Far East	233	4,905	21	224	254	5,129
Administrative Center Pusan, Korea	9	172		1	9	173
Division Administrative Center, 1st Armd Amph TracBn, 17-year-olds and casuals at Kobe, Japan	59	1,268	3	14	62	1,282
Total	301	6,345	24	239	325	6,584

APPENDIX G

Summary of Operation Orders Issued by 1st Marine Division for the Inchon-Seoul Campaign

1–50	9 Aug 50	Movement of the Division to the Far East
2–50	4 Sep 50	Inchon Landing
3–50	15 Sep 50 (2328)	Seizure of Objective O–3 short of the FBHL
4–50	16 Sep 50 (1045)	Seizure of FBHL
5–50	16 Sep 50 (1600)	Capture of Kimpo Airfield. Prepare to seize Corps Phase Line C–C
6–50	18 Sep 50 (1814)	Seizure and preparation of crossing of Han River by 5th Marines. 1st Marines to continue attack relieved on the right (south) flank by the 32nd Infantry now attached to 1st MarDiv
7–50	19 Sep 50 (1430)	Crossing of the Han River by the 5th Marines and uncovering crossing sites by 1st Marines
8–50	20 Sep 50	Continuation of attack by 5th Marines toward Seoul to uncover the northern approaches of the main Seoul bridge sites. Continuation of attack by 1st Marines to seize the southern and western approaches and the Seoul bridge sites, prepared to cross the Han River in that vicinity
9–50	23 Sep 50 (1200)	Continuation of attack by 1st Marines to seize high ground south of the road and rail bridges leading to Seoul prepared to cross the Han River. Continuation of attack by 5th Marines to uncover the bridge sites. Crossing of the Han River at Haengju by the 7th Marines to seize objectives covering the north flank of the Division

10–50	23Sep50 (2200)	Crossing of the Han River by the 1st Marines. Continuation of the attack by the 5th Marines. 7th Marines to continue or Mission assigned by 1st MarDiv OpnO 9–50
11–50	24Sep50 (2400)	Continuation of the attack with all three regiments to capture Seoul and the high ground north thereof
12–50	26Sep50 (1230)	Continuation of the attack to capture Seoul. Boundary between 5th and 7th Marines changed to pinch out 5th Marines beyond the Government Palace. The 7th Marines to make an enveloping attack from the northwest
13–50	29Sep50 (2000)	Continuation of the attack to the east to secure Seoul and conduct a reconnaissance in force to the northwest prepared to relieve elements of the 7th Infantry Division north of the Han River. Seizure of prescribed Corps blocking positions
14–50	30Sep50 (1500)	Continuation of the attack and prescription of blocking positions to be occupied by the Division
15–50	5Oct50	Movement of the Division to staging area in the vicinity of Inchon in anticipation of the move in assault shipping to Wonsan

Enemy Units During the Inchon-Seoul Campaign

The enemy's method of operation, except for a brief determined stand near and in Seoul, consisted of moderate to strong delaying actions. The first reaction following the initial disorganization at Inchon was an attempt to contain our advance until such time as sufficient reinforcements could arrive to warrant initiating a counteroffensive. In view of the scarcity of reinforcements and our own rapid advances, this never materialized.

The Order of Battle of the units which opposed the advance of the Division from the time of the landing at Inchon until the capture of Uijong-bu, north of Seoul, is given below:

Unit	POWs cap- tured	Area of employment	Strength	Remarks
226th Marine Regt....	183	Inchon...........	2,000	In the Inchon area prior to the landing. Newly conscripted and poorly trained.
918th (Coast) Art Regt (Elements).	2(?)	.....do...........	200	In the Inchon area prior to the landing. 8 76mm guns. Wiped out or scattered by naval and air bombardment.
Air Force Division....	91	Kimpo Airfield....	(1)	When our troops approached the airfield area part of the personnel from this unit withdrew across the Han River.
42d Mech (Tank) Regt.	11	Between Inchon and Seoul.	500	Arrived in Seoul from Sinuiju in early Sept. 18 T-34 tanks.
107th Security Regt...	270	Kimpo Area........	2,500	In the Kimpo area when we landed. A quasi-military organization.
Rehabilitation Bn (Special Cultural Bn)	16	West of Yongdung-po.	230	This unit was organized on 19 Sept and contained NK prisoners serving sentence in Seoul. Officers were also former prisoners. Most were serving sentence for desertion.
3d Regt, 9th Rifle Div.	23	Yongdungpo	2,000	Remainder of the division on the southern front.
25th Inf Brig........	179	Seoul.............	4,000– 5,000	Arrived from Chorwon on 20 Sept. An excellent unit which opposed the 5th Marines on the western approaches to Seoul.

Unit	POWs cap-tured	Area of employment	Strength	Remarks
18th Rifle Div	301	Seoul and Yong-dungpo.	8,000–10,000	Arrived from Chorwon in mid-August. Known as the Seoul Defense Division. It was the only unit of division strength in the area.
43d Tank Regt	56	Seoul	500	Arrived from Wonsan 23 Sept. 10–15 T–34 tanks.
19th AA Regt	5	....do	1,200	In Seoul when we landed. 37mm, 85mm, and 12.7mm AT guns.
76th Ind Regt, 42d Div	218	....do	3,000	Arrived from Wonsan after 17 Sept. Was opposite the 5th Marines but withdrew from Seoul almost intact.
78th Ind Regt	528	....do	2,000	Arrived from Sariwon on 20 Sept. Opposed the 5th and 1st Marines. Put up stubborn defense and suffered heavy losses.
513th Art Regt	33	....do	1,500	Arrived from Chorwon on 23 Sept. 1 76mm and 5 45mm guns. Most of the regiment served as infantry.
10th Railroad Regt	17	....do	900	In Seoul when we landed. Its mission was to maintain the security of the railroad lines and keep them in operation. It participated in the defense of Seoul.
31st Rifle Div/or Seoul City Regt.	345	....do	3,600	In Seoul when we landed. Formed as a division on 20 Sept by an amalgamation of units in Seoul. Participated in the defense of Seoul and delayed our advance north to Uijong-bu.
36th Bn, 111th Security Regt.	32	....do	750	In Seoul when we landed.
2d Regt 17th Rifle Div (Reinforced).	41	Seoul-Uijongbu	3,500	Withdrawn from the southern front after the landing at Inchon.
75th Ind Regt	16	Uijongbu	2,000	Arrived from Hamhung on 30 Sept. Used as a covering force to cover the withdrawal through Uijong-bu.
27th Inf Brig	123	Suyuhyon	5,000	Arrived from Kumchon on 1 Oct. Withdrew in the face of the advance of the 5th Marines to Suyuhyon, 17 miles northwest of Seoul.
Total Enemy Strength			44,380.	

¹ Unknown.

A total of 428 prisoners interrogated did not know enough of their own units to be further identified. Approximately 1,000 prisoners were not interrogated due to the heavy initial influx.

Prisoners were captured from some 24 units not listed above, but the number of prisoners captured from individual units was not sufficient to accept the presence of the unit. Further, many of these POWs were deserters or wounded from the southern front.

The identification, by date, of North Korean units opposing the 1st Marine Division is indicated below:

15 September....	226th Ind Marine Regt (2 Bns).	2,000 defending Wolmi-do and Inchon
16 September....	918th Art Regt (2 Cos).....	200 defending Wolmi-do
	18th Rifle Div (Opposing 1st Marines)	300 POWs and 1,350 enemy casualties for the first two days, 15 and 16 Sep
17 September....	42d Mech (Tank) Regt (Opposing 1st Marines)	Lost 14 T–34 tanks
	107th Security Regt (Kimpo) (Opposing KMC & 5th Marines)	400 POWs and 350 enemy casualties
18 September....	NK Air Force EngBn (Opposing 5th Marines)	197 POWs and 450 enemy casualties
19 September....	No additional identifications on fronts of 1st and 5th Marines	126 POWs and 600 enemy casualties
20 September....	78th Ind Regt (Opposing 5th Marines) No additional identifications on front of 1st Marines	326 POWs and 600 enemy casualties
21 September.....	No additional identifications	355 POWs and 1,350 enemy casualties
22 September.....	Rehabilitation Bn (Opposing 1st Marines).	395 POWs and 1,250 casualties
	25th Inf Brig (Opposing 5th Marines)	
	31st Rifle Div (Seoul City Regt) (Opposing 5th Marines)	
23 September.....	No additional identifications	169 POWs and 900 casualties
24 September.....	.....do.................	67 POWs and 950 casualties

25 September....	.....do..................	142 POWs and 1,750 casualties
26 September.....	76th Ind Regt............. 43d Tank Regt 19th AA Regt 513th Art Regt 17th Rifle Div (Opposing 1st & 5th Marines)	407 POWs and 950 casualties
27 September.....	No additional identifications	139 POWs and 1,252 casualties
28 September.....	.....do..................	206 POWs and 332 casualties
29 September.....	.....do..................	507 POWs and 102 casualties
30 September.....	.....do..................	328 POWs and 305 casualties
1 October.......	.....do..................	124 POWs and 75 casualties
2 October.......	27th Inf Brig (Opposing 5th Marines) 75th Ind Regt (Opposing 7th Marines)	82 POWs and 350 casualties
3 October.......	No additional identifications	103 POWs and 800 casualties
4 October.......	.....do..................	118 POWs
5 October.......	.....do..................	57 POWs
6 October.......	.....do..................	144 POWs

In the above tabulation, a unit is shown only for the first day upon which it was identified by the capture of prisoners. In the cases of most of the units there were recurring captures of prisoners.

APPENDIX I

Congratulatory Messages

The following messages, of a commendatory nature, were transmitted to the 1st Marine Division by the X Corps upon completion of the Inchon-Seoul Campaign.

From CG, X Corps to CG, 1st Marine Division under date of 28 September 1950

"On this date the X Corps attained one of its distinct objectives—the securing of the city of Seoul. In recognition of the heroic efforts of the officers and men of the 1st Marine Division I extend my deepest thanks and my continuing admiration for a task well done." Signed Edward M. Almond, Major General, United States Army, Commanding.

From the President to General MacArthur

"I know that I speak for the entire American people when I send you my warmest congratulations on the victory which has been achieved under your leadership in Korea. Few operations in military history can match either the delaying action where you traded space for time in which to build up your forces, or the brilliant maneuver which has now resulted in the liberation of Seoul. I am particularly impressed by the splendid cooperation of our Army, Navy, and Air Force. I wish you would extend my thanks and congratulations to the commanders of those services—Lieutenant General Walton H. Walker, Vice Admiral Charles T. Joy and Lieutenant General George E. Stratemeyer. The unification of our arms established by you and by them has set a shining example. My thanks and the thanks of the people of all the free nations go out to your gallant forces—soldiers, sailors, Marines and airmen—from the United States and the other countries fighting for freedom under the United Nations Banner. I salute you all, and say to all of you from all of us at home, 'well and nobly done.'" Signed Harry S. Truman.

From the Joint Chiefs of Staff to General MacArthur

"The Joint Chiefs of Staff are proud of the great successes you have achieved. We realize that they would have been impossible without brilliant and audacious leadership and without the full coordination and the fighting spirit of all forces and all arms. From the sudden initiation of hostilities you have exploited to the utmost all capabilities and opportunities. Your transition from defensive to offensive operations was magnificently planned, timed, and executed. You have given new inspiration to the freedom-loving peoples of the world. We remain completely confident that the great task entrusted to you by the United Nations will be carried to a successful conclusion."

From CG, X Corps to all units of the X Corps under date of 2 October 1950

"It is desired that this message be disseminated to all members of your command. The achievements of the U. N. forces comprising the X Corps should be a pride and inspiration to all who participated in the recent operations so successfully concluded and which resulted in the liberation of Seoul, the capital city of Korea. Your efforts have greatly contributed in freeing the Republic of Korea of the forces of Communism that threatened to enslave her people. Koreans may now take their rightful place among the freedom-loving people of the world. History will long remember the feat of arms that you, through your untiring efforts and superb valor have accomplished. I am proud of the units comprising the X Corps. Each of you should be proud of the unit in which you serve, the nation it represents, and your part in this military operation. I am confident that the tasks that are before us will be accomplished with the same splendid cooperation, leadership, and determination that you have so recently displayed." Signed Major General Edward M. Almond, Commanding General, X Corps.

Division Commander's Message to the 1st Marine Division upon Completion of the Inchon-Seoul Campaign

On 8 October 1950, the Division Commander issued Division Memorandum No. 192–50, quoted below, in recognition of the accomplishments of the 1st Marine Division during the Inchon-Seoul Campaign:

"1. Upon completion of the campaign in the Inchon-Seoul area of Korea I desire to express my appreciation and admiration of the superb manner in which all hands have cooperated in bringing to a successful conclusion a very difficult operation.

"2. From the time the decision was made to bring the Division to war strength and to commit it in Korea until the city of Seoul was captured, urgency has been the order of the day. Urgency has been necessary because tidal conditions dictated that a landing at Inchon be made on September 15th. For the Division this meant that its elements in the United States had to be brought to war strength immediately, had to be re-equipped and, in the absence of amphibious shipping, had to be loaded on such other ships as could hurriedly be made available. Upon arrival in Kobe, Japan, there was the pressing necessity of reloading in minimum time in amphibious shipping, with the disruption caused by a destructve typhoon. Elements of the Division comprising the First Provisional Marine Brigade were not released from combat in South Korea until midnight of September 5th and between that date and September 12th were required to move to Pusan, re-equip and mount out.

"3. It is now history that the First Marine Division did meet its commitments, did land at Inchon on September 15th under conditions which required the maximum of coordination, aggressive action, and devotion to duty; went on to capture the Kimpo airfield three days after landing, to effect a difficult amphibious crossing of the Han River, and to liberate the city of Seoul by driving the North Korean invaders far beyond its limits.

"4. I fully appreciate, and I am sure the American people now fully appreciate and realize, that only well-trained and determined troops, completely devoted to duty, could have accomplished what the First Marine Division did in Korea. You have established your place in history. The memory of those who made the supreme sacrifice in the accomplishment of this mission will forever remain an inspiration to all Marines."

Casualties During the Inchon-Seoul Campaign

Following is a daily breakdown of the casualties suffered by the 1st Marine Division during the Inchon-Seoul Campaign (15 September–7 October 1950), together with a tabulation of the number of POWs captured by the Division and the estimated casualties inflicted on the enemy.

Date	KIA [1]	DOW [1]	MIA [1]	WIA [1]	Total battle casualties	POWs captured [2]	Estimated enemy casualties [3]
15 Sep	20	1	1	174	196	([3])	([4])
16 Sep	2	1	1	22	26	300	[4] 1,350
17 Sep	6	0	0	70	76	400	350
18 Sep	7	3	0	92	102	197	450
19 Sep	10	1	0	61	72	126	600
20 Sep	24	1	3	119	147	326	600
21 Sep	30	3	0	198	231	355	1,350
22 Sep	27	3	0	135	165	395	1,200
23 Sep	19	7	0	117	143	169	900
24 Sep	68	4	0	217	289	67	950
25 Sep	33	4	1	238	276	142	1,750
26 Sep	29	7	0	167	203	407	950
27 Sep	33	3	0	153	189	139	1,252
28 Sep	8	4	0	31	43	206	332
29 Sep	19	1	0	49	69	507	102
30 Sep	11	2	0	48	61	328	.305
1 Oct	2	1	0	16	19	124	75
2 Oct	15	1	0	81	97	82	350
3 Oct	2	1	0	35	38	103	800
4 Oct	0	0	0	3	3	118	0
5 Oct	1	1	0	3	5	57	0
6 Oct	0	0	0	0	0	144	0
7 Oct	0	0	0	0	0	0	0
Total	366	49	6	2,029	2,450	6,492	13,666

[1] Based on compilation on 15 March 1951 by Casualty Reporting Officer.

[2] Based on G–2 Report included in the Special Action Report for the Inchon-Seoul Campaign. The figures shown are less than the total of regimental reports of captures, as only those POWs remaining after processing by the G–2 were counted. Oftentimes civilians were turned over to the G–2 as POWs. A lag is also reflected in the figures of the G–2 Section. Both regiments captured prisoners on D–Day, 15 September, but the prisoners were not processed until 16 September.

[3] Estimated enemy casualties do not include POWs. Figures shown are based on the G–2 Report included in the Special Action Report for the Inchon-Seoul Campaign.

[4] The figure shown for 16 September includes the casualties inflicted on the enemy on 15 September.

APPENDIX K

Comments on Close Air Support Provided by 1st Marine Aircraft Wing

HEADQUARTERS

7TH INFANTRY DIVISION ARTILLERY

Office of the Commanding General

APO 7

10 January 1951

Subject: Marine Air Support

To: Commandant, United States Marine Corps, Washington 25, D. C.

Thru: Commanding General, 7th Infantry Division, APO 7.

1. In my capacity as Division Artillery Commander and Fire Support Coordinator of the Seventh Infantry Division I have been able to observe closely the most effective system of close air support currently used by the Marines. During the period 19 September to 20 December 1950, close air support of this division was furnished almost exclusively by the First Marine Air Wing.

2. In an effort to parallel as nearly as possible the Marine system of controlling close support air this division had attached to it the Far East Detachment, ANGLICO, FMF, Atlantic. This detachment was augmented by nine (9) Tactical Air Control Parties, Fifth U. S. Air Force, trained in the Marine system of control by the ANGLICO detachment. This enabled the placement of Tactical Air Control Parties with each infantry battalion. Such placement proved to be ideal and gave the battalion commander a means of controlling and coordinating the close air support he received.

3. It is worthy to note that in 57 days of combat 1024 sorties were flown by Marine Aircraft in close support of the division without a single casualty among our own troops due to friendly air action. This record I attribute to the fact that adequate control was available with front line units. In many instances Marine planes were bombing and strafing within 200 yards of our front lines.

4. I wish to express my appreciation for the superior cooperation of Captain Charles E. Crew, 023897, USMC, Far East Detachment, ANGLICO, FMF, Atlantic and his enlisted assistants during the period 19 September 1950 to 20 December 1950. In his capacity as Marine Air Liaison Officer to the Seventh Infantry Division Captain Crew functioned as a member of the division team with a common objective. The excellent air support received by this division was due

in no small part to the enthusiastic manner in which Captain Crew performed. Unfortunately, I was not able to observe the work of the other two Marine Forward Air Controllers attached to the division. Reports indicate that they performed equally as well.

5. Again, allow me to reemphasize my appreciation for the outstanding air support received by this division. The Marine system of control, in my estimation, approaches the ideal and I firmly believe that a similar system should be adopted as standard for Army Divisions.

(s) HOMER W. KIEFER
Brigadier General, USA
Commanding

[1st Endorsement]

Subject: Marine Air Support
Headquarters, 7th Infantry Division, APO 7 12 January 1951
To: Commanding General, X Corps, APO 909

I wish to express my own appreciation to all members of the 1st Marine Air Wing who assisted in the fine air support given to the 7th Infantry Division and also to commend Forward Air Controllers, Captain Edward P. Stamford and 1st Lieutenant Jack R. Grey as well as Captain Crew for outstanding performances of duty in connection with the support.

(s) DAVID G. BARR
Maj Gen., USA
Commanding

[2nd Endorsement]

Headquarters, X Corps, APO 909, 16 January 1951
To: Commanding General, Eighth United States Army, APO 301

1. The effective close air support rendered by the 1st Marine Air Wing through the Forward Air Controllers with the 7th Infantry Division greatly aided in the successful accomplishment of X Corps operations. The actions of the personnel concerned are worthy of commendation, and I wish to add my appreciation for their assistance.

2. Further, I wish to emphasize the statements of General Kiefer in paragraph 5, basic letter, in which he endorses the Marine system of Tactical Air Control. It has proved itself on every occasion.

(s) EDWARD M. ALMOND
Major General, United States Army
Commanding

[3rd Endorsement]

CHO FEC–SCAP
AG RECORDS
FIEDAG 330.13
4795

AG 373 KAR (10 Jan 51)
Subject: Marine Air Support
Hq Eighth U. S. Army Korea (EU AK), APO 301 30 JAN 1951
TO: Commander-in-Chief, Far East, APO 500

I note with gratification the splendid spirit of cooperation that existed between the 1st Marine Air Wing and the 7th Infantry Division in recent combat operations. I congratulate not only Captain Crew, Captain Stamford, and Lieutenant Grey but all officers and men of the 1st Marine Air Wing for their magnificent performance.

(s)   M. B. Ridgway
Lieutenant General, United States Army
Commanding

[4th Endorsement]

AG 330.13 (10 Jan 51) GA
General Headquarters, Far East Command, APO 500, 4 February 1951
To: Commander, United States Naval Forces, Far East, Navy No. 1165

Commander-in-Chief, Far East, takes pleasure in forwarding this correspondence which again illustrated the outstanding support that Marine Air is providing ground forces in the Korean operations.

By Command of General MacArthur

(s)   K. B. Bush
Brigadier General, USA
Adjutant General

CNFE/P15   05/RVW/the
Serial: 1213   12 Feb 1951
Fifth Endorsement on CG, 7th INFDIVART ltr of 10 Jan 1951
From: Commander Naval Forces, Far East
To: Commandant, United States Marine Corps
Via: (1) Commanding General, First Marine Air Wing
        (2) Commander in Chief, Pacific Fleet
Subj: Marine Air Support

1. Readdressed and forwarded.

2. Commander, Naval Forces, Far East, takes great pleasure in forwarding correspondence and desires to recognize also the outstanding performance of duty of Marine Corps personnel concerned.

(s)   C. T. Joy

APPENDIX L

Presidential Unit Citation

THE SECRETARY OF THE NAVY

Washington

The President of the United States takes pleasure in presenting the Presidential Unit Citation to the

First Marine Division, Reinforced

for service as set forth in the following Citation:

"For extraordinary heroism in action against enemy aggressor forces in Korea from 15 September to 11 October 1950. In the face of a determined enemy and against almost insurmountable obstacles, including disadvantageous tidal and beach conditions on the western coast of Korea, the First Marine Division, Reinforced, rapidly and successfully effected the amphibious seizure of Inch'on in an operation without parallel in the history of amphibious warfare. Fully aware that the precarious situation of friendly ground forces fighting desperately against the continued heavy pressure of a numerically superior hostile force necessitated the planning and execution of this extremely hazardous operation within a period of less than thirty days, and cognizant of the military importance of its assigned target, the Division moved quickly into action and, on 15 September, by executing three well-coordinated attacks over highly treacherous beach approaches defended by resolute enemy troops, captured the island of Wolmi-do, the city of Inch'on and Kimp'o Airfield, and rendered invaluable assistance in the capture of Seoul. As a result of its aggressive attack, the Division drove the hostile forces in hasty retreat over thirty miles in the ensuing ten days, completely severed vital hostile communication and supply lines and greatly relieved enemy pressure on other friendy ground units, thereby permitting these units to break out from their Pusan beachhead and contributing materially to the total destruction of hostile ground forces in southern Korea. The havoc and destruction wrought on an enemy flushed with previous victories and the vast accomplishments in turning the tide of battle from a weakening defensive to a vigorous offensive action reflect the highest credit upon the officers and men of the First Marine Division, Reinforced, and the United States Naval Service."

The following reinforcing units of the First Marine Division participated in operations against enemy aggressor forces in Korea from 15 September to 11 October 1950:

Fleet Marine Force Units and Detachments: Radio Relay Platoon, 1st Signal Operations Company; Battery C, 1st 4.5 Inch Rocket Battalion; 1st Amphibian Truck Company; 1st Amphibian Tractor Battalion (less Company "D"); 1st

339

Combat Service Group, Service Command; 1st Fumigation and Bath Platoon; 1st Aerial Delivery Platoon; 7th Motor Transport Battalion, Service Command; 1st Armored Amphibian Battalion; Detachment Marine Tactical Air Control Squadron Two; Team #1, First Provisional Historical Platoon; Marine Observation Squadron Six; Marine Aircraft Group Thirty-Three, Reinforced, including Headquarters Squadron Thirty-Three, Marine Service Squadron Thirty-Three, Marine Ground Control Intercept Squadron One, Marine Fighter Squadron Two Hundred Twelve, Marine Fighter Squadron Two Hundred Fourteen, Marine Fighter Squadron Three Hundred Twelve, Marine Fighter Squadron Three Hundred Twenty-Three, Marine Night Fighter Squadron Five Hundred Thirteen, and Marine Night Fighter Squadron Five Hundred Forty-Two.

United States Navy Units: Naval Beach Group One.

United States Army Units: Detachment 205th Signal Repair Company; Detachment 4th Signal Battalion; 163rd Military Intelligence Service Detachment; Company "A" Reinforced, 56th Amphibian Tractor Battalion; 96th Field Artillery Battalion; 441st Counter-Intelligence Corps Detachment; 2nd Engineer Special Brigade; 73rd Engineer (C) Battalion; 50th Engineer Port Construction Company; 65th Ordnance Ammunition Company; 32nd Regimental Combat Team; Special Operations Company; 3rd Battalion, 187th Airborne Regimental Combat Team; and the 50th Antiaircraft Artillery Air Warning Battalion.

For the President,

(s)   DAN A. KIMBALL
Secretary of the Navy

Bibliography

Documents

Earney, William R. Maj, USMC. Notes on operations of Third Battalion, Seventh Marines, in South Korea. MS. Manuscript File, Records and Research Section, Historical Branch, G–3, Headquarters Marine Corps (HQMC Historical).

Forney, Edward H. Col, USMC. Transcript of special report. n. d. MS. Manuscript File, HQMC Historical.

Smith, Oliver P. MajGen, USMC. Chronicle of the operations of the 1st Marine Division during the first nine months of the Korean War, 1950–1951. MS. Manuscript File, HQMC Historical.

———. Notes on the operations of the 1st Marine Division during the first nine months of the Korean War, 1950–1951. MS. Manuscript File, HQMC Historical.

U. S. Congress. *National Security Act of 1947.* 61 *U. S. Stat. at L.* 495.

Joint Army-Navy Intelligence Survey. No. 75. Copy at HQMC Secret and Confidential Files, Naval Records Management Center, Alexandria, Va. (S&C Files, NRMC).

Joint Landing Force Board. Study on the conduct of training of landing forces for joint amphibious operations during World War II. Project no. 13–52. Copy at HQMC S&C Files, NRMC.

U. S. Marine Corps. U. S. Marine Corps Board. An evaluation of the influence of Marine Corps forces on the course of the Korean War (4 Aug 50–15 Dec 50). Processed; copy in HQMC Historical. 2 v.

———. Interviews with participants in the Korean War, 1951–54. Interviews (Korea) File, HQMC Historical.

———. Headquarters Marine Corps incoming and outgoing dispatches, 1949–50. HQMC S&C Files, NRMC.

———. Letters and memoranda to Historical Branch, G–3, concerning Korean operations. Monograph and Comments File, HQMC Historical.

Commander in Chief, U. S. Pacific Fleet. Interim Evaluation report no. 1. Period 25 June to 15 November 1950. 20 January 1951. v. XV: Annexes.

    ZEBRA. Fleet Marine Force Pacific. A report on activities of Fleet Marine Force, Pacific, from 25 June 1950 to the amphibious assault at Inchon. n. d.

    ABLE ABLE. Commander Amphibious Group ONE (CTF 90). Report of ComPhibGru ONE (CTF 90) operations for period 25 June 1950 to 1 January 1951. 17 January 1951.

    BAKER BAKER. Commanding General, Aircraft, Fleet Marine Force, Pacific. Historical report. 24 November 1950.

    CHARLIE CHARLIE. Operations of 1st Marine Air Wing, FMF, in Korea. 25 June–15 November 1950. n. d.

DOG DOG. Headquarters, 1st Marine Division (Reinf), FMF. Special report, 1st Marine Division (Reinf), FMF. Period 1 August–15 November 1950. n. d. Processed; copy in HQMC Historical.

Fleet Marine Force Pacific. Historical diary, 1–31 August 1950. Historical Diary (Korea) File, HQMC Historical.

Commanding General, 1st Marine Air Wing, FMF. Special action report for period 7 September to October 1950. 20 February 1951.

Basic report

Annexes

ABLE	Tactical Air Command, X Corps, USA.
BAKER	G–1
CHARLIE	G–2
DOG	G–3
EASY	G–4
ITEM	Marine Air Group 33

Basic report

Annexes

Able	Personnel
Baker	Intelligence (including combat narrative)
Charlie	Operations
Dog	Supply
Easy	Communications
Fox	Logistics
George	Medical
How	Public Information
Item	Buildings and Grounds
Jig	Ordnance
King	Transportation
Love	Base Security
Mike	Electronics
Nan	Photographic Unit
Oboe	Engineering
Peter	Comments and recommendations
Queen	VMF–312
Roger	VMF–212
Sugar	VMF(n)–542
Tare	MGCIS–1
Uncle	MTACS–2

JIG	Marine Aircraft Group 12.

Basic report

Annexes

Able	Personnel
Baker	Intelligence
Charlie	Operations
Dog	Supply

JIG   Annexes
     Easy VMF–214
     Fox   VMF–323
     George VMF(N)–513
     How Logistics
     Item Medical
     Jig   Communications
     King Building and Grounds
     Love Engineering
     Mike Ordnance
     Nan Transportation
     Oboe Base Security
     Peter Electronics
     Queen Mess
     Roger Plans and Directives

"SAR" File (Korea), USMC Historical.

1st Marine Division, FMF. Field journals, correspondence, dispatches, orders, reports, and miscellaneous matter. August–October 1950. Classified Correspondence File, (1st Marine Division) HQMC Historical.

1st Marine Division. 1st Korean Marine Corps Regiment and its relationship to the 1st Marine Division. "SAR" File (Korea), Type "C" Reports, HQMC Historical.

1st Marine Division, FMF. Special action report for the Inchon-Seoul operation, 15 September–7 October 1950. 2 May 1951. 3 sections:

 1. Division (20 April 1951.)
 2. Commanding General's remarks on comments and recommendations
 3. Annexes
    ABLE   G–1
    BAKER   G–2
    CHARLIE   G–3
    DOG   G–4
    EASY   Adjutant
    FOX   Anti-Tank
    GEORGE   Chaplain
    HOW   Chemical Warfare & Radiological Defense
    ITEM   Dental
    JIG   Embarkation
    KING   Engineer
    LOVE   Headquarters Commandant
    MIKE   Food Director
    NAN   Historical
    OBOE   Inspector
    PETER   Legal

QUEEN	Medical
ROGER	Motor Transport
SUGAR	Ordnance
TARE	Post Exchange
UNCLE	Public Information
VICTOR	Signal
WILLIAM	Special Services
XRAY	Supply
YOKE	Disbursing
ZEBRA	Civil Affairs
ABLE ABLE	Division Administration Center
BAKER BAKER	Fire Support Coordination Center
CHARLIE CHARLIE	Air & Air Observers
DOG DOG	Naval Gunfire
EASY EASY	Headquarters Bn
FOX FOX	1st Service Bn
GEORGE GEORGE	1st Signal Bn
HOW HOW	1st Medical Bn
ITEM ITEM	1st Motor Transport Bn
JIG JIG	1st Amphibious Truck Co
LOVE LOVE	1st Ordnance Bn
MIKE MIKE	1st Shore Party Bn
NAN NAN	1st Engineer Bn
OBOE OBOE	1st Tank Bn
PETER PETER	1st Marines
QUEEN QUEEN	5th Marines
ROGER ROGER	7th Marines
SUGAR SUGAR	11th Marines
TARE TARE	1st Amphibious Tractor Bn
UNCLE UNCLE	1st Combat Service Group
VICTOR VICTOR	7th Motor Transport Bn
WILLIAM WILLIAM	Marine Observation Squadron 6

· "SAR" File (Korea), HQMC Historical

7th Infantry Division.   War diaries, supporting documents, histories, and general and special staff activities reports, September 1950. Army Record Group 207-0.3, Code 307, Departmental Records Branch, The Adjutant General's Office, Alexandria, Va.

Commander Air Support Group and Commander Carrier Division 15.   Report of operations, 6–21 September 1950. Classified Correspondence File (1st Marine Division) HQMC Historical.

2d Battalion, 1st Marines. Special action report for Inchon-Seoul operation. "SAR" File (Korea), HQMC Historical.
3d Battalion, 1st Marines. Special action report for Inchon-Seoul operation. "SAR" File (Korea), HQMC Historical.

Books and Periodicals

Almond, Edward M. LtGen, USA. *Conference on United Nations Military Operations in Korea, 29 June 1950–31 December 1951.* Carlisle Barracks, Pennsylvania: The Army War College. 1952.
Cole, Eli K. BGen, USMC. "Joint Overseas Operations." *U. S. Naval Institute Proceedings,* 35, no. 321:927–937 (November, 1929).
Condit, Kenneth W. "Marine Supply in Korea." *Marine Corps Gazette,* 37, no. 1:48–55 (January, 1953).
Fuller, J. F. C. MajGen, British Army. *The Second World War.* London: Hutchinson, 1948.
Geer, Andrew. *The New Breed: The Story of the U. S. Marines in Korea.* New York: Harper and Brothers, 1952.
Giusti, Ernest H. *The Mobilization of the Marine Corps Reserve in the Korean Conflict.* Washington: Historical Branch, G–3, HQMC, 1952.
———, and Condit, Kenneth W. "Marine Air Over Inchon-Seoul," *Marine Corps Gazette,* 36, no. 6:19–27 (June, 1952).
Gugeler, Russell A. Capt, USA. *Combat Actions in Korea.* Washington: Combat Forces Press, 1954.
Isely, Jeter A., and Crowl, Philip A. *The U. S. Marines and Amphibious War.* Princeton: Princeton University Press, 1951.
Karig, Walter, Capt, USN, Cagle, Malcolm, Cdr, USN, and Manson, Frank A., LtCdr. *Battle Report: The War in Korea.* New York: Rinehart, 1952.
Montross, Lynn. *Cavalry of the Sky: The Story of U. S. Marine Combat Helicopters.* New York: Harper and Brothers, 1954.
——— "Fleet Marine Force Korea." *U. S. Naval Institute Proceedings,* 37, no. 8:836–839 (August, 1953).
——— "They Make Men Whole Again." *Marine Corps Gazette,* 36, no. 12:42–49 (December, 1952).
Sleger, J., Jr. 2dLt, USA. Report to Dr. A. D. Coax, n. d. Department of the Army, Operations Research Office.
U. S. Department of Defense, Office of Armed Forces Information and Education. *The United States Marine Corps.* Washington: Department of Defense Printing, 1950. (Armed Forces Talk No. 317.)
———, Department of the Army, Office of the Chief of Military History. The Korean conflict. By James F. Schnabel. Maj, USA. MS. v. I.

U. S. Marine Corps, Fleet Marine Force Pacific. *Historical Outline of the Development of FMFPac 1941–1950 (Preliminary)*. Processed; copy at HQMC Historical.

U. S. Military Academy, Department of Military Art and Engineering. *Operations in Korea*. West Point: U. S. Military Academy, 1953.

U. S. Department of State. *Guide to the U. N. in Korea*. Washington: U. S. Government Printing Office, 1951.

————, Office of the Solicitor. *Right To Protect Citizens in Foreign Countries by Landing Forces*. 3d revised edition with supplementary appendix to 1933. Washington: U. S. Government Printing Office, 1934. (State Dept. Publication No. 538.)

Index

SET AND PRINTED FOR THE UNITED STATES
MARINE CORPS BY THE UNITED STATES GOV-
ERNMENT PRINTING OFFICE: 1955. TEXT SET
IN 12-POINT GRANJON AND PRINTED ON
OFFSET VELLUM STOCK.

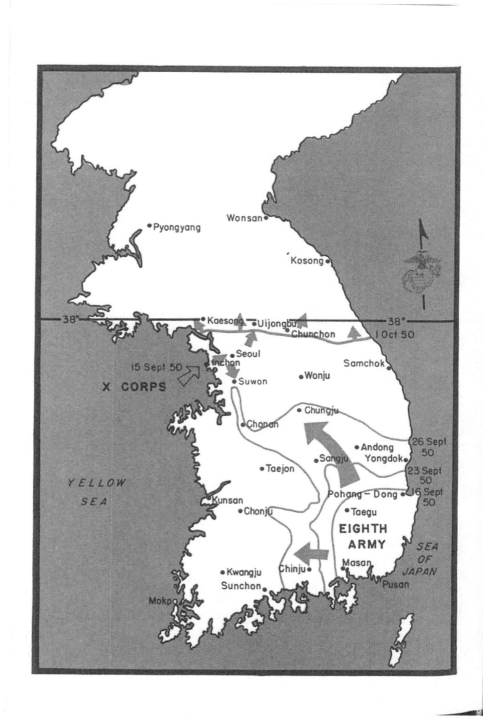

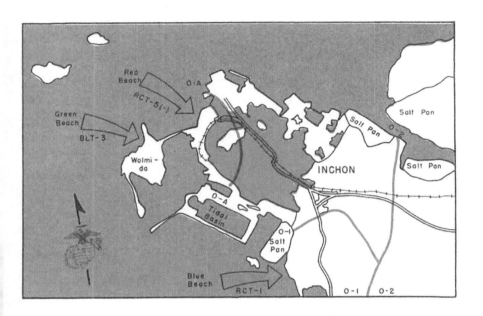

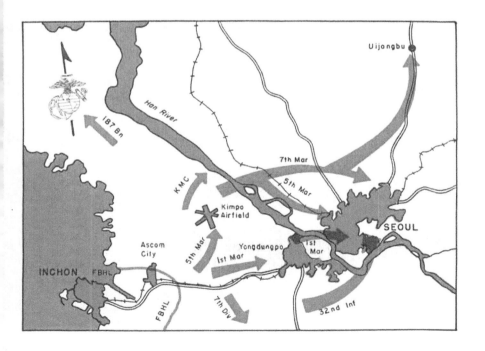

Made in the USA
Middletown, DE
07 September 2023

37975365R00225